Shojo Beat

# Yona of the Dawn

# 17

### Story & Art by

# Mizuho Kusanagi

# yona of the Dawn

**Volume 17**

## CONTENTS

# Yona
## of the
# Dawn

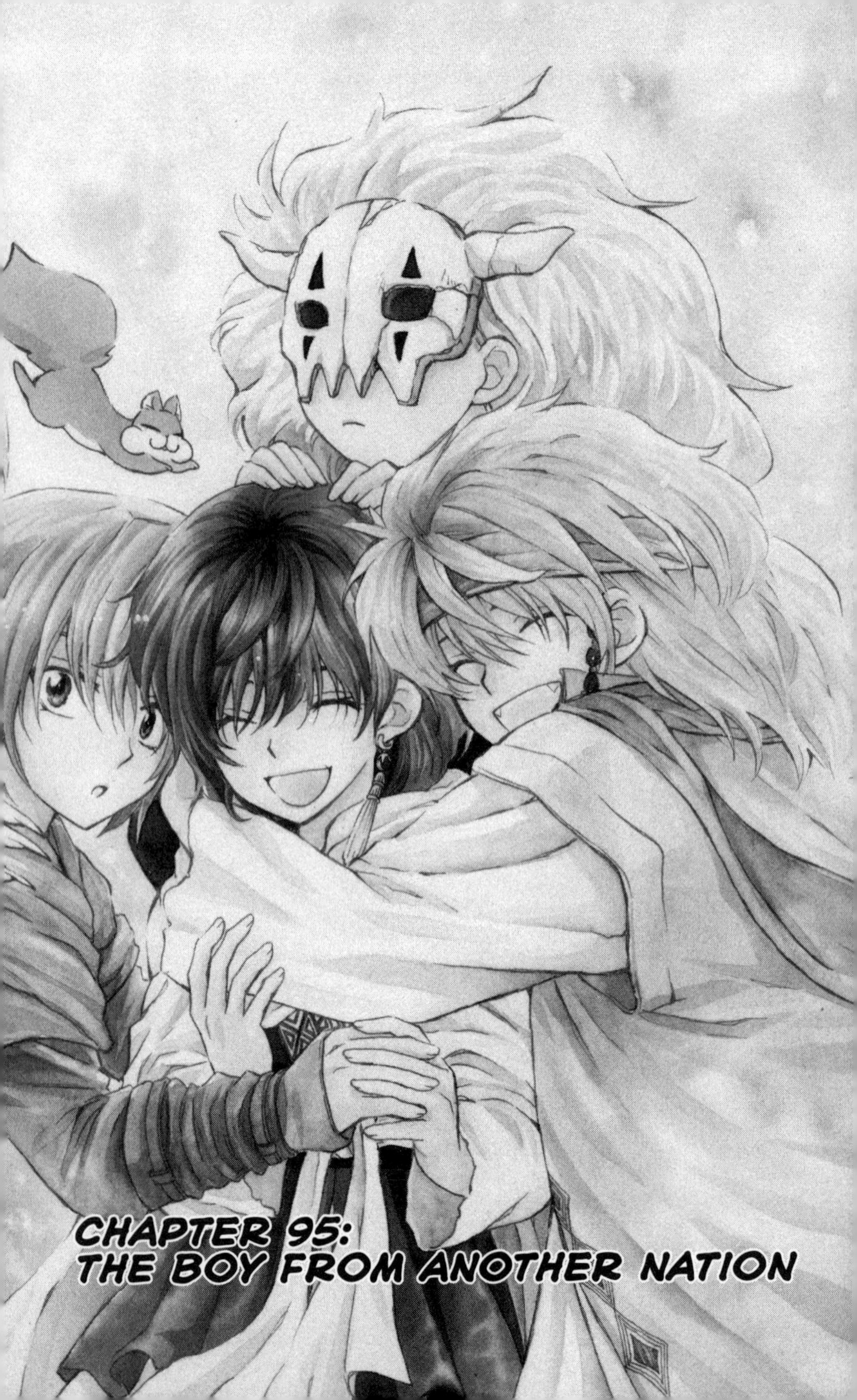

## CHAPTER 95:
## THE BOY FROM ANOTHER NATION

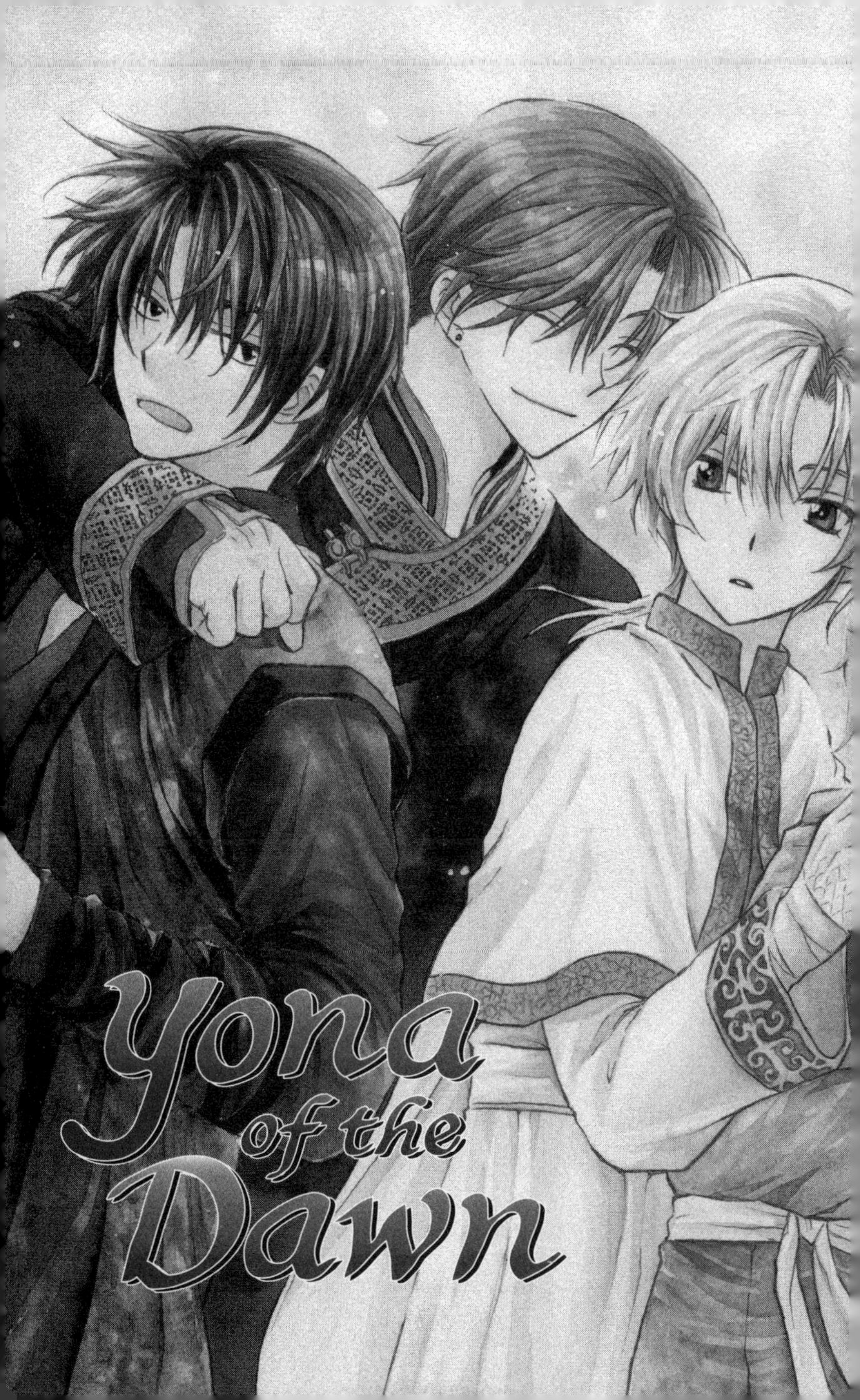
Yona
of the
Dawn

# A True Story!

My editor asked me to do some art for a magazine supplement.

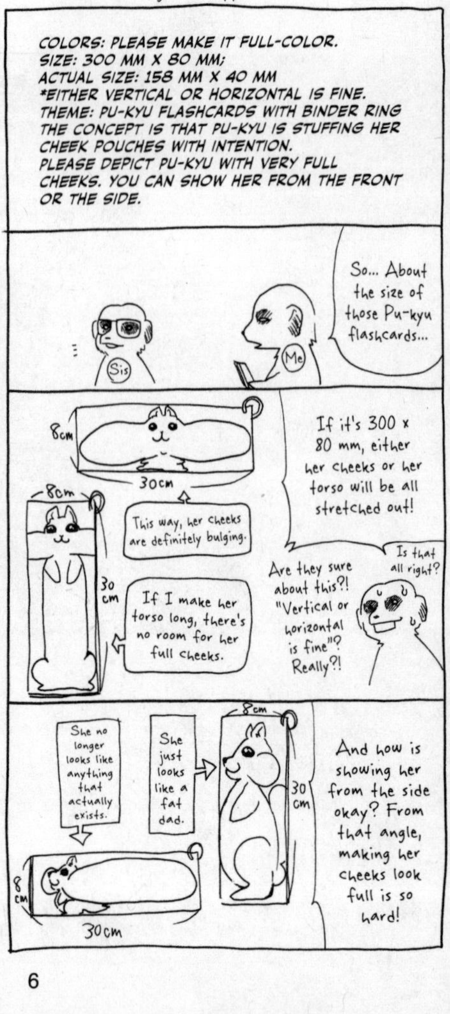
COLORS: PLEASE MAKE IT FULL-COLOR.
SIZE: 300 MM X 80 MM;
ACTUAL SIZE: 158 MM X 40 MM
*EITHER VERTICAL OR HORIZONTAL IS FINE.
THEME: PU-KYU FLASHCARDS WITH BINDER RING
THE CONCEPT IS THAT PU-KYU IS STUFFING HER CHEEK POUCHES WITH INTENTION.
PLEASE DEPICT PU-KYU WITH VERY FULL CHEEKS. YOU CAN SHOW HER FROM THE FRONT OR THE SIDE.
So... About the size of those Pu-kyu flashcards...
Me
Sis
If it's 300 x 80 mm, either her cheeks or her torso will be all stretched out!
Is that all right?
Are they sure about this?! "Vertical or horizontal is fine"? Really?!
8cm
30cm
This way, her cheeks are definitely bulging.
8cm
30 cm
If I make her torso long, there's no room for her full cheeks.
And how is showing her from the side okay? From that angle, making her cheeks look full is so hard!
8cm
30 cm
She just looks like a fat dad.
She no longer looks like anything that actually exists.
8 cm
30cm

My editor asked me to do some art for a magazine supplement. (Part 2)

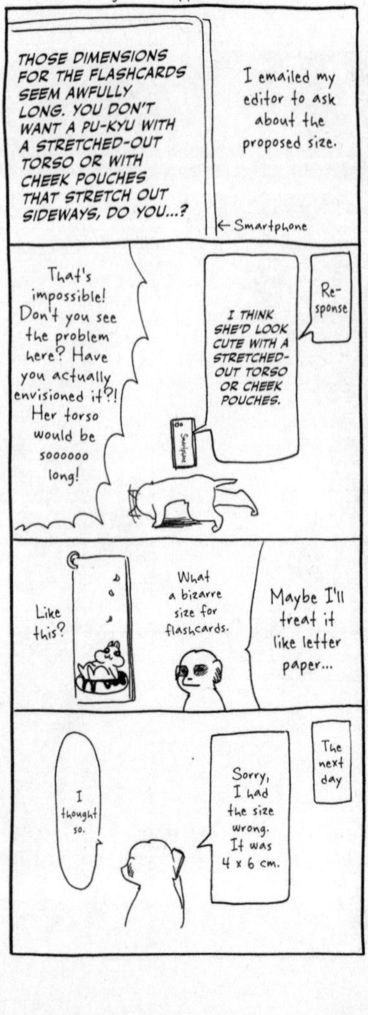
I emailed my editor to ask about the proposed size.
THOSE DIMENSIONS FOR THE FLASHCARDS SEEM AWFULLY LONG. YOU DON'T WANT A PU-KYU WITH A STRETCHED-OUT TORSO OR WITH CHEEK POUCHES THAT STRETCH OUT SIDEWAYS, DO YOU...?
← Smartphone
Re-sponse
I THINK SHE'D LOOK CUTE WITH A STRETCHED-OUT TORSO OR CHEEK POUCHES.
That's impossible! Don't you see the problem here? Have you actually envisioned it?! Her torso would be soooooo long!
Maybe I'll treat it like letter paper...
What a bizarre size for flashcards.
Like this?
The next day
Sorry, I had the size wrong. It was 4 x 6 cm.
I thought so.

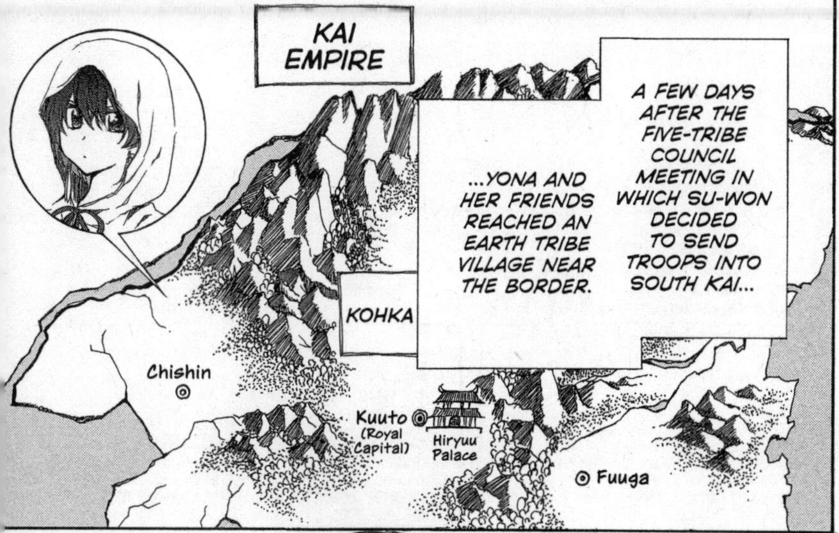
A FEW DAYS AFTER THE FIVE-TRIBE COUNCIL MEETING IN WHICH SU-WON DECIDED TO SEND TROOPS INTO SOUTH KAI...
...YONA AND HER FRIENDS REACHED AN EARTH TRIBE VILLAGE NEAR THE BORDER.
KAI EMPIRE
KOHKA
Chishin
Kuuto (Royal Capital)
Hiryuu Palace
Fuuga

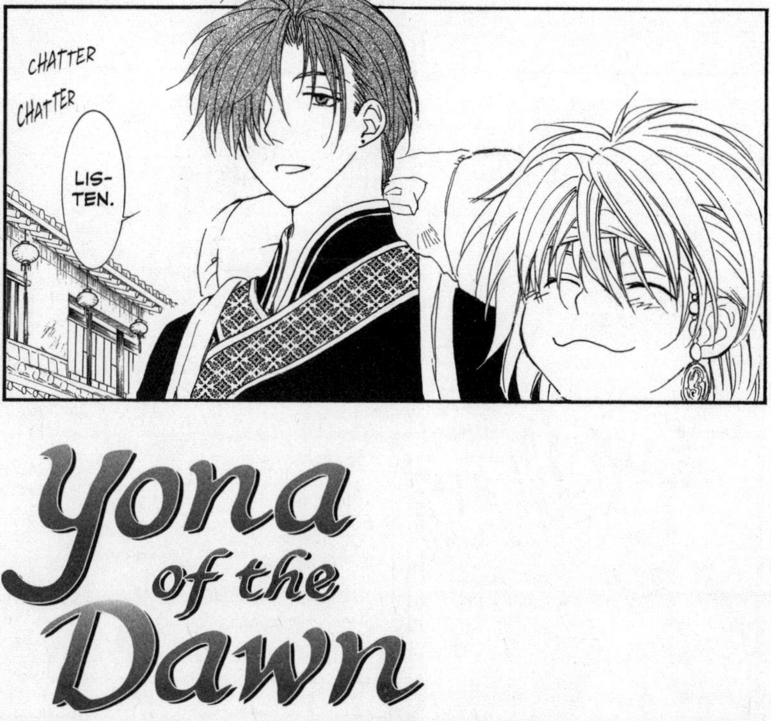
LIS-TEN.
CHATTER
CHATTER

# Yona of the Dawn

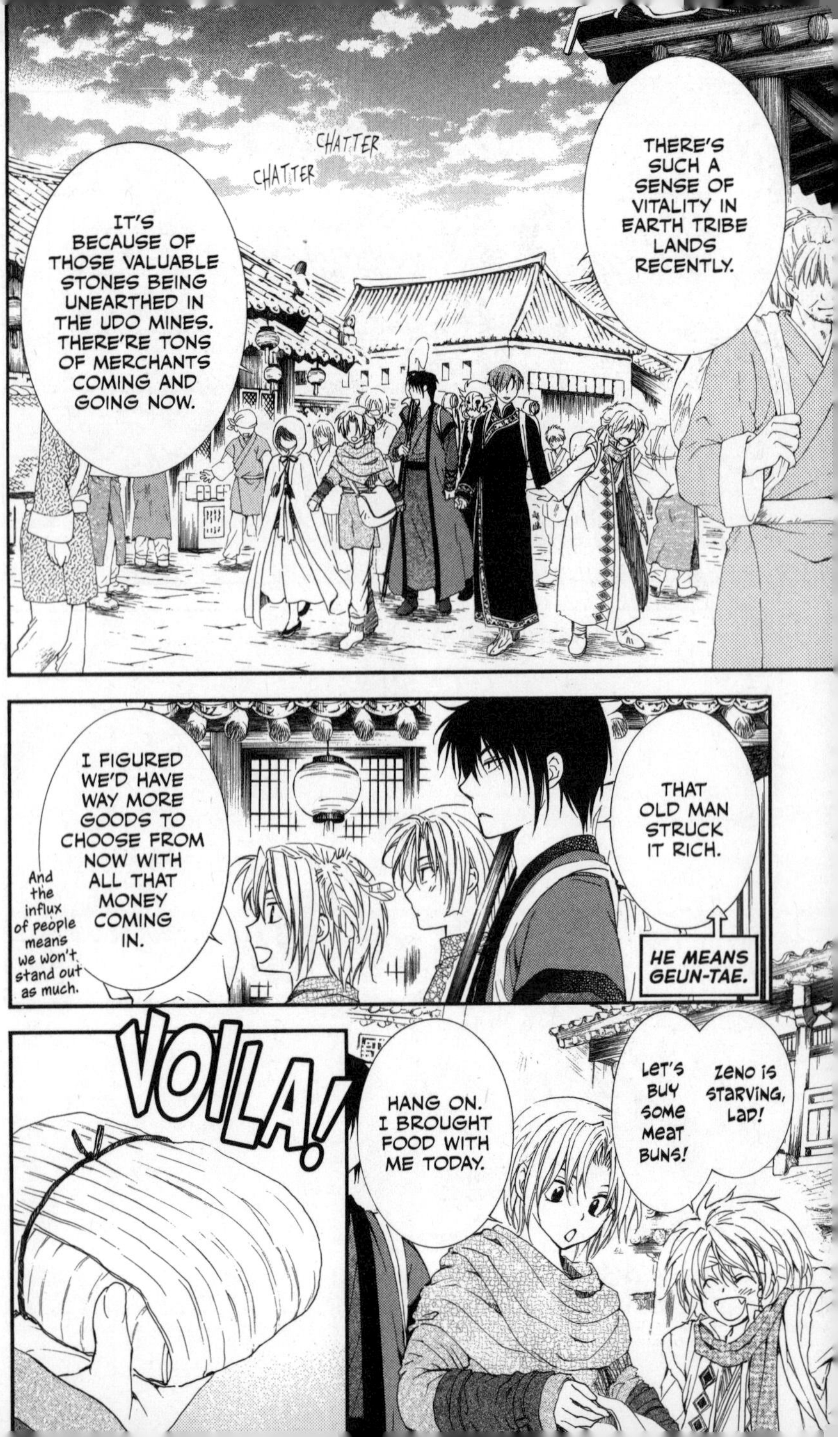
THERE'S SUCH A SENSE OF VITALITY IN EARTH TRIBE LANDS RECENTLY.
CHATTER
CHATTER
IT'S BECAUSE OF THOSE VALUABLE STONES BEING UNEARTHED IN THE UDO MINES. THERE'RE TONS OF MERCHANTS COMING AND GOING NOW.
THAT OLD MAN STRUCK IT RICH.
HE MEANS GEUN-TAE.
I FIGURED WE'D HAVE WAY MORE GOODS TO CHOOSE FROM NOW WITH ALL THAT MONEY COMING IN.
And the influx of people means we won't stand out as much.
Zeno is starving, lad!
Let's buy some meat buns!
HANG ON. I BROUGHT FOOD WITH ME TODAY.
VOILA!

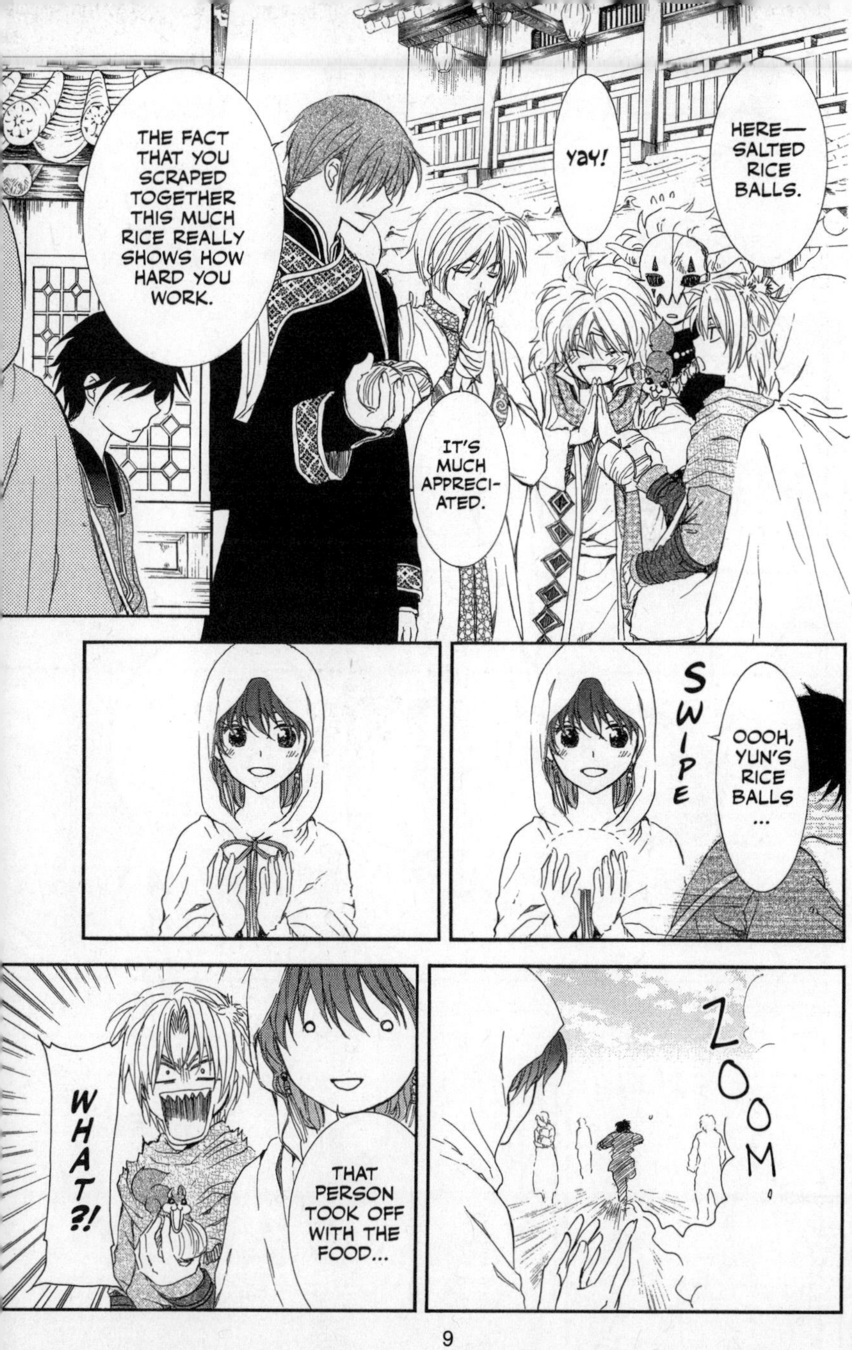
HERE—SALTED RICE BALLS.
YAY!
THE FACT THAT YOU SCRAPED TOGETHER THIS MUCH RICE REALLY SHOWS HOW HARD YOU WORK.
IT'S MUCH APPRECIATED.
SWIPE
OOOH, YUN'S RICE BALLS...
ZOOM
THAT PERSON TOOK OFF WITH THE FOOD...
WHAT?!

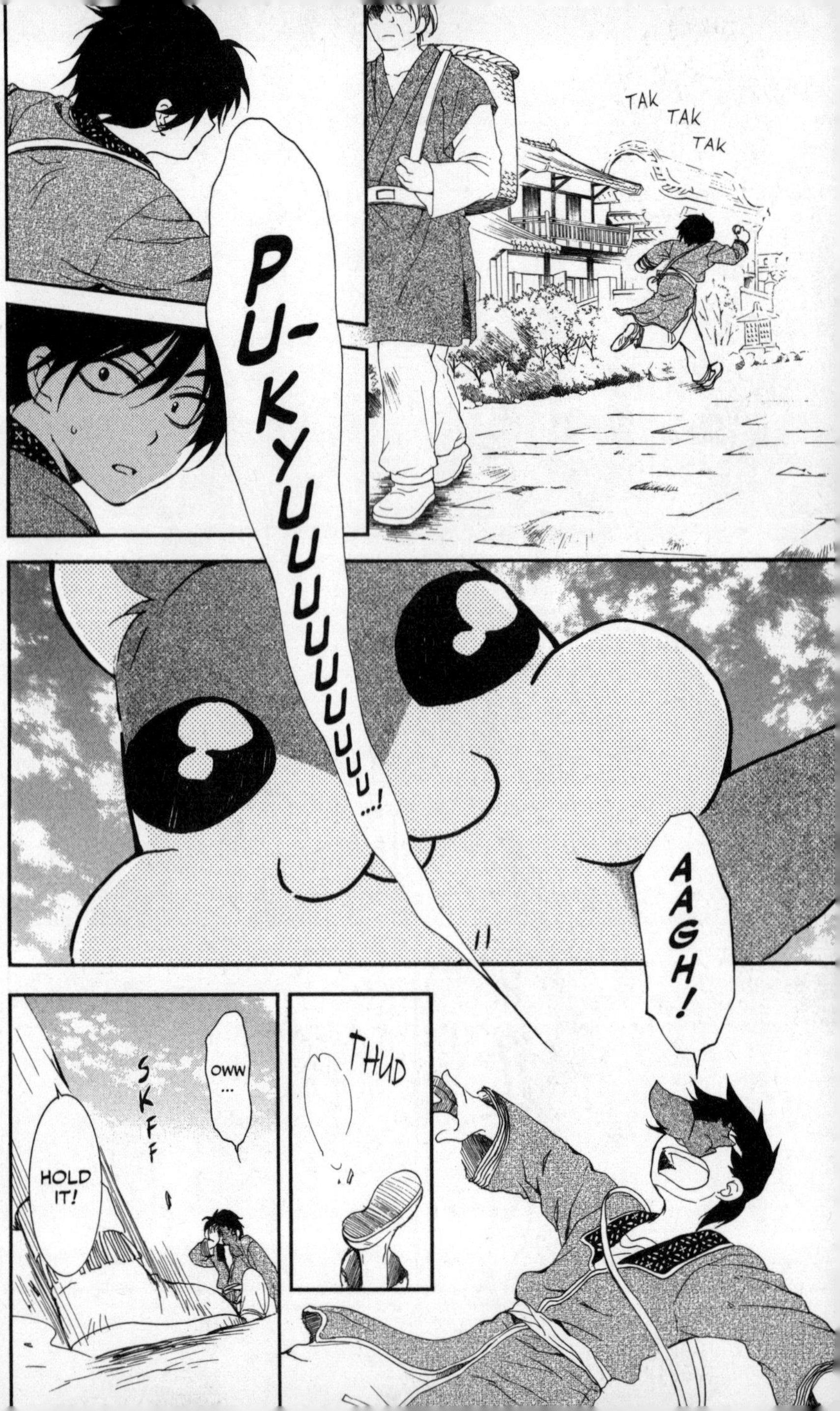
TAK
TAK
TAK
PU-KYUUUUUUUUUU...!
AAGH!
THUD
OWW...
SKFF
HOLD IT!

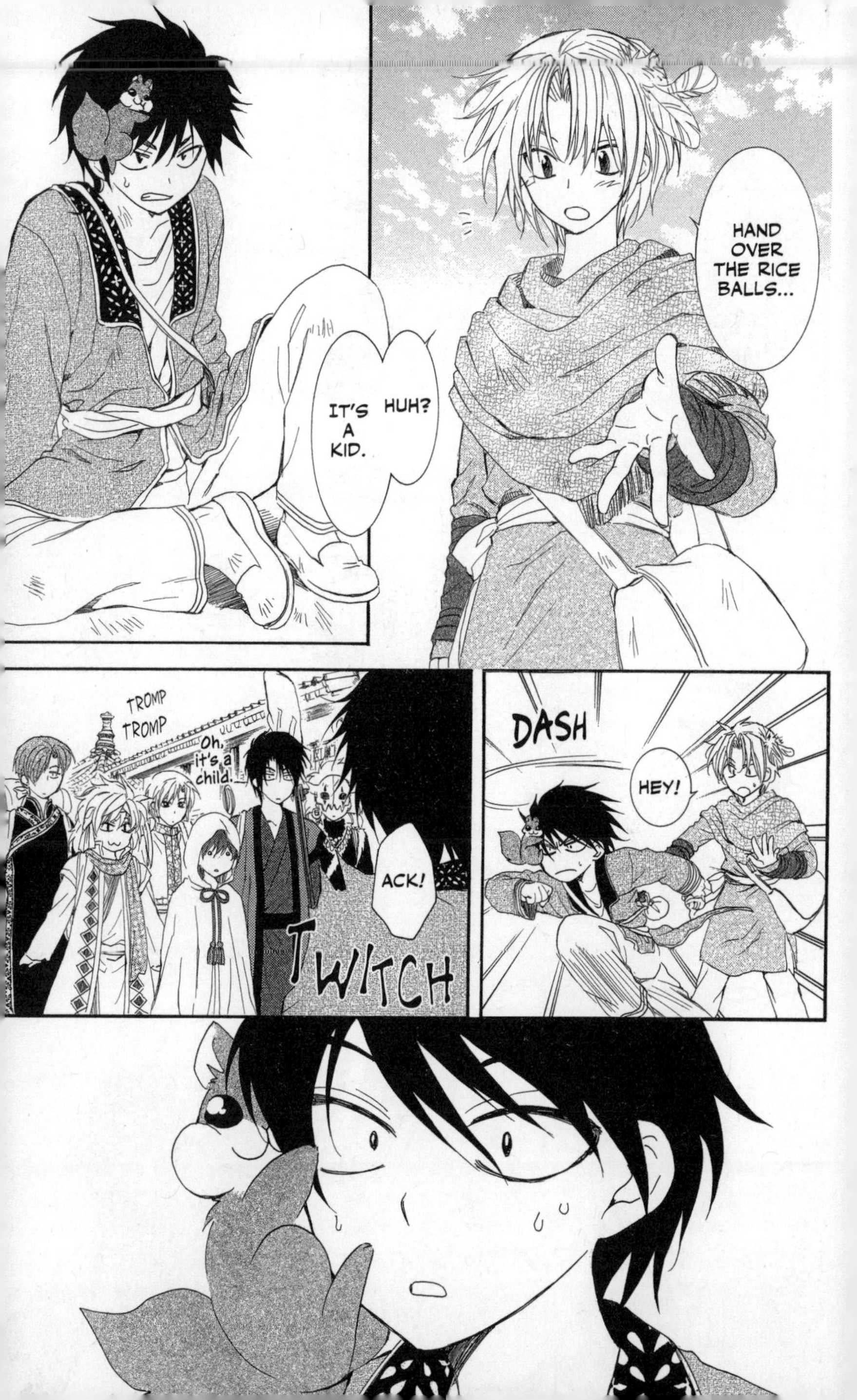
HAND OVER THE RICE BALLS...
HUH?
IT'S A KID.
DASH
HEY!
TROMP TROMP
Oh, it's a child.
ACK!
TWITCH

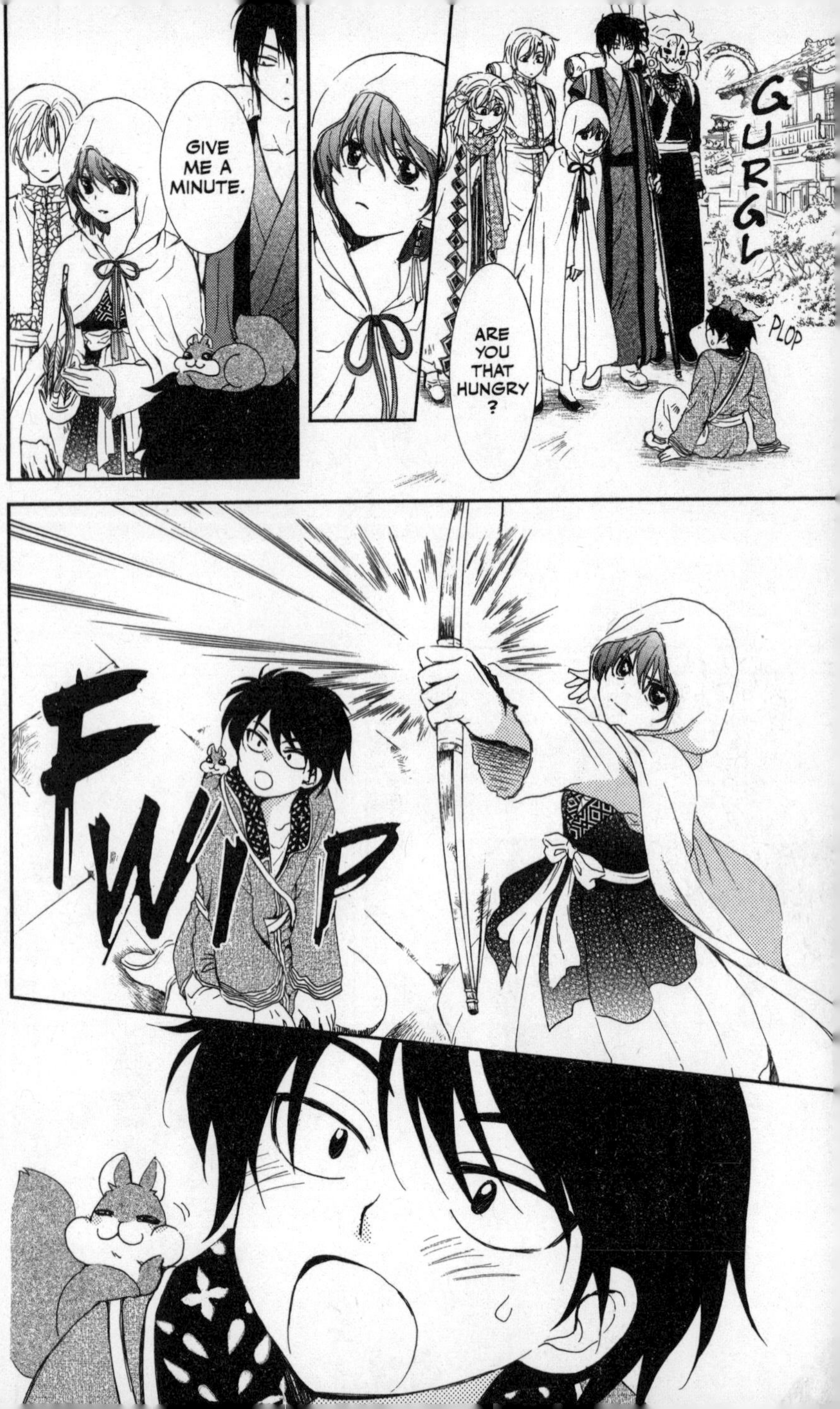
GURGL
PLOP
ARE YOU THAT HUNGRY?
GIVE ME A MINUTE.
FWIP

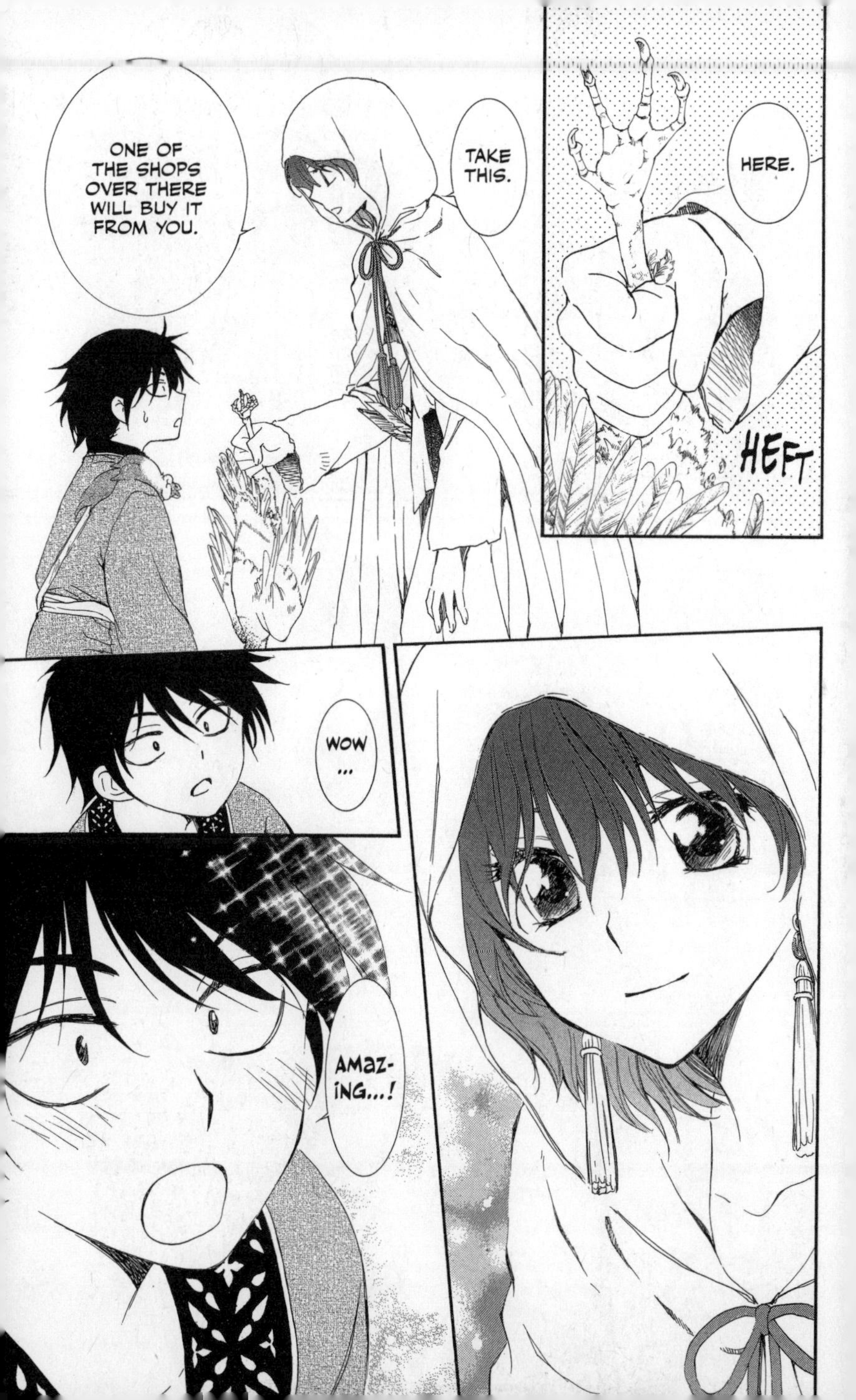
HERE.
HEFT
TAKE THIS.
ONE OF THE SHOPS OVER THERE WILL BUY IT FROM YOU.
WOW ...
AMAZ-ING...!

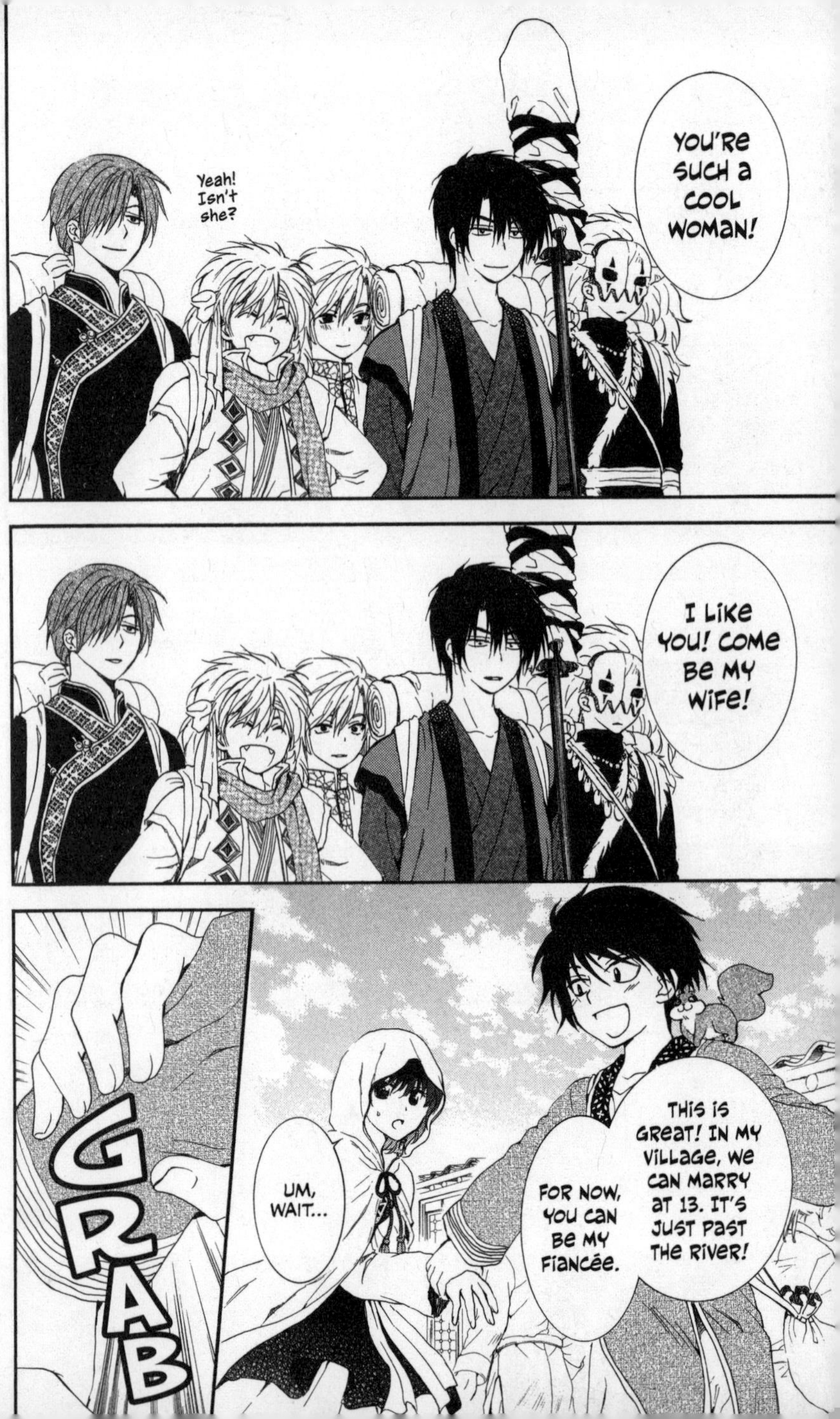
YOU'RE SUCH A COOL WOMAN!
Yeah! Isn't she?
I LIKE YOU! COME BE MY WIFE!
THIS IS GREAT! IN MY VILLAGE, WE CAN MARRY AT 13. IT'S JUST PAST THE RIVER!
FOR NOW, YOU CAN BE MY FIANCÉE.
UM, WAIT...
GRAB

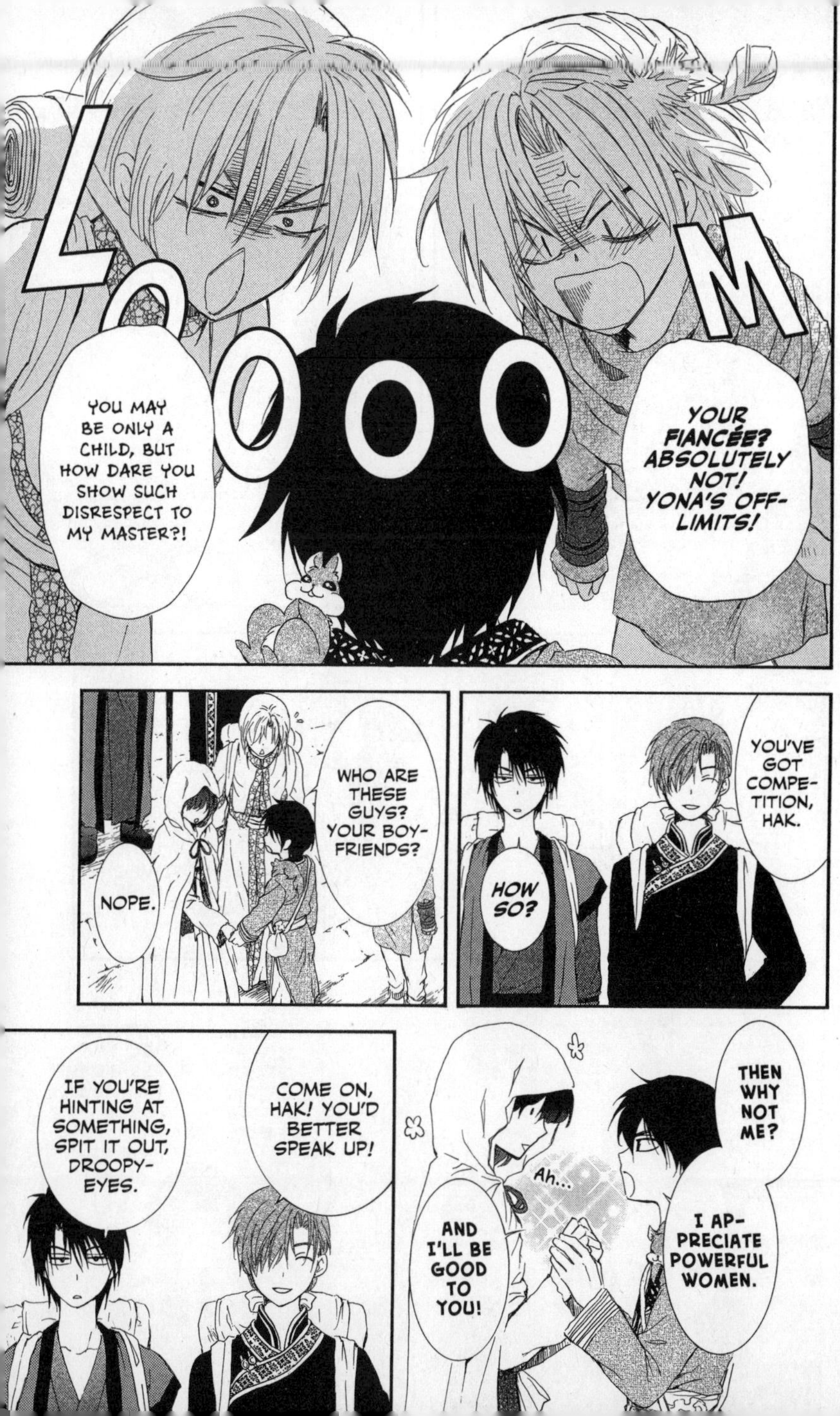
YOUR FIANCÉE? ABSOLUTELY NOT! YONA'S OFF-LIMITS!
LOOOOM
YOU MAY BE ONLY A CHILD, BUT HOW DARE YOU SHOW SUCH DISRESPECT TO MY MASTER?!
YOU'VE GOT COMPETITION, HAK.
HOW SO?
WHO ARE THESE GUYS? YOUR BOYFRIENDS?
NOPE.
THEN WHY NOT ME?
I APPRECIATE POWERFUL WOMEN.
Ah...
AND I'LL BE GOOD TO YOU!
COME ON, HAK! YOU'D BETTER SPEAK UP!
IF YOU'RE HINTING AT SOMETHING, SPIT IT OUT, DROOPY-EYES.

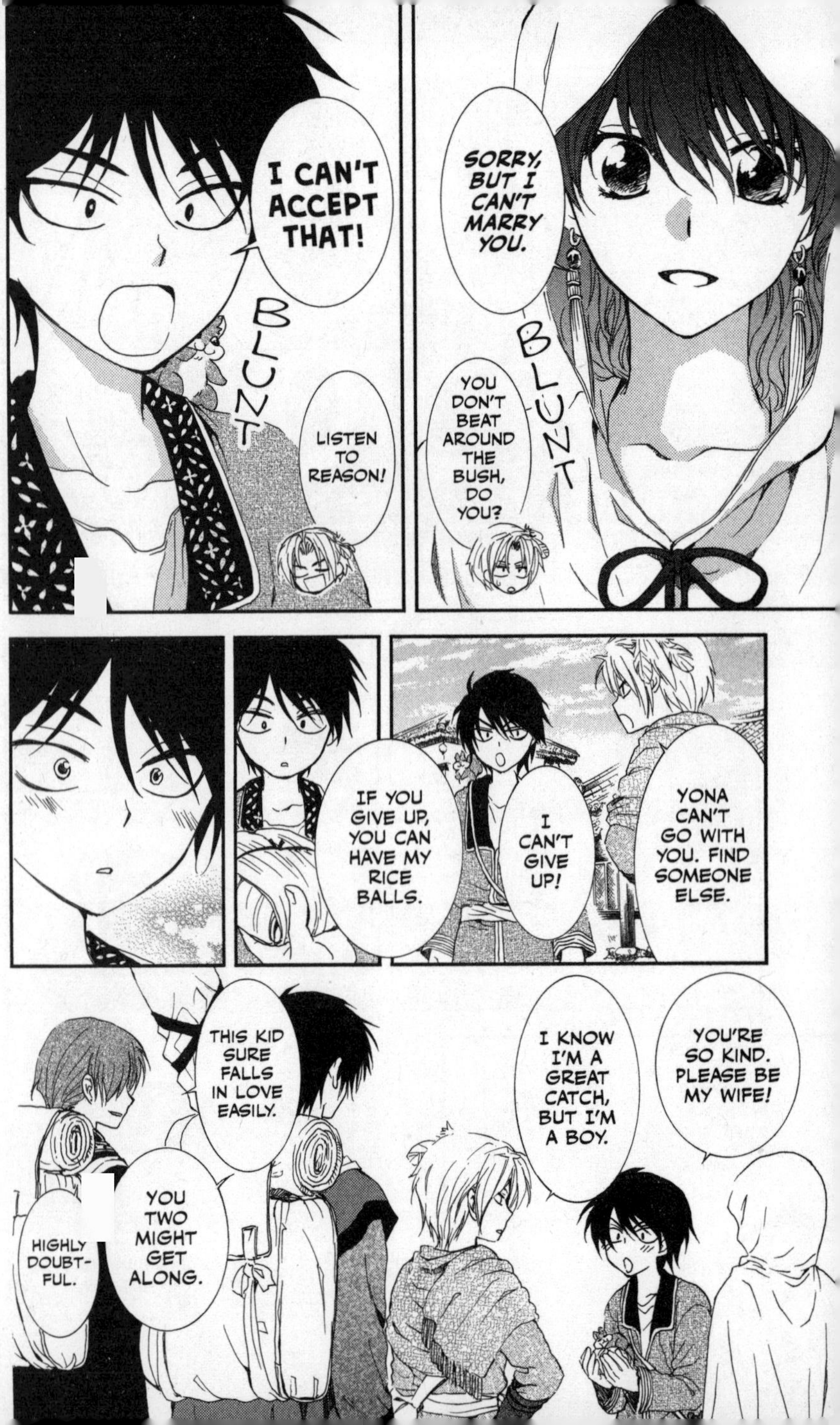
SORRY, BUT I CAN'T MARRY YOU.
BLUNT
YOU DON'T BEAT AROUND THE BUSH, DO YOU?
I CAN'T ACCEPT THAT!
BLUNT
LISTEN TO REASON!
YONA CAN'T GO WITH YOU. FIND SOMEONE ELSE.
I CAN'T GIVE UP!
IF YOU GIVE UP, YOU CAN HAVE MY RICE BALLS.
YOU'RE SO KIND. PLEASE BE MY WIFE!
I KNOW I'M A GREAT CATCH, BUT I'M A BOY.
THIS KID SURE FALLS IN LOVE EASILY.
YOU TWO MIGHT GET ALONG.
HIGHLY DOUBT-FUL.

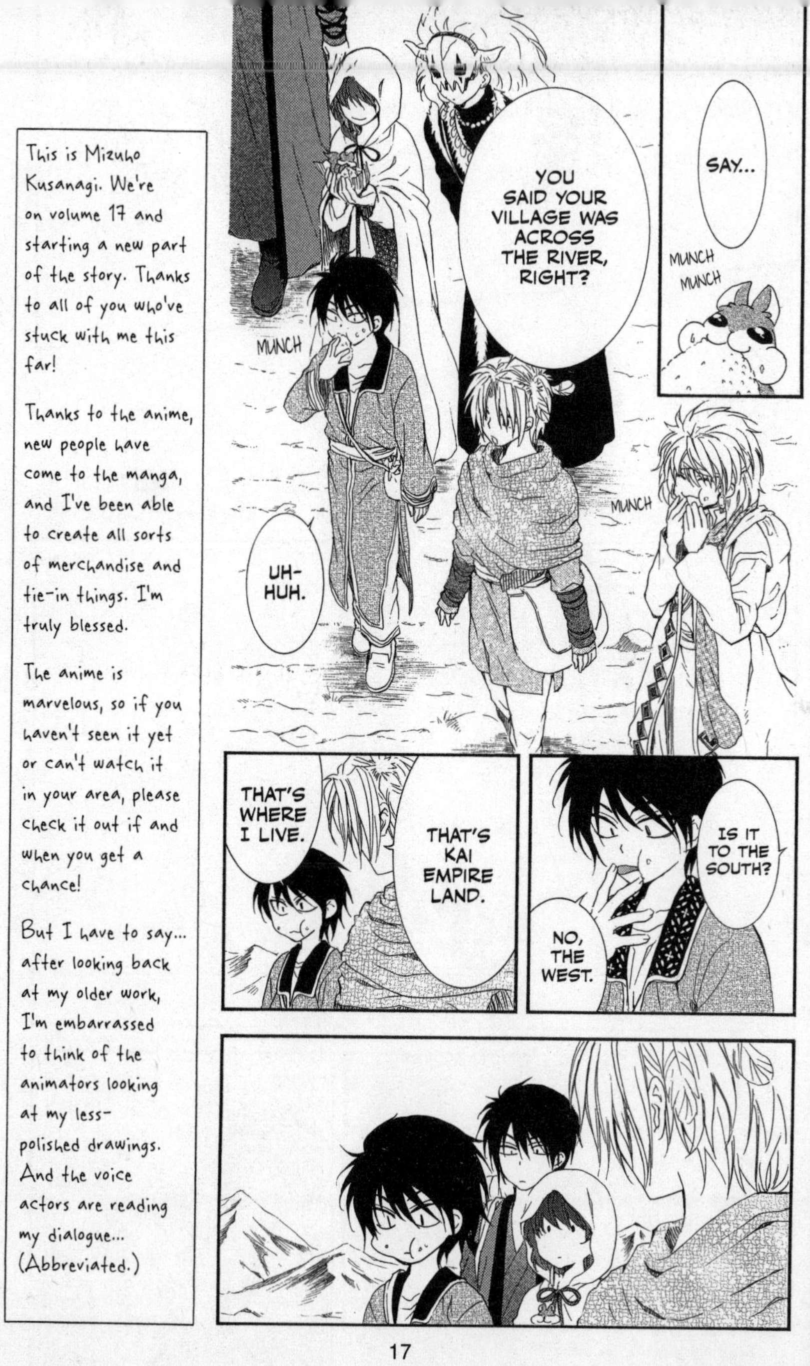

SAY...
MUNCH
MUNCH
YOU SAID YOUR VILLAGE WAS ACROSS THE RIVER, RIGHT?
MUNCH
MUNCH
UH-HUH.
IS IT TO THE SOUTH?
NO, THE WEST.
THAT'S KAI EMPIRE LAND.
THAT'S WHERE I LIVE.


This is Mizuho Kusanagi. We're on volume 17 and starting a new part of the story. Thanks to all of you who've stuck with me this far!

Thanks to the anime, new people have come to the manga, and I've been able to create all sorts of merchandise and tie-in things. I'm truly blessed.

The anime is marvelous, so if you haven't seen it yet or can't watch it in your area, please check it out if and when you get a chance!

But I have to say... after looking back at my older work, I'm embarrassed to think of the animators looking at my less-polished drawings. And the voice actors are reading my dialogue... (Abbreviated.)

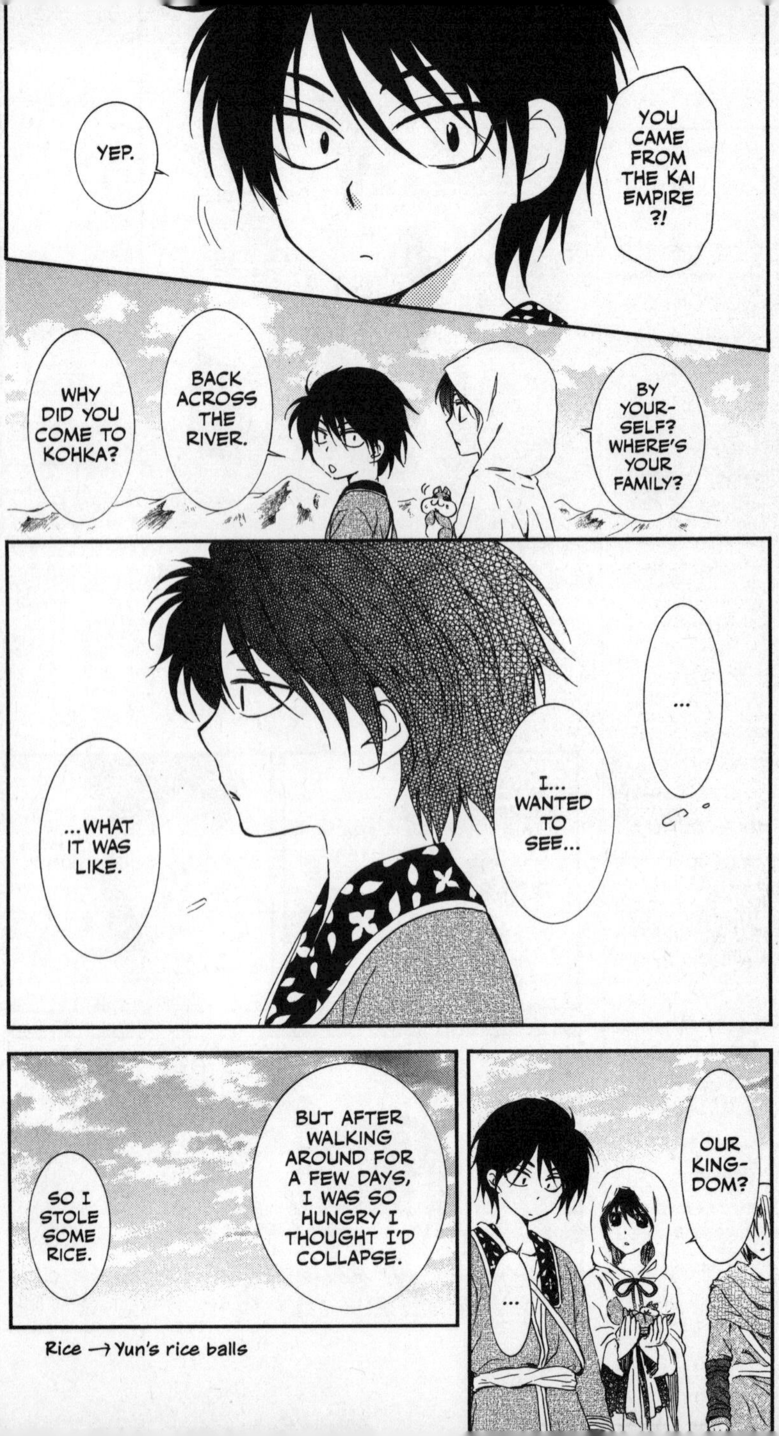
YOU CAME FROM THE KAI EMPIRE ?!
YEP.
BY YOUR-SELF? WHERE'S YOUR FAMILY?
BACK ACROSS THE RIVER.
WHY DID YOU COME TO KOHKA?
...
I... WANTED TO SEE...
...WHAT IT WAS LIKE.
OUR KING-DOM?
...
BUT AFTER WALKING AROUND FOR A FEW DAYS, I WAS SO HUNGRY I THOUGHT I'D COLLAPSE.
SO I STOLE SOME RICE.

Rice → Yun's rice balls

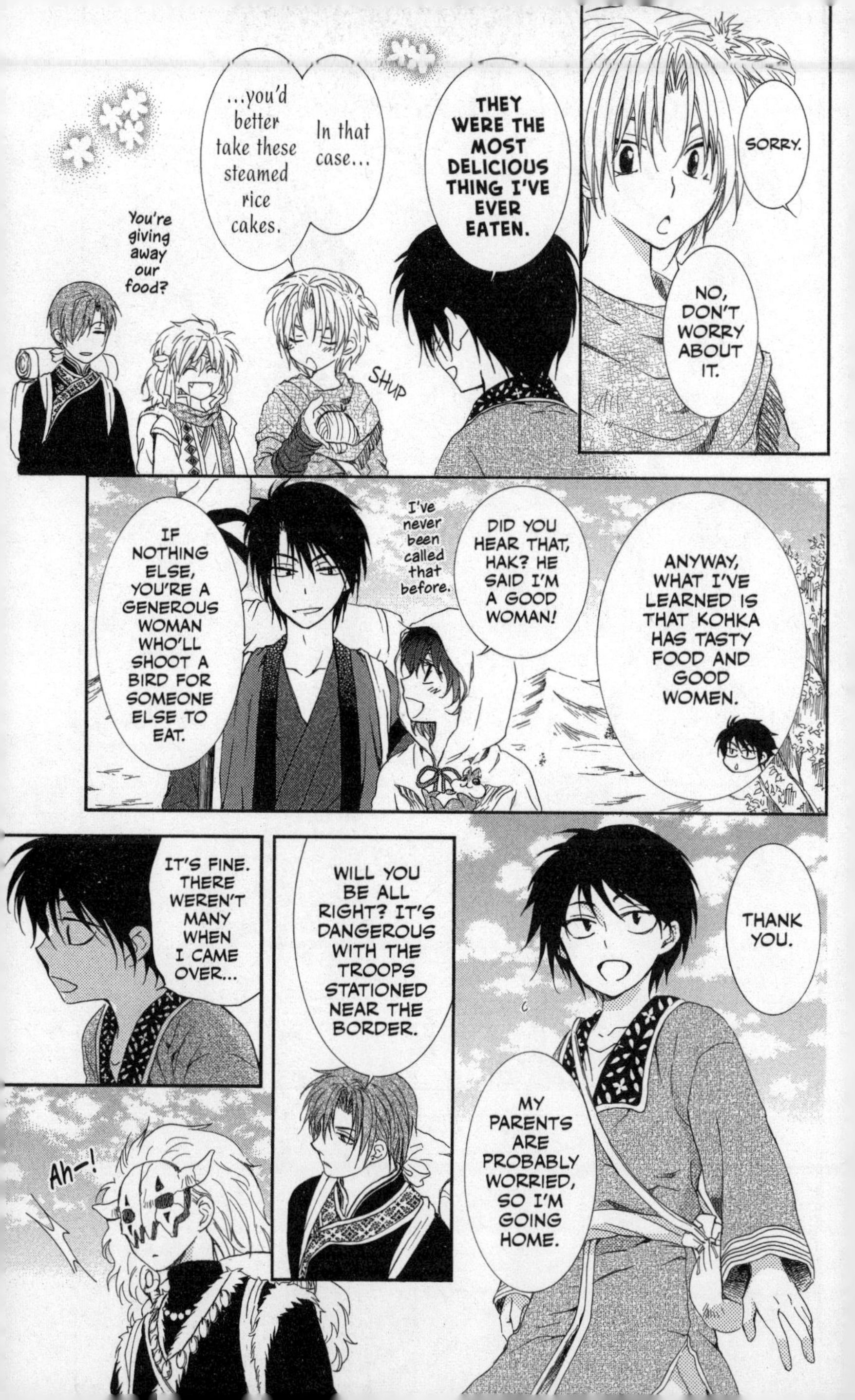
SORRY.
NO, DON'T WORRY ABOUT IT.
THEY WERE THE MOST DELICIOUS THING I'VE EVER EATEN.
In that case...
...you'd better take these steamed rice cakes.
SHUP
You're giving away our food?
ANYWAY, WHAT I'VE LEARNED IS THAT KOHKA HAS TASTY FOOD AND GOOD WOMEN.
DID YOU HEAR THAT, HAK? HE SAID I'M A GOOD WOMAN!
I've never been called that before.
IF NOTHING ELSE, YOU'RE A GENEROUS WOMAN WHO'LL SHOOT A BIRD FOR SOMEONE ELSE TO EAT.
THANK YOU.
MY PARENTS ARE PROBABLY WORRIED, SO I'M GOING HOME.
WILL YOU BE ALL RIGHT? IT'S DANGEROUS WITH THE TROOPS STATIONED NEAR THE BORDER.
IT'S FINE. THERE WEREN'T MANY WHEN I CAME OVER...
Ah—!

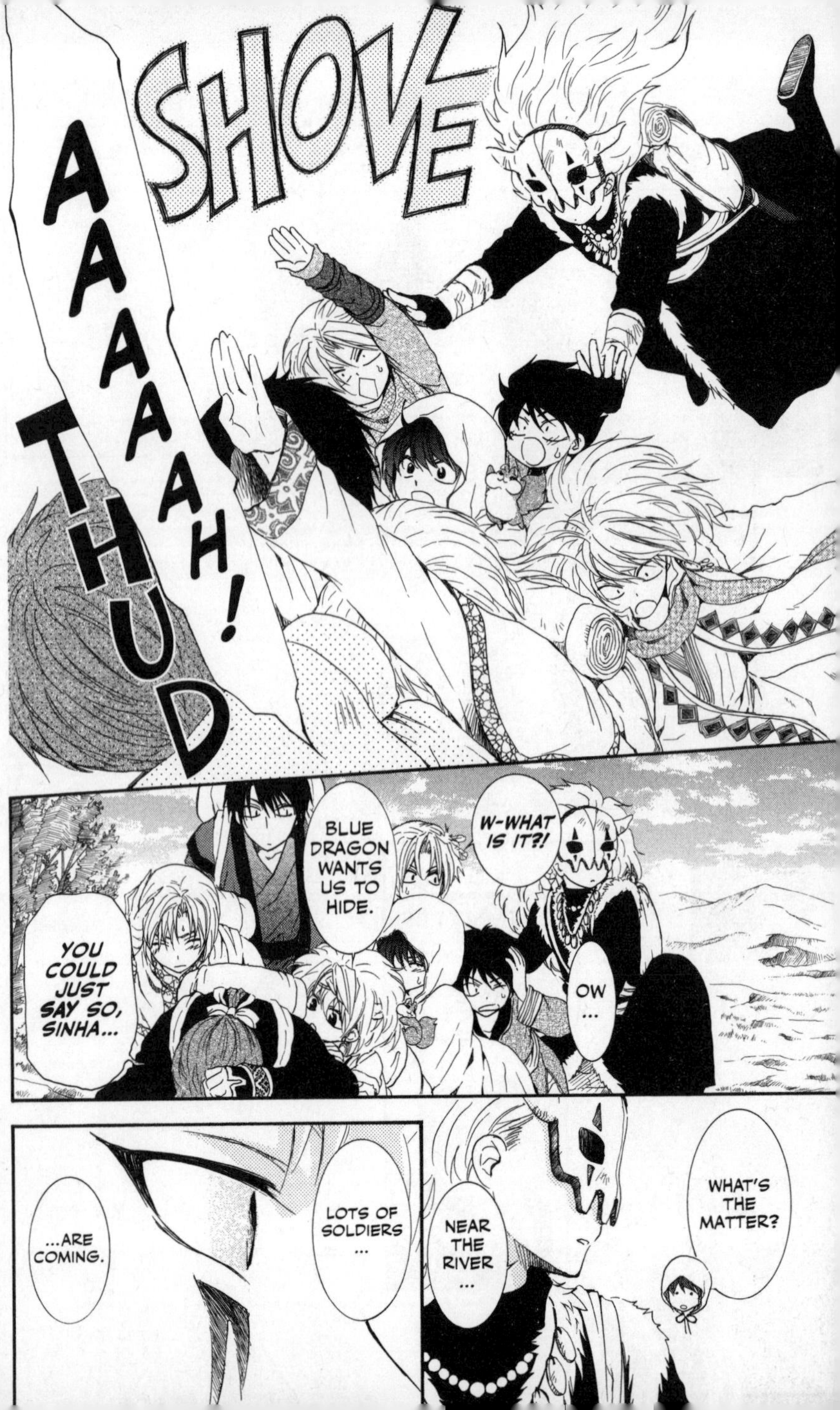
SHOVE
AAAAAH!
THUD
W-WHAT IS IT?!
BLUE DRAGON WANTS US TO HIDE.
OW ...
YOU COULD JUST SAY SO, SINHA...
WHAT'S THE MATTER?
NEAR THE RIVER ...
LOTS OF SOLDIERS ...
...ARE COMING.

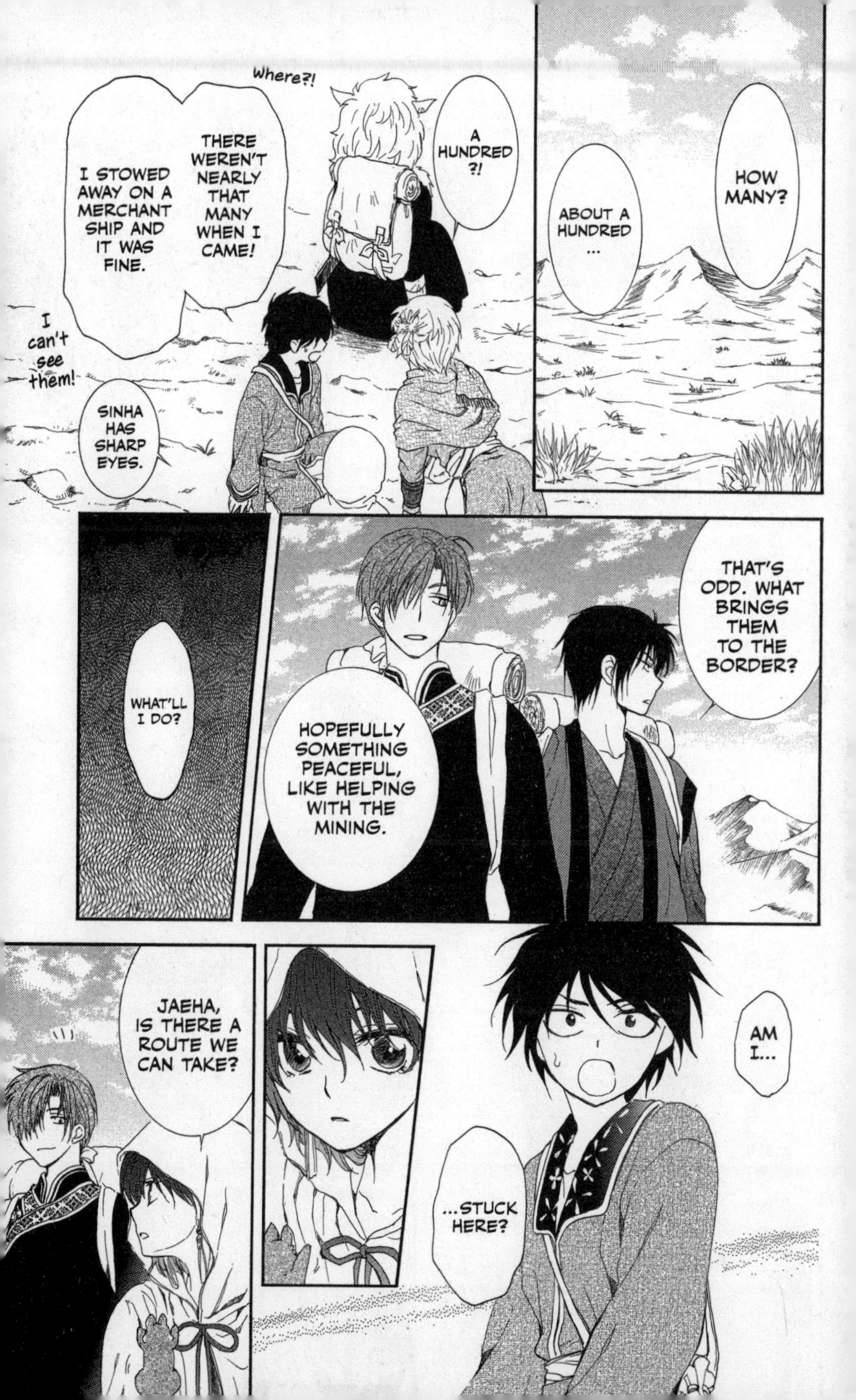
HOW MANY?
ABOUT A HUNDRED...
A HUNDRED?!
Where?!
THERE WEREN'T NEARLY THAT MANY WHEN I CAME!
I STOWED AWAY ON A MERCHANT SHIP AND IT WAS FINE.
I can't see them!
SINHA HAS SHARP EYES.
THAT'S ODD. WHAT BRINGS THEM TO THE BORDER?
HOPEFULLY SOMETHING PEACEFUL, LIKE HELPING WITH THE MINING.
WHAT'LL I DO?
AM I...
...STUCK HERE?
JAEHA, IS THERE A ROUTE WE CAN TAKE?

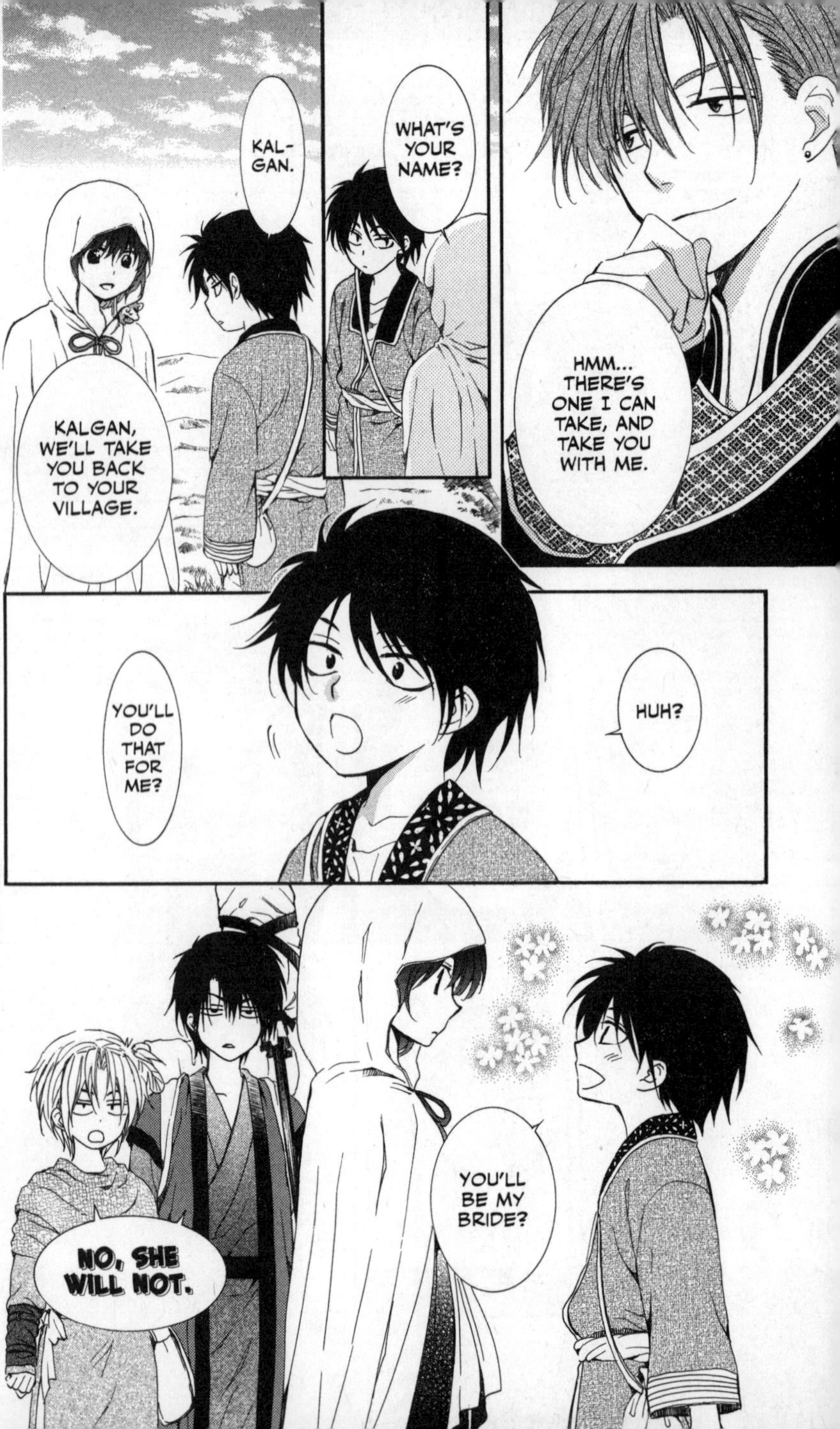
HMM... THERE'S ONE I CAN TAKE, AND TAKE YOU WITH ME.
WHAT'S YOUR NAME?
KAL-GAN.
KALGAN, WE'LL TAKE YOU BACK TO YOUR VILLAGE.
HUH?
YOU'LL DO THAT FOR ME?
YOU'LL BE MY BRIDE?
NO, SHE WILL NOT.

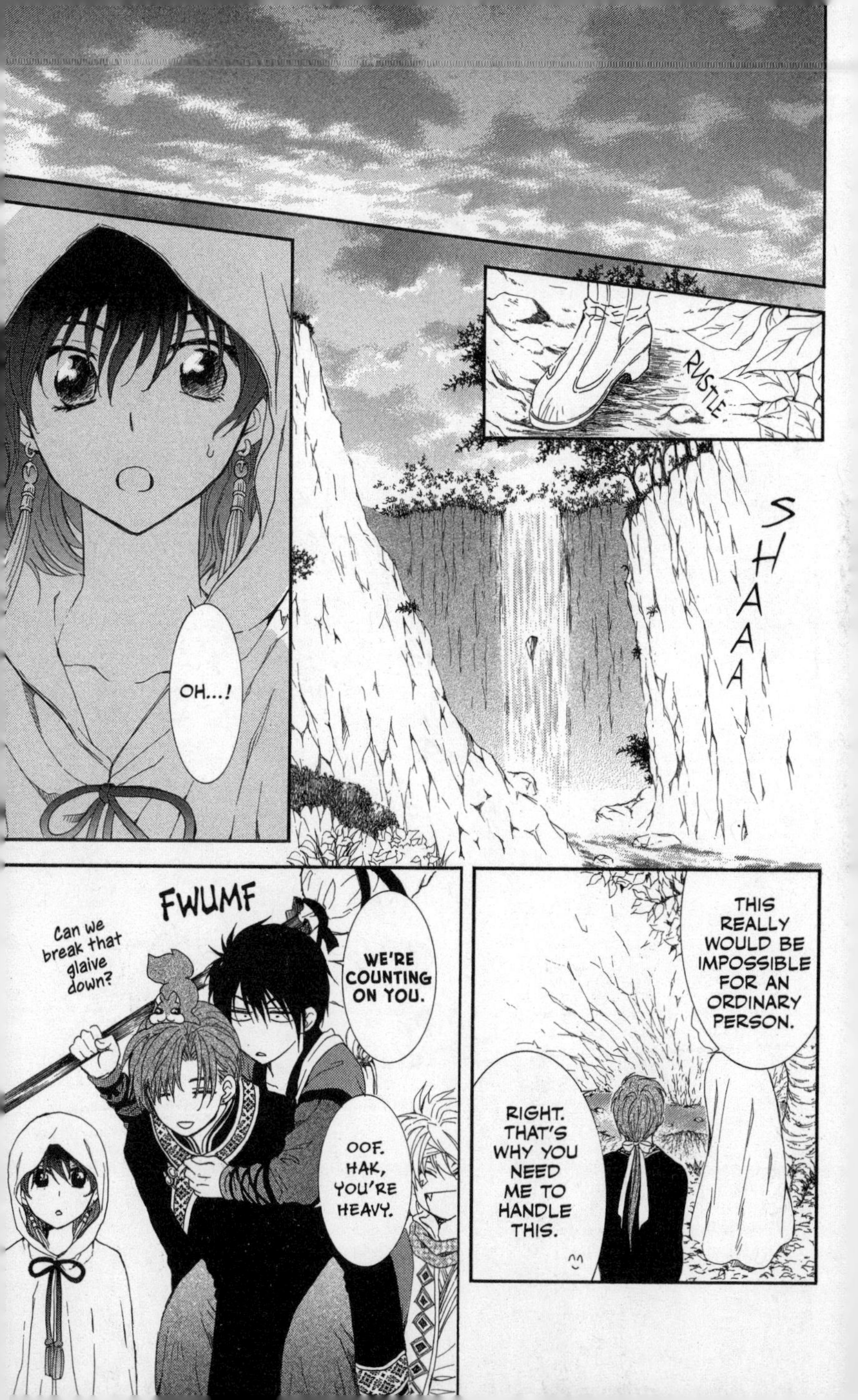
RUSTLE
SHAAAA
OH...!
THIS REALLY WOULD BE IMPOSSIBLE FOR AN ORDINARY PERSON.
RIGHT. THAT'S WHY YOU NEED ME TO HANDLE THIS.
WE'RE COUNTING ON YOU.
FWUMF
OOF. HAK, YOU'RE HEAVY.
Can we break that glaive down?

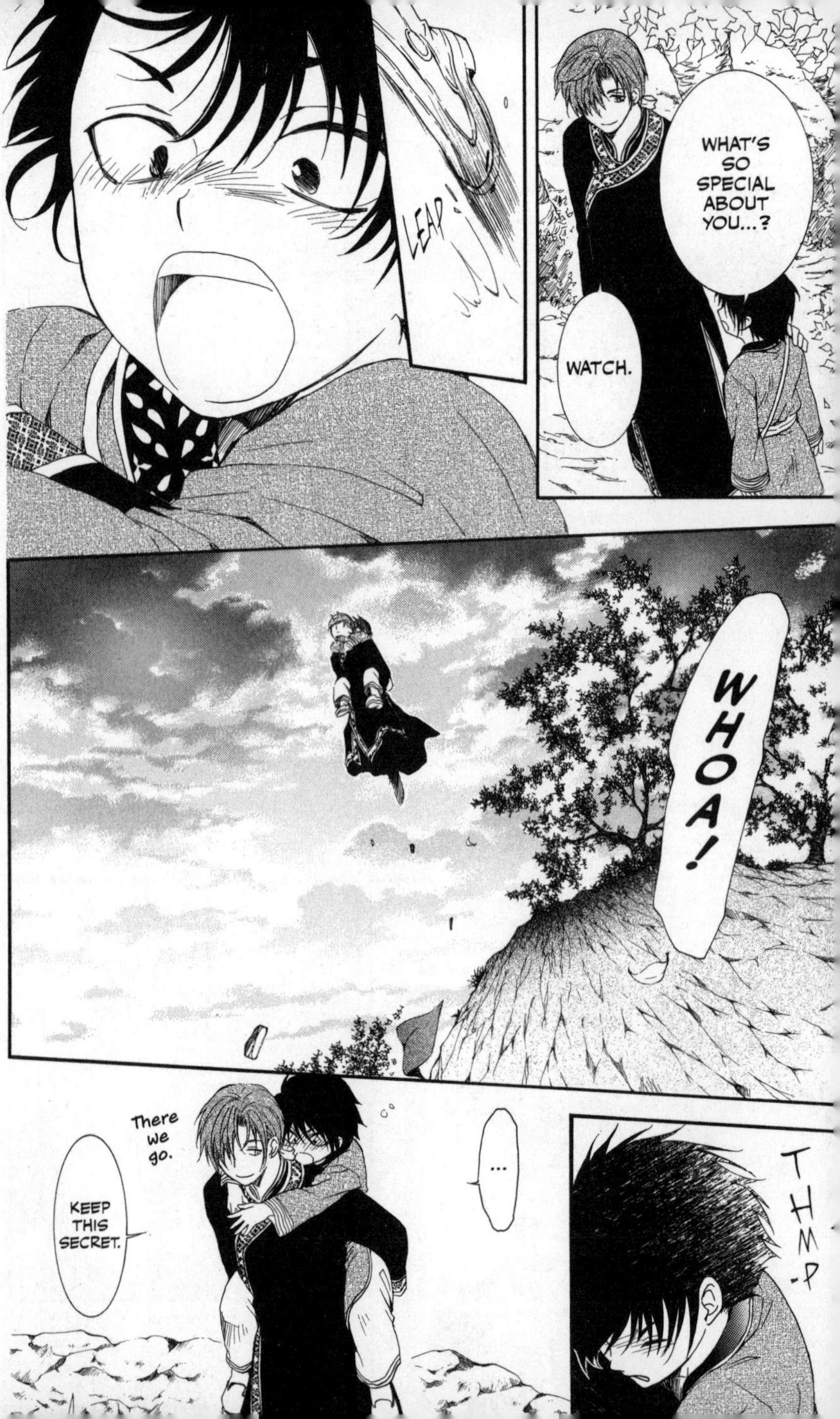

WHAT'S SO SPECIAL ABOUT YOU...?
WATCH.
LEAP!
WHOA!
THMP
...
There we go.
KEEP THIS SECRET.

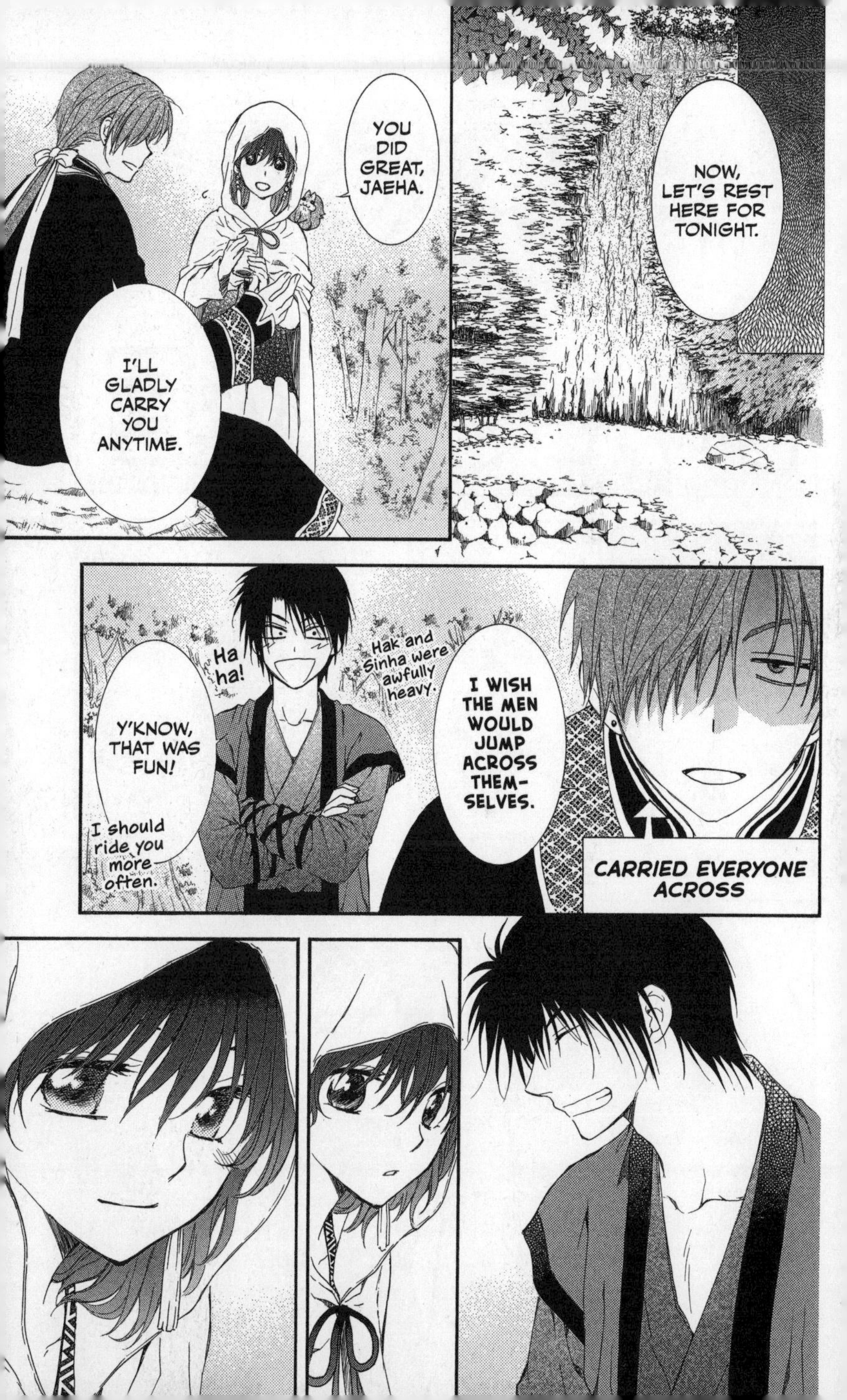
NOW, LET'S REST HERE FOR TONIGHT.
YOU DID GREAT, JAEHA.
I'LL GLADLY CARRY YOU ANYTIME.
I WISH THE MEN WOULD JUMP ACROSS THEM-SELVES.
CARRIED EVERYONE ACROSS
Hak and Sinha were awfully heavy.
Ha ha!
Y'KNOW, THAT WAS FUN!
I should ride you more often.

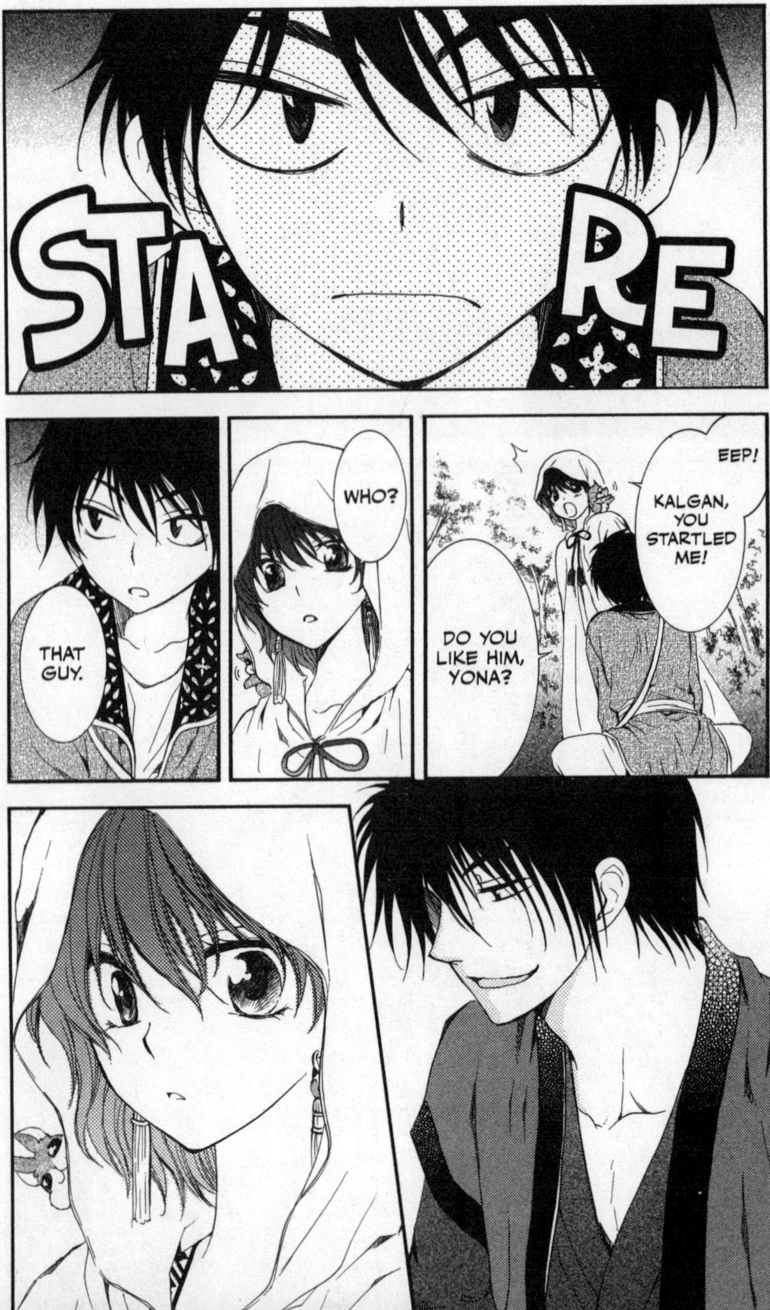
STARE
EEP!
KALGAN, YOU STARTLED ME!
DO YOU LIKE HIM, YONA?
WHO?
THAT GUY.

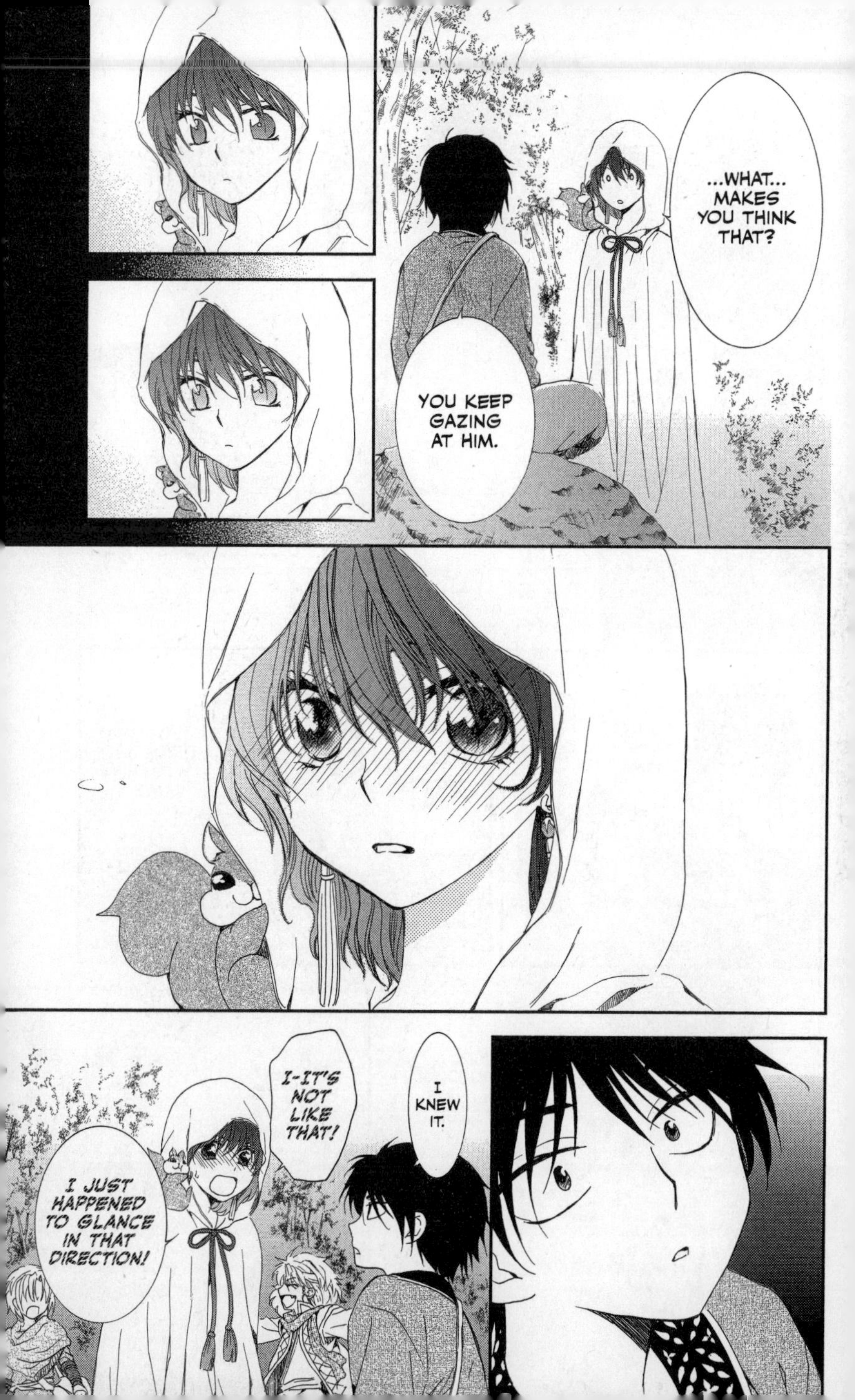
...WHAT... MAKES YOU THINK THAT?
YOU KEEP GAZING AT HIM.
I KNEW IT.
I-IT'S NOT LIKE THAT!
I JUST HAPPENED TO GLANCE IN THAT DIRECTION!

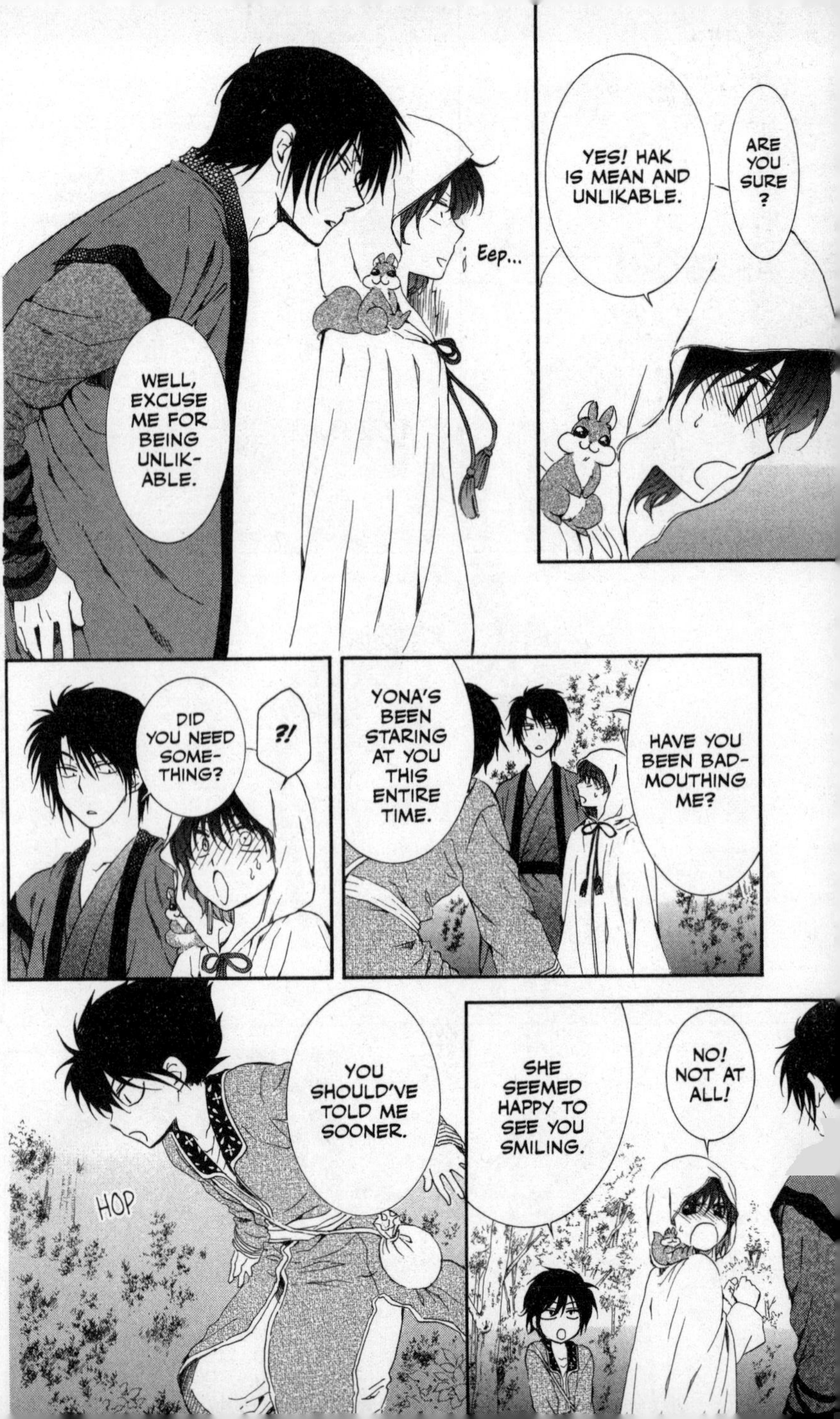
ARE YOU SURE?
YES! HAK IS MEAN AND UNLIKABLE.
Eep...
WELL, EXCUSE ME FOR BEING UNLIKABLE.
HAVE YOU BEEN BAD-MOUTHING ME?
YONA'S BEEN STARING AT YOU THIS ENTIRE TIME.
?!
DID YOU NEED SOMETHING?
NO! NOT AT ALL!
SHE SEEMED HAPPY TO SEE YOU SMILING.
YOU SHOULD'VE TOLD ME SOONER.
HOP

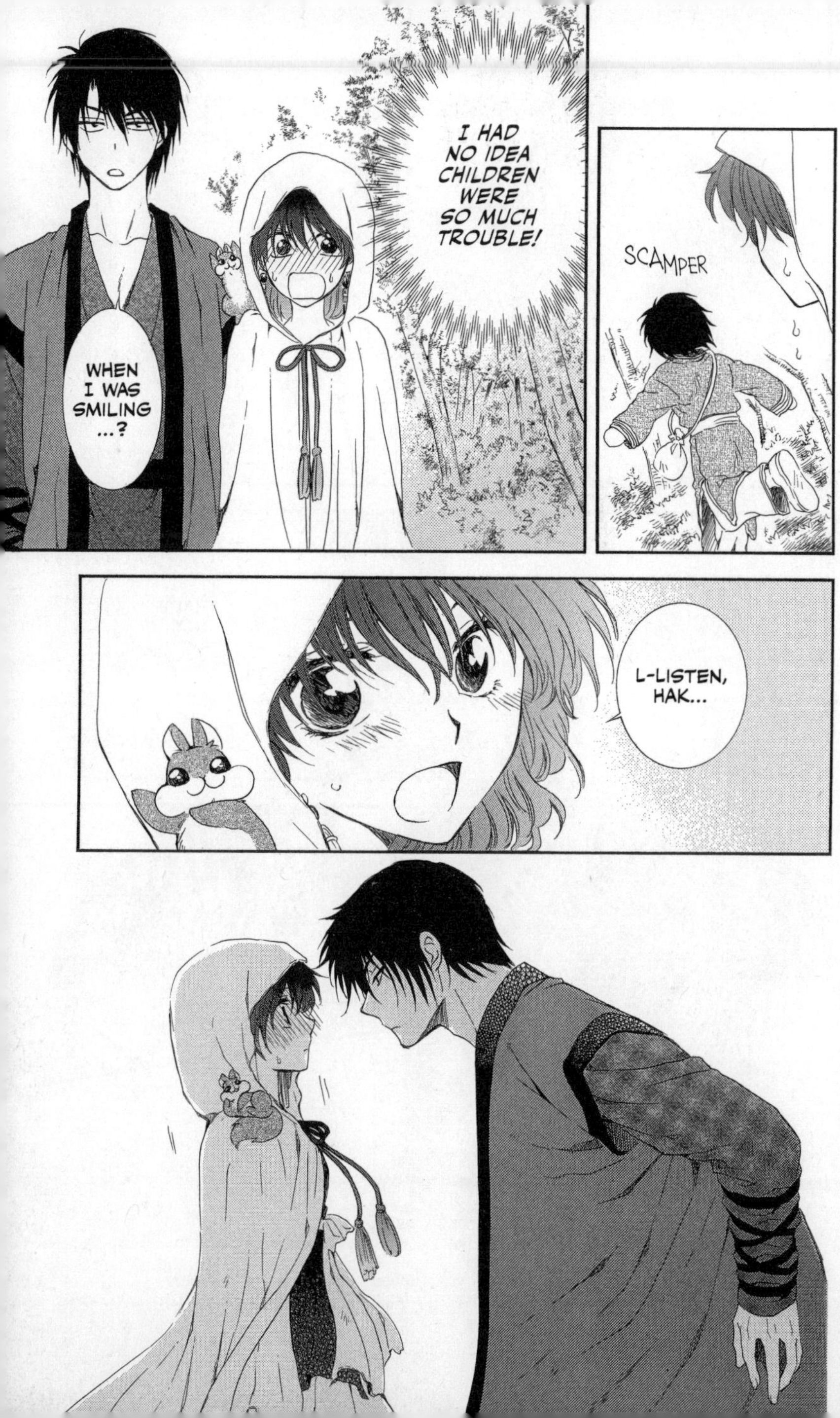
SCAMPER
I HAD NO IDEA CHILDREN WERE SO MUCH TROUBLE!
WHEN I WAS SMILING ...?
L-LISTEN, HAK...

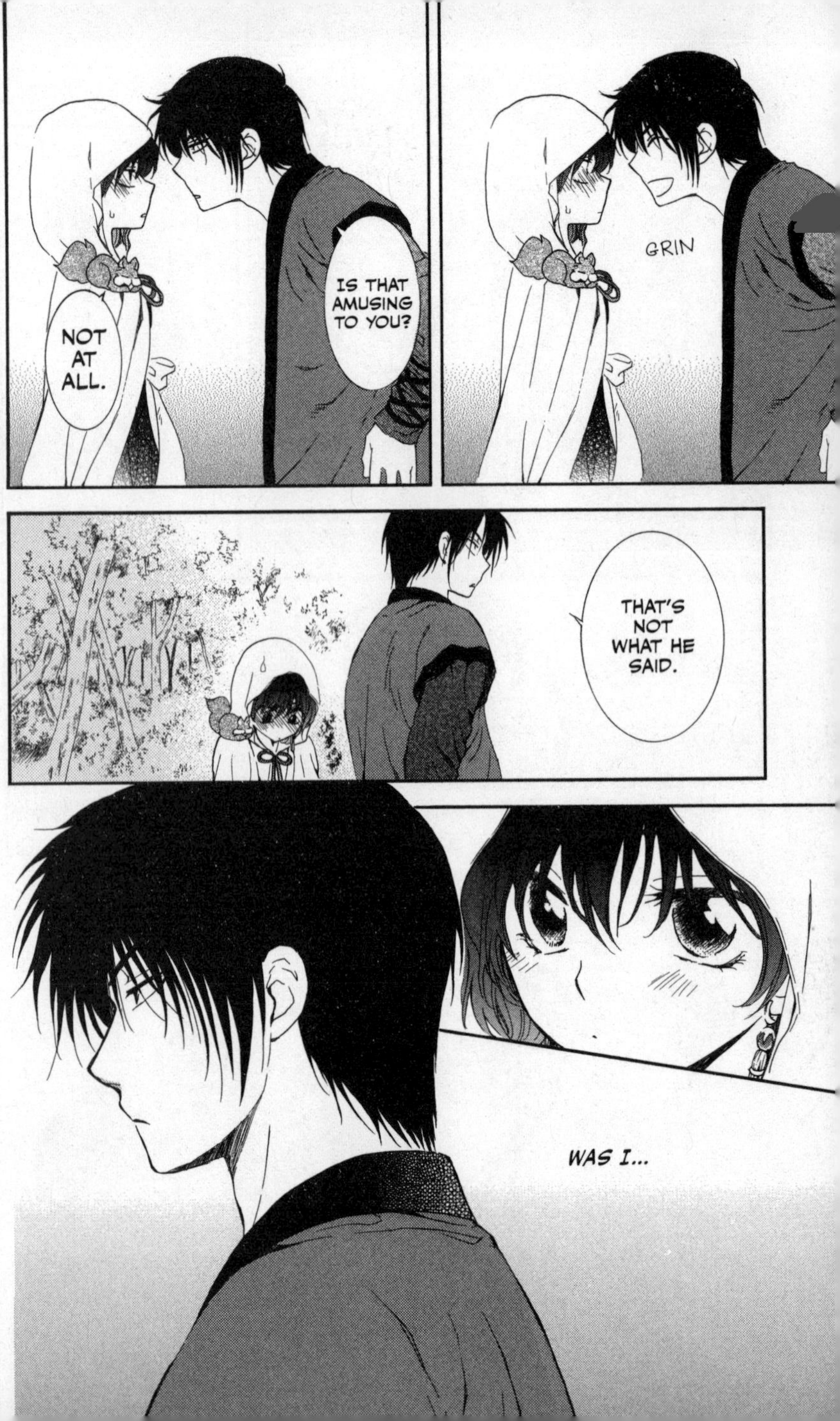
GRIN
IS THAT AMUSING TO YOU?
NOT AT ALL.
THAT'S NOT WHAT HE SAID.
WAS I...

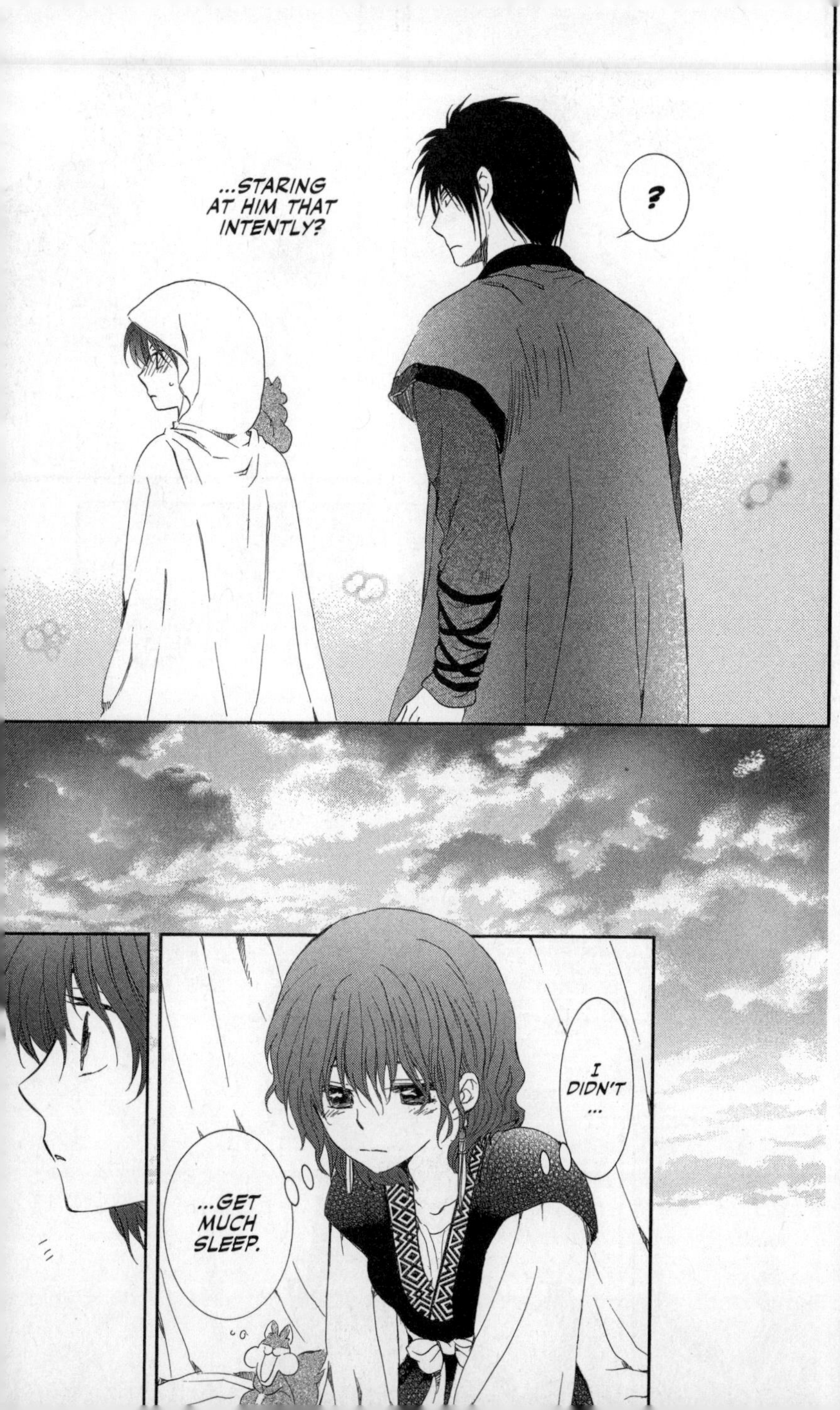
?
...STARING AT HIM THAT INTENTLY?
I DIDN'T ...
...GET MUCH SLEEP.

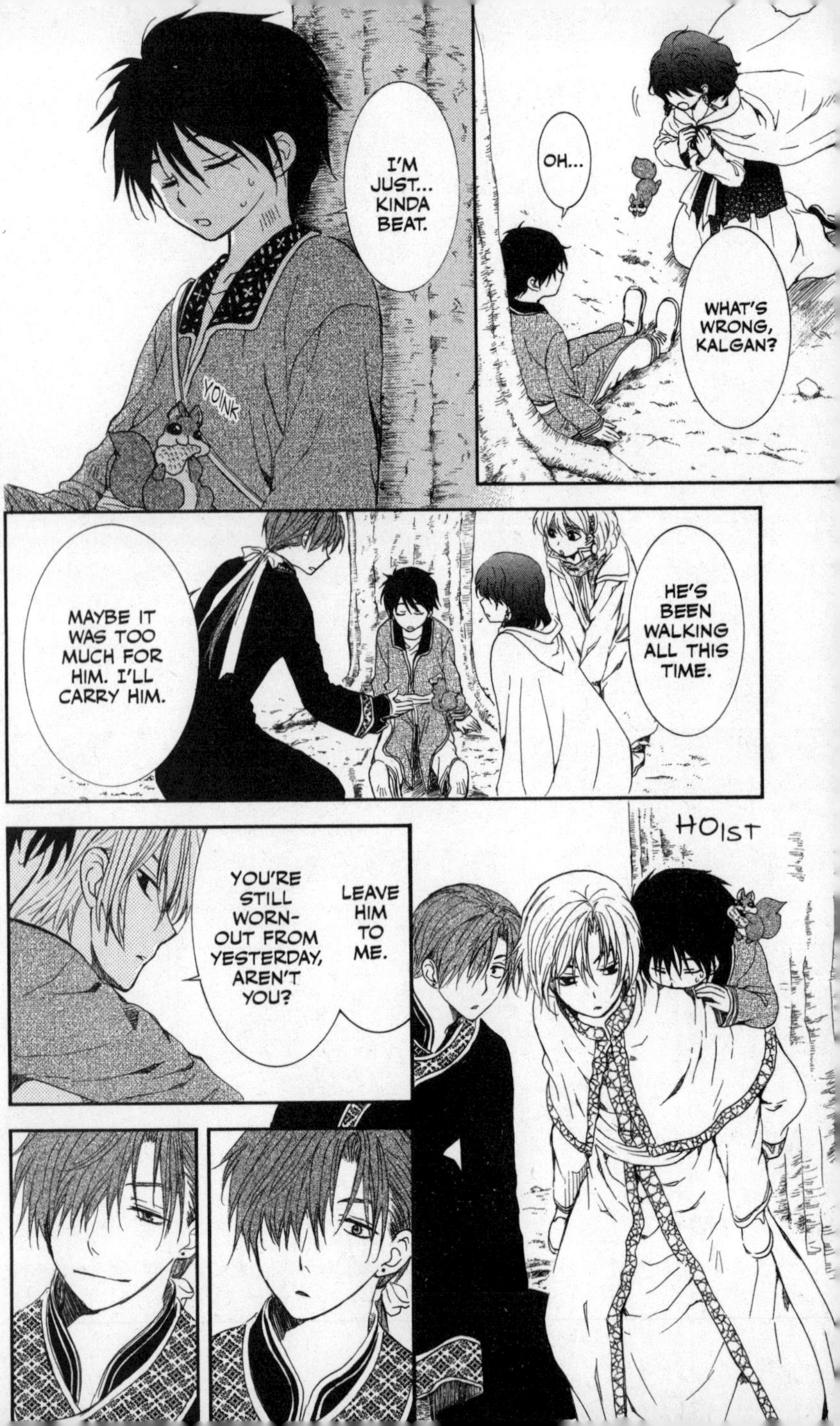
OH...
WHAT'S WRONG, KALGAN?
I'M JUST... KINDA BEAT.
YOINK
HE'S BEEN WALKING ALL THIS TIME.
MAYBE IT WAS TOO MUCH FOR HIM. I'LL CARRY HIM.
HOIST
LEAVE HIM TO ME.
YOU'RE STILL WORN-OUT FROM YESTERDAY, AREN'T YOU?

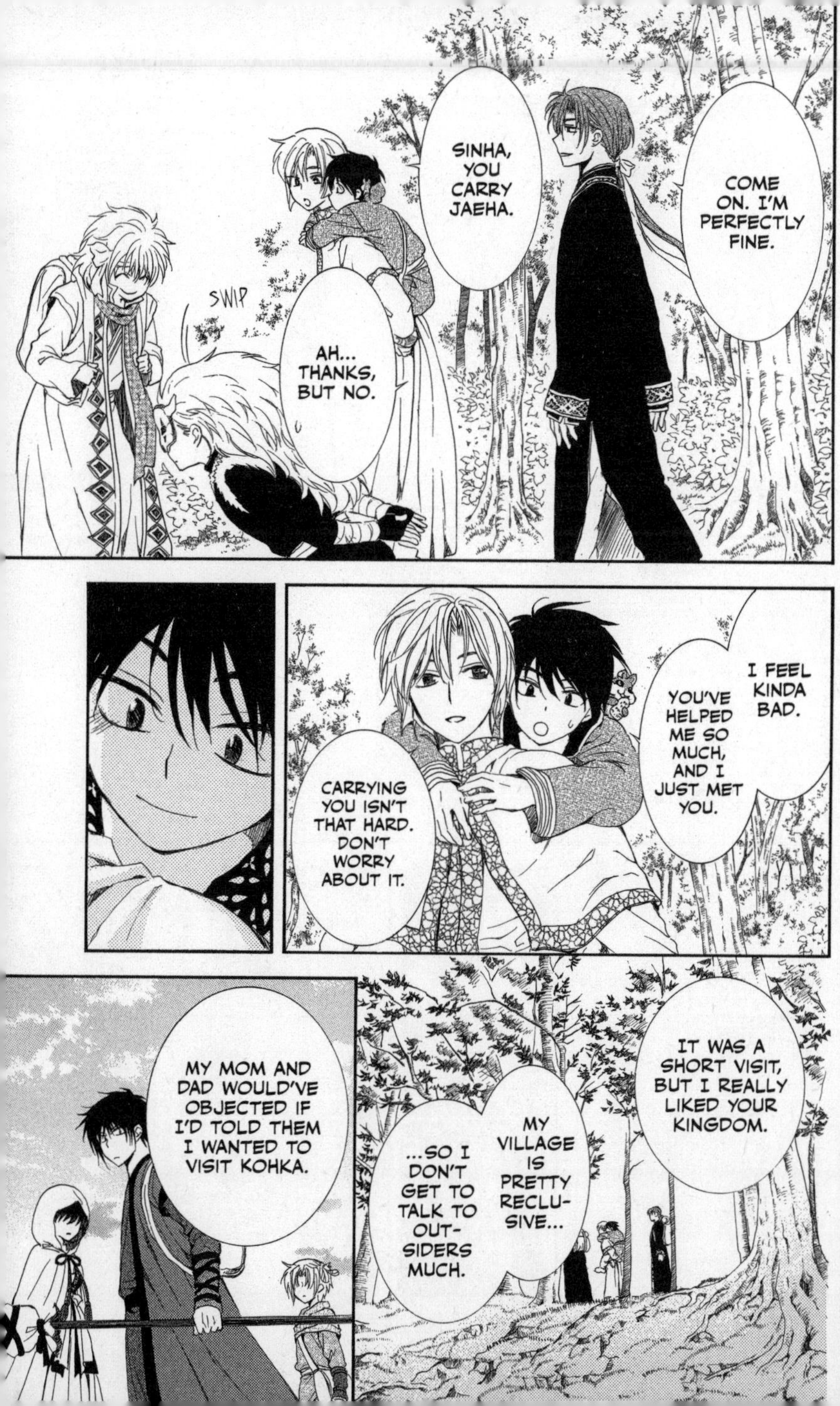
COME ON. I'M PERFECTLY FINE.
SINHA, YOU CARRY JAEHA.
AH... THANKS, BUT NO.
SWIP
I FEEL KINDA BAD.
YOU'VE HELPED ME SO MUCH, AND I JUST MET YOU.
CARRYING YOU ISN'T THAT HARD. DON'T WORRY ABOUT IT.
IT WAS A SHORT VISIT, BUT I REALLY LIKED YOUR KINGDOM.
MY VILLAGE IS PRETTY RECLU-SIVE...
...SO I DON'T GET TO TALK TO OUT-SIDERS MUCH.
MY MOM AND DAD WOULD'VE OBJECTED IF I'D TOLD THEM I WANTED TO VISIT KOHKA.

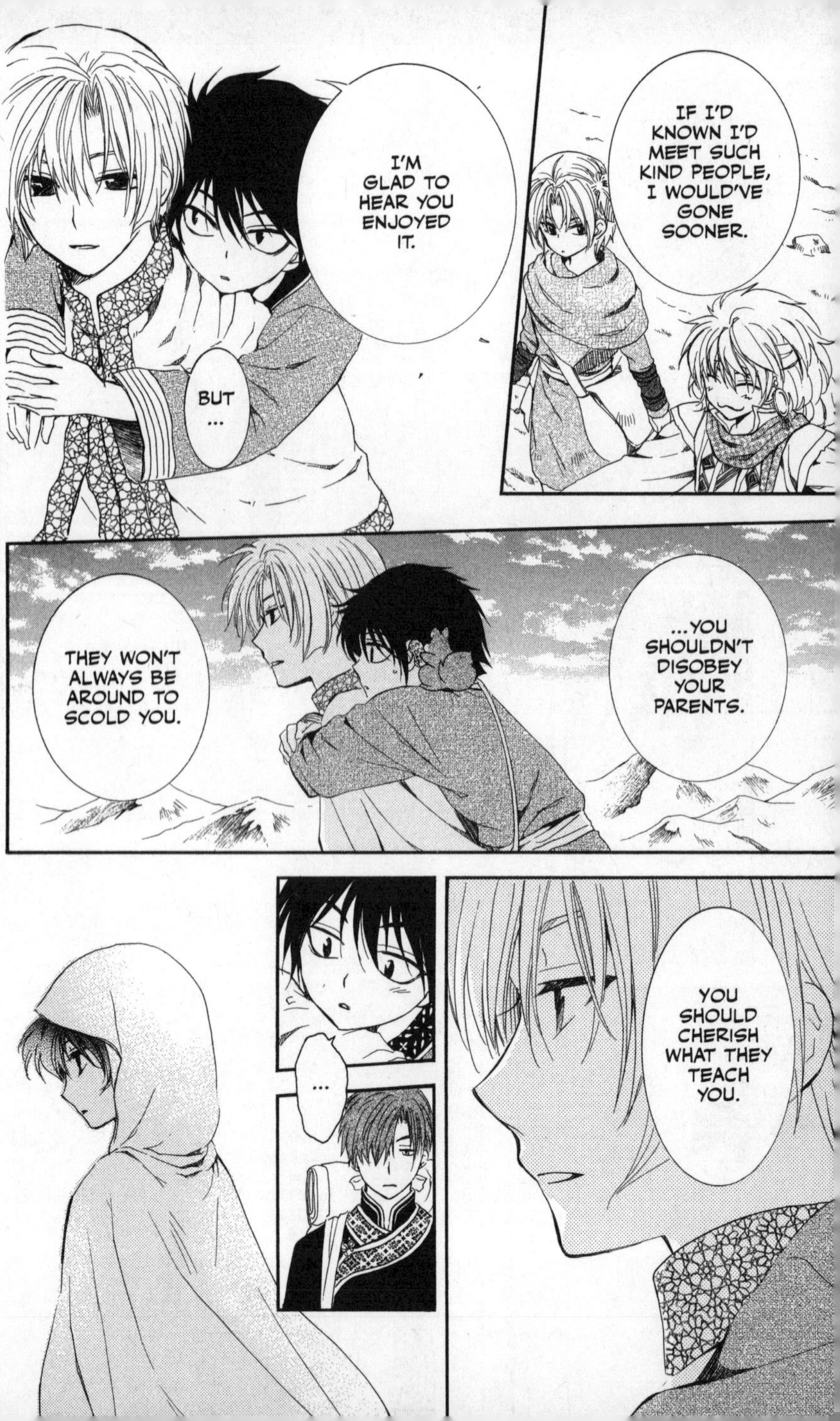
IF I'D KNOWN I'D MEET SUCH KIND PEOPLE, I WOULD'VE GONE SOONER.
I'M GLAD TO HEAR YOU ENJOYED IT.
BUT ...
...YOU SHOULDN'T DISOBEY YOUR PARENTS.
THEY WON'T ALWAYS BE AROUND TO SCOLD YOU.
YOU SHOULD CHERISH WHAT THEY TEACH YOU.
...

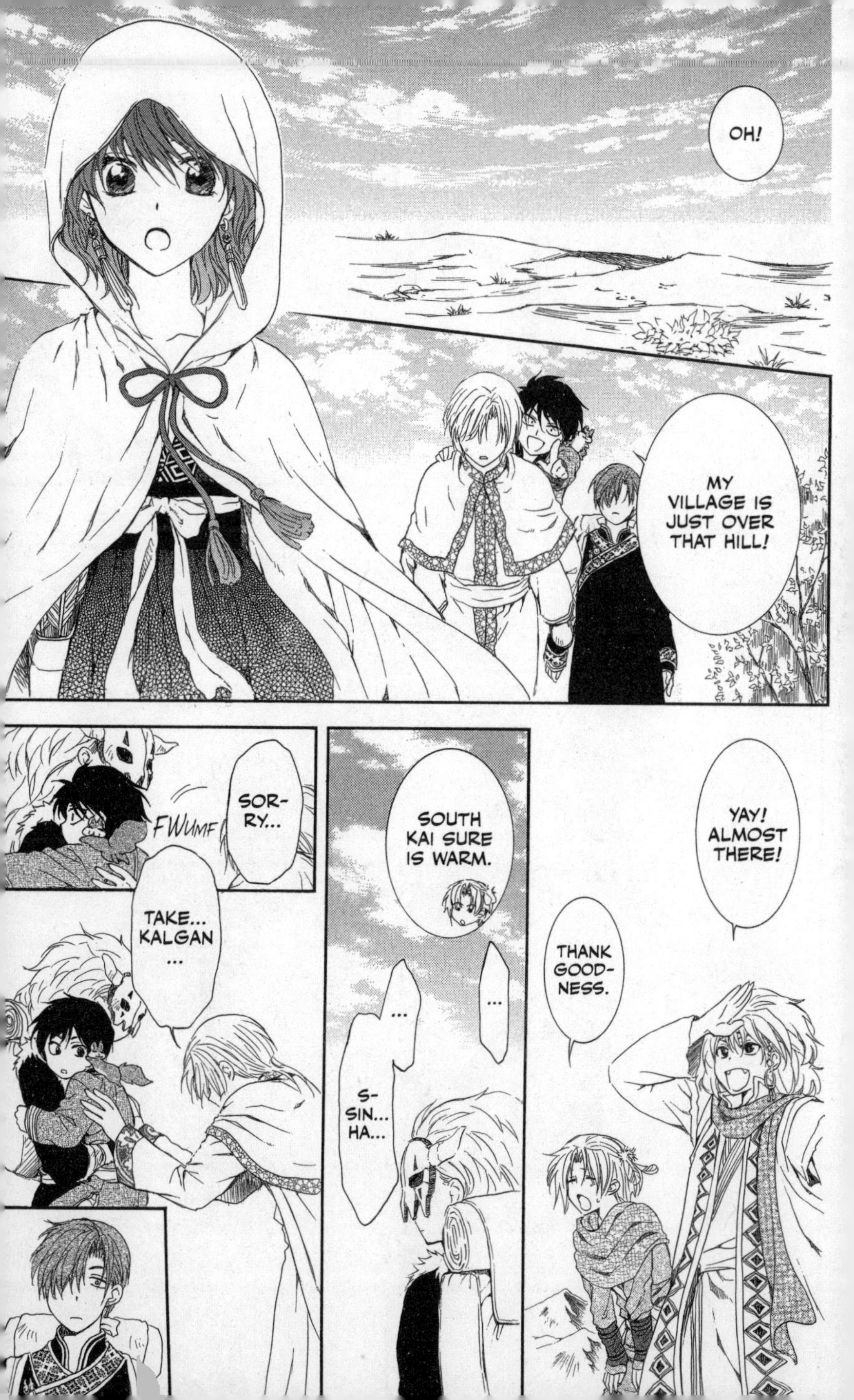
OH!
MY VILLAGE IS JUST OVER THAT HILL!
YAY! ALMOST THERE!
THANK GOOD-NESS.
SOUTH KAI SURE IS WARM.
...
...
S-SIN... HA...
SOR-RY...
FWUMF
TAKE... KALGAN...

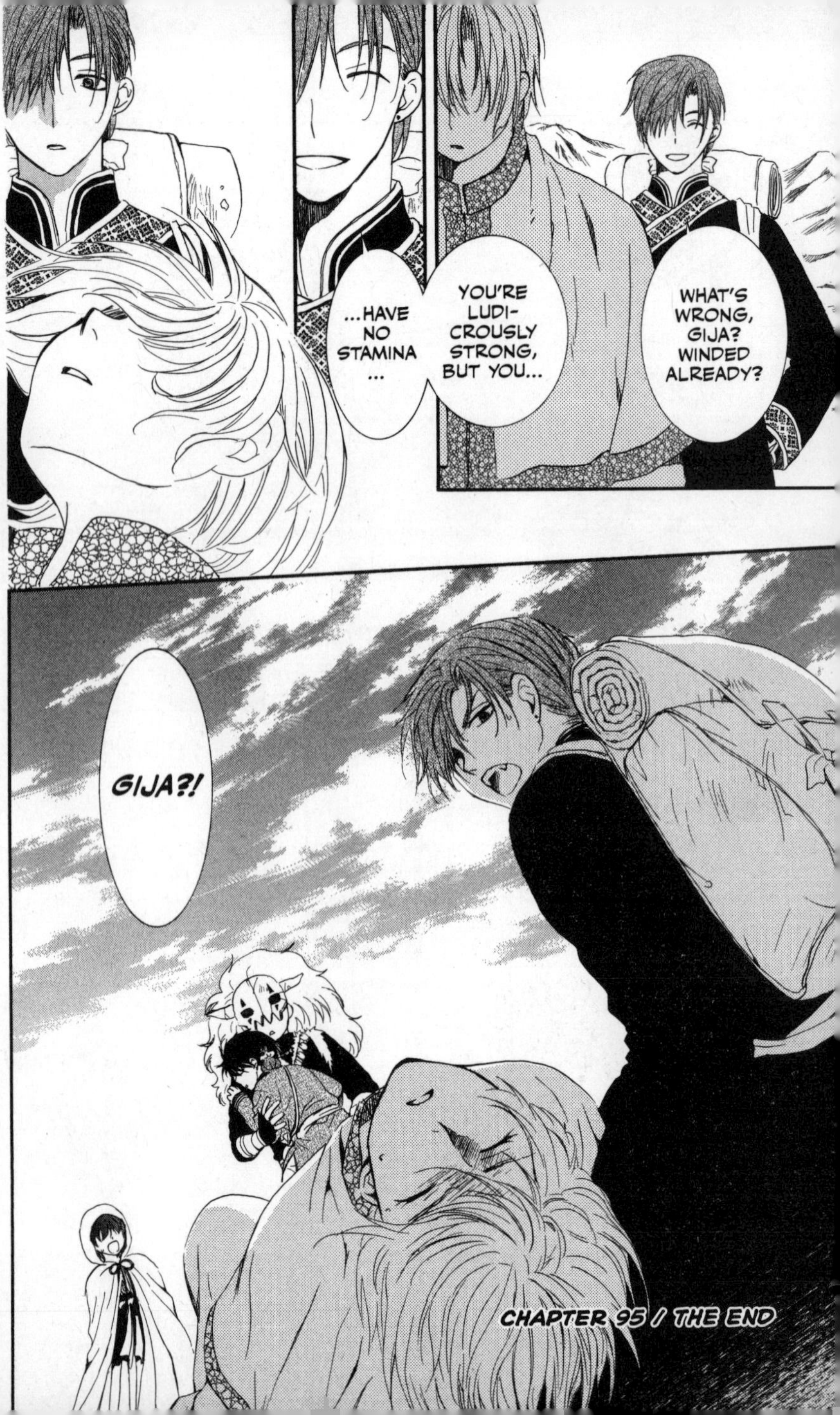
WHAT'S WRONG, GIJA? WINDED ALREADY?
YOU'RE LUDI-CROUSLY STRONG, BUT YOU...
...HAVE NO STAMINA ...
GIJA?!
CHAPTER 95 / THE END

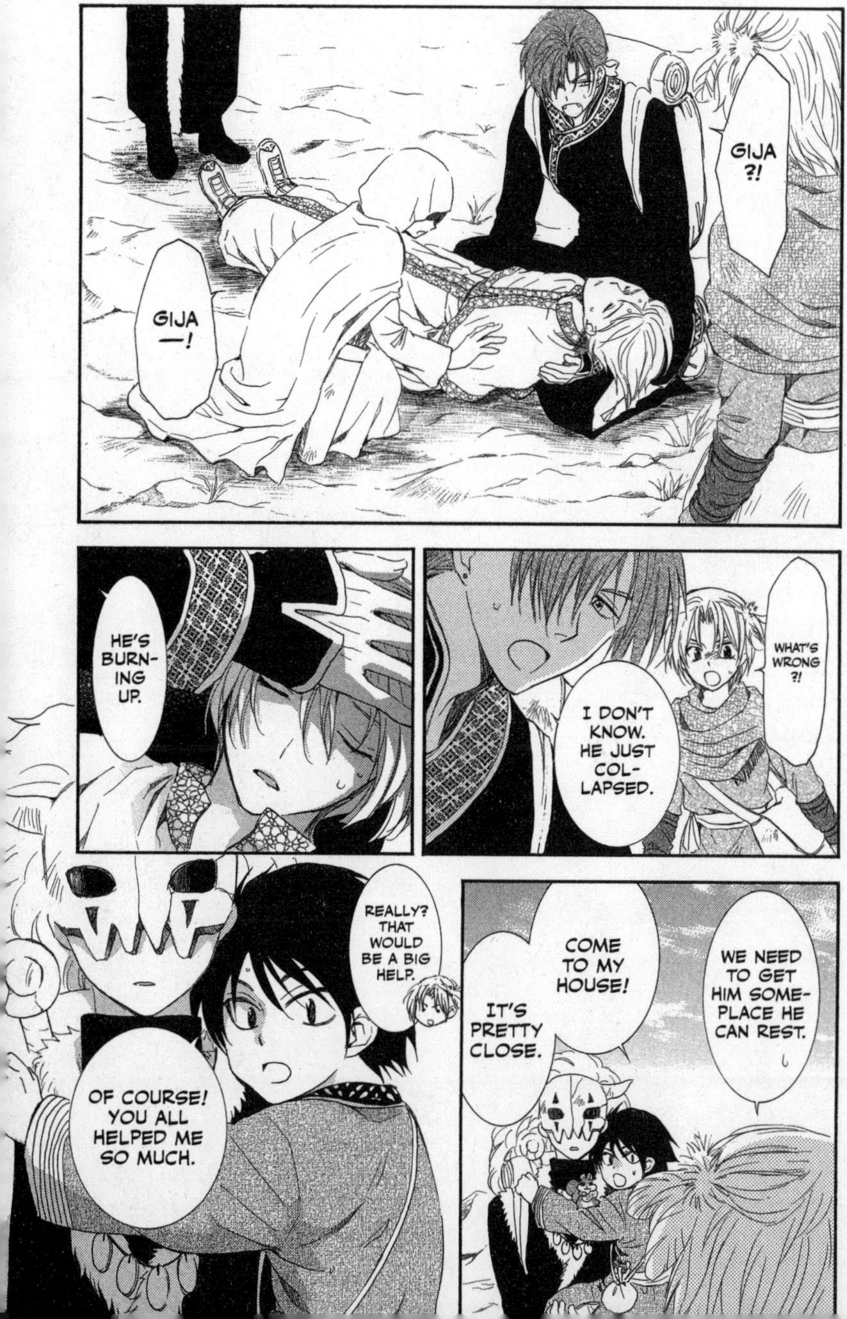
GIJA ?!
GIJA—!
WHAT'S WRONG ?!
I DON'T KNOW. HE JUST COL-LAPSED.
HE'S BURN-ING UP.
WE NEED TO GET HIM SOME-PLACE HE CAN REST.
COME TO MY HOUSE!
IT'S PRETTY CLOSE.
REALLY? THAT WOULD BE A BIG HELP.
OF COURSE! YOU ALL HELPED ME SO MUCH.

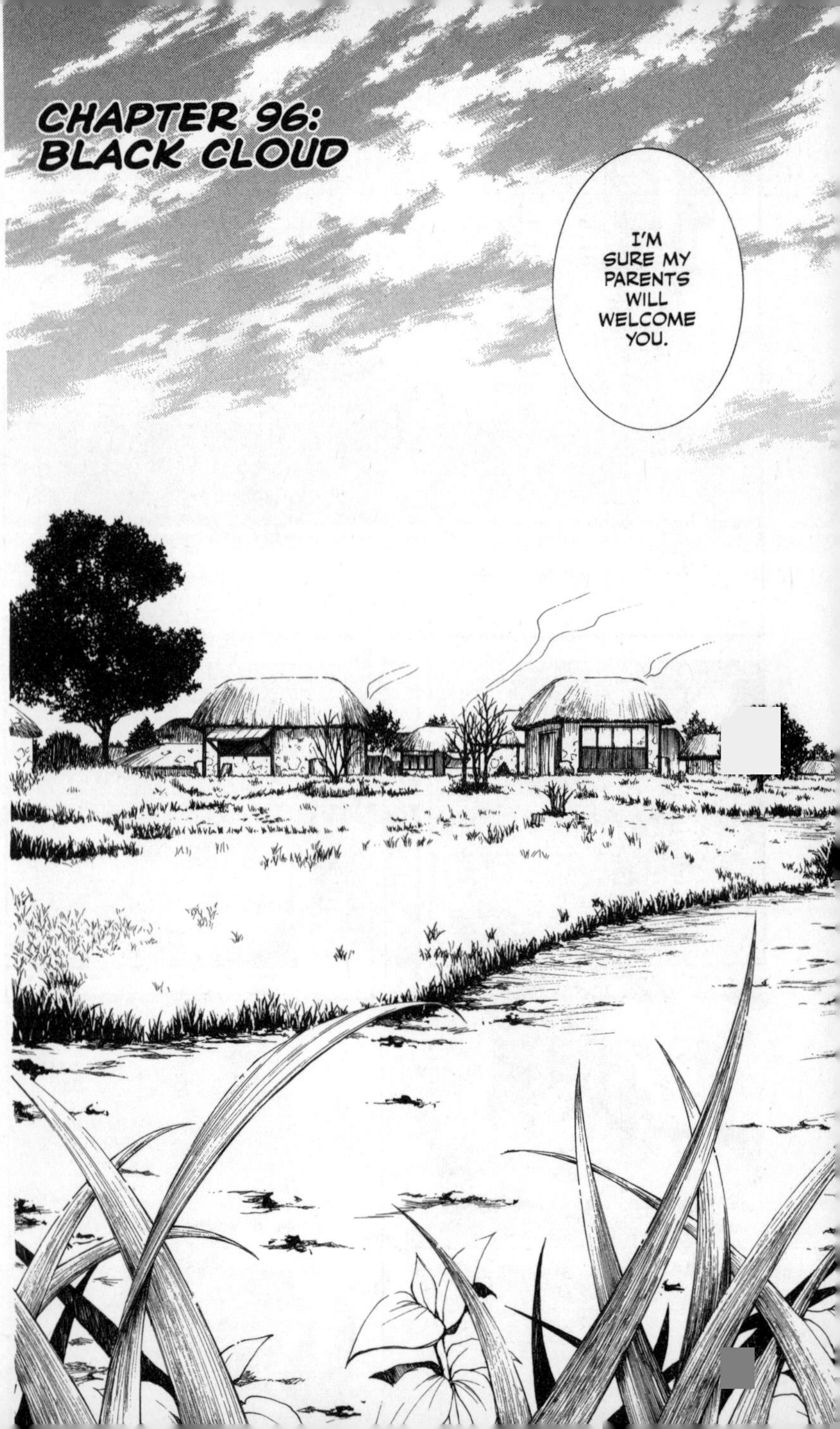
CHAPTER 96:
BLACK CLOUD
I'M SURE MY PARENTS WILL WELCOME YOU.

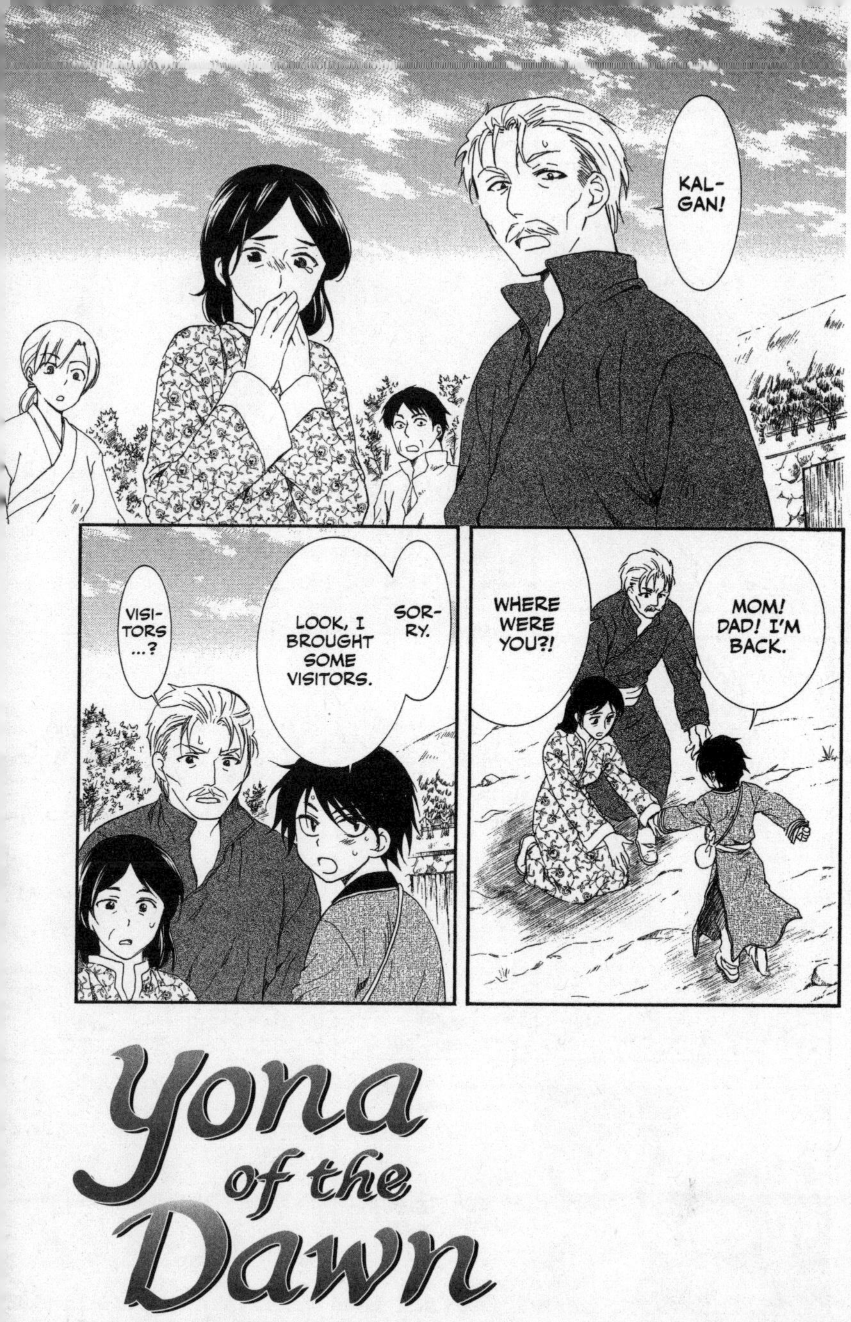
KALGAN!
MOM! DAD! I'M BACK.
WHERE WERE YOU?!
SORRY.
LOOK, I BROUGHT SOME VISITORS.
VISITORS ...?

Yona of the Dawn

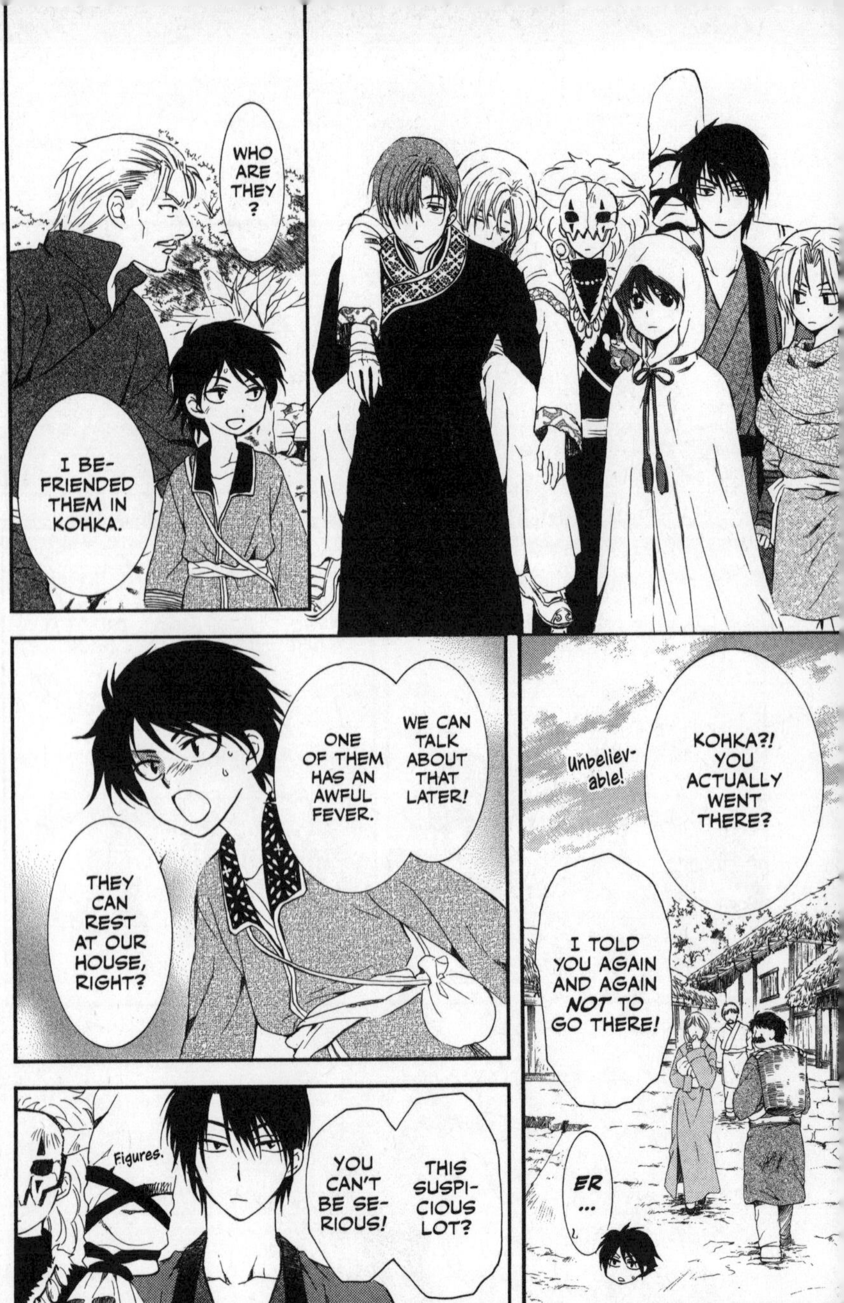
WHO ARE THEY?
I BE-FRIENDED THEM IN KOHKA.
KOHKA?! YOU ACTUALLY WENT THERE?
Unbeliev-able!
I TOLD YOU AGAIN AND AGAIN *NOT* TO GO THERE!
ER...
WE CAN TALK ABOUT THAT LATER!
ONE OF THEM HAS AN AWFUL FEVER.
THEY CAN REST AT OUR HOUSE, RIGHT?
THIS SUSPI-CIOUS LOT?
YOU CAN'T BE SE-RIOUS!
Figures.

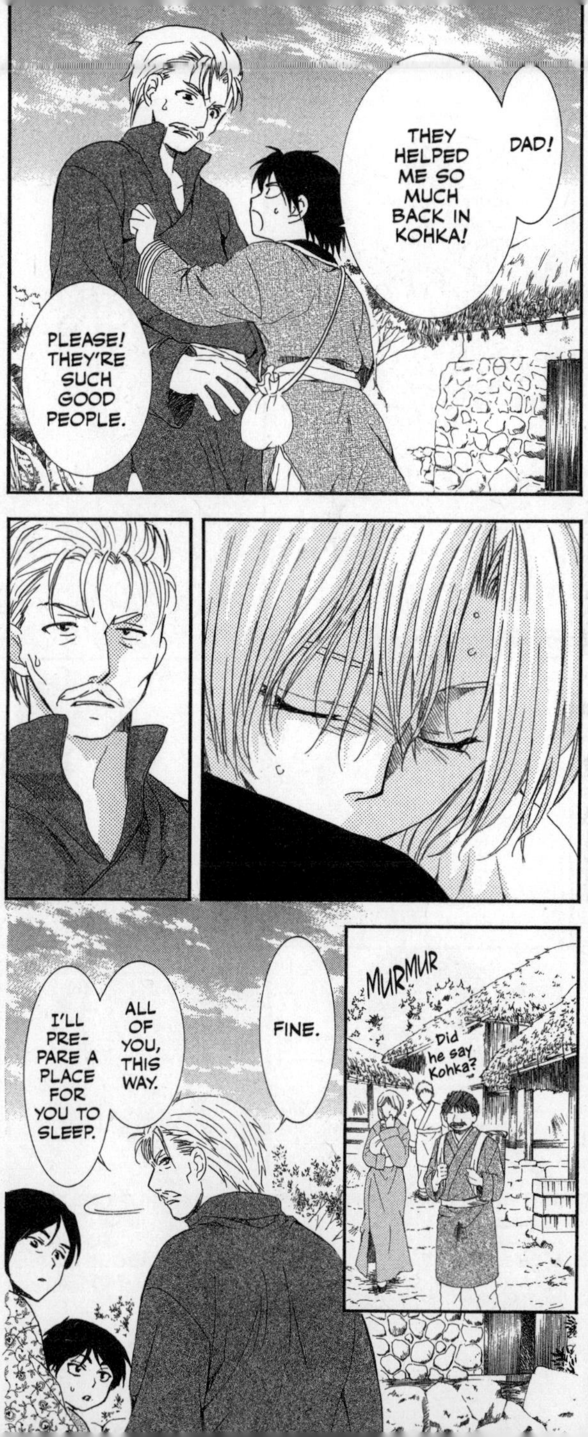
DAD!
THEY HELPED ME SO MUCH BACK IN KOHKA!
PLEASE! THEY'RE SUCH GOOD PEOPLE.
MURMUR
Did he say Kohka?
FINE.
ALL OF YOU, THIS WAY.
I'LL PREPARE A PLACE FOR YOU TO SLEEP.

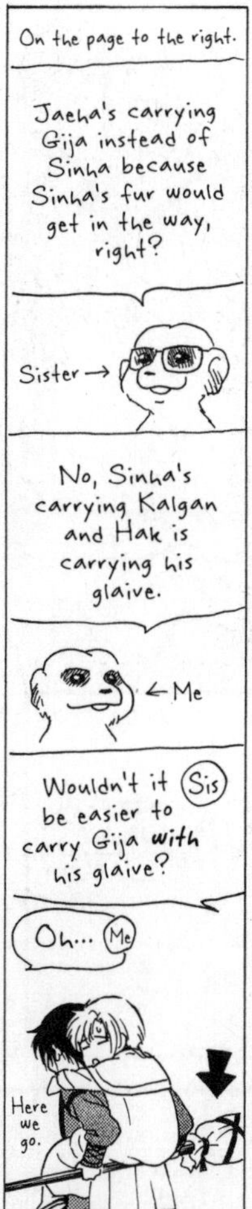
On the page to the right.
Jaeha's carrying Gija instead of Sinha because Sinha's fur would get in the way, right?
Sister →
No, Sinha's carrying Kalgan and Hak is carrying his glaive.
← Me
Wouldn't it be easier to carry Gija with his glaive?
Sis
Oh...
Me
Here we go.
Carrying Gija with his glaive...?
Assistants

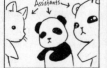

To be continued

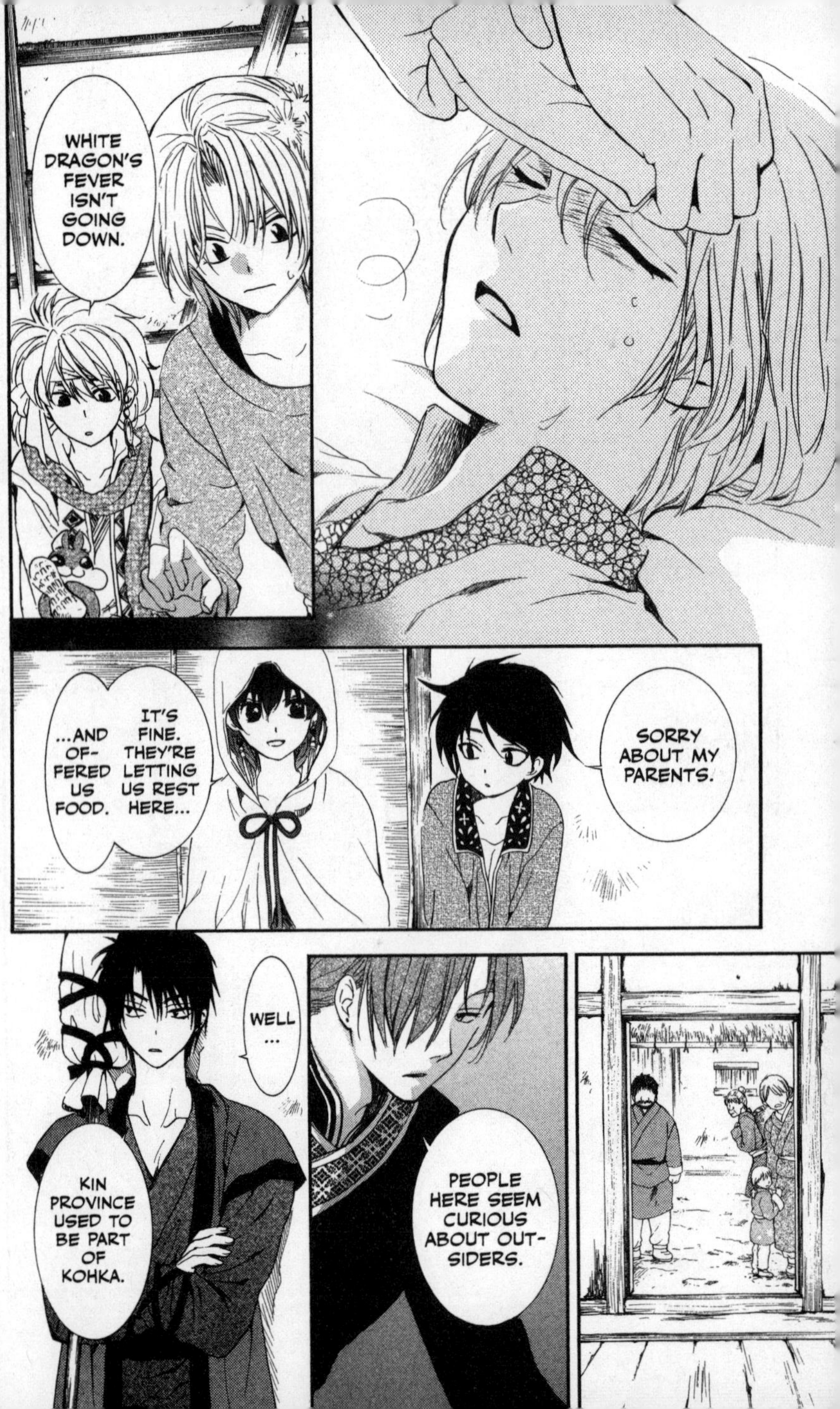
WHITE DRAGON'S FEVER ISN'T GOING DOWN.
SORRY ABOUT MY PARENTS.
IT'S FINE. THEY'RE LETTING US REST HERE...
...AND OF-FERED US FOOD.
PEOPLE HERE SEEM CURIOUS ABOUT OUT-SIDERS.
WELL...
KIN PROVINCE USED TO BE PART OF KOHKA.

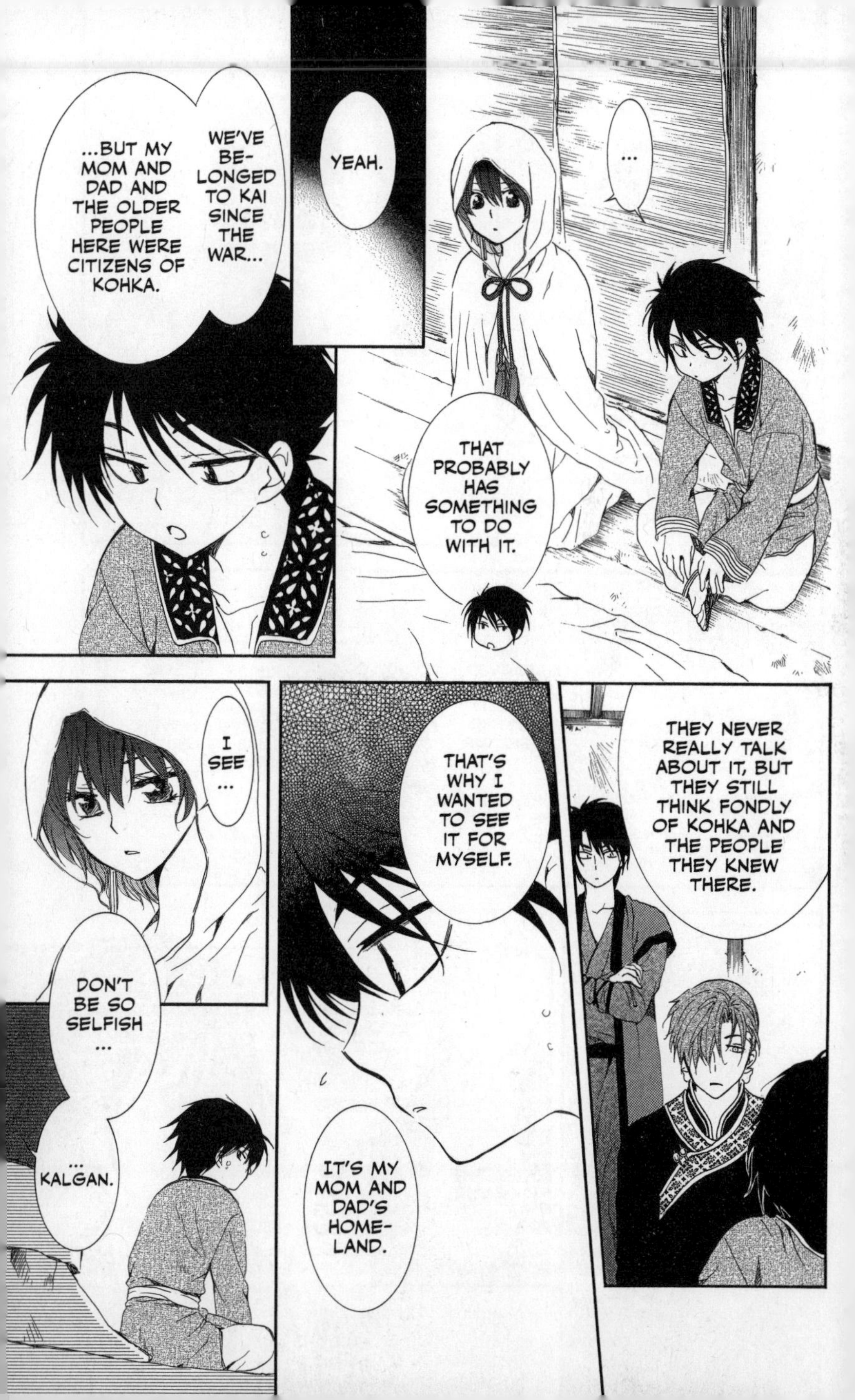
...
THAT PROBABLY HAS SOMETHING TO DO WITH IT.
YEAH.
WE'VE BE-LONGED TO KAI SINCE THE WAR...
...BUT MY MOM AND DAD AND THE OLDER PEOPLE HERE WERE CITIZENS OF KOHKA.
THEY NEVER REALLY TALK ABOUT IT, BUT THEY STILL THINK FONDLY OF KOHKA AND THE PEOPLE THEY KNEW THERE.
THAT'S WHY I WANTED TO SEE IT FOR MYSELF.
IT'S MY MOM AND DAD'S HOME-LAND.
I SEE...
DON'T BE SO SELFISH...
...KALGAN.

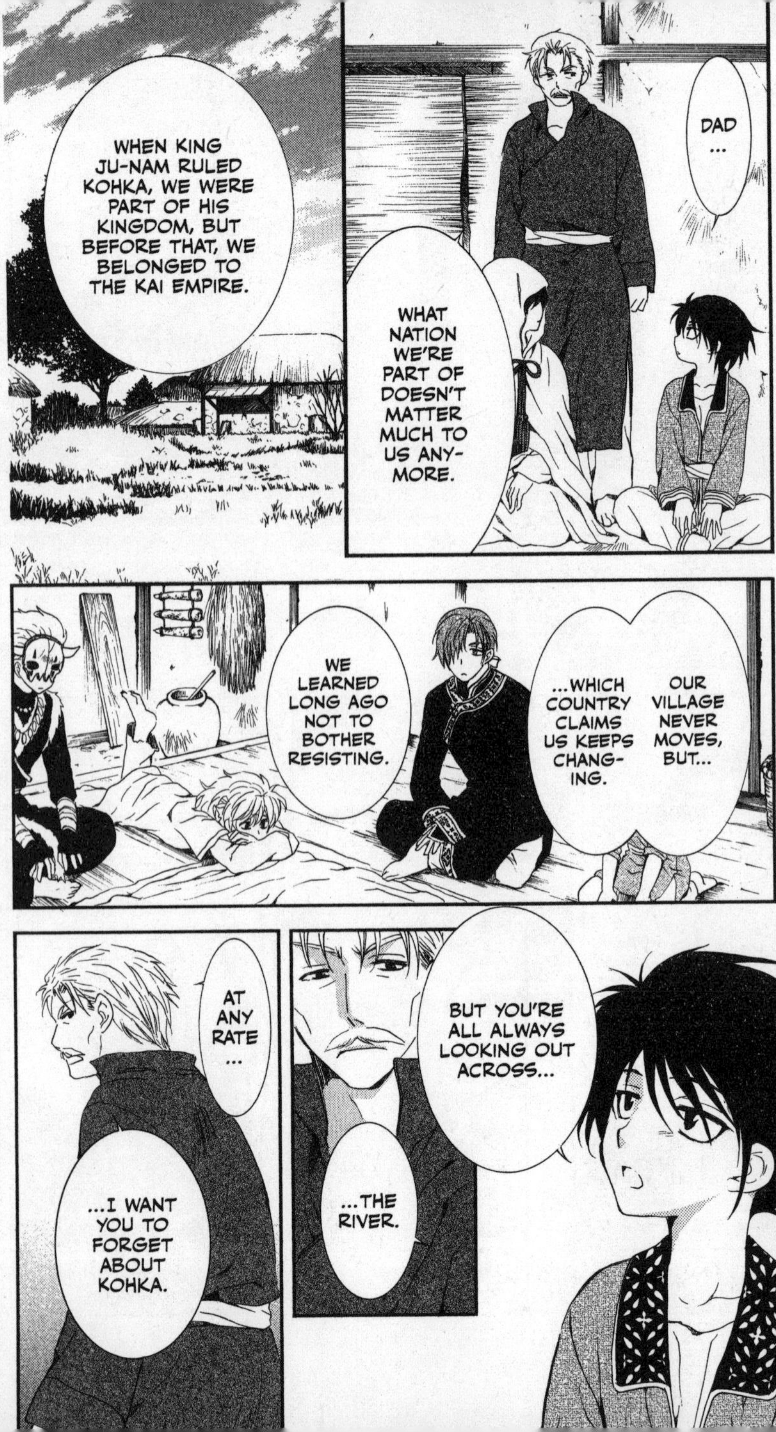
DAD ...
WHAT NATION WE'RE PART OF DOESN'T MATTER MUCH TO US ANY-MORE.
WHEN KING JU-NAM RULED KOHKA, WE WERE PART OF HIS KINGDOM, BUT BEFORE THAT, WE BELONGED TO THE KAI EMPIRE.
OUR VILLAGE NEVER MOVES, BUT...
...WHICH COUNTRY CLAIMS US KEEPS CHANG-ING.
WE LEARNED LONG AGO NOT TO BOTHER RESISTING.
BUT YOU'RE ALL ALWAYS LOOKING OUT ACROSS...
...THE RIVER.
AT ANY RATE ...
...I WANT YOU TO FORGET ABOUT KOHKA.

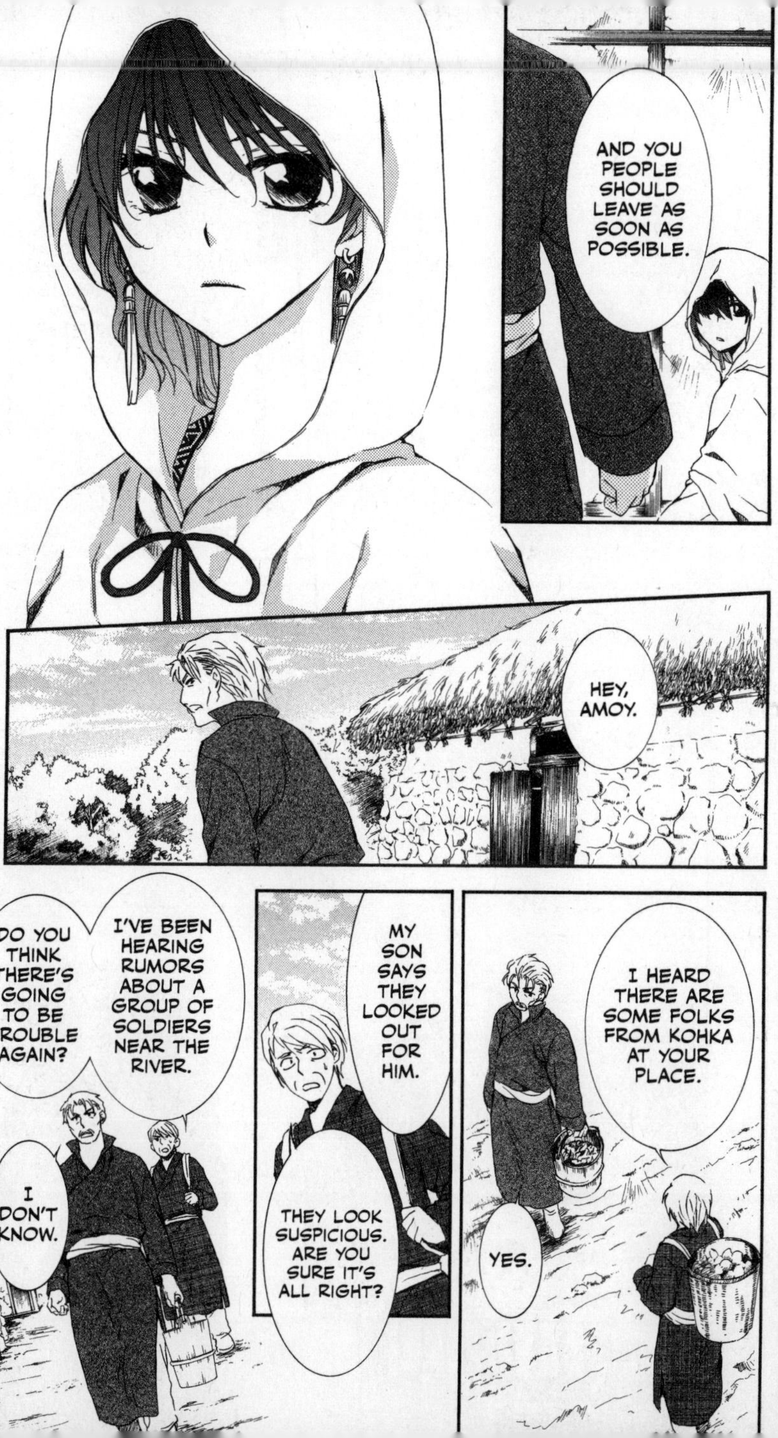
AND YOU PEOPLE SHOULD LEAVE AS SOON AS POSSIBLE.
HEY, AMOY.
I HEARD THERE ARE SOME FOLKS FROM KOHKA AT YOUR PLACE.
YES.
MY SON SAYS THEY LOOKED OUT FOR HIM.
THEY LOOK SUSPICIOUS. ARE YOU SURE IT'S ALL RIGHT?
I'VE BEEN HEARING RUMORS ABOUT A GROUP OF SOLDIERS NEAR THE RIVER.
DO YOU THINK THERE'S GOING TO BE TROUBLE AGAIN?
I DON'T KNOW.

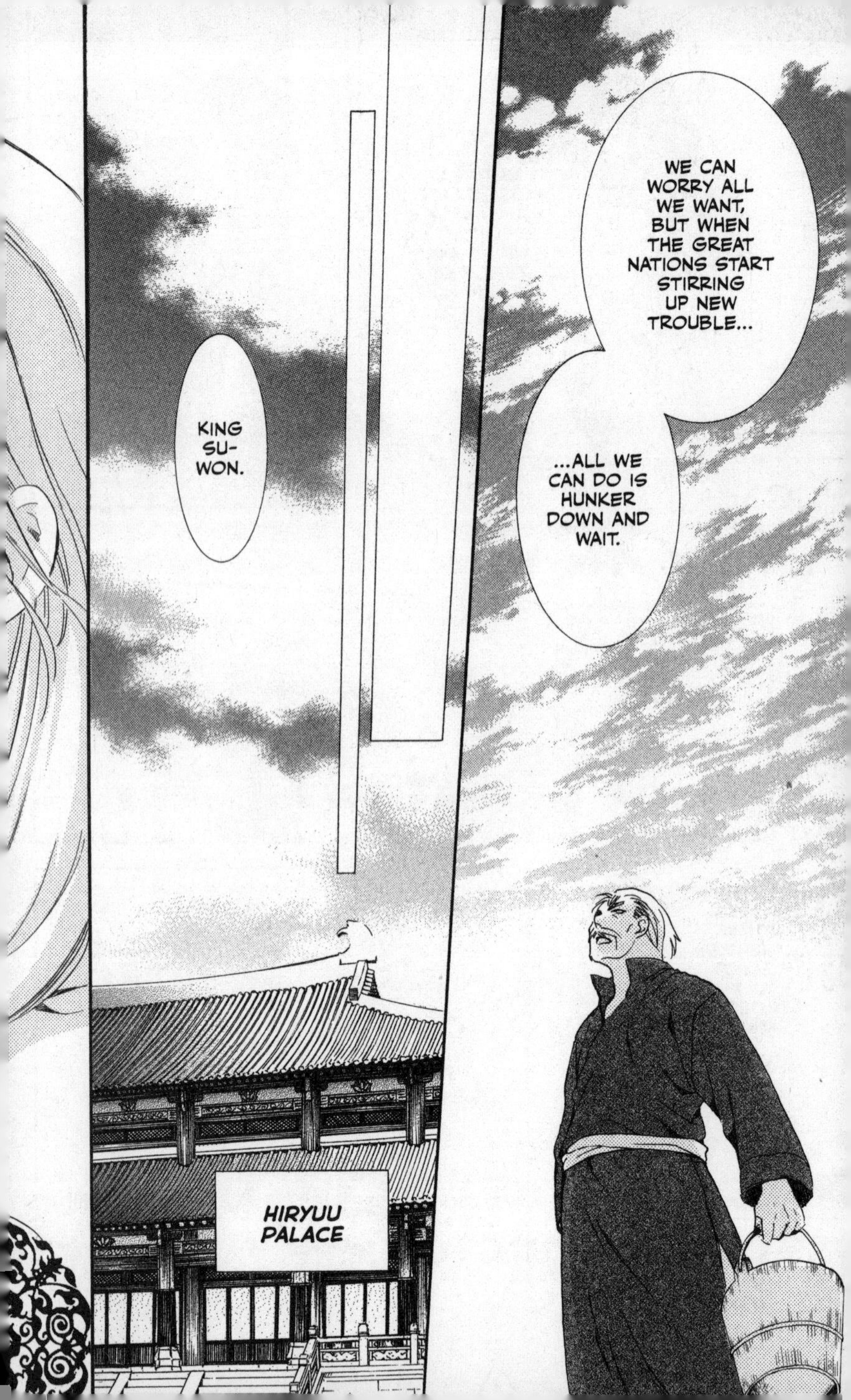
WE CAN WORRY ALL WE WANT, BUT WHEN THE GREAT NATIONS START STIRRING UP NEW TROUBLE...
...ALL WE CAN DO IS HUNKER DOWN AND WAIT.
KING SU-WON.
HIRYUU PALACE

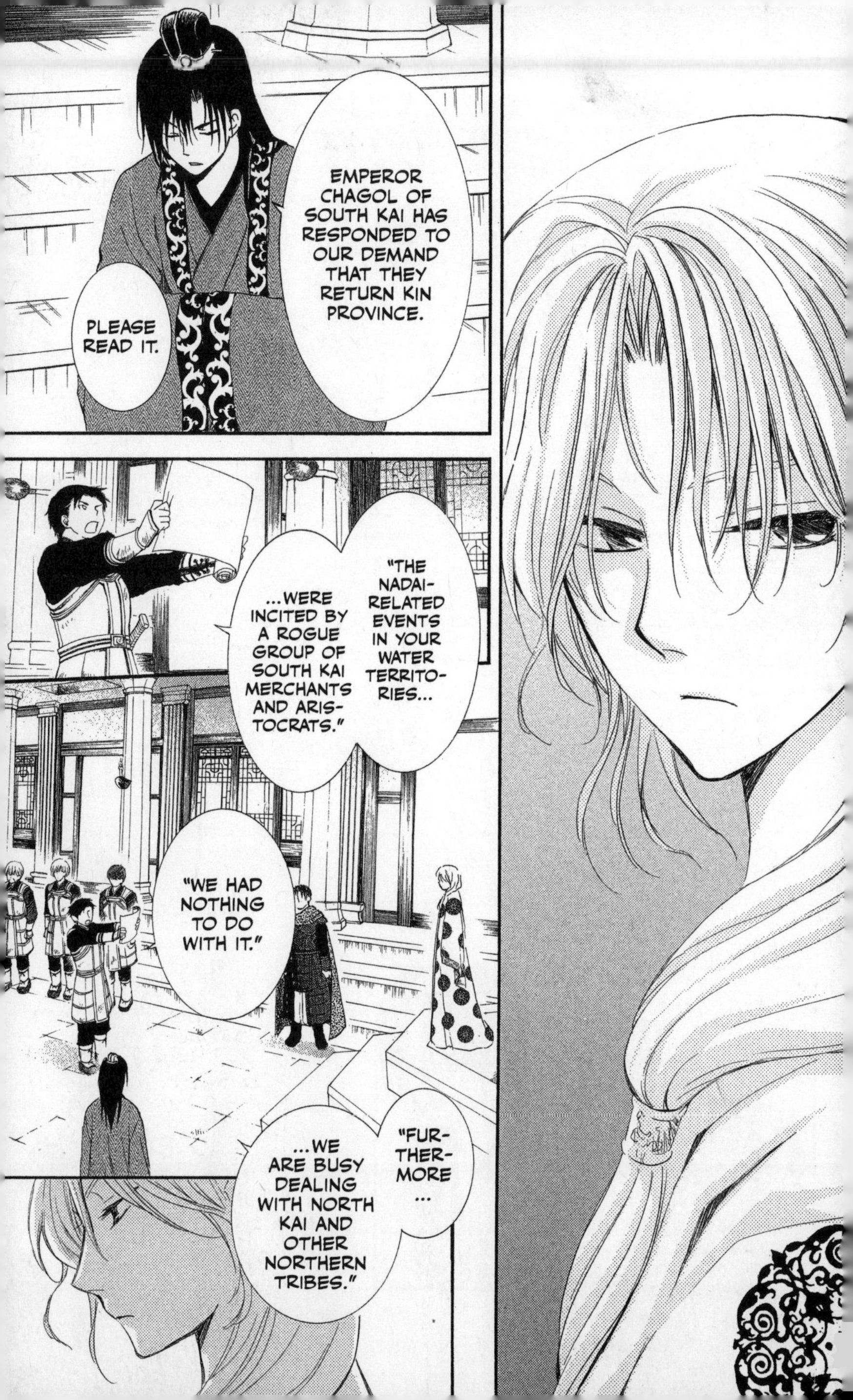
EMPEROR CHAGOL OF SOUTH KAI HAS RESPONDED TO OUR DEMAND THAT THEY RETURN KIN PROVINCE.
PLEASE READ IT.
"THE NADAI-RELATED EVENTS IN YOUR WATER TERRITO-RIES...
...WERE INCITED BY A ROGUE GROUP OF SOUTH KAI MERCHANTS AND ARIS-TOCRATS."
"WE HAD NOTHING TO DO WITH IT."
"FUR-THER-MORE...
...WE ARE BUSY DEALING WITH NORTH KAI AND OTHER NORTHERN TRIBES."

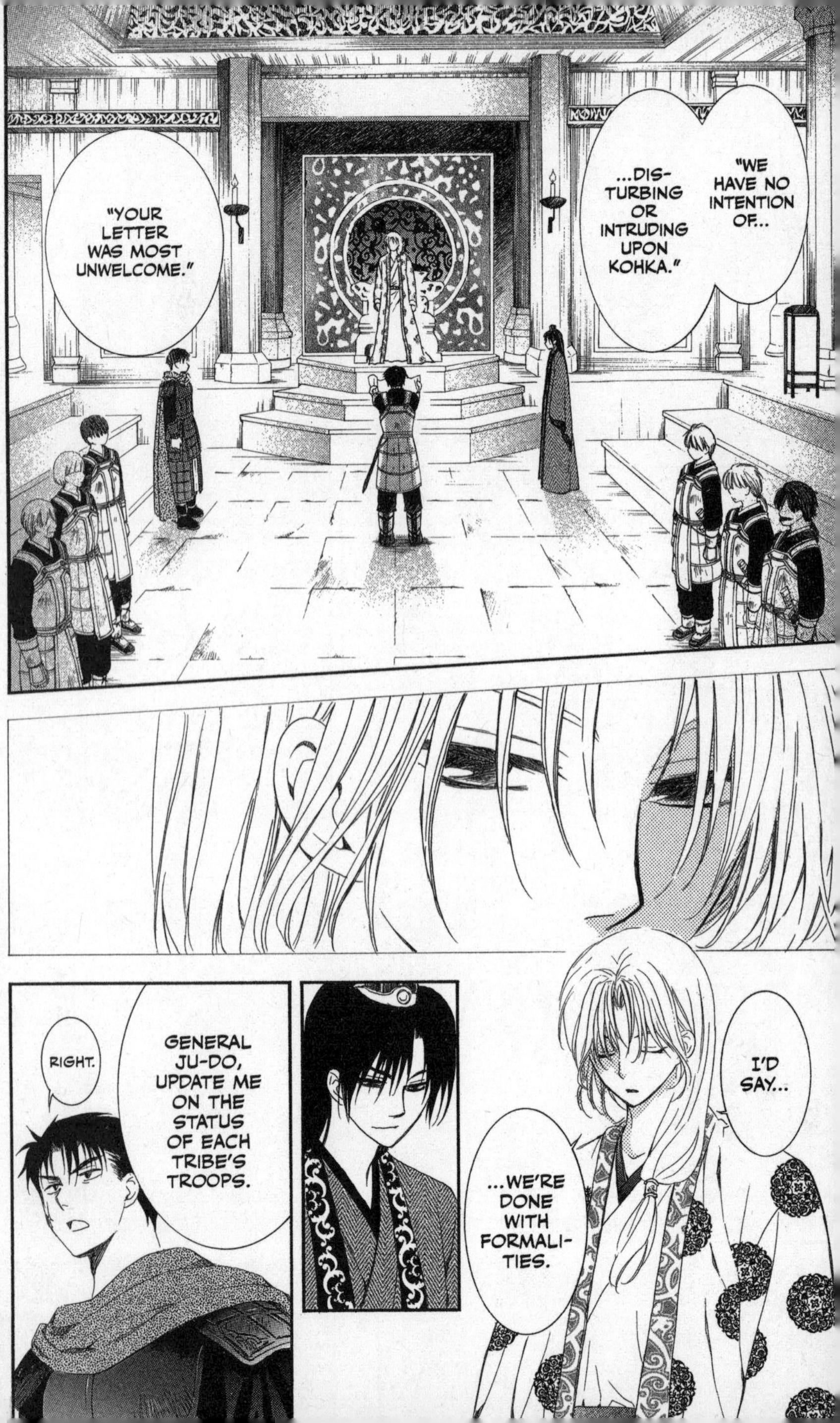
"WE HAVE NO INTENTION OF...
...DIS-TURBING OR INTRUDING UPON KOHKA."
"YOUR LETTER WAS MOST UNWELCOME."
I'D SAY...
...WE'RE DONE WITH FORMALI-TIES.
GENERAL JU-DO, UPDATE ME ON THE STATUS OF EACH TRIBE'S TROOPS.
RIGHT.

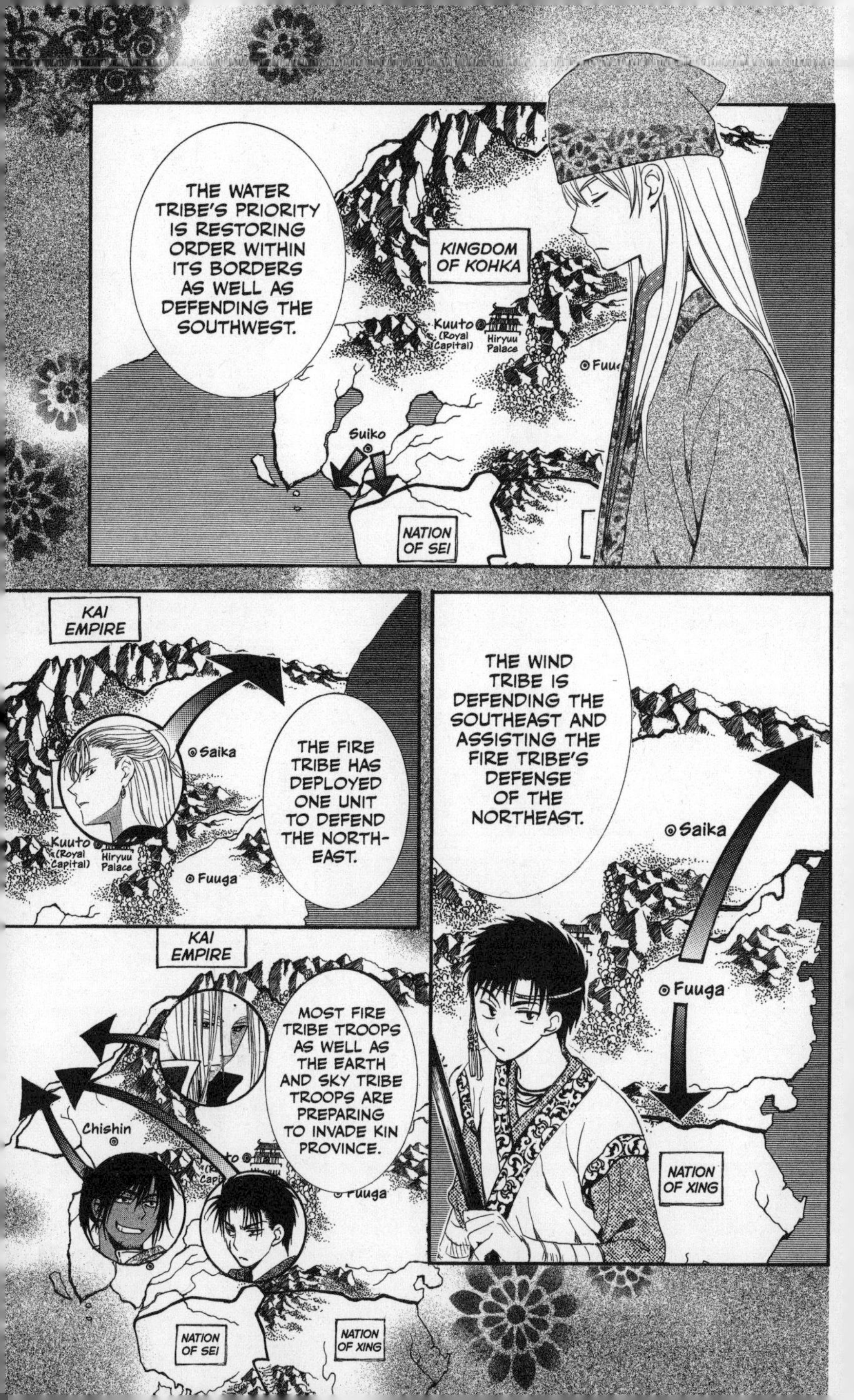
THE WATER TRIBE'S PRIORITY IS RESTORING ORDER WITHIN ITS BORDERS AS WELL AS DEFENDING THE SOUTHWEST.
KINGDOM OF KOHKA
Kuuto (Royal Capital)
Hiryuu Palace
Suiko
NATION OF SEI
THE WIND TRIBE IS DEFENDING THE SOUTHEAST AND ASSISTING THE FIRE TRIBE'S DEFENSE OF THE NORTHEAST.
Saika
Fuuga
NATION OF XING
KAI EMPIRE
THE FIRE TRIBE HAS DEPLOYED ONE UNIT TO DEFEND THE NORTH-EAST.
Saika
Kuuto (Royal Capital)
Hiryuu Palace
Fuuga
KAI EMPIRE
MOST FIRE TRIBE TROOPS AS WELL AS THE EARTH AND SKY TRIBE TROOPS ARE PREPARING TO INVADE KIN PROVINCE.
Chishin
NATION OF SEI
NATION OF XING

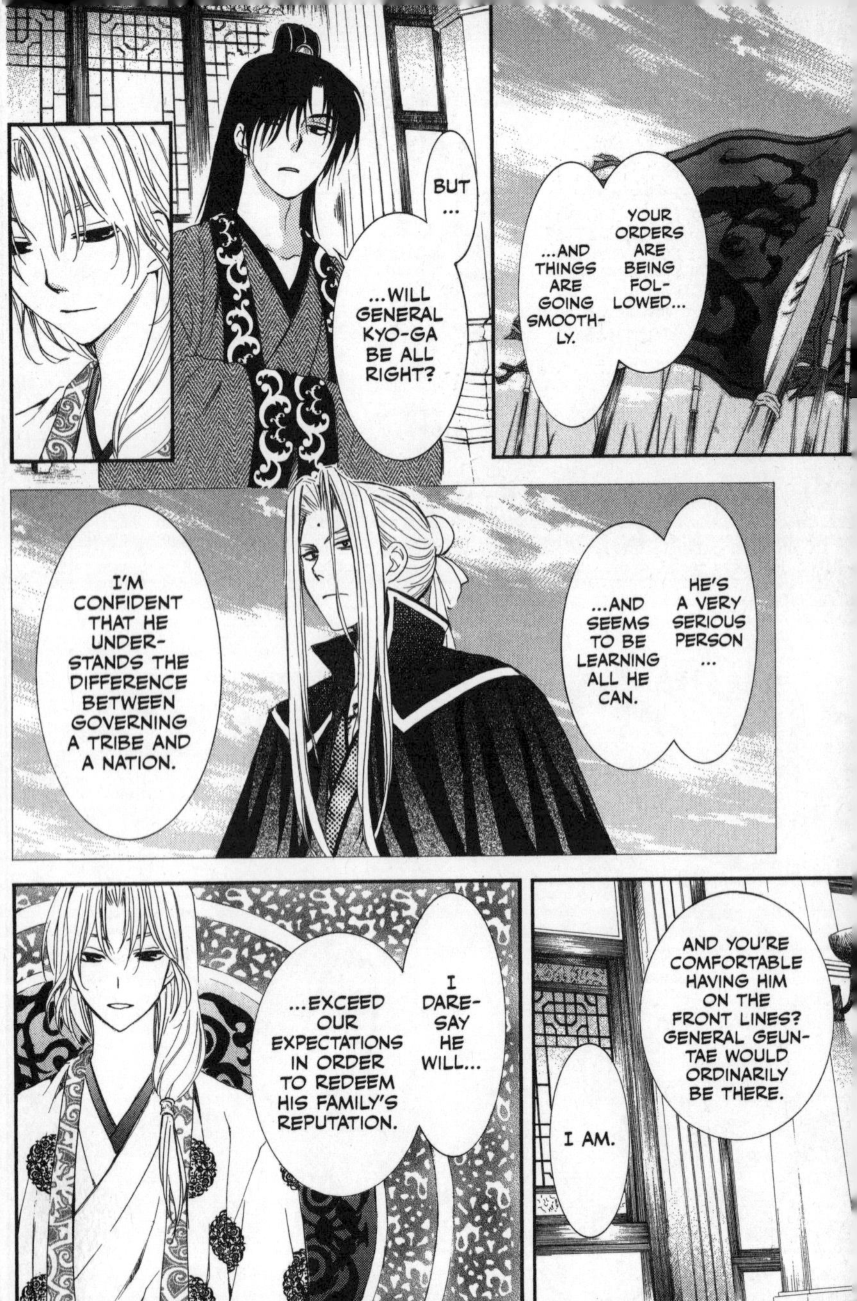

YOUR ORDERS ARE BEING FOLLOWED...
...AND THINGS ARE GOING SMOOTHLY.
BUT...
...WILL GENERAL KYO-GA BE ALL RIGHT?
HE'S A VERY SERIOUS PERSON...
...AND SEEMS TO BE LEARNING ALL HE CAN.
I'M CONFIDENT THAT HE UNDERSTANDS THE DIFFERENCE BETWEEN GOVERNING A TRIBE AND A NATION.
AND YOU'RE COMFORTABLE HAVING HIM ON THE FRONT LINES? GENERAL GEUN-TAE WOULD ORDINARILY BE THERE.
I AM.
I DARESAY HE WILL...
...EXCEED OUR EXPECTATIONS IN ORDER TO REDEEM HIS FAMILY'S REPUTATION.

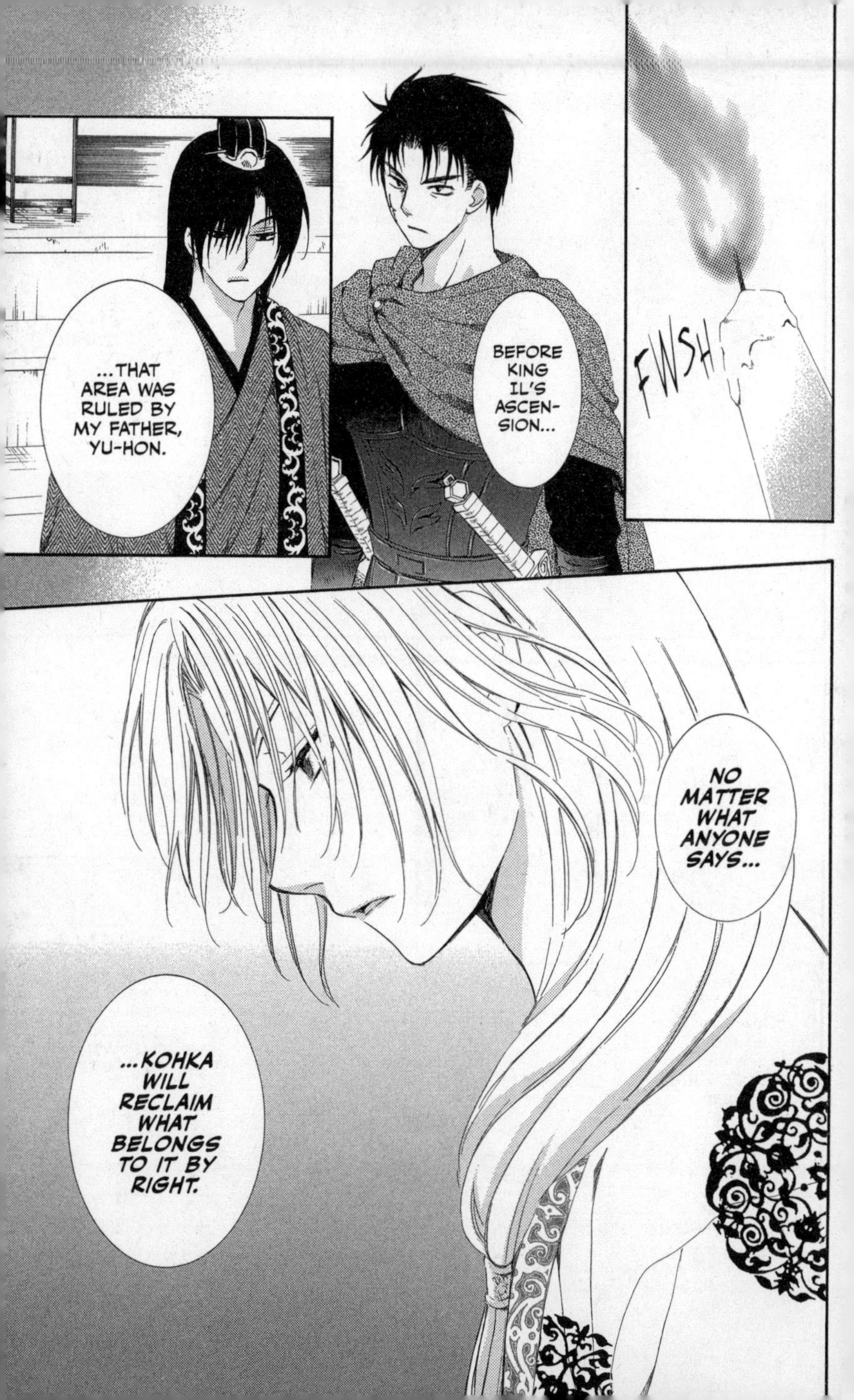
FWSH
BEFORE KING IL'S ASCENSION...
...THAT AREA WAS RULED BY MY FATHER, YU-HON.
NO MATTER WHAT ANYONE SAYS...
...KOHKA WILL RECLAIM WHAT BELONGS TO IT BY RIGHT.

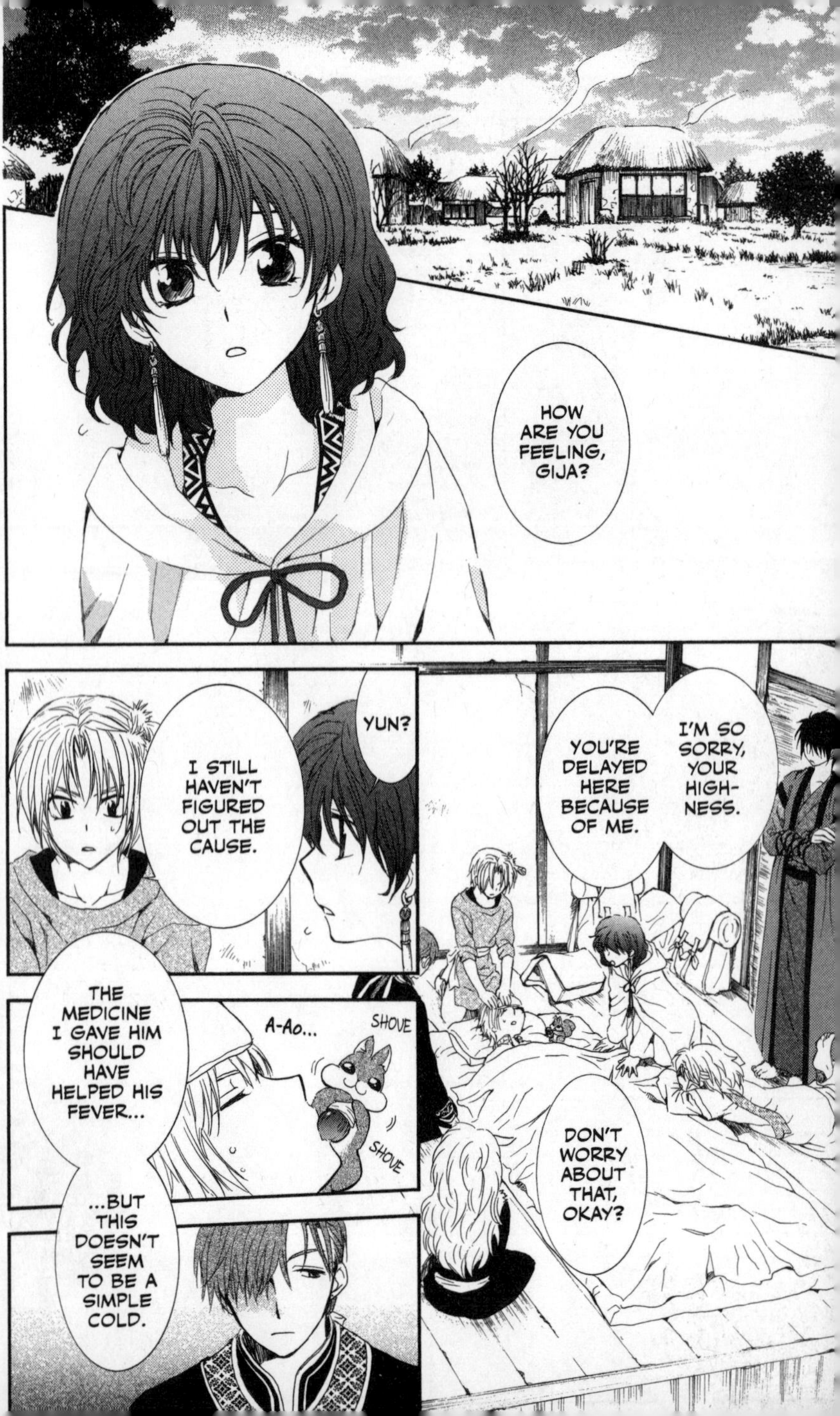
HOW ARE YOU FEELING, GIJA?
I'M SO SORRY, YOUR HIGHNESS.
YOU'RE DELAYED HERE BECAUSE OF ME.
DON'T WORRY ABOUT THAT, OKAY?
YUN?
I STILL HAVEN'T FIGURED OUT THE CAUSE.
SHOVE
A-Ao...
SHOVE
THE MEDICINE I GAVE HIM SHOULD HAVE HELPED HIS FEVER...
...BUT THIS DOESN'T SEEM TO BE A SIMPLE COLD.

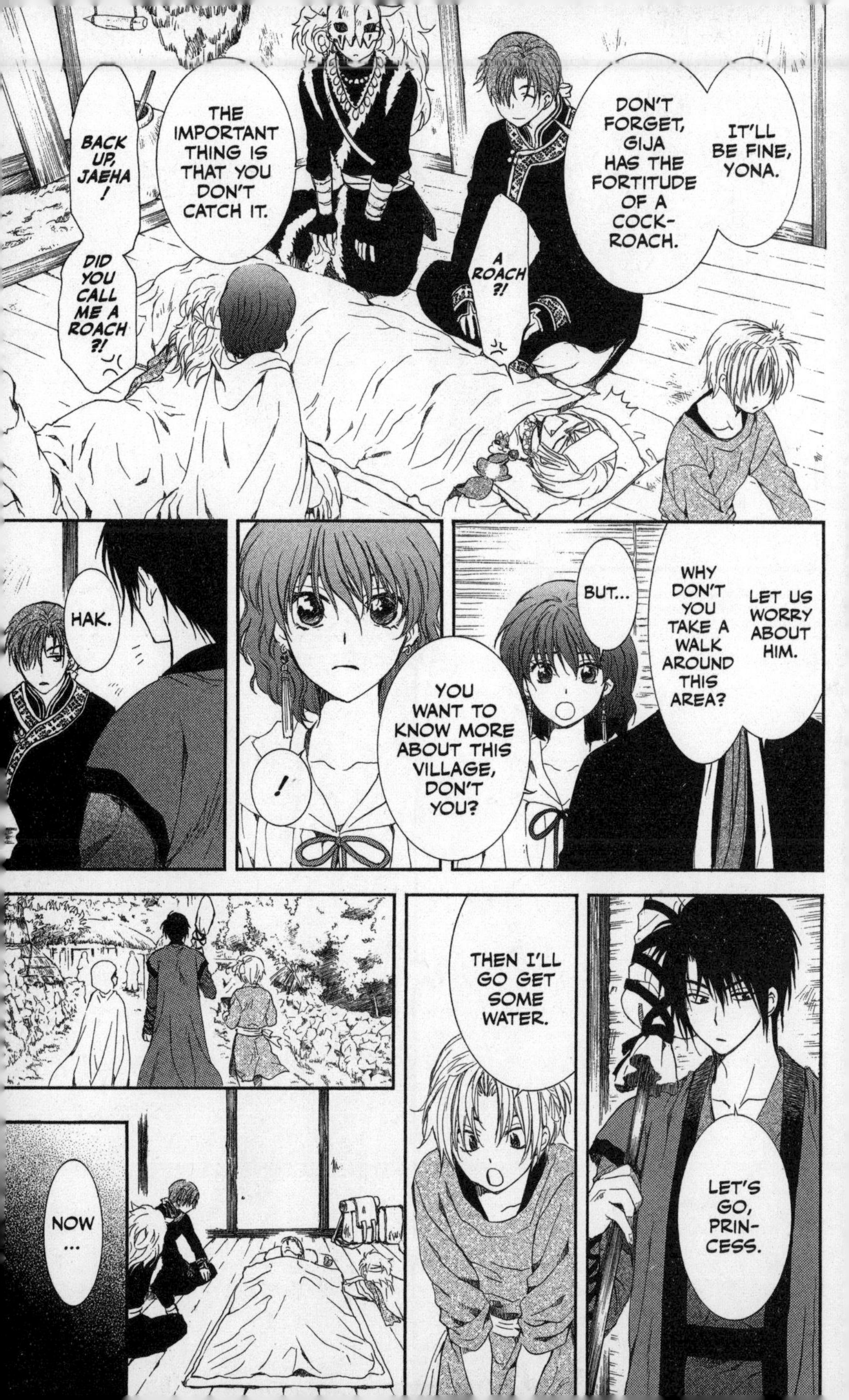
IT'LL BE FINE, YONA.
DON'T FORGET, GIJA HAS THE FORTITUDE OF A COCK-ROACH.
A ROACH?!
THE IMPORTANT THING IS THAT YOU DON'T CATCH IT.
BACK UP, JAEHA!
DID YOU CALL ME A ROACH?!
LET US WORRY ABOUT HIM.
WHY DON'T YOU TAKE A WALK AROUND THIS AREA?
BUT...
YOU WANT TO KNOW MORE ABOUT THIS VILLAGE, DON'T YOU?
!
HAK.
LET'S GO, PRIN-CESS.
THEN I'LL GO GET SOME WATER.
NOW...

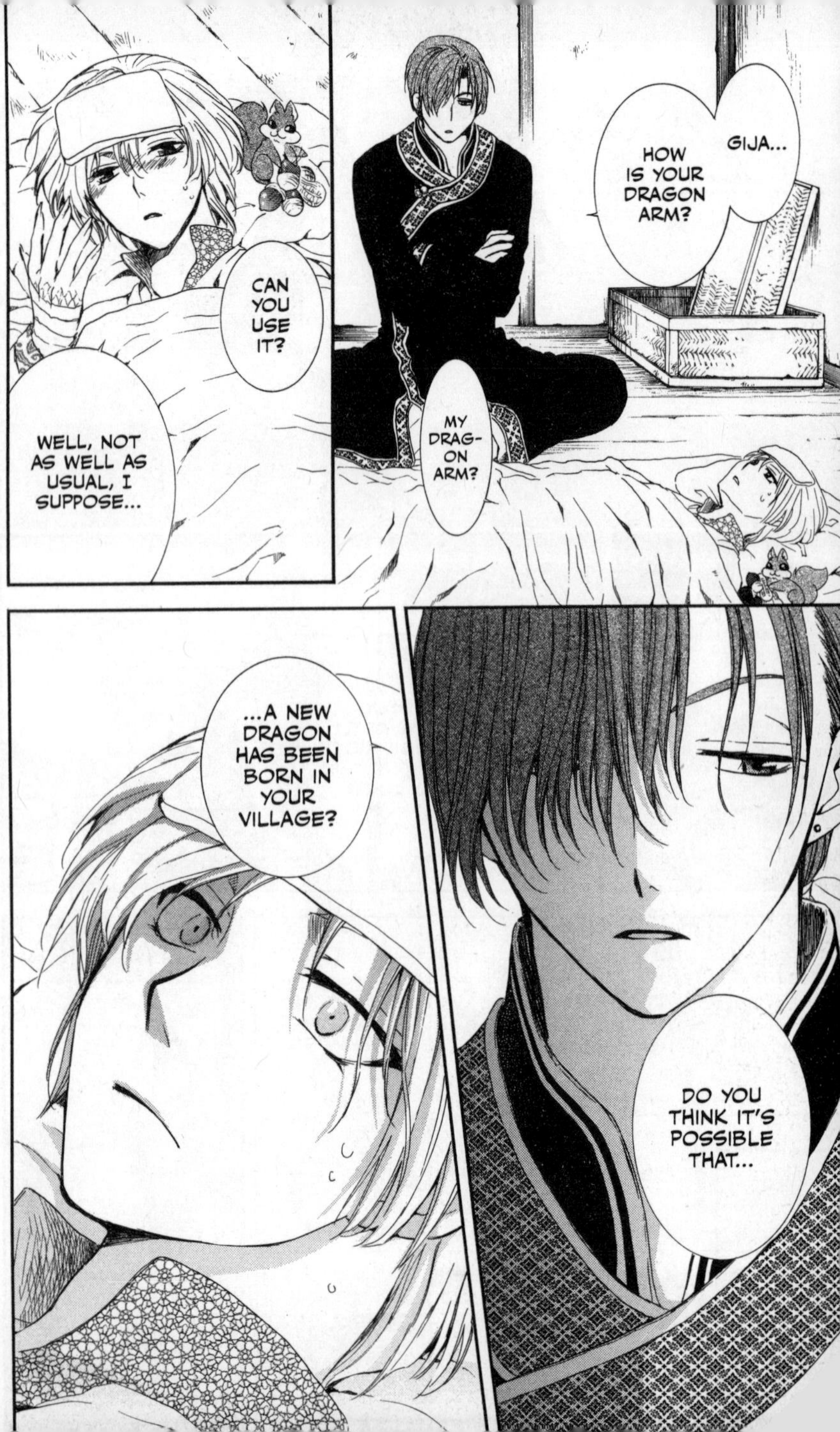
GIJA... HOW IS YOUR DRAGON ARM?
MY DRAG-ON ARM?
CAN YOU USE IT?
WELL, NOT AS WELL AS USUAL, I SUPPOSE...
DO YOU THINK IT'S POSSIBLE THAT...
...A NEW DRAGON HAS BEEN BORN IN YOUR VILLAGE?

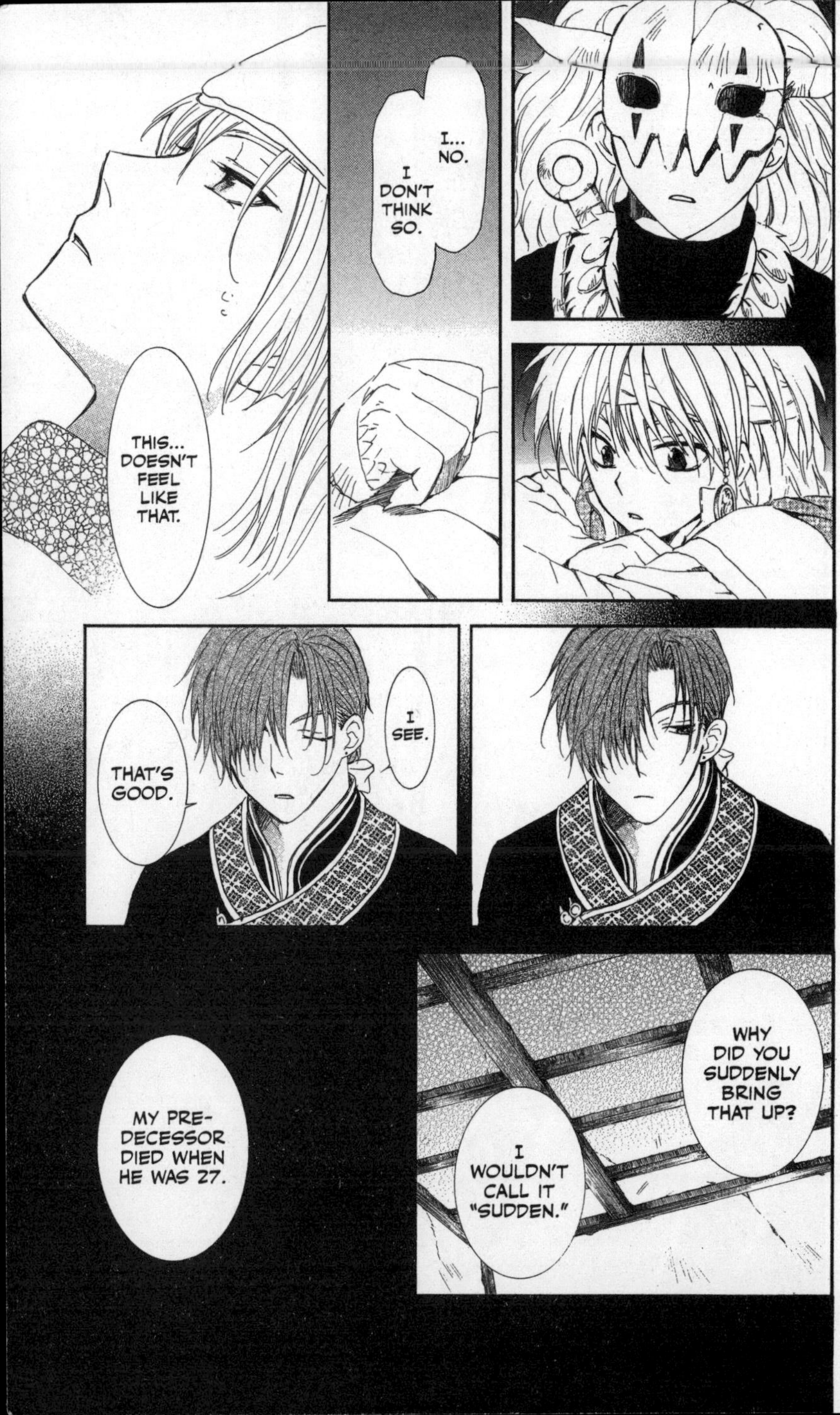
I... NO. I DON'T THINK SO.
THIS... DOESN'T FEEL LIKE THAT.
I SEE.
THAT'S GOOD.
WHY DID YOU SUDDENLY BRING THAT UP?
I WOULDN'T CALL IT "SUDDEN."
MY PRE-DECESSOR DIED WHEN HE WAS 27.

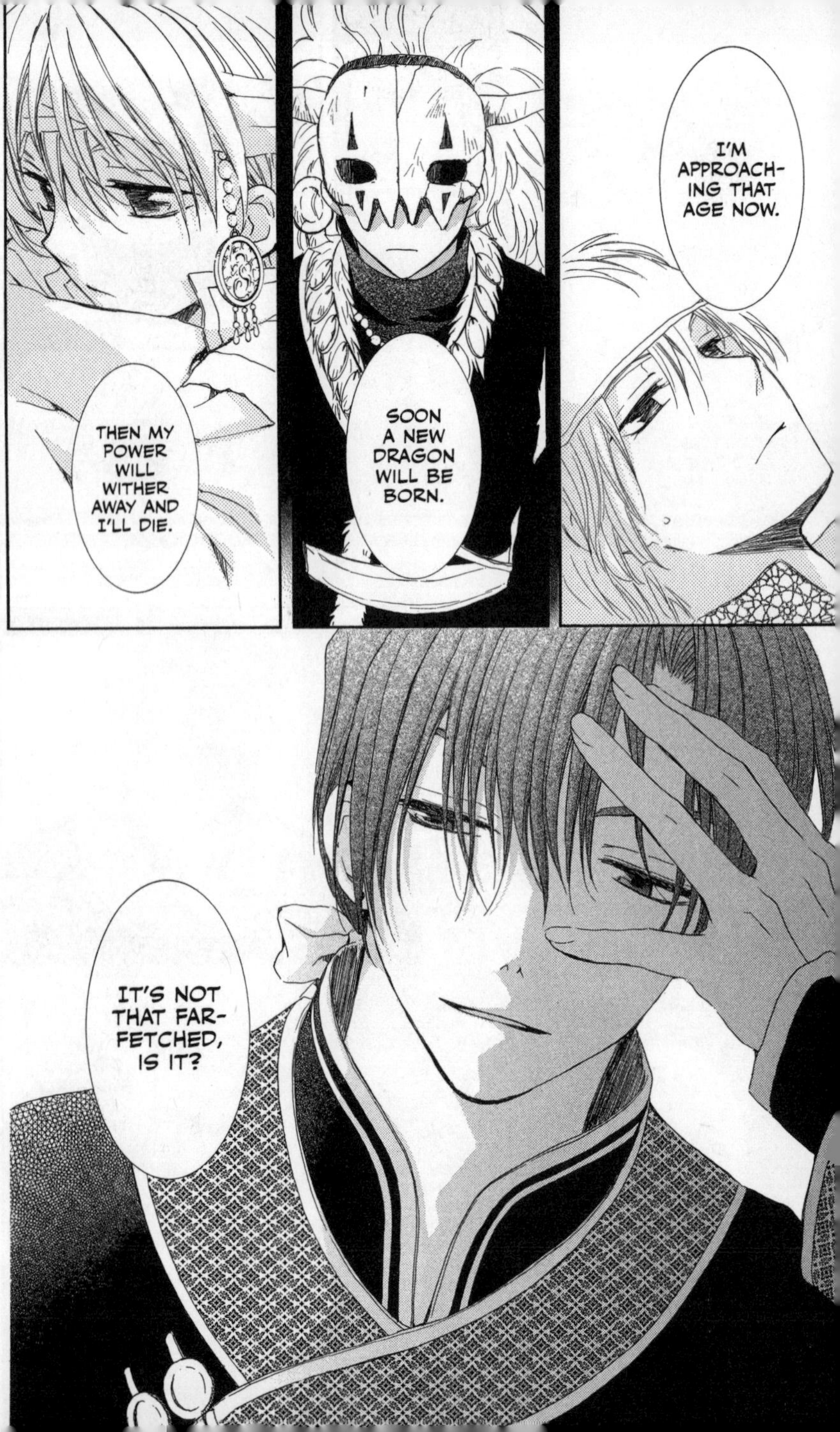
I'M APPROACHING THAT AGE NOW.
SOON A NEW DRAGON WILL BE BORN.
THEN MY POWER WILL WITHER AWAY AND I'LL DIE.
IT'S NOT THAT FAR-FETCHED, IS IT?

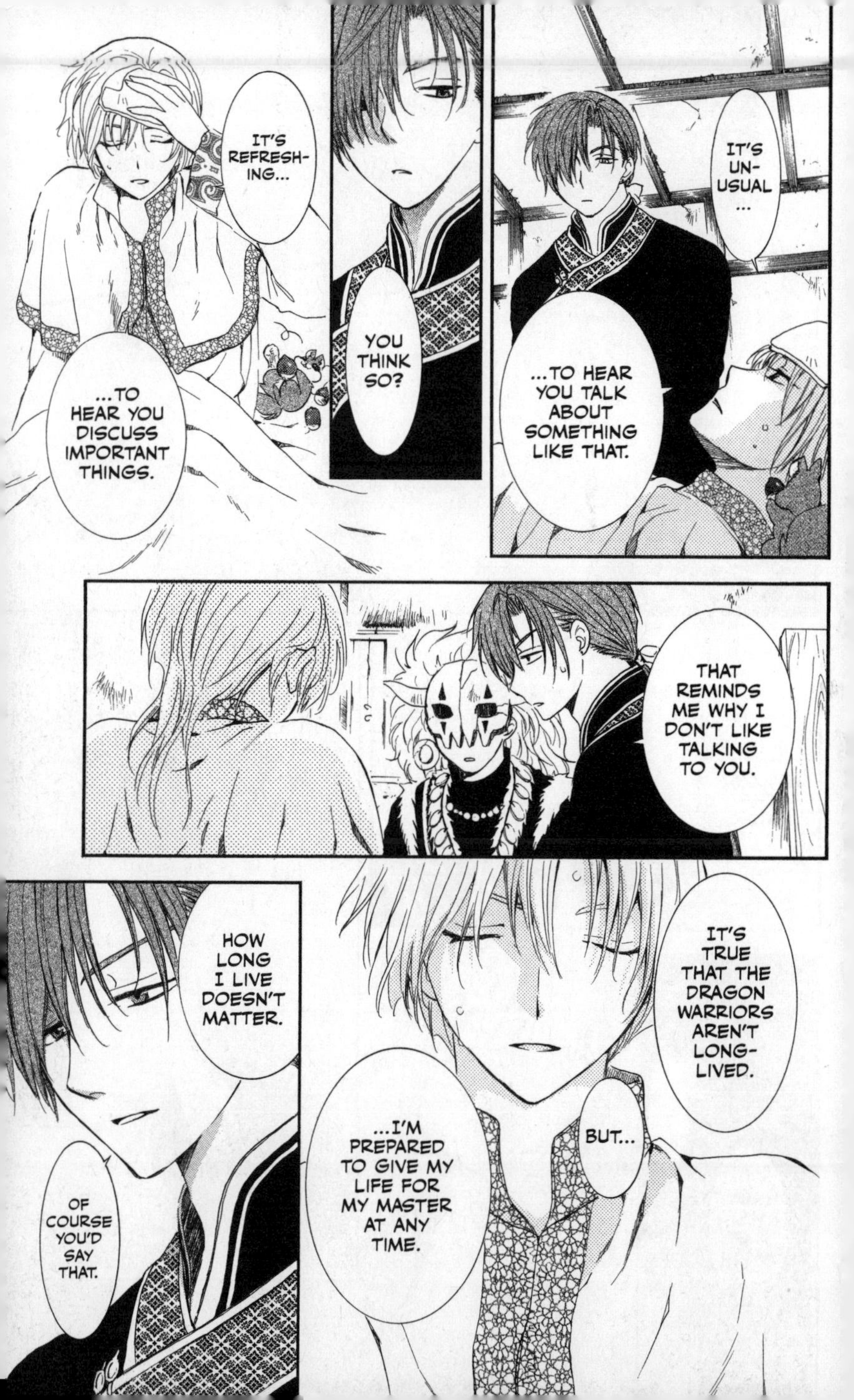
IT'S UN-USUAL...
...TO HEAR YOU TALK ABOUT SOMETHING LIKE THAT.
YOU THINK SO?
IT'S REFRESH-ING...
...TO HEAR YOU DISCUSS IMPORTANT THINGS.
THAT REMINDS ME WHY I DON'T LIKE TALKING TO YOU.
IT'S TRUE THAT THE DRAGON WARRIORS AREN'T LONG-LIVED.
BUT...
...I'M PREPARED TO GIVE MY LIFE FOR MY MASTER AT ANY TIME.
HOW LONG I LIVE DOESN'T MATTER.
OF COURSE YOU'D SAY THAT.

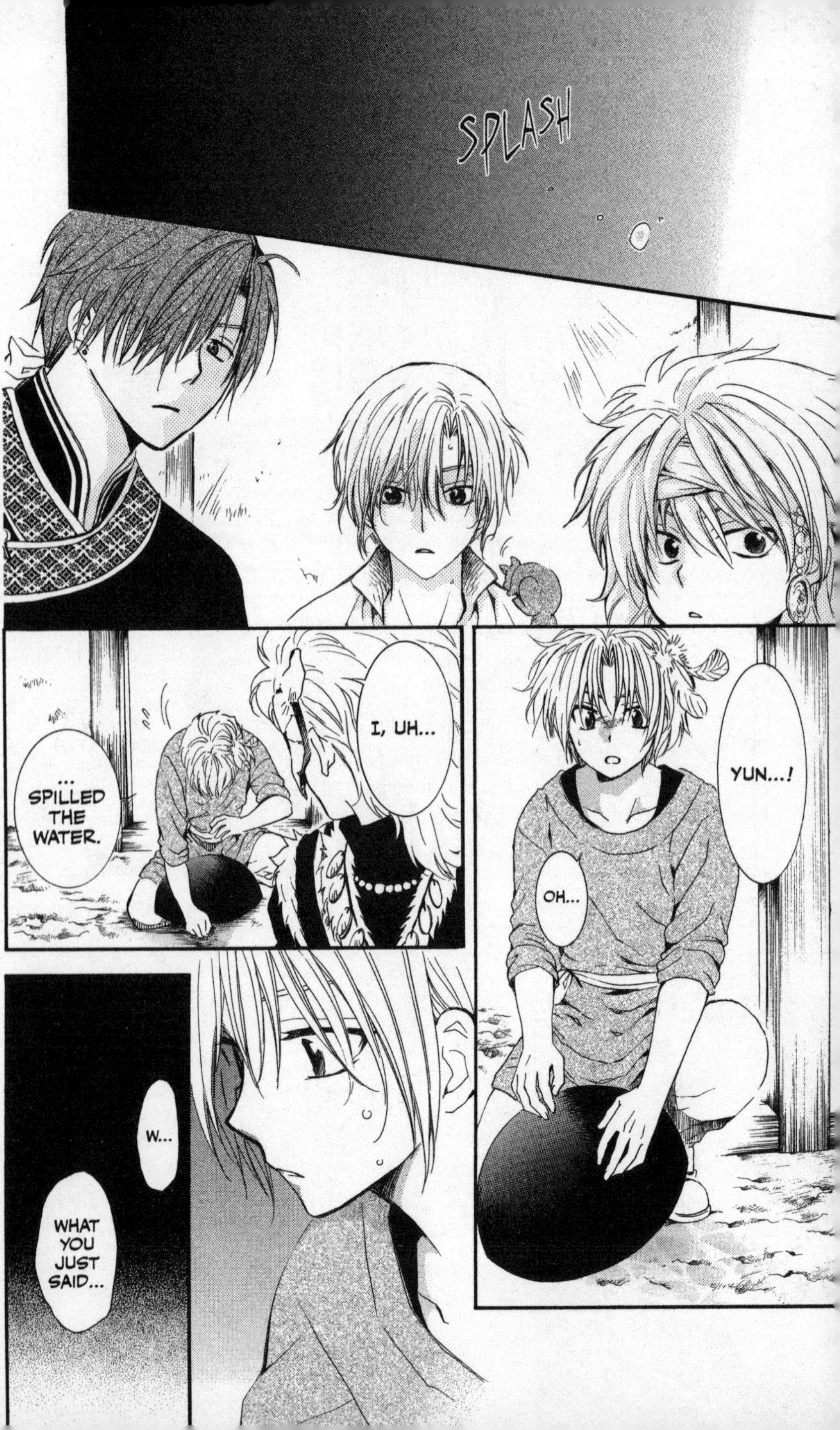
SPLASH
YUN...!
OH...
I, UH...
...SPILLED THE WATER.
W...
WHAT YOU JUST SAID...

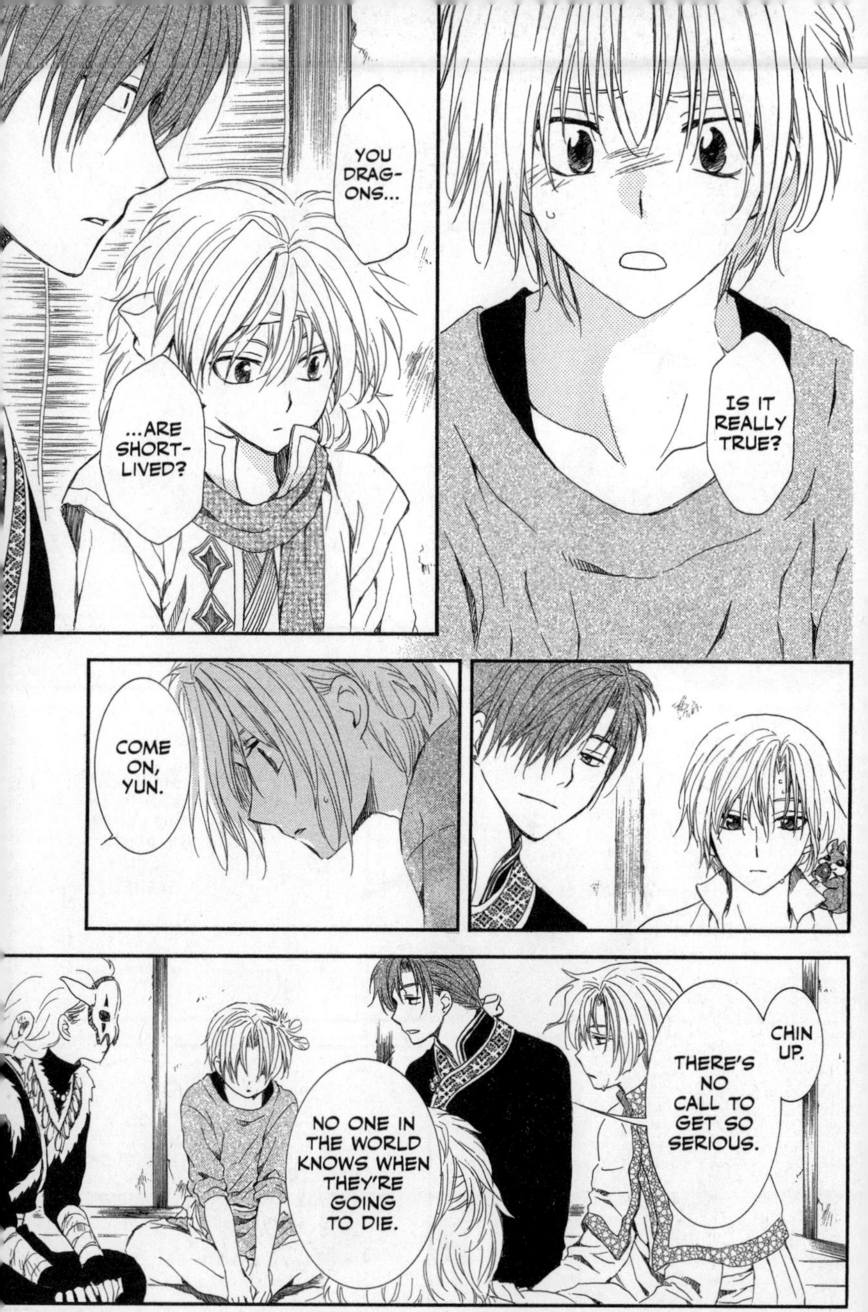
IS IT REALLY TRUE?
YOU DRAGONS...
...ARE SHORT-LIVED?
COME ON, YUN.
CHIN UP.
THERE'S NO CALL TO GET SO SERIOUS.
NO ONE IN THE WORLD KNOWS WHEN THEY'RE GOING TO DIE.

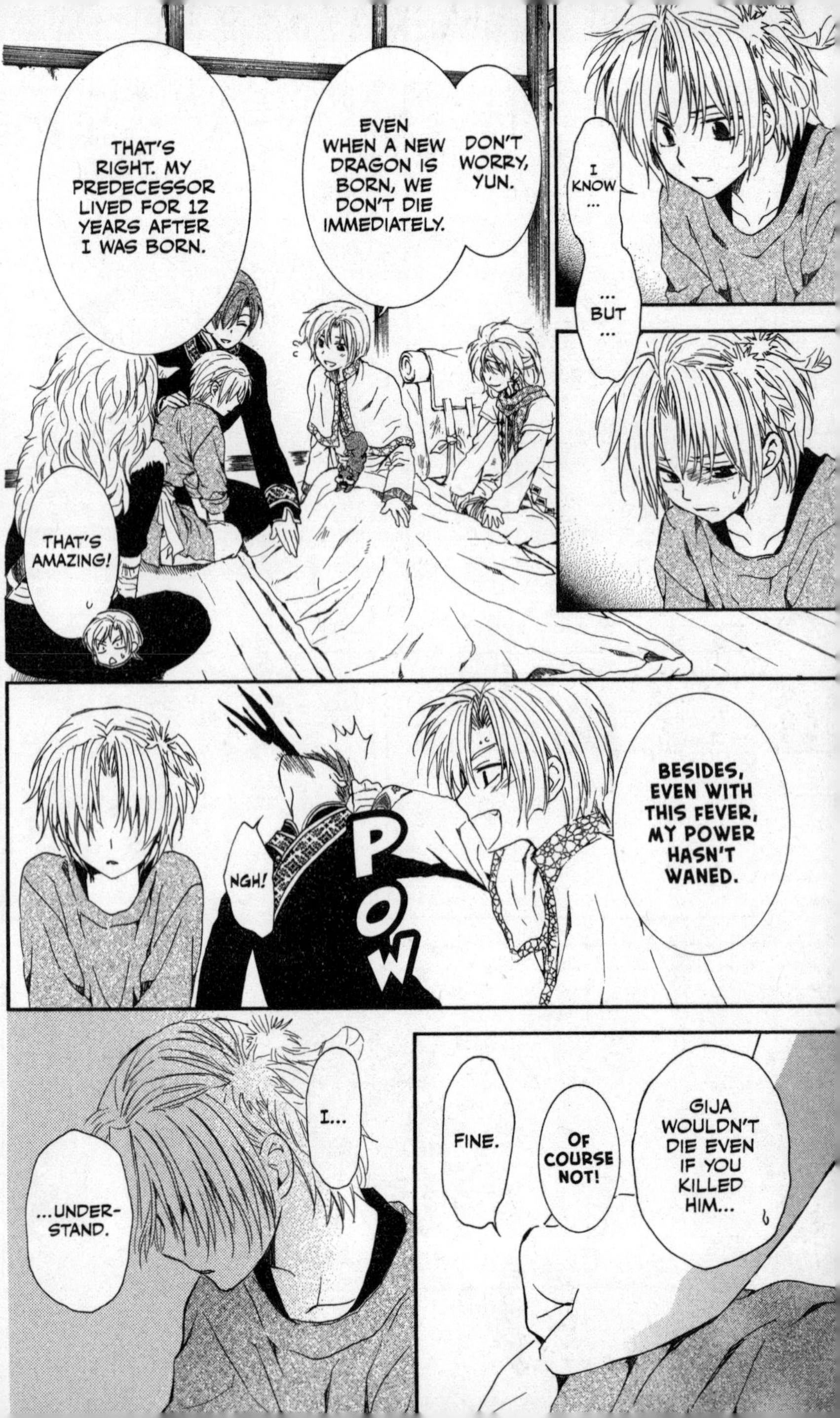
I KNOW...
...BUT...
DON'T WORRY, YUN.
EVEN WHEN A NEW DRAGON IS BORN, WE DON'T DIE IMMEDIATELY.
THAT'S RIGHT. MY PREDECESSOR LIVED FOR 12 YEARS AFTER I WAS BORN.
THAT'S AMAZING!
BESIDES, EVEN WITH THIS FEVER, MY POWER HASN'T WANED.
POW
NGH!
GIJA WOULDN'T DIE EVEN IF YOU KILLED HIM...
OF COURSE NOT!
FINE.
I...
...UNDER-STAND.

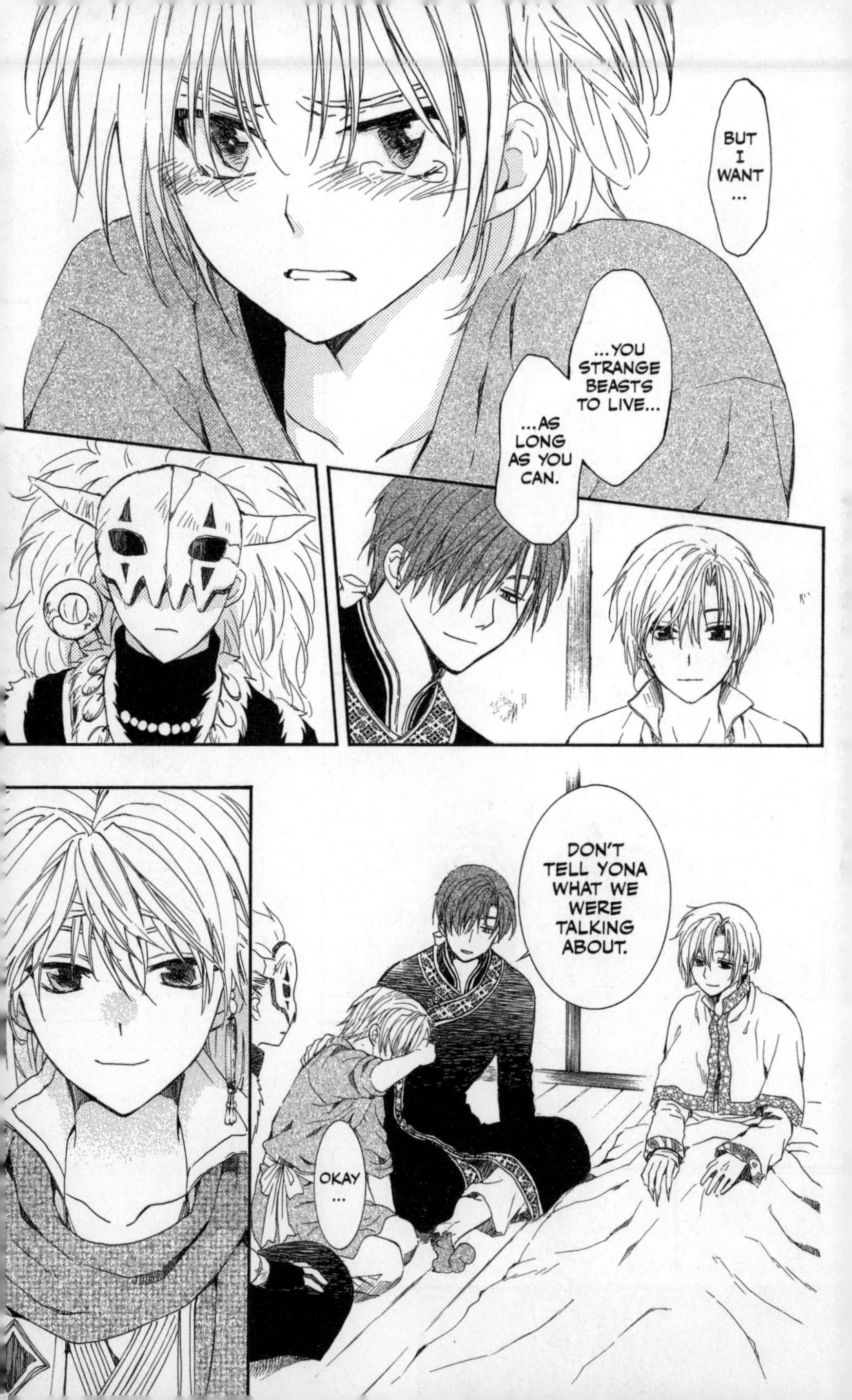
BUT I WANT ...
...YOU STRANGE BEASTS TO LIVE...
...AS LONG AS YOU CAN.
DON'T TELL YONA WHAT WE WERE TALKING ABOUT.
OKAY ...

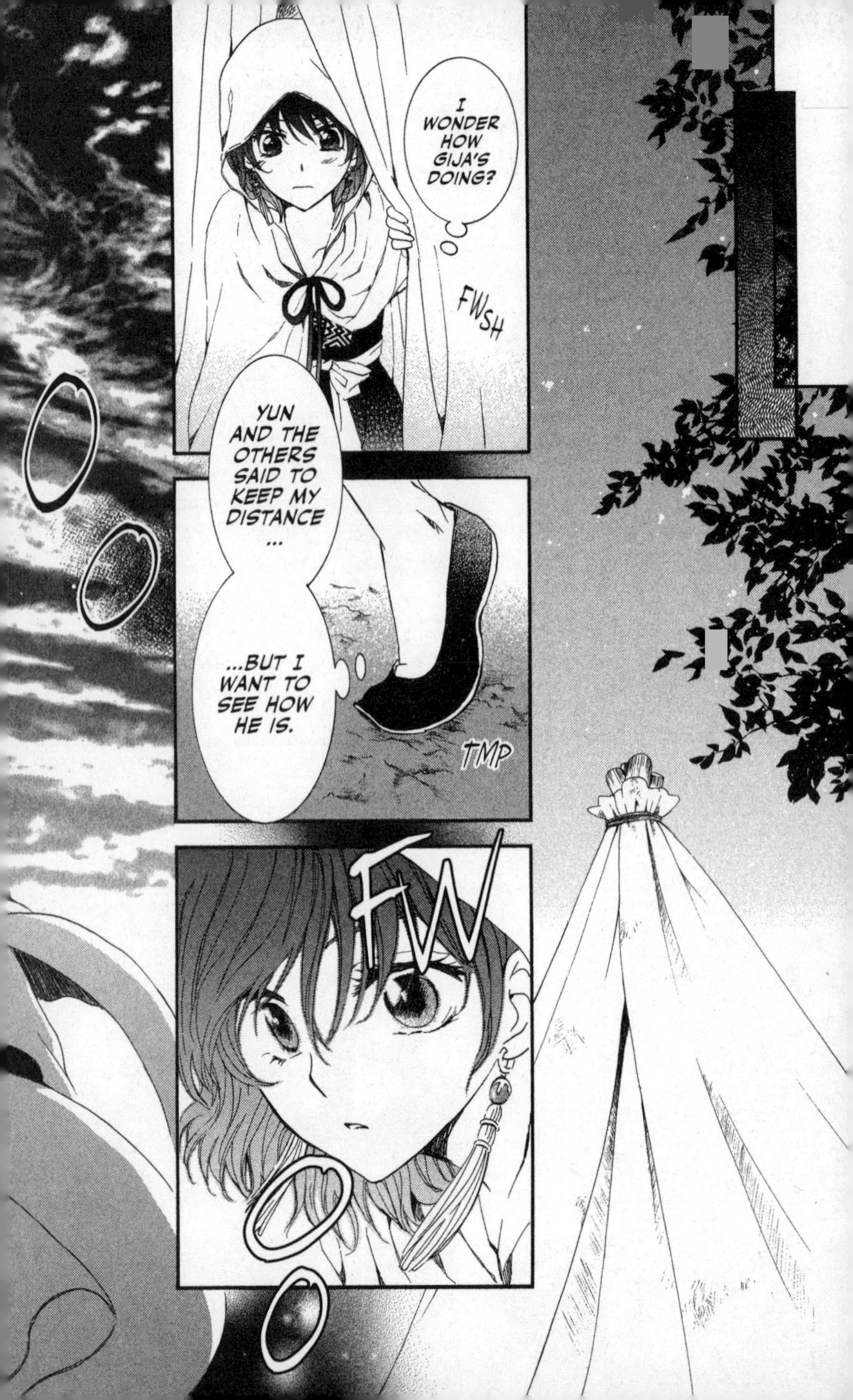
I WONDER HOW GIJA'S DOING?
FWSH
YUN AND THE OTHERS SAID TO KEEP MY DISTANCE...
...BUT I WANT TO SEE HOW HE IS.
TMP
FW

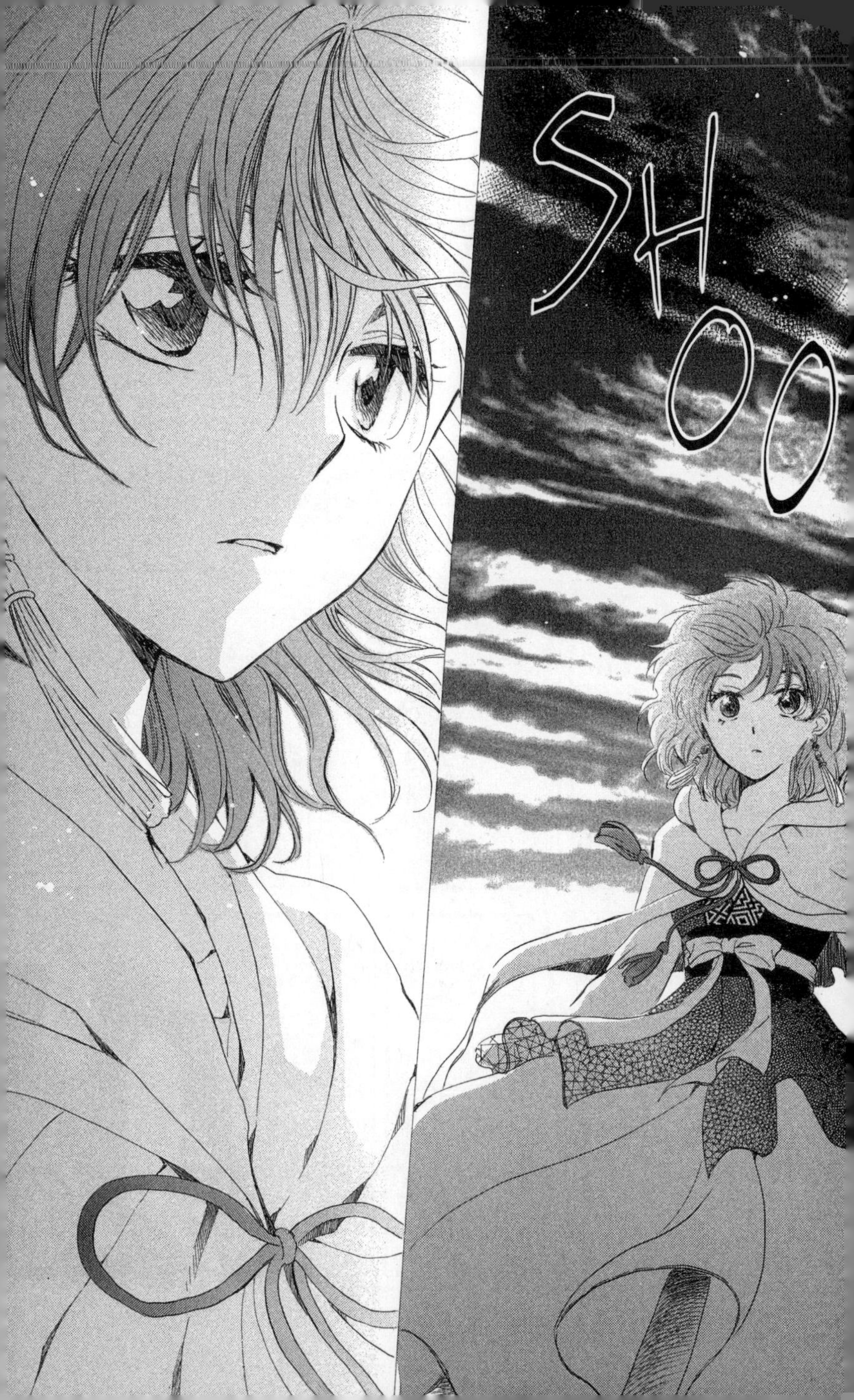
SHOO

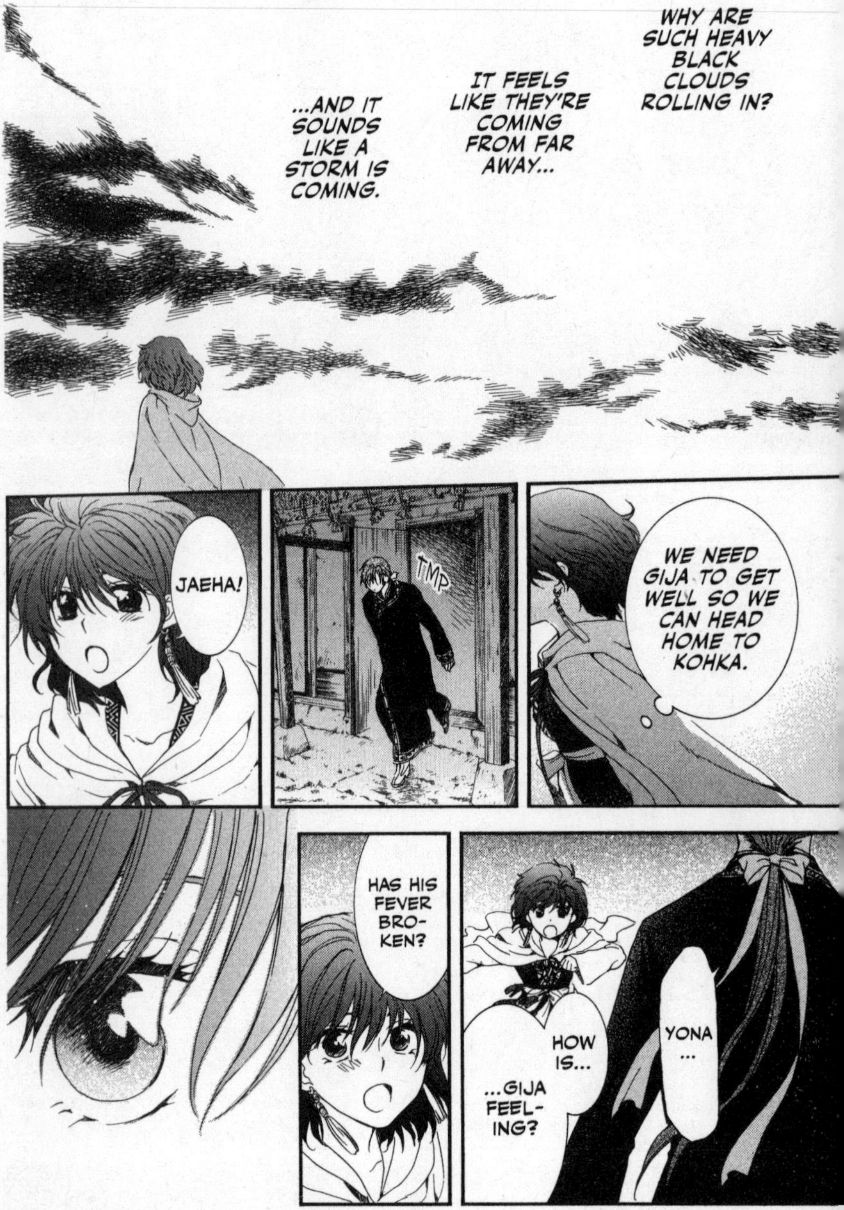
WHY ARE SUCH HEAVY BLACK CLOUDS ROLLING IN?
IT FEELS LIKE THEY'RE COMING FROM FAR AWAY...
...AND IT SOUNDS LIKE A STORM IS COMING.
WE NEED GIJA TO GET WELL SO WE CAN HEAD HOME TO KOHKA.
TMP
JAEHA!
YONA ...
HOW IS... ...GIJA FEELING?
HAS HIS FEVER BROKEN?

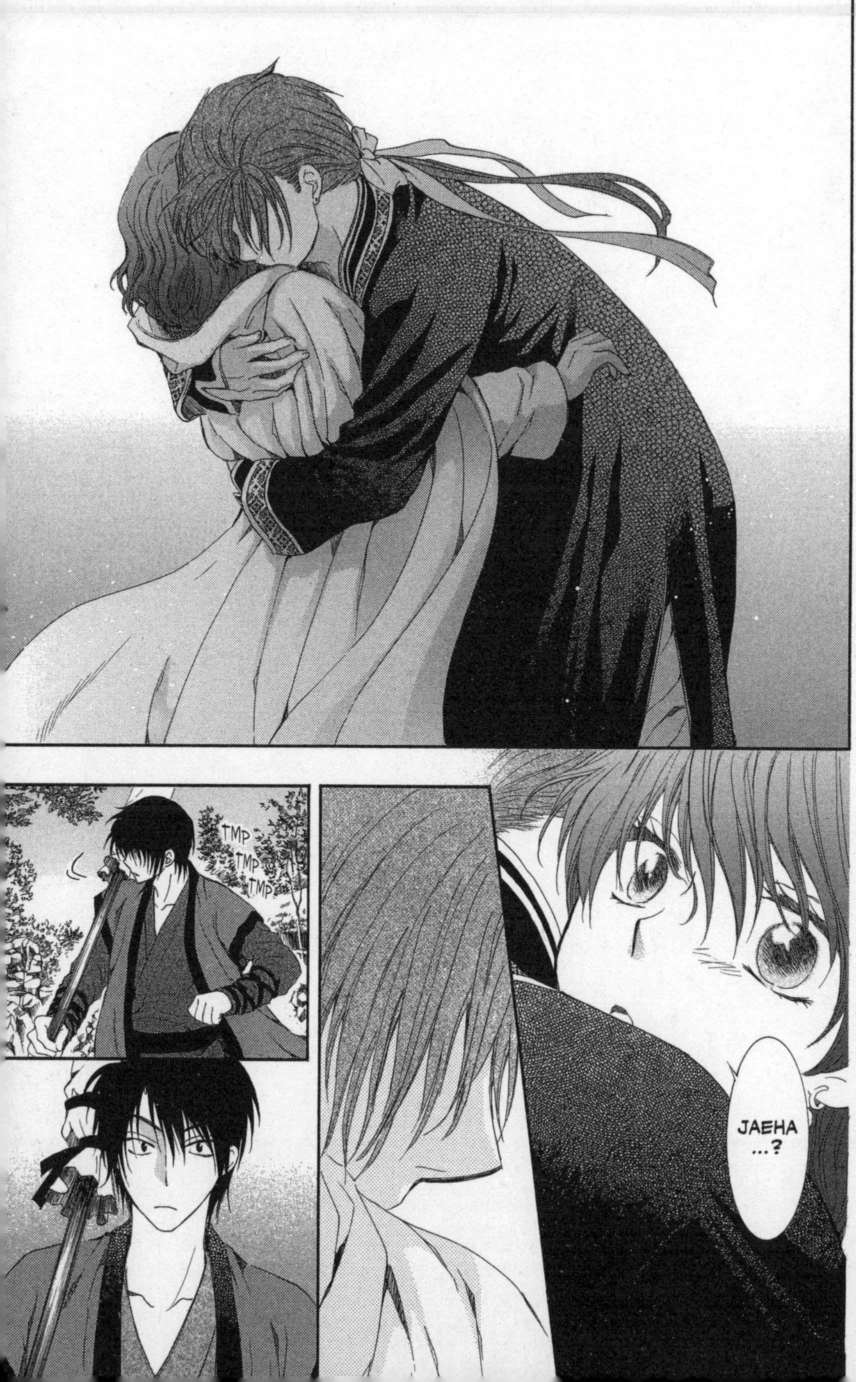
JAEHA ...?
TMP TMP TMP

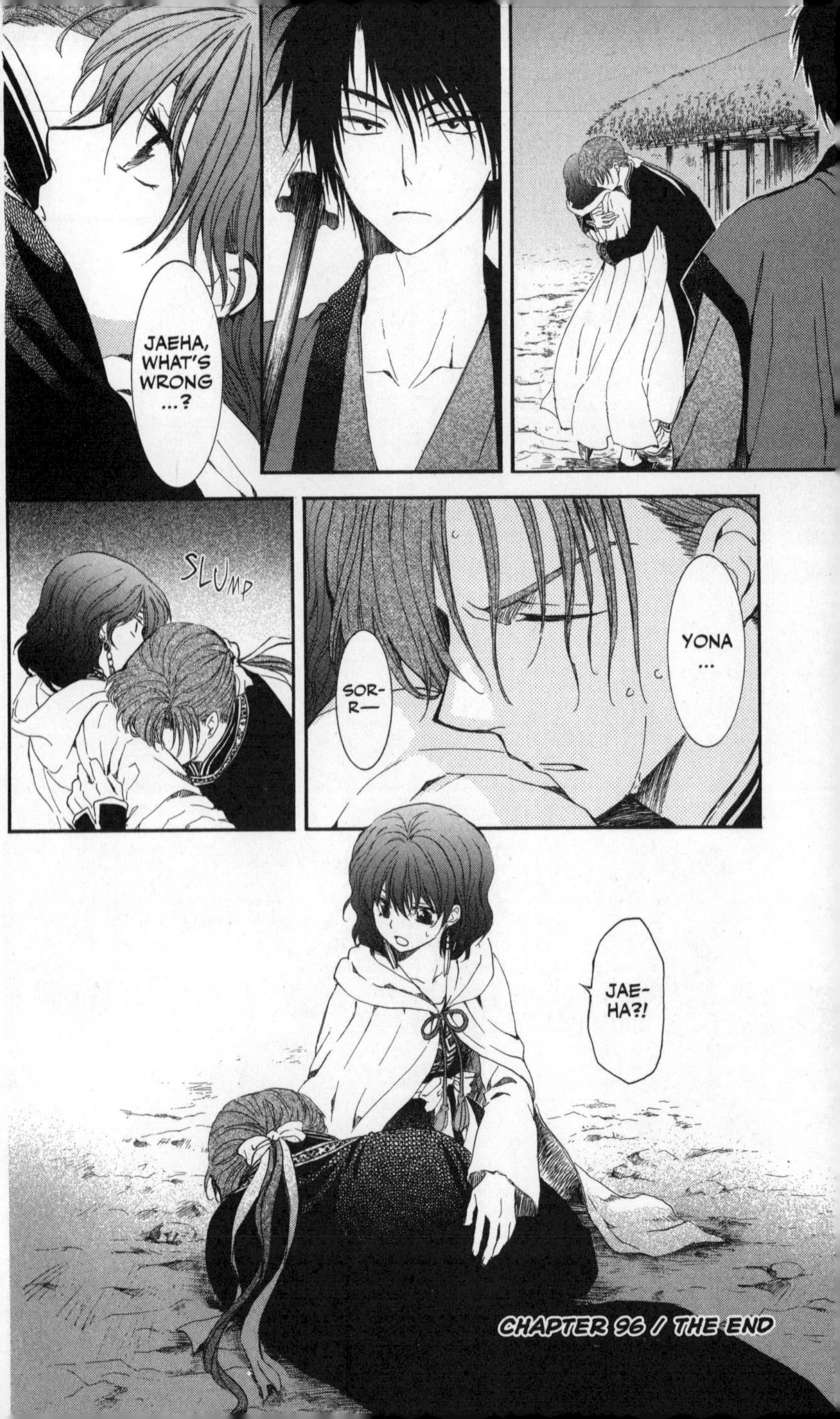
JAEHA, WHAT'S WRONG ...?
YONA ...
SORR—
SLUMP
JAE-HA?!
CHAPTER 96 / THE END

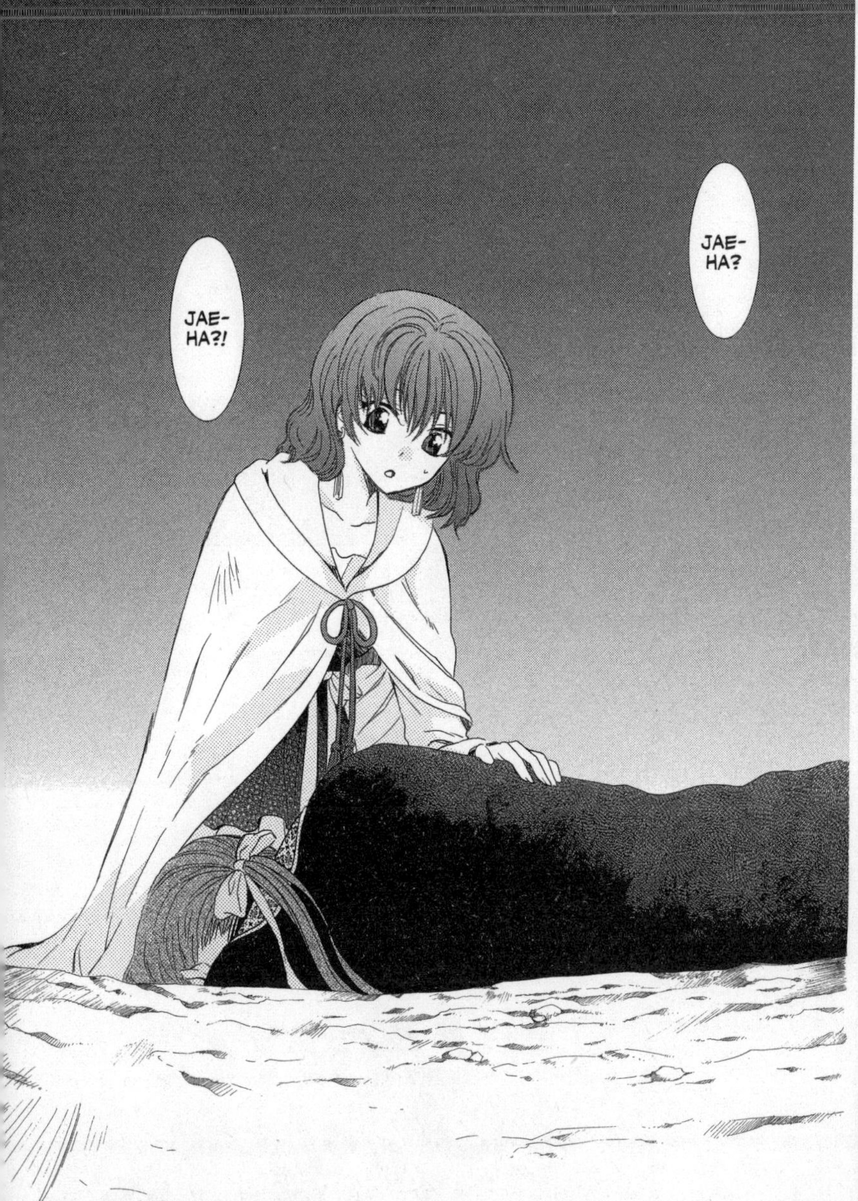
JAE-HA?
JAE-HA?!

## CHAPTER 97: SEARCHING FOR ANSWERS

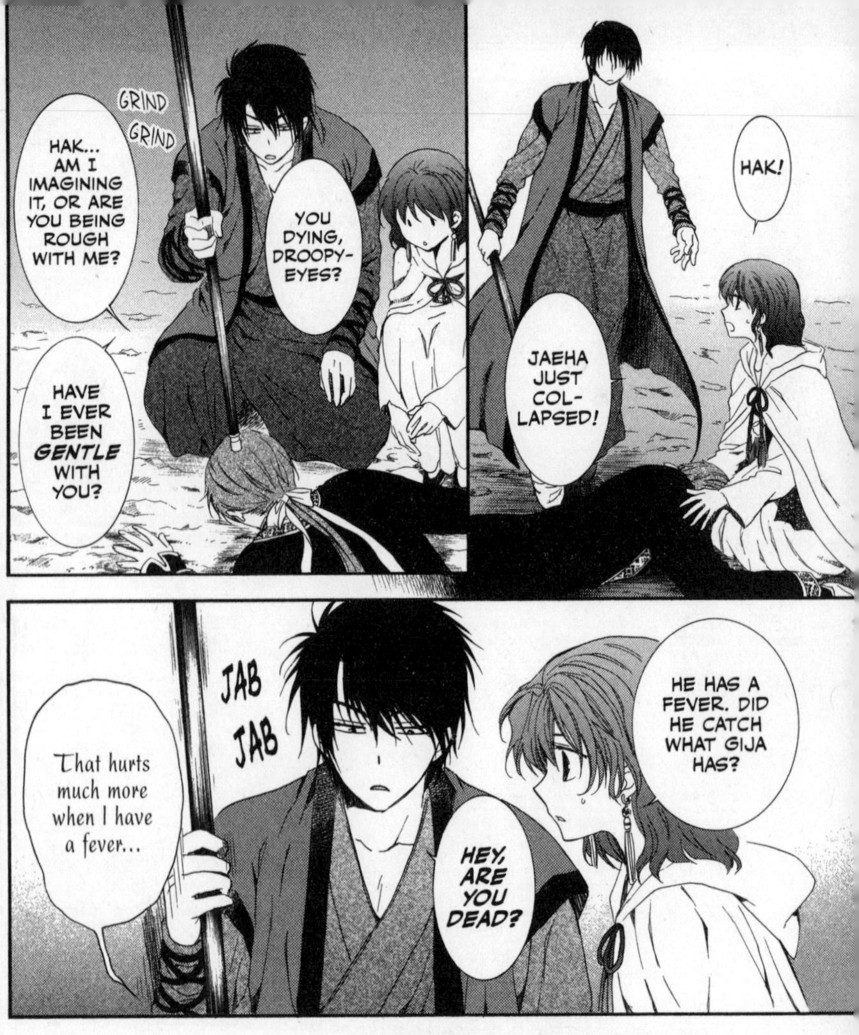
HAK!
JAEHA JUST COL-LAPSED!
GRIND GRIND
YOU DYING, DROOPY-EYES?
HAK... AM I IMAGINING IT, OR ARE YOU BEING ROUGH WITH ME?
HAVE I EVER BEEN GENTLE WITH YOU?
HE HAS A FEVER. DID HE CATCH WHAT GIJA HAS?
HEY, ARE YOU DEAD?
JAB JAB
That hurts much more when I have a fever...

# Yona of the Dawn

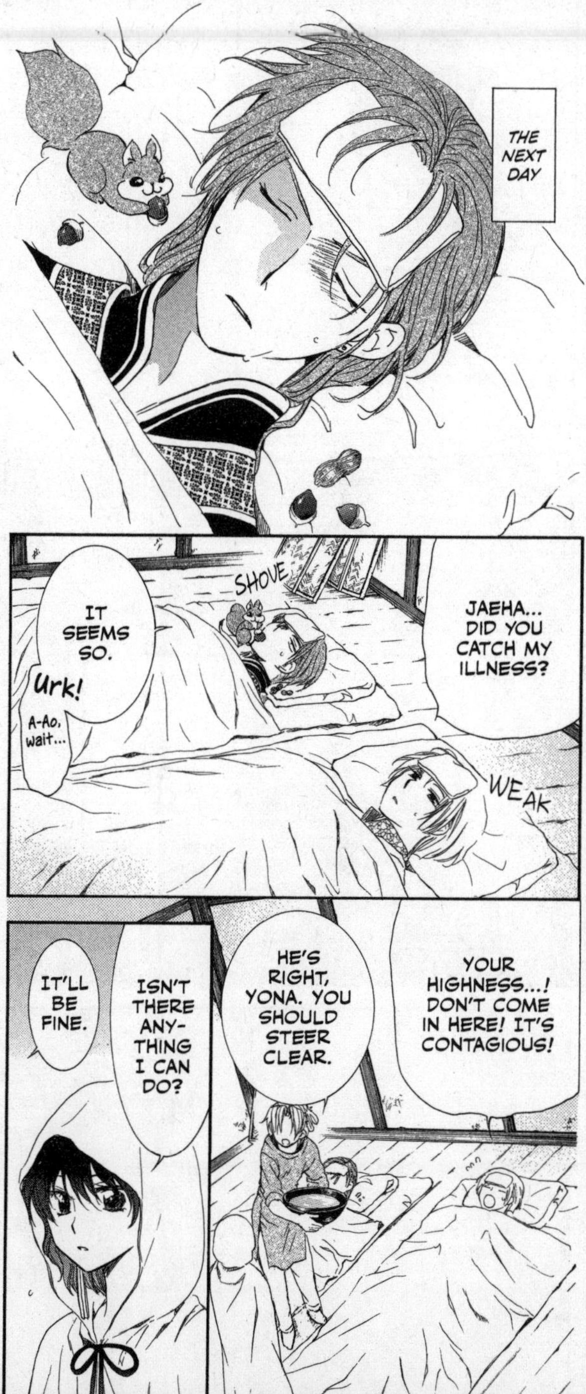
THE NEXT DAY
JAEHA... DID YOU CATCH MY ILLNESS?
SHOVE
IT SEEMS SO.
Urk!
A-Ao, wait...
WEAK
YOUR HIGHNESS...! DON'T COME IN HERE! IT'S CONTAGIOUS!
HE'S RIGHT, YONA. YOU SHOULD STEER CLEAR.
ISN'T THERE ANYTHING I CAN DO?
IT'LL BE FINE.

Continuation

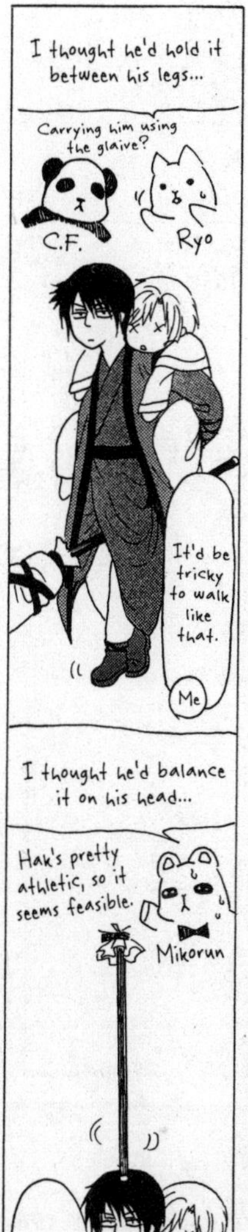
I thought he'd hold it between his legs...
Carrying him using the glaive?
C.F.
Ryo
It'd be tricky to walk like that.
Me
I thought he'd balance it on his head...
Hak's pretty athletic, so it seems feasible.
Mikorun
On his head?! Why?!
Me

To be continued

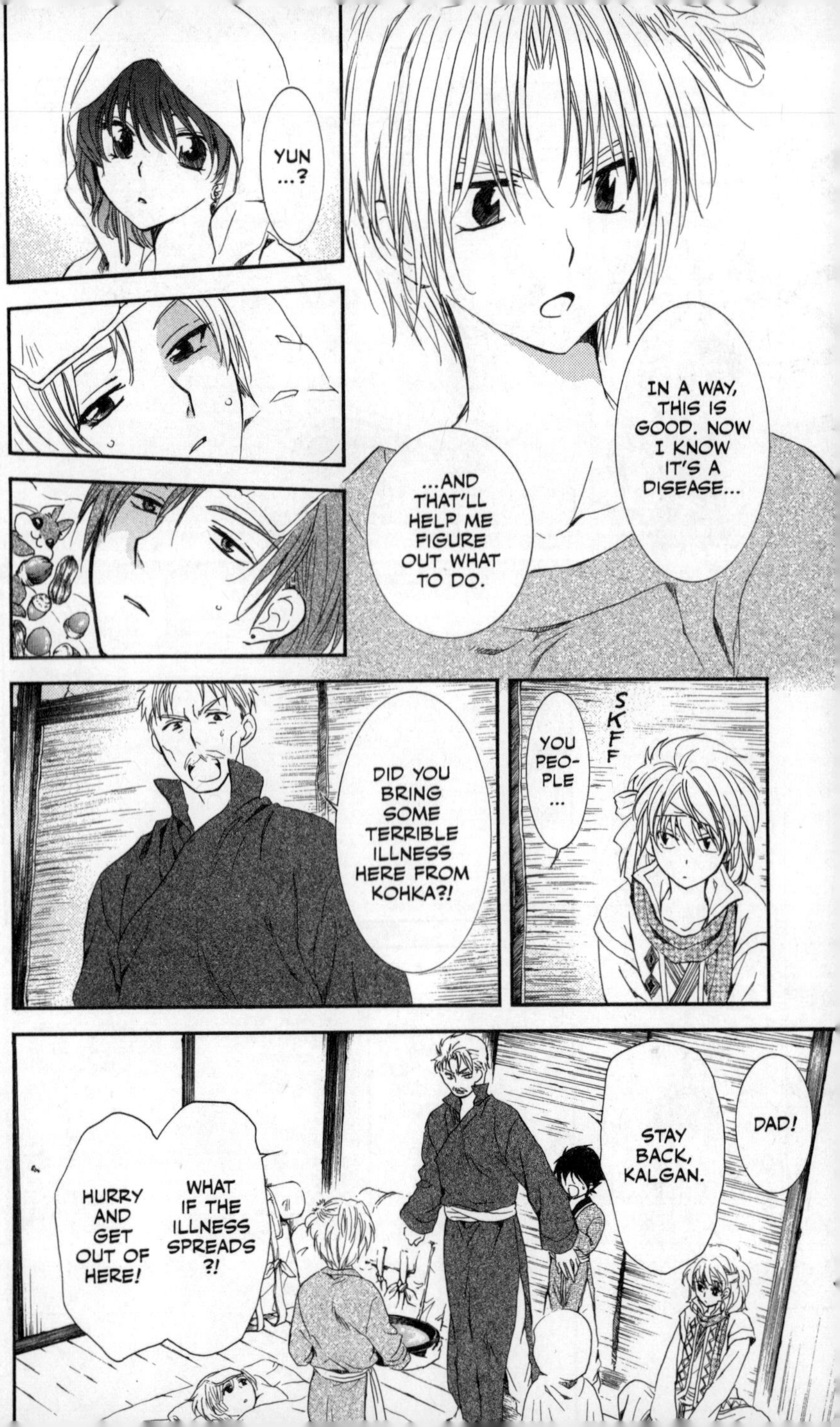
IN A WAY, THIS IS GOOD. NOW I KNOW IT'S A DISEASE...
...AND THAT'LL HELP ME FIGURE OUT WHAT TO DO.
YUN ...?
SKFF
YOU PEO-PLE ...
DID YOU BRING SOME TERRIBLE ILLNESS HERE FROM KOHKA?!
DAD!
STAY BACK, KALGAN.
WHAT IF THE ILLNESS SPREADS ?!
HURRY AND GET OUT OF HERE!

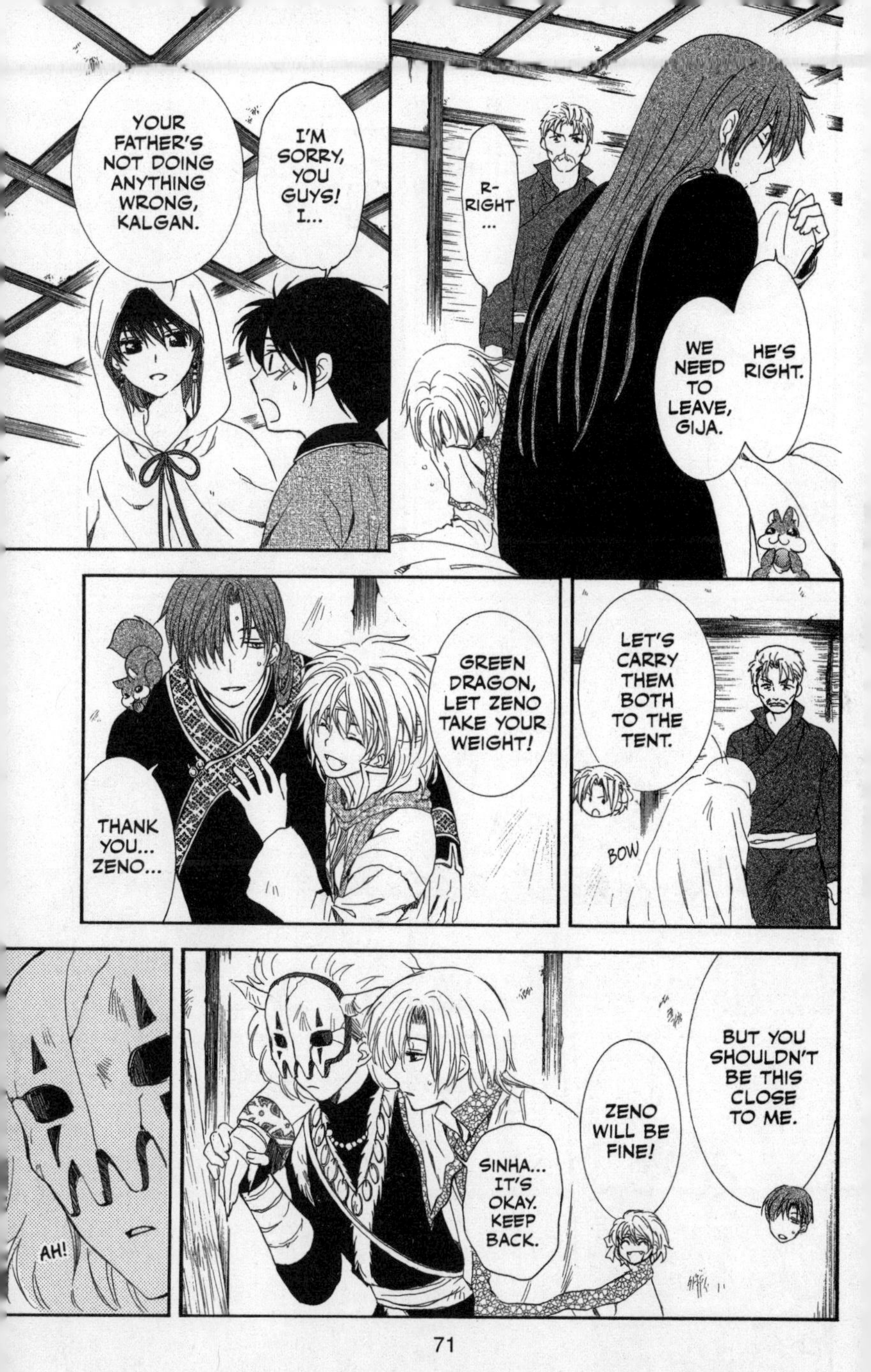
HE'S RIGHT.
WE NEED TO LEAVE, GIJA.
R-RIGHT...
I'M SORRY, YOU GUYS! I...
YOUR FATHER'S NOT DOING ANYTHING WRONG, KALGAN.
LET'S CARRY THEM BOTH TO THE TENT.
BOW
GREEN DRAGON, LET ZENO TAKE YOUR WEIGHT!
THANK YOU... ZENO...
BUT YOU SHOULDN'T BE THIS CLOSE TO ME.
ZENO WILL BE FINE!
SINHA... IT'S OKAY. KEEP BACK.
AH!

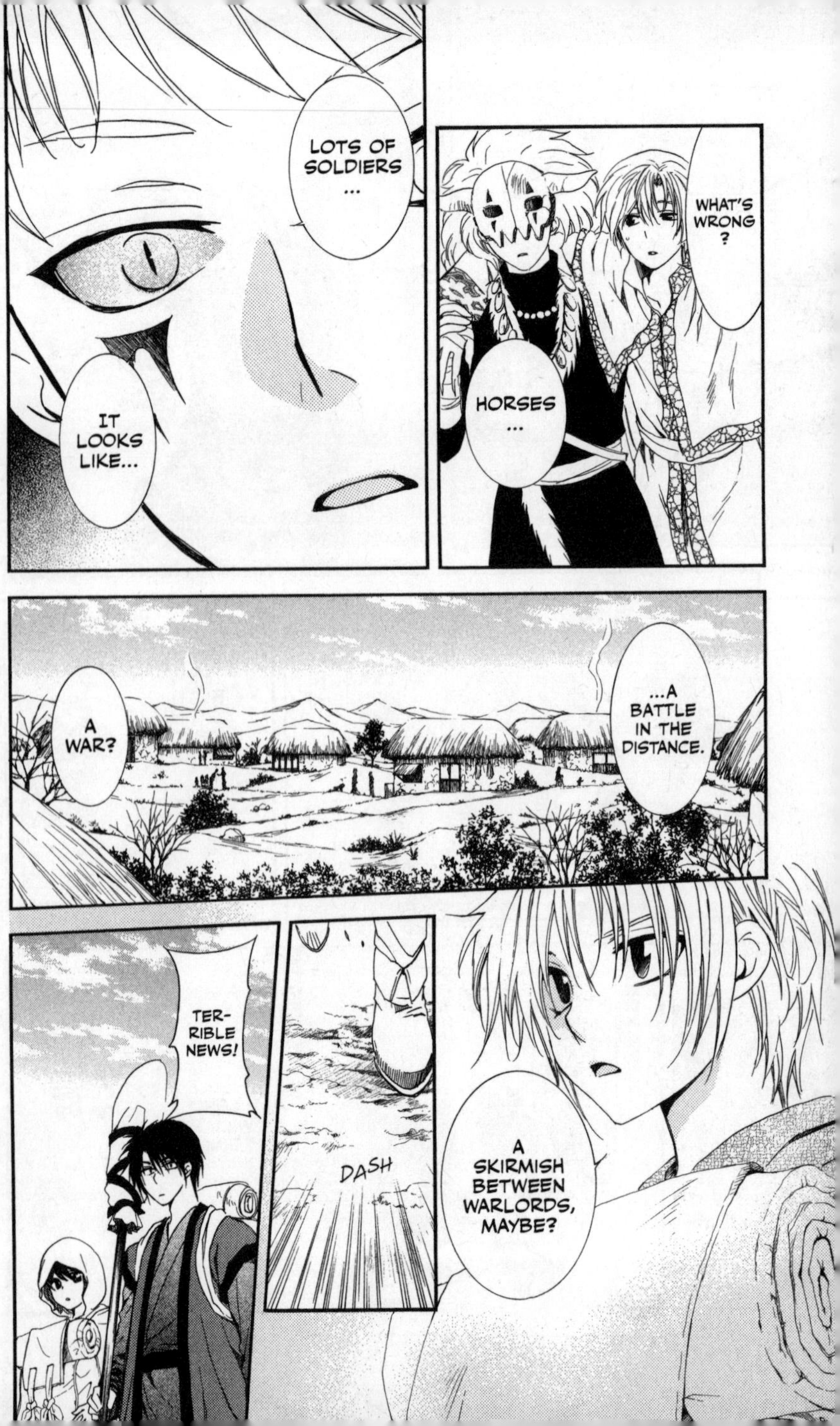
WHAT'S WRONG ?
HORSES ...
LOTS OF SOLDIERS ...
IT LOOKS LIKE...
...A BATTLE IN THE DISTANCE.
A WAR?
A SKIRMISH BETWEEN WARLORDS, MAYBE?
DASH
TER-RIBLE NEWS!

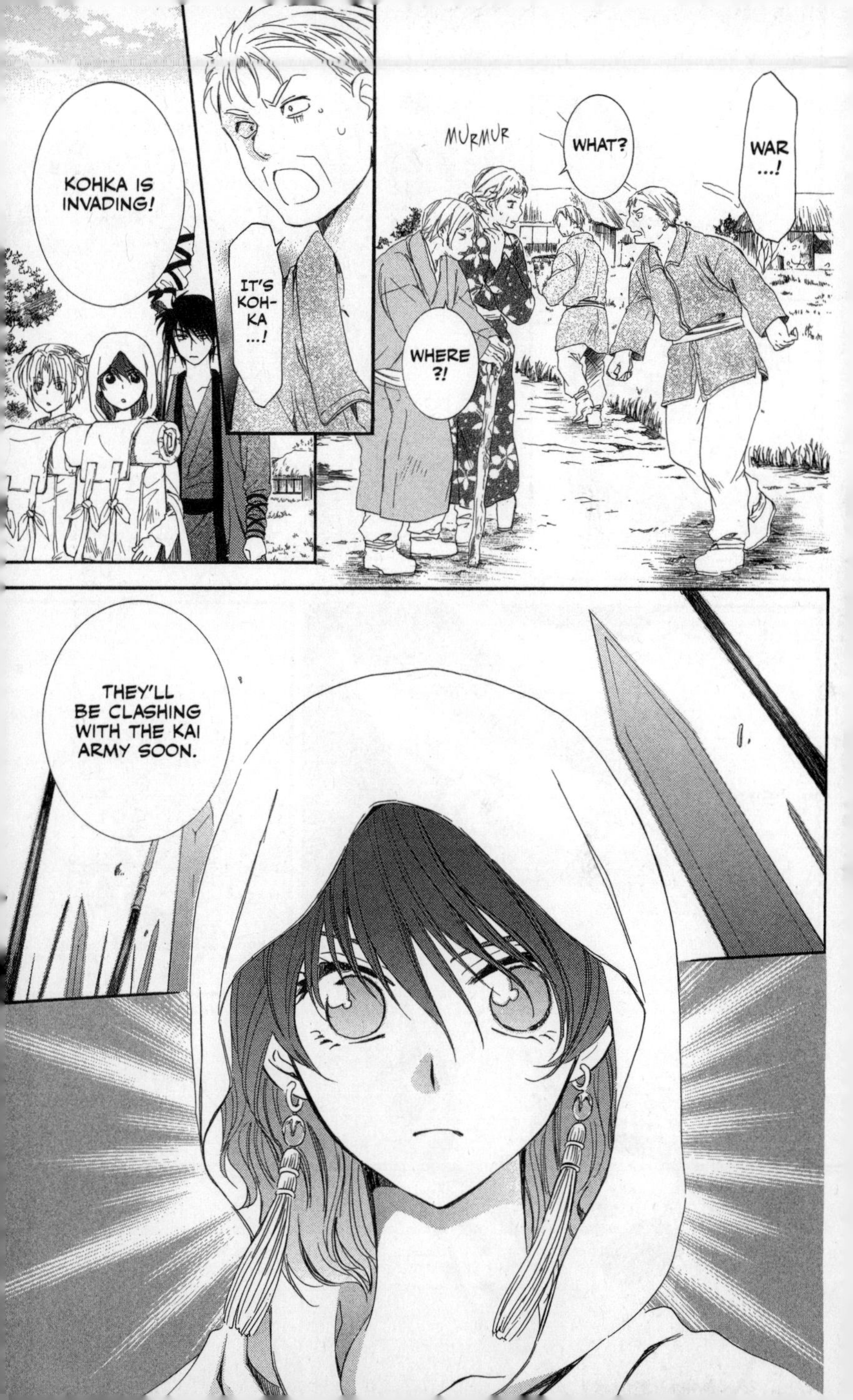
WAR ...!
WHAT?
MURMUR
WHERE ?!
IT'S KOHKA ...!
KOHKA IS INVADING!
THEY'LL BE CLASHING WITH THE KAI ARMY SOON.

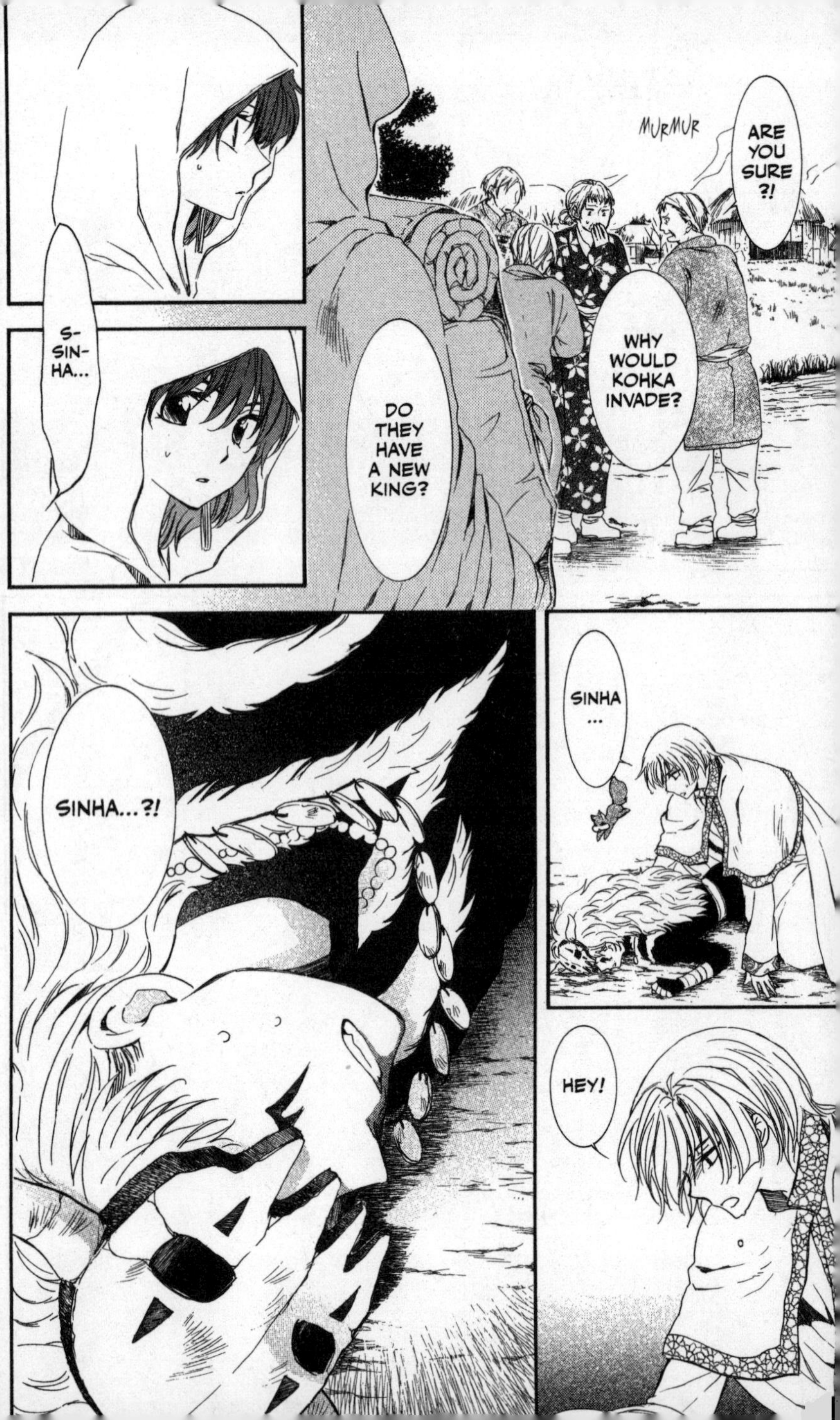
MURMUR
ARE YOU SURE?!
WHY WOULD KOHKA INVADE?
DO THEY HAVE A NEW KING?
S-SINHA...
SINHA...
HEY!
SINHA...?!
...

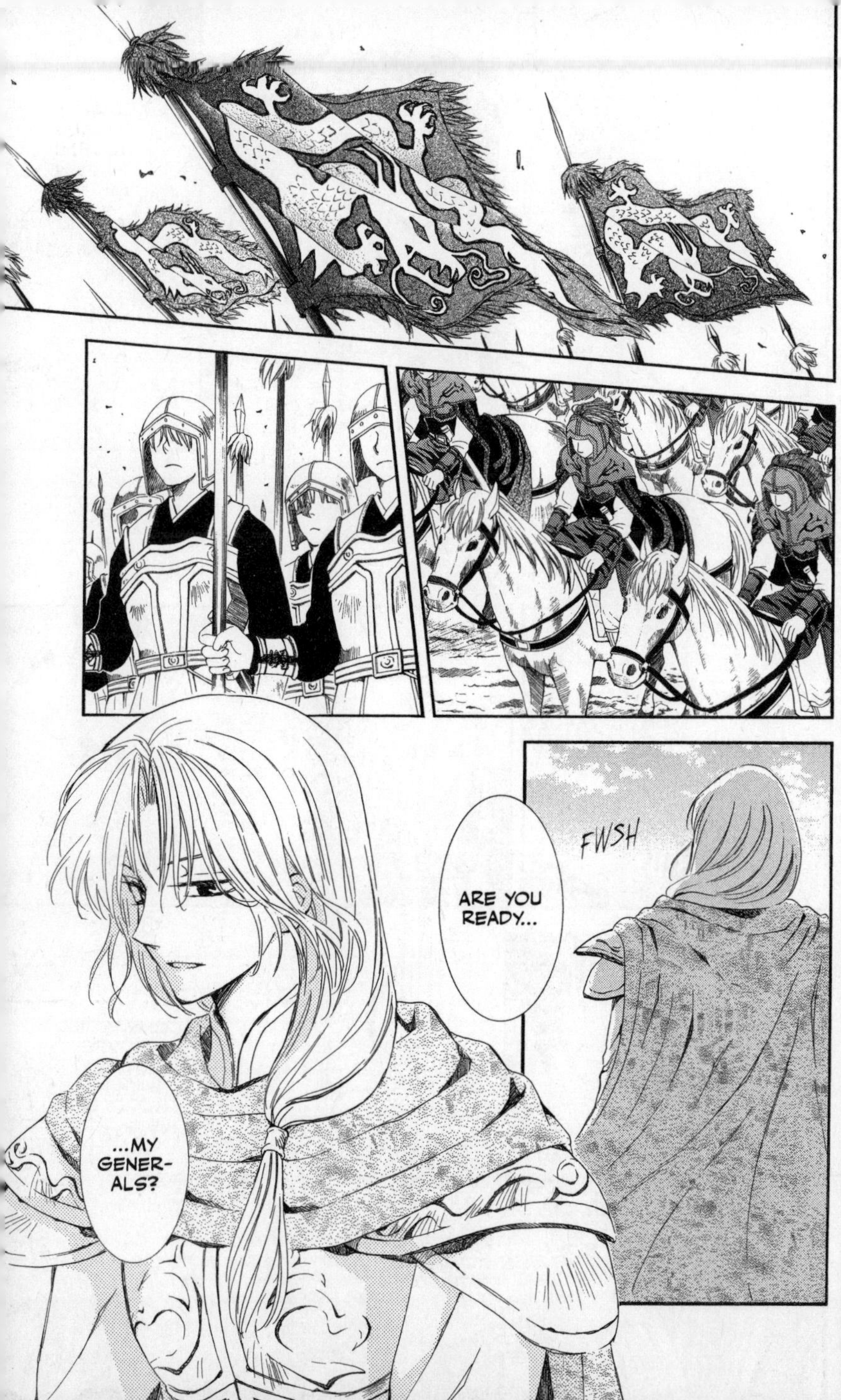
FWSH
ARE YOU READY...
...MY GENER-ALS?

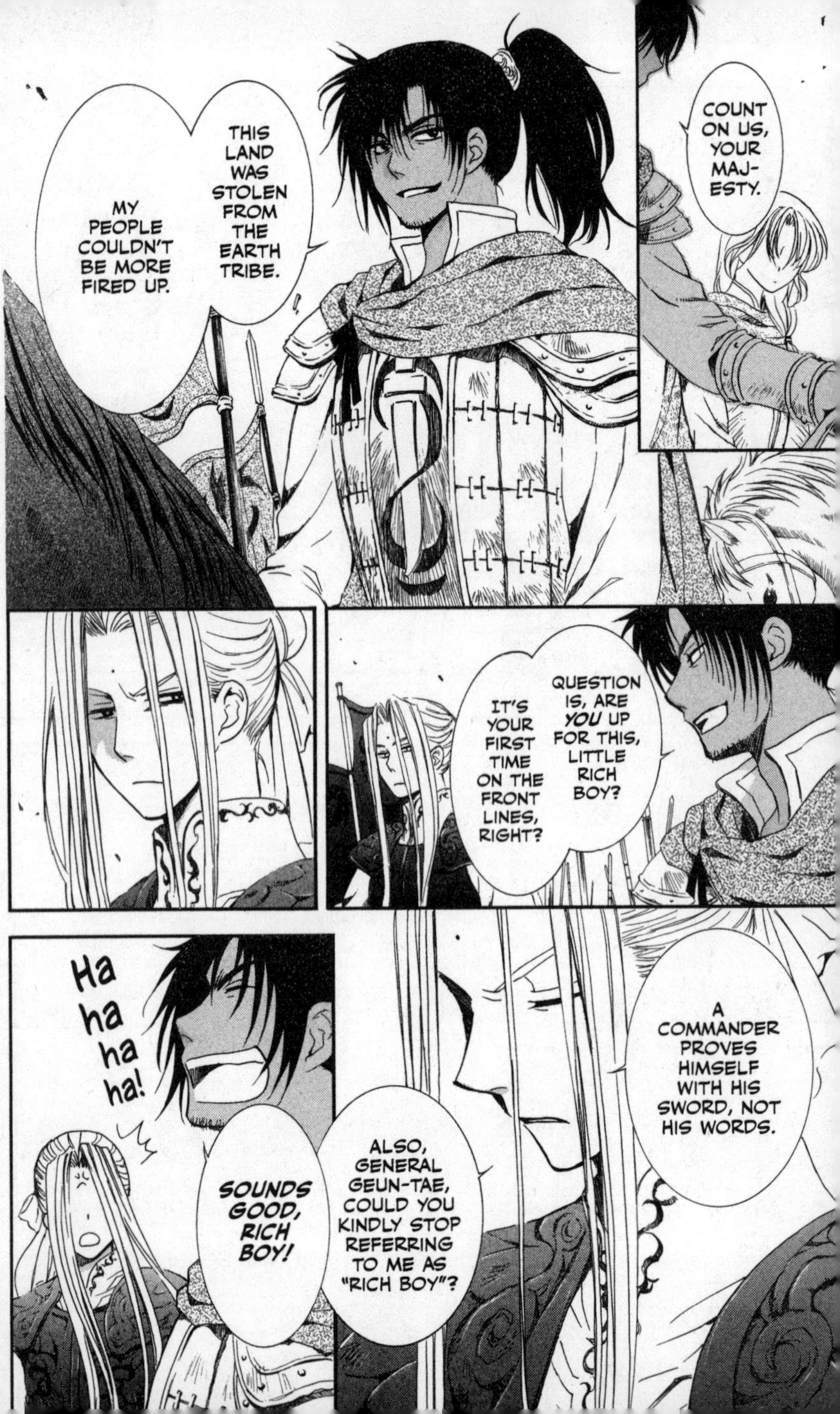
COUNT ON US, YOUR MAJ-ESTY.
THIS LAND WAS STOLEN FROM THE EARTH TRIBE.
MY PEOPLE COULDN'T BE MORE FIRED UP.
QUESTION IS, ARE *YOU* UP FOR THIS, LITTLE RICH BOY?
IT'S YOUR FIRST TIME ON THE FRONT LINES, RIGHT?
A COMMANDER PROVES HIMSELF WITH HIS SWORD, NOT HIS WORDS.
ALSO, GENERAL GEUN-TAE, COULD YOU KINDLY STOP REFERRING TO ME AS "RICH BOY"?
Ha ha ha ha!
*SOUNDS GOOD, RICH BOY!*

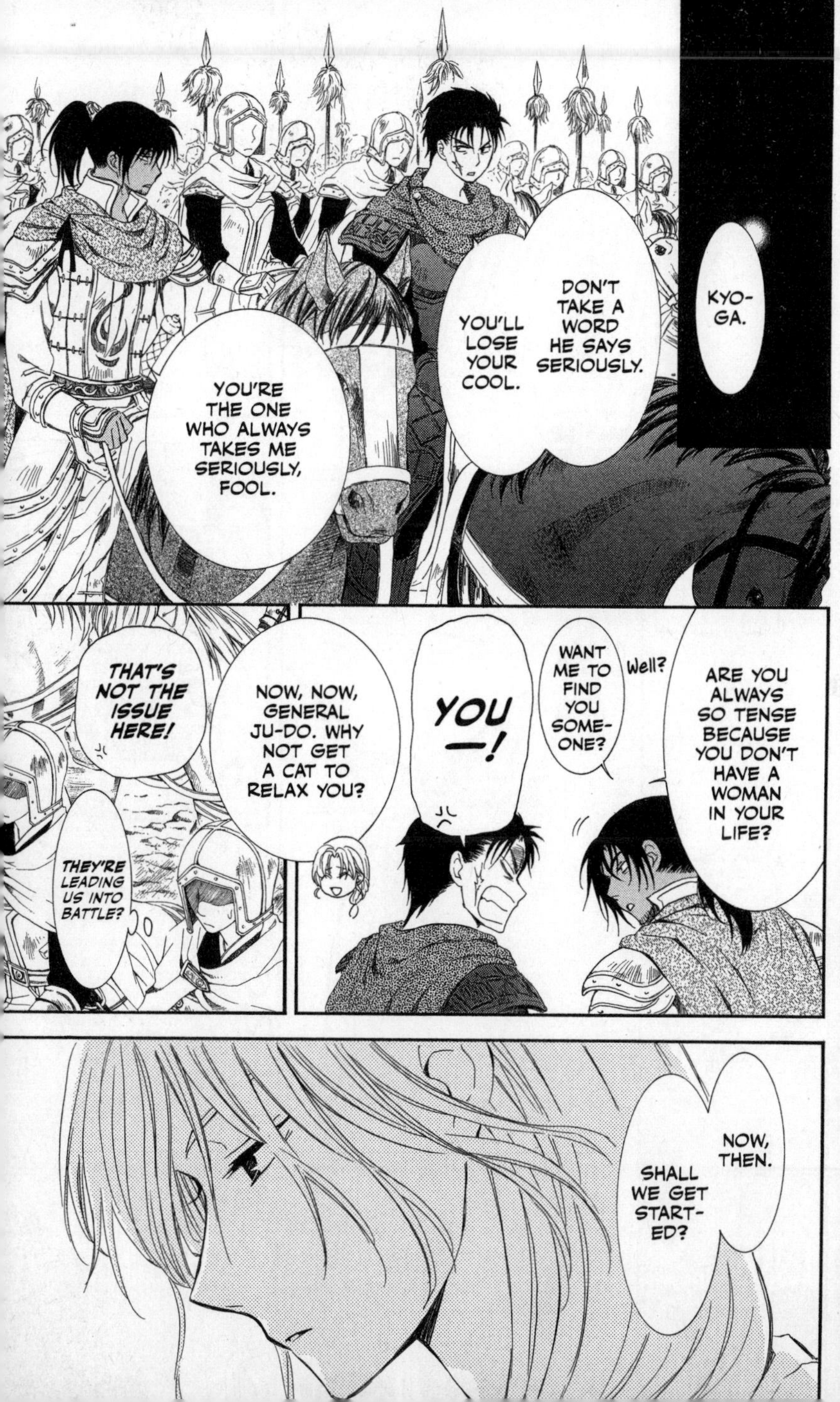
KYO-GA.
DON'T TAKE A WORD HE SAYS SERIOUSLY.
YOU'LL LOSE YOUR COOL.
YOU'RE THE ONE WHO ALWAYS TAKES ME SERIOUSLY, FOOL.
ARE YOU ALWAYS SO TENSE BECAUSE YOU DON'T HAVE A WOMAN IN YOUR LIFE?
Well?
WANT ME TO FIND YOU SOME-ONE?
YOU—!
NOW, NOW, GENERAL JU-DO. WHY NOT GET A CAT TO RELAX YOU?
THAT'S NOT THE ISSUE HERE!
THEY'RE LEADING US INTO BATTLE?
NOW, THEN.
SHALL WE GET START-ED?

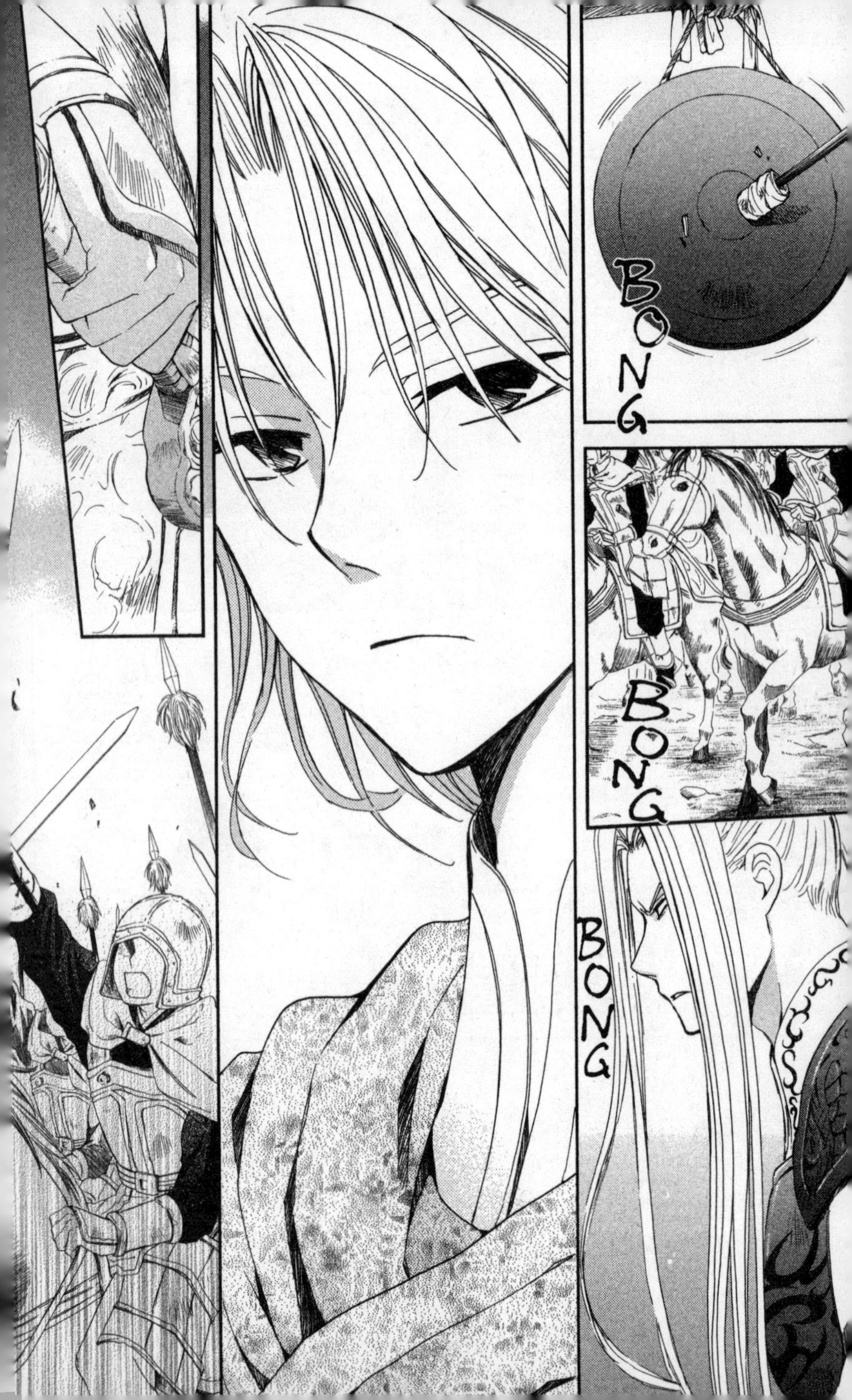
BONG
BONG
BONG

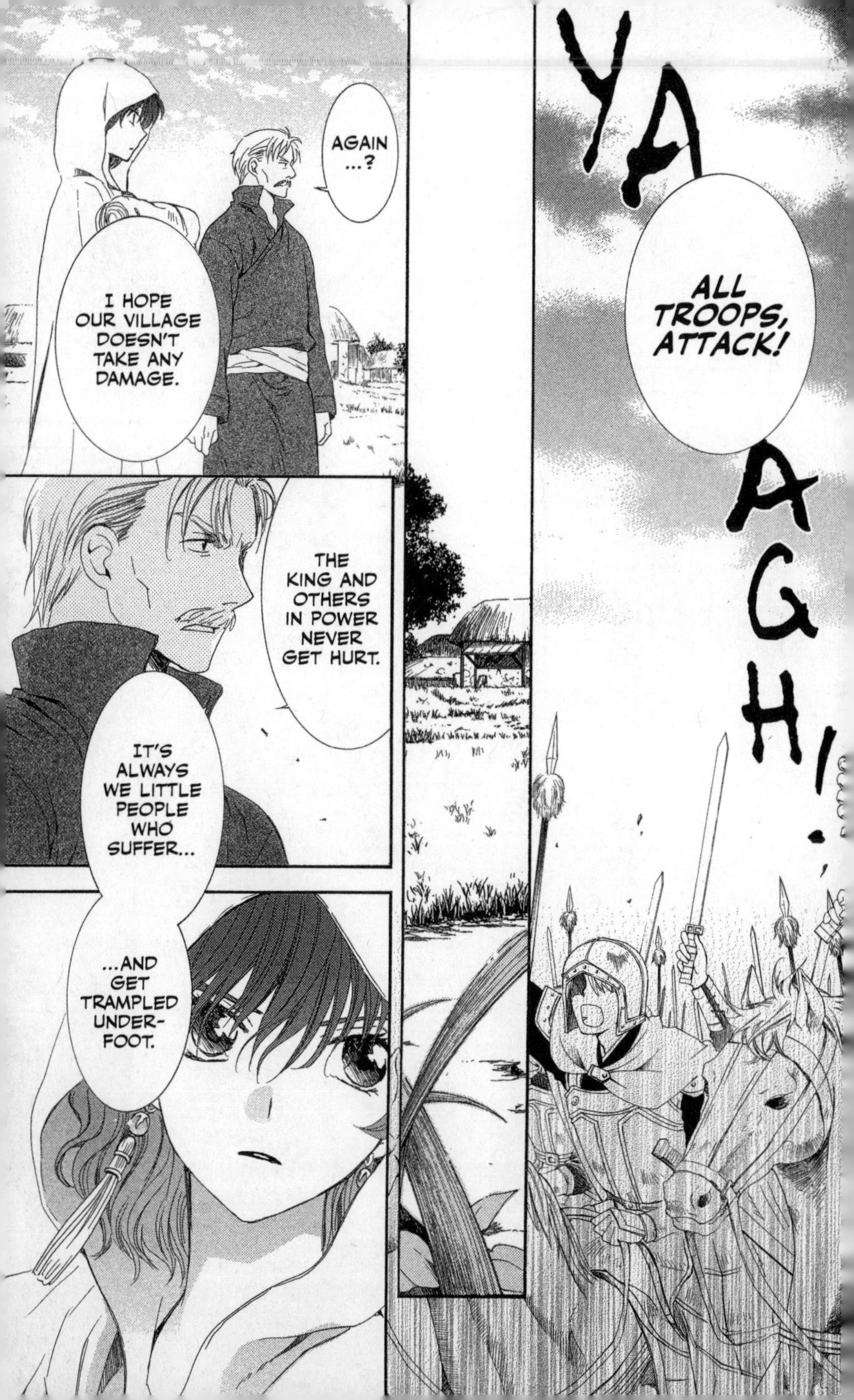
YAAGH!!
ALL TROOPS, ATTACK!
AGAIN ...?
I HOPE OUR VILLAGE DOESN'T TAKE ANY DAMAGE.
THE KING AND OTHERS IN POWER NEVER GET HURT.
IT'S ALWAYS WE LITTLE PEOPLE WHO SUFFER...
...AND GET TRAMPLED UNDER-FOOT.

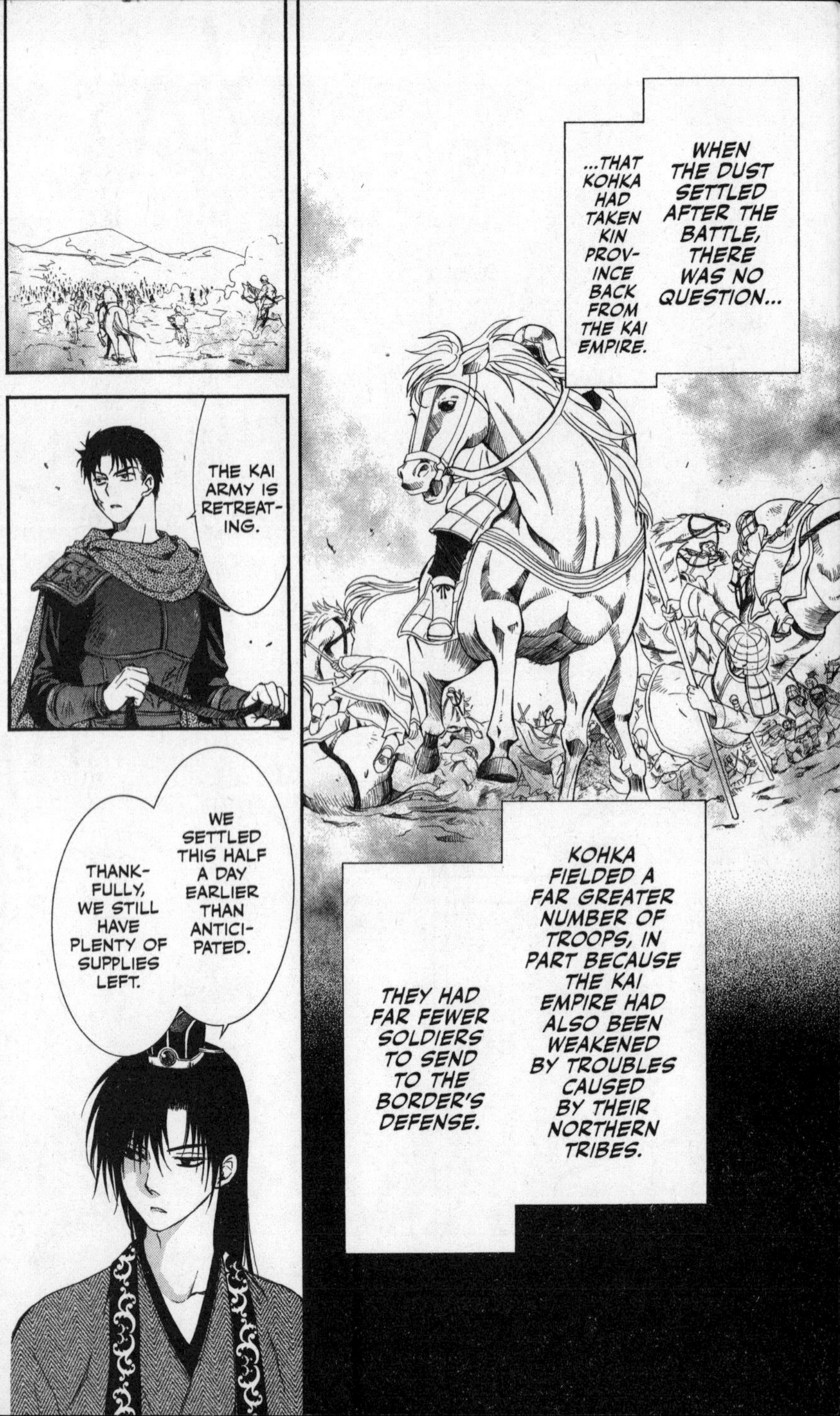
WHEN THE DUST SETTLED AFTER THE BATTLE, THERE WAS NO QUESTION...
...THAT KOHKA HAD TAKEN KIN PROVINCE BACK FROM THE KAI EMPIRE.
KOHKA FIELDED A FAR GREATER NUMBER OF TROOPS, IN PART BECAUSE THE KAI EMPIRE HAD ALSO BEEN WEAKENED BY TROUBLES CAUSED BY THEIR NORTHERN TRIBES.
THEY HAD FAR FEWER SOLDIERS TO SEND TO THE BORDER'S DEFENSE.
THE KAI ARMY IS RETREATING.
WE SETTLED THIS HALF A DAY EARLIER THAN ANTICIPATED.
THANKFULLY, WE STILL HAVE PLENTY OF SUPPLIES LEFT.

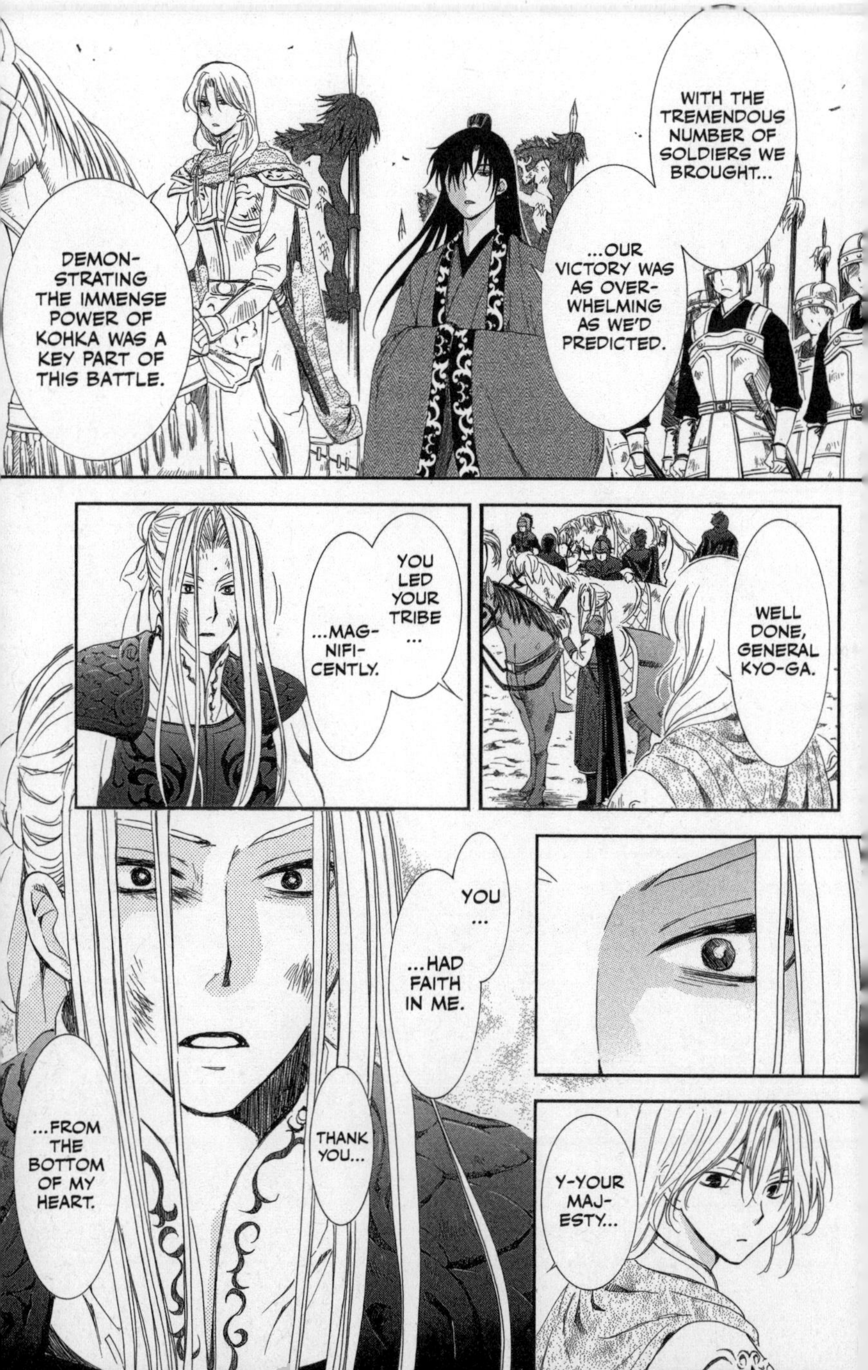

WITH THE TREMENDOUS NUMBER OF SOLDIERS WE BROUGHT...
...OUR VICTORY WAS AS OVERWHELMING AS WE'D PREDICTED.
DEMONSTRATING THE IMMENSE POWER OF KOHKA WAS A KEY PART OF THIS BATTLE.
WELL DONE, GENERAL KYO-GA.
YOU LED YOUR TRIBE ...
...MAGNIFICENTLY.
Y-YOUR MAJESTY...
YOU ...
...HAD FAITH IN ME.
THANK YOU...
...FROM THE BOTTOM OF MY HEART.

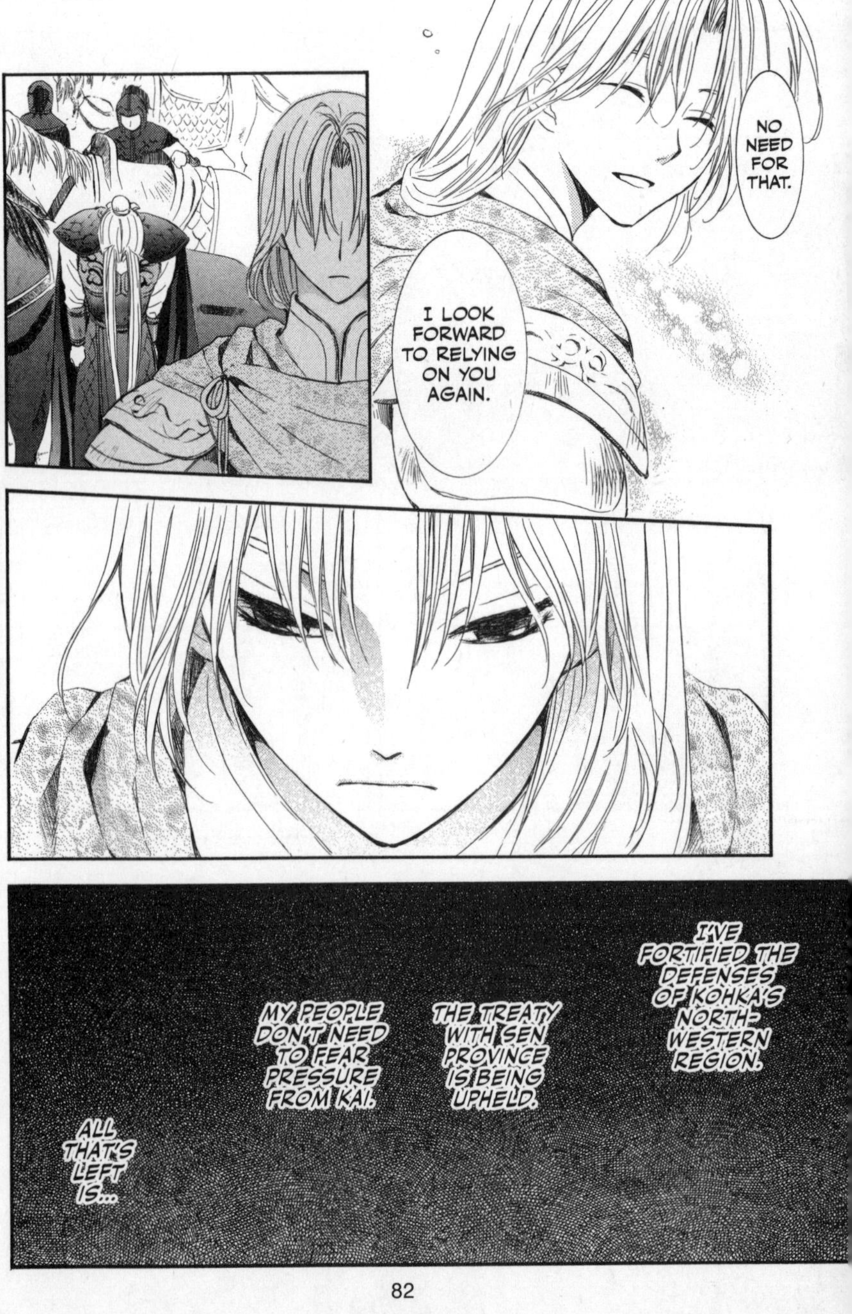
NO NEED FOR THAT.
I LOOK FORWARD TO RELYING ON YOU AGAIN.
I'VE FORTIFIED THE DEFENSES OF KOHKA'S NORTH-WESTERN REGION.
THE TREATY WITH SEN PROVINCE IS BEING UPHELD.
MY PEOPLE DON'T NEED TO FEAR PRESSURE FROM KAI.
ALL THAT'S LEFT IS...

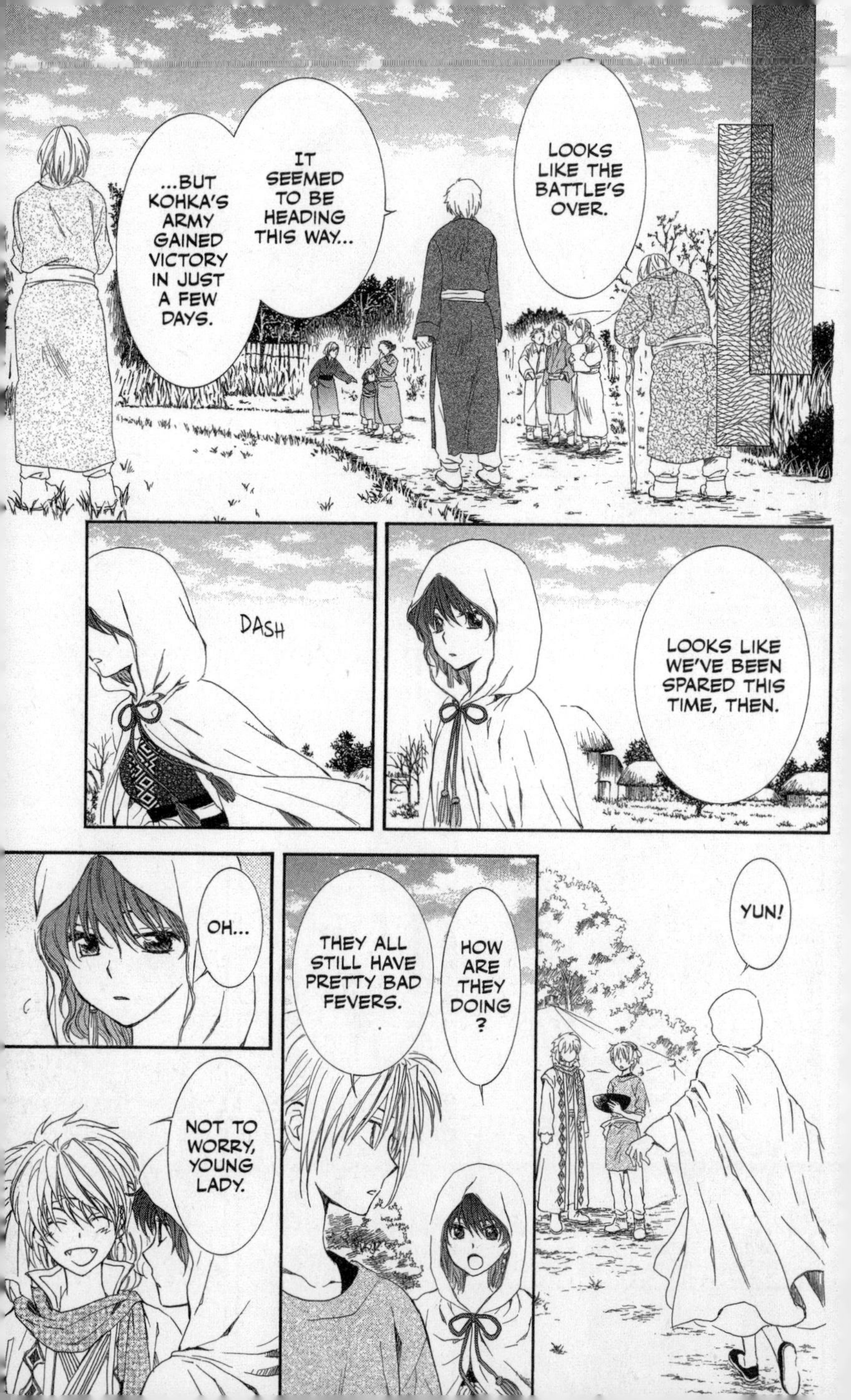
LOOKS LIKE THE BATTLE'S OVER.
IT SEEMED TO BE HEADING THIS WAY...
...BUT KOHKA'S ARMY GAINED VICTORY IN JUST A FEW DAYS.
LOOKS LIKE WE'VE BEEN SPARED THIS TIME, THEN.
DASH
YUN!
HOW ARE THEY DOING?
THEY ALL STILL HAVE PRETTY BAD FEVERS.
OH...
NOT TO WORRY, YOUNG LADY.

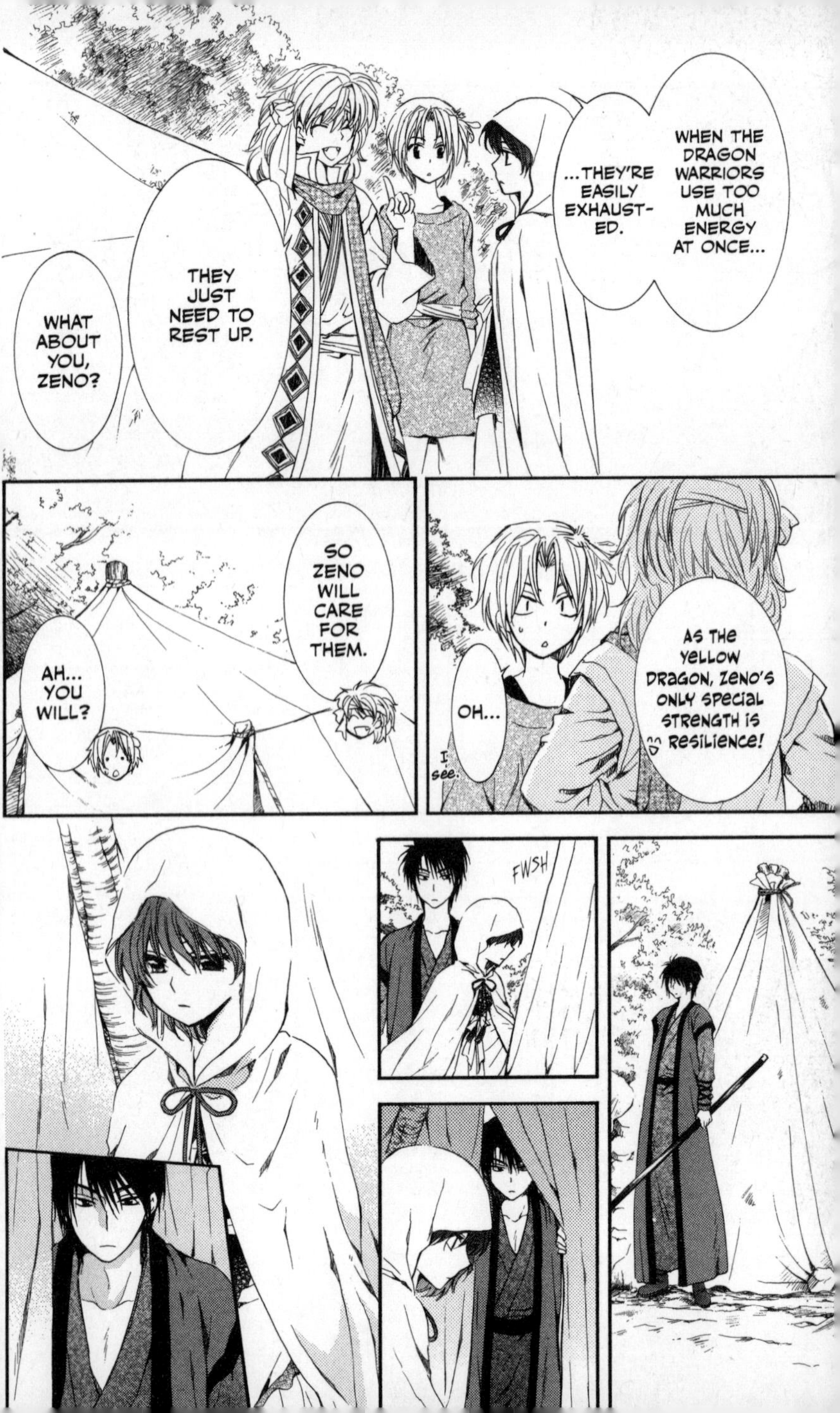
WHEN THE DRAGON WARRIORS USE TOO MUCH ENERGY AT ONCE...
...THEY'RE EASILY EXHAUST-ED.
THEY JUST NEED TO REST UP.
WHAT ABOUT YOU, ZENO?
AS THE YELLOW DRAGON, ZENO'S ONLY SPECIAL STRENGTH IS RESILIENCE!
OH...
I see.
SO ZENO WILL CARE FOR THEM.
AH... YOU WILL?
FWSH

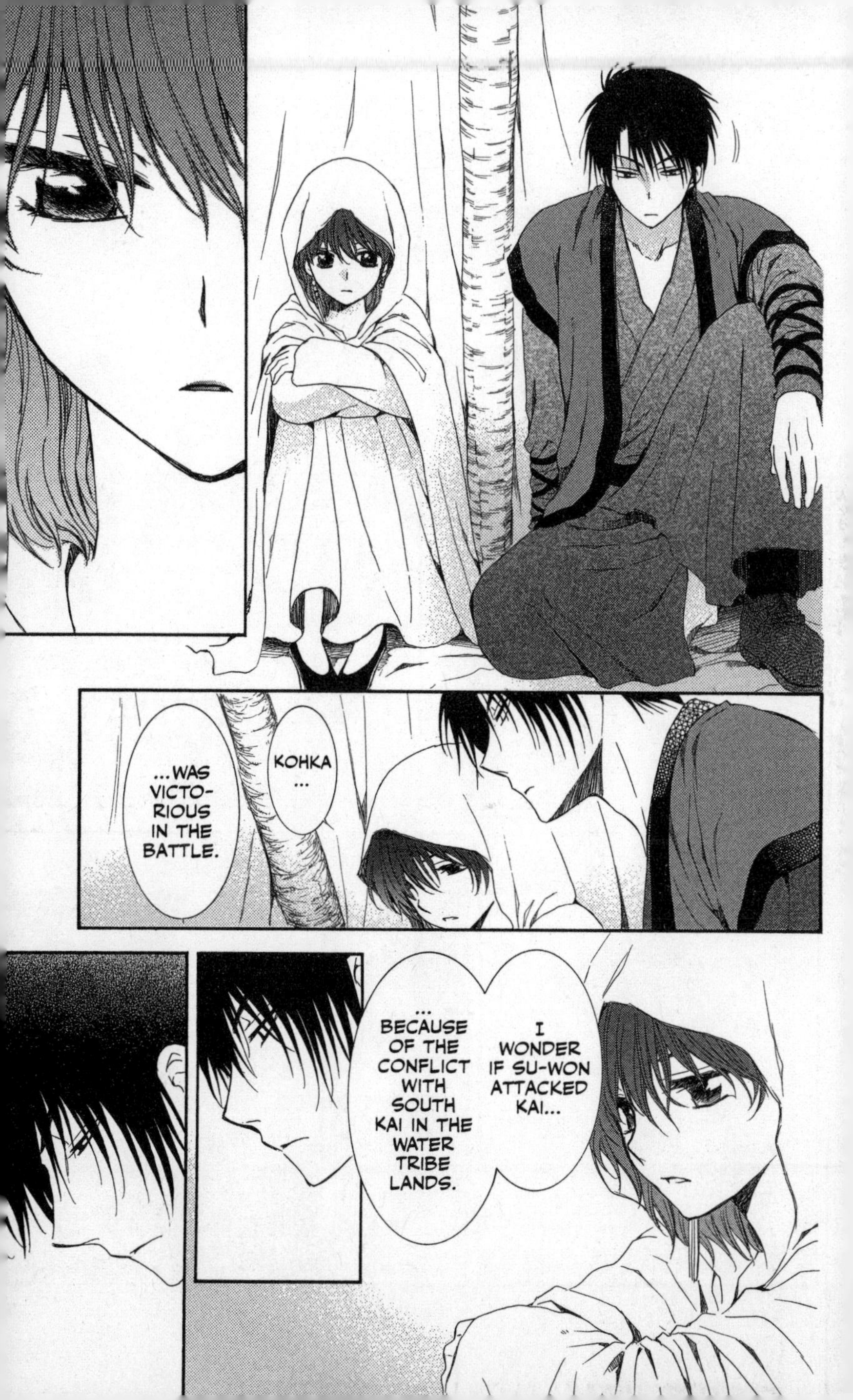
KOHKA...
...WAS VICTORIOUS IN THE BATTLE.
I WONDER IF SU-WON ATTACKED KAI...
...BECAUSE OF THE CONFLICT WITH SOUTH KAI IN THE WATER TRIBE LANDS.

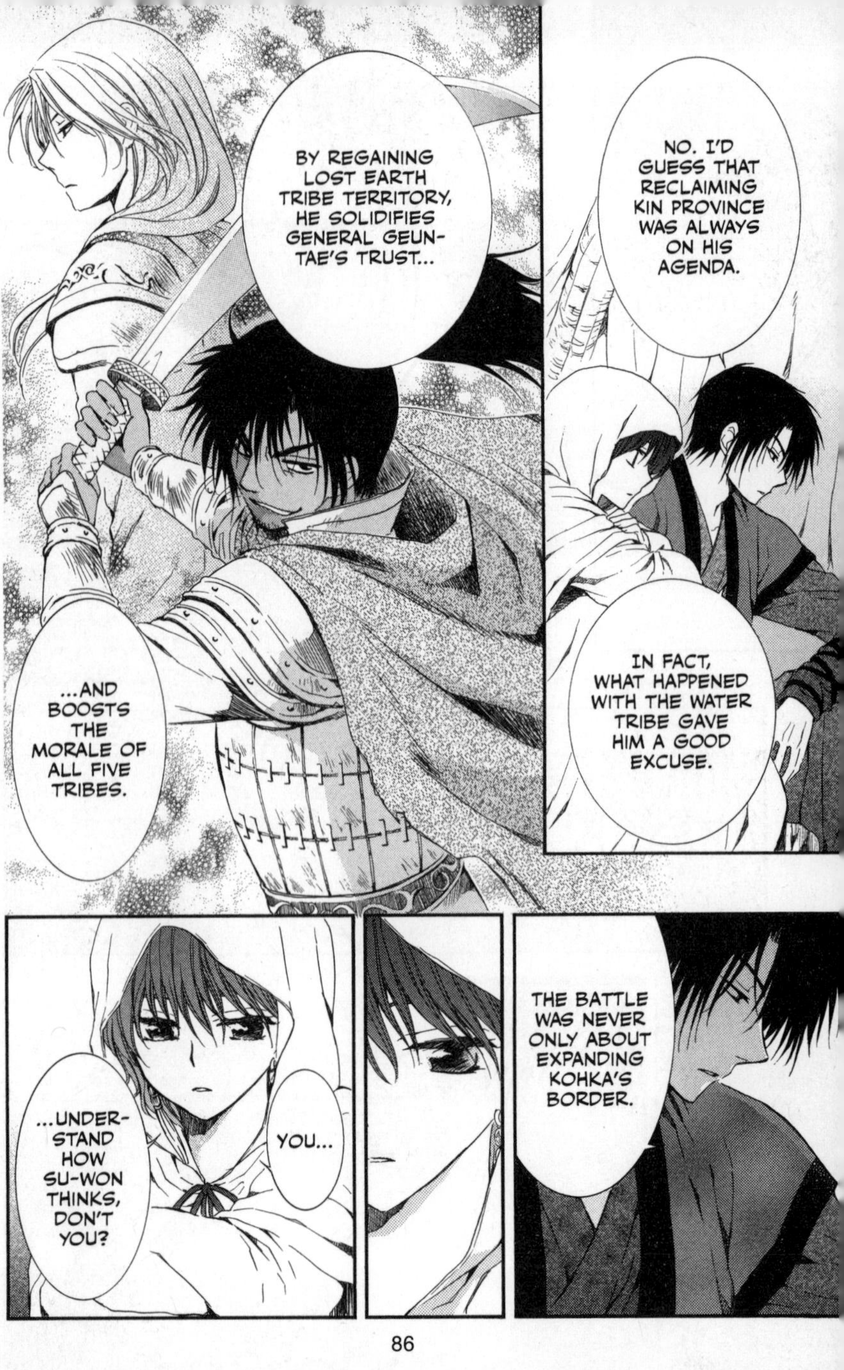
NO. I'D GUESS THAT RECLAIMING KIN PROVINCE WAS ALWAYS ON HIS AGENDA.
IN FACT, WHAT HAPPENED WITH THE WATER TRIBE GAVE HIM A GOOD EXCUSE.
BY REGAINING LOST EARTH TRIBE TERRITORY, HE SOLIDIFIES GENERAL GEUN-TAE'S TRUST...
...AND BOOSTS THE MORALE OF ALL FIVE TRIBES.
THE BATTLE WAS NEVER ONLY ABOUT EXPANDING KOHKA'S BORDER.
YOU...
...UNDER-STAND HOW SU-WON THINKS, DON'T YOU?

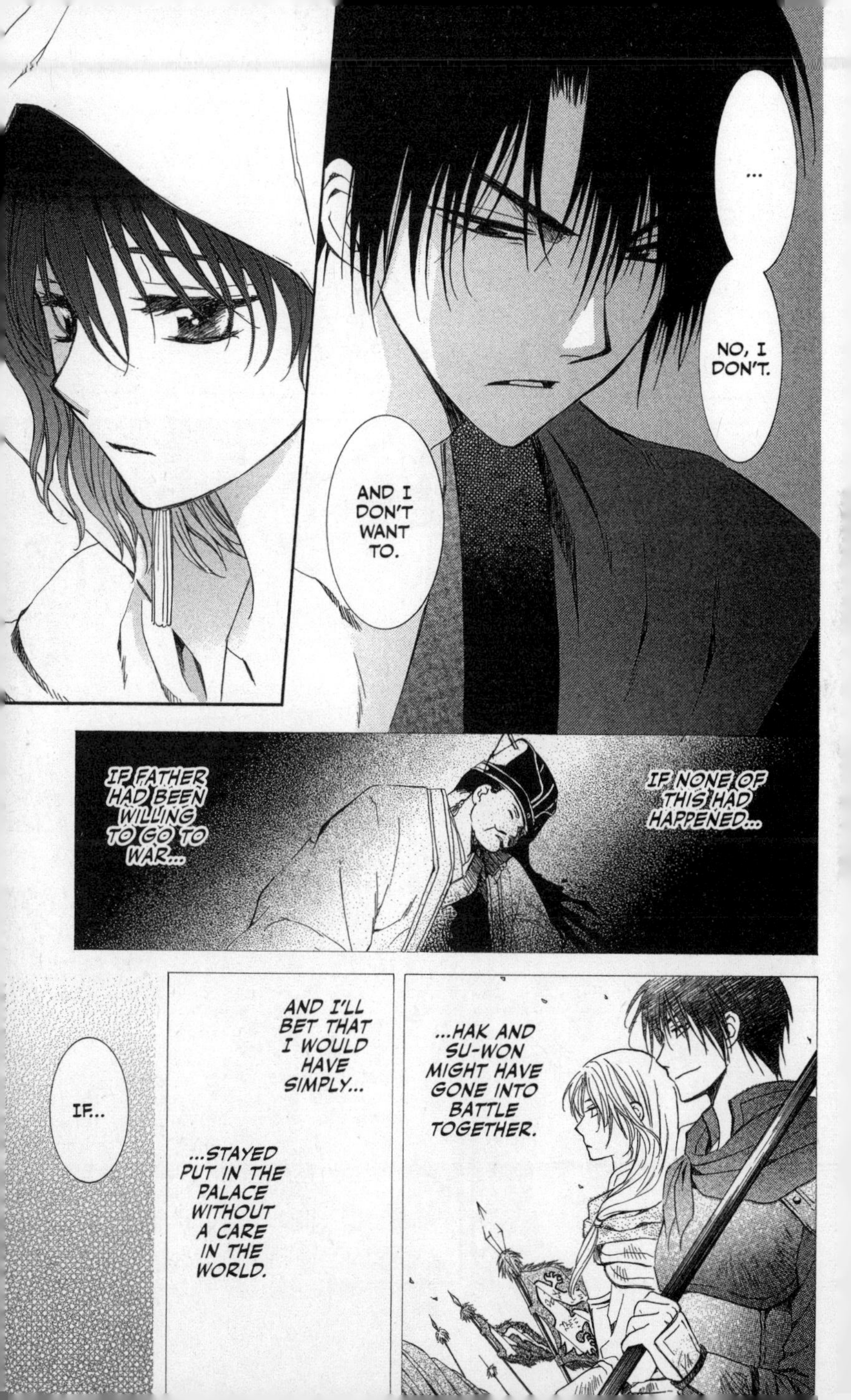
...
NO, I DON'T.
AND I DON'T WANT TO.
IF NONE OF THIS HAD HAPPENED...
IF FATHER HAD BEEN WILLING TO GO TO WAR...
...HAK AND SU-WON MIGHT HAVE GONE INTO BATTLE TOGETHER.
AND I'LL BET THAT I WOULD HAVE SIMPLY...
...STAYED PUT IN THE PALACE WITHOUT A CARE IN THE WORLD.
IF...

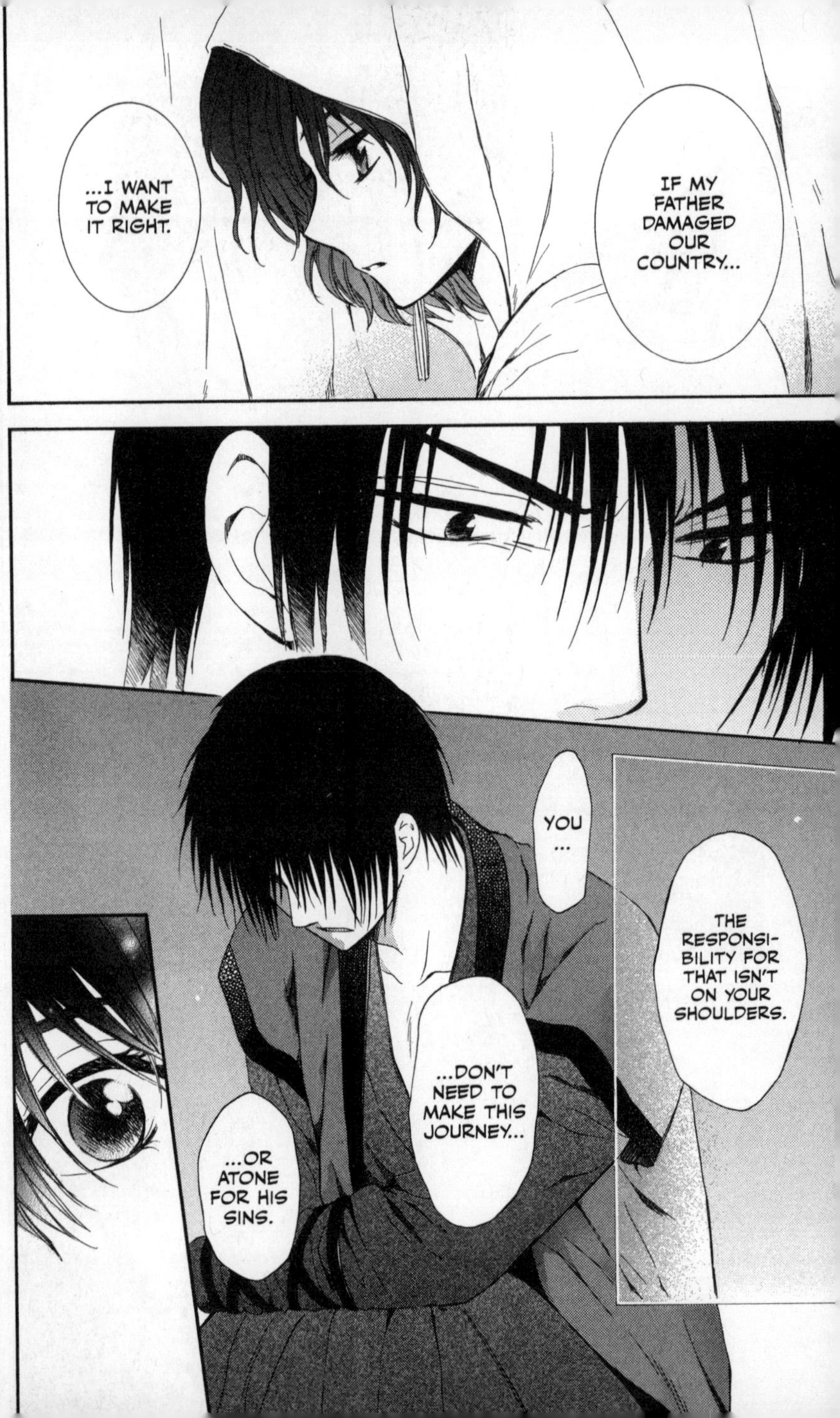
IF MY FATHER DAMAGED OUR COUNTRY...
...I WANT TO MAKE IT RIGHT.
YOU ...
...DON'T NEED TO MAKE THIS JOURNEY...
...OR ATONE FOR HIS SINS.
THE RESPONSIBILITY FOR THAT ISN'T ON YOUR SHOULDERS.

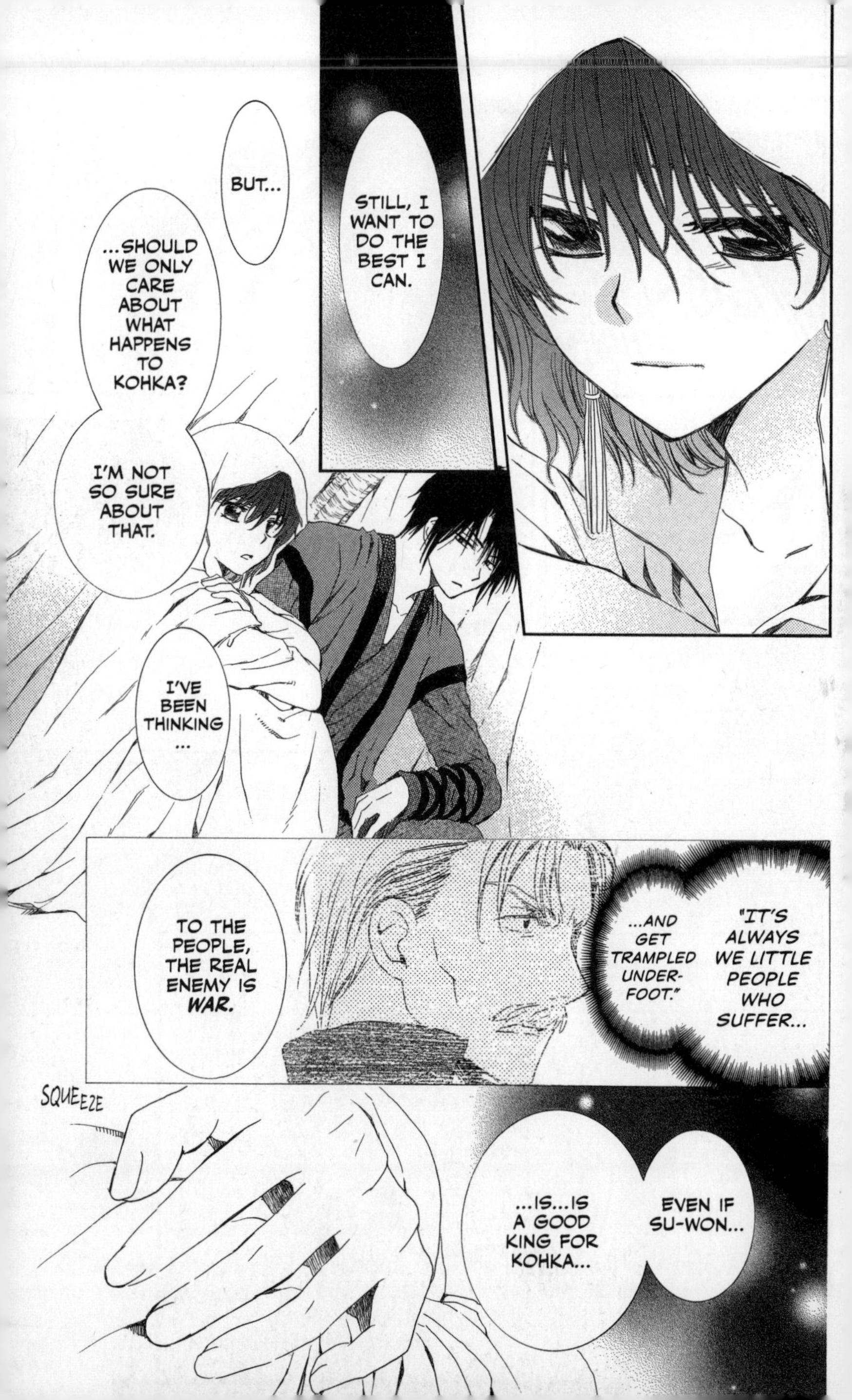
STILL, I WANT TO DO THE BEST I CAN.
BUT...
...SHOULD WE ONLY CARE ABOUT WHAT HAPPENS TO KOHKA?
I'M NOT SO SURE ABOUT THAT.
I'VE BEEN THINKING ...
"IT'S ALWAYS WE LITTLE PEOPLE WHO SUFFER...
...AND GET TRAMPLED UNDER-FOOT."
TO THE PEOPLE, THE REAL ENEMY IS *WAR.*
EVEN IF SU-WON...
...IS...IS A GOOD KING FOR KOHKA...
SQUEEZE

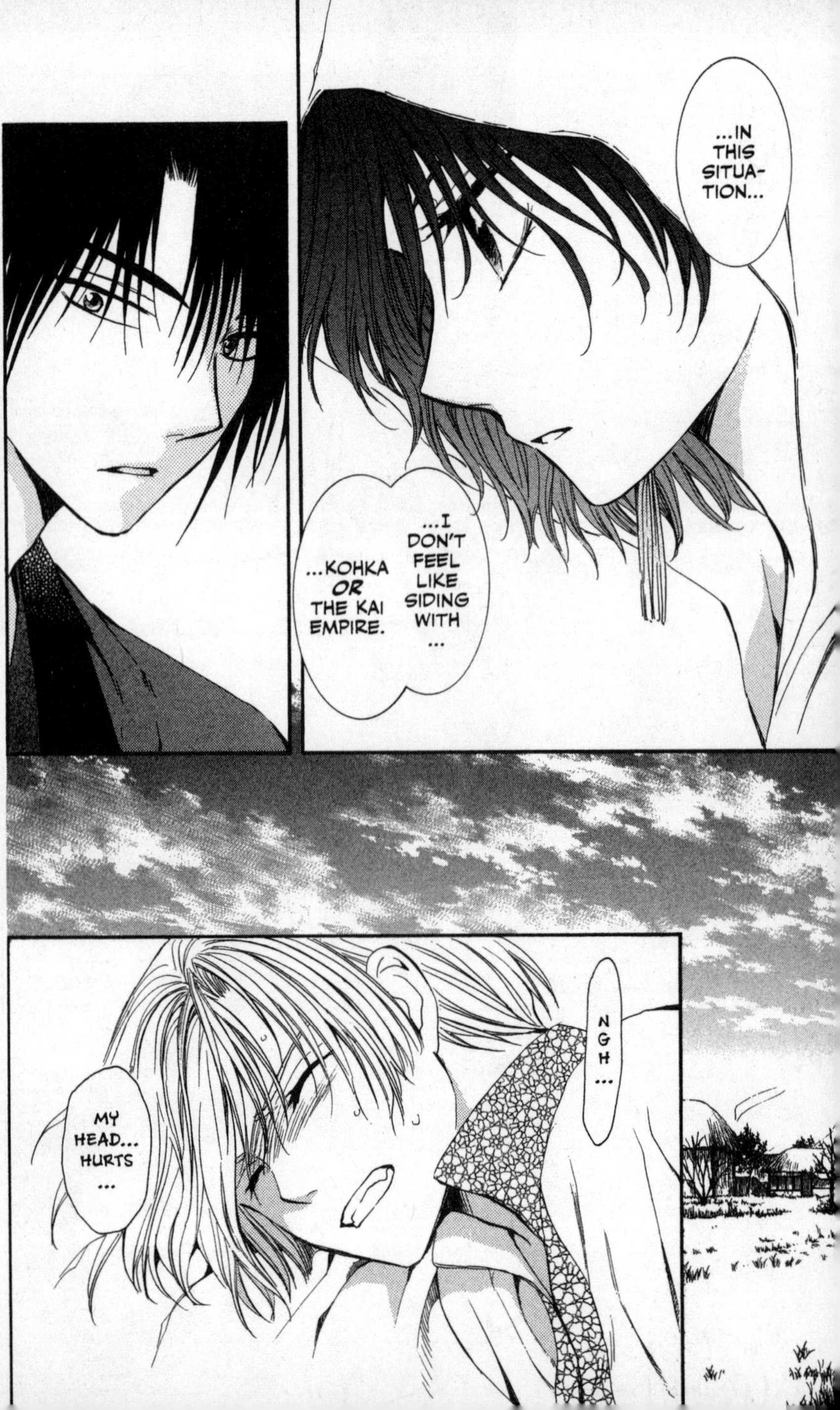
...IN THIS SITUATION...
...I DON'T FEEL LIKE SIDING WITH ...
...KOHKA *OR* THE KAI EMPIRE.
NGH ...
MY HEAD... HURTS ...

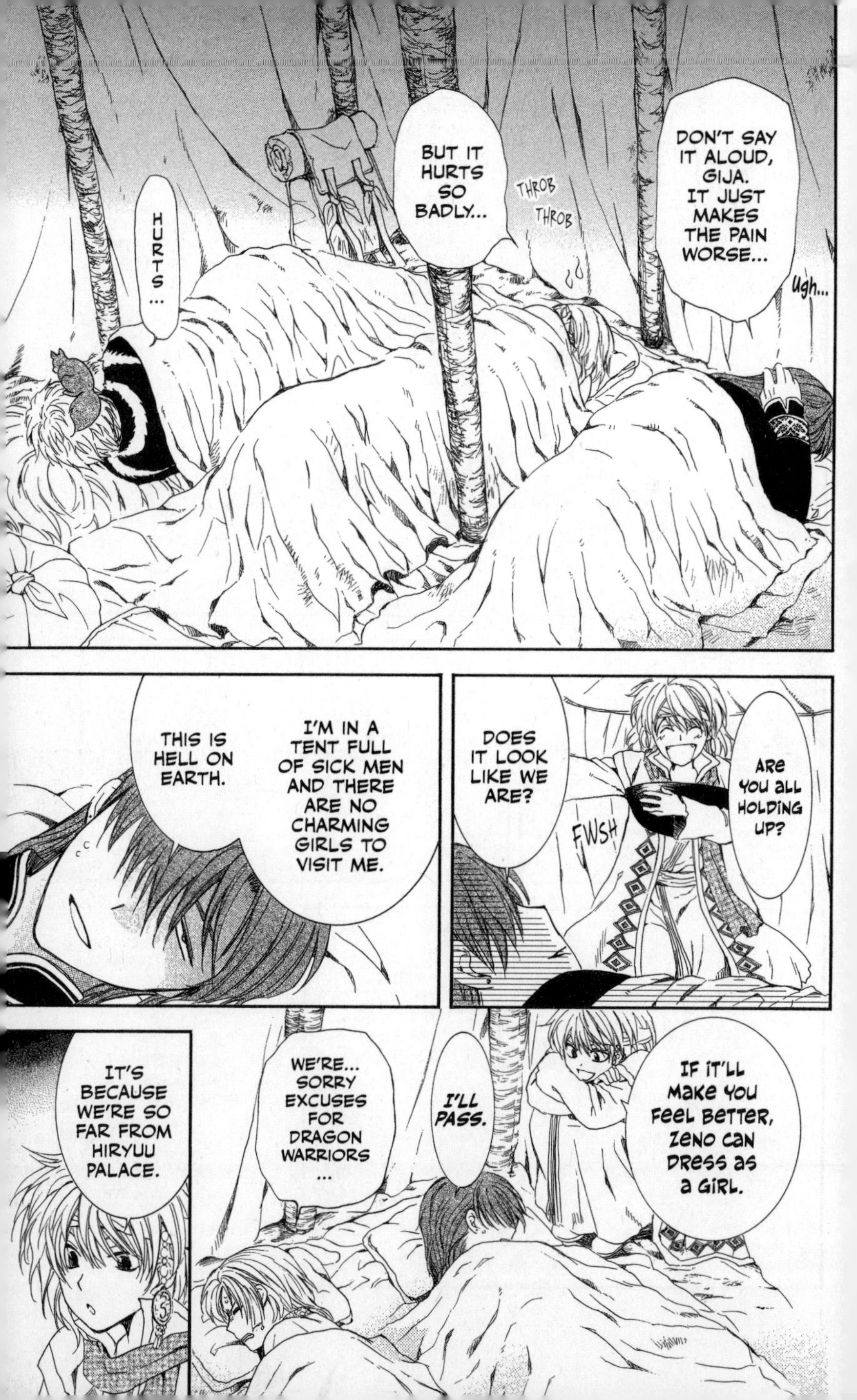
DON'T SAY IT ALOUD, GIJA. IT JUST MAKES THE PAIN WORSE...
Ugh...
THROB THROB
BUT IT HURTS SO BADLY...
HURTS...
Are you all HOLDING UP?
FWSH
DOES IT LOOK LIKE WE ARE?
I'M IN A TENT FULL OF SICK MEN AND THERE ARE NO CHARMING GIRLS TO VISIT ME.
THIS IS HELL ON EARTH.
IF IT'LL MAKE YOU FEEL BETTER, ZENO CAN DRESS AS A GIRL.
I'LL PASS.
WE'RE... SORRY EXCUSES FOR DRAGON WARRIORS...
IT'S BECAUSE WE'RE SO FAR FROM HIRYUU PALACE.

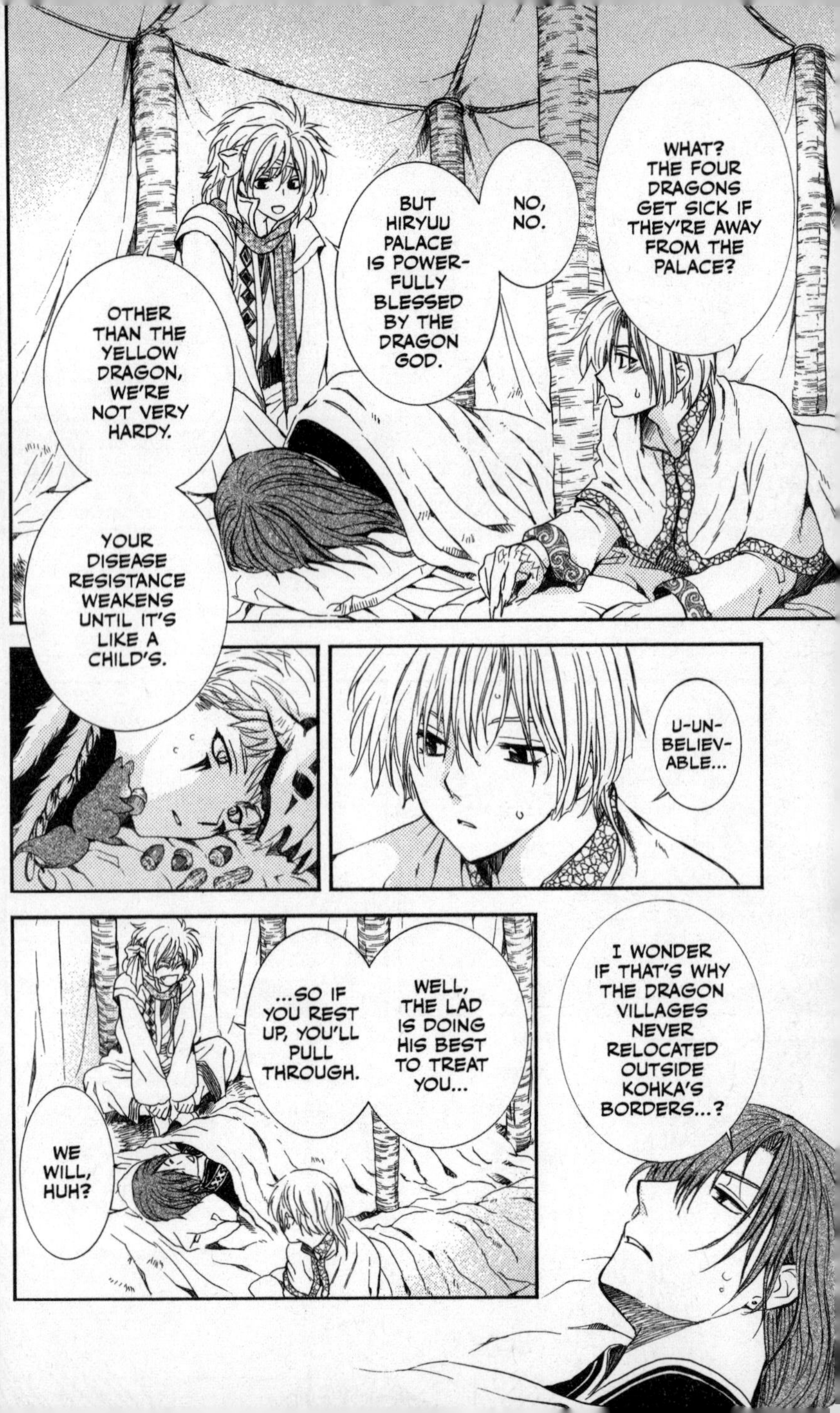
WHAT? THE FOUR DRAGONS GET SICK IF THEY'RE AWAY FROM THE PALACE?
NO, NO.
BUT HIRYUU PALACE IS POWER-FULLY BLESSED BY THE DRAGON GOD.
OTHER THAN THE YELLOW DRAGON, WE'RE NOT VERY HARDY.
YOUR DISEASE RESISTANCE WEAKENS UNTIL IT'S LIKE A CHILD'S.
U-UN-BELIEV-ABLE...
I WONDER IF THAT'S WHY THE DRAGON VILLAGES NEVER RELOCATED OUTSIDE KOHKA'S BORDERS...?
WELL, THE LAD IS DOING HIS BEST TO TREAT YOU...
...SO IF YOU REST UP, YOU'LL PULL THROUGH.
WE WILL, HUH?

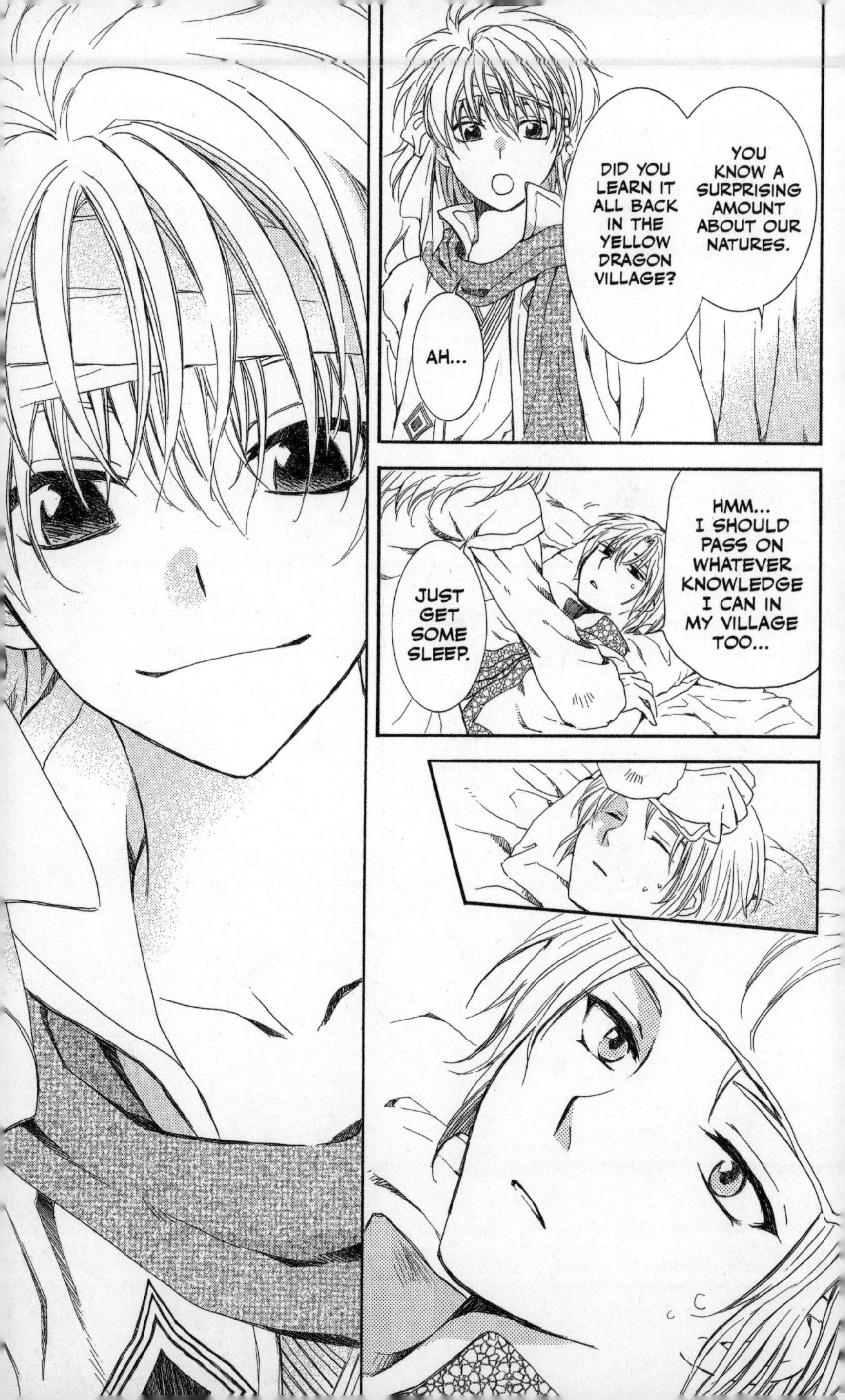
YOU KNOW A SURPRISING AMOUNT ABOUT OUR NATURES.
DID YOU LEARN IT ALL BACK IN THE YELLOW DRAGON VILLAGE?
AH...
HMM... I SHOULD PASS ON WHATEVER KNOWLEDGE I CAN IN MY VILLAGE TOO...
JUST GET SOME SLEEP.

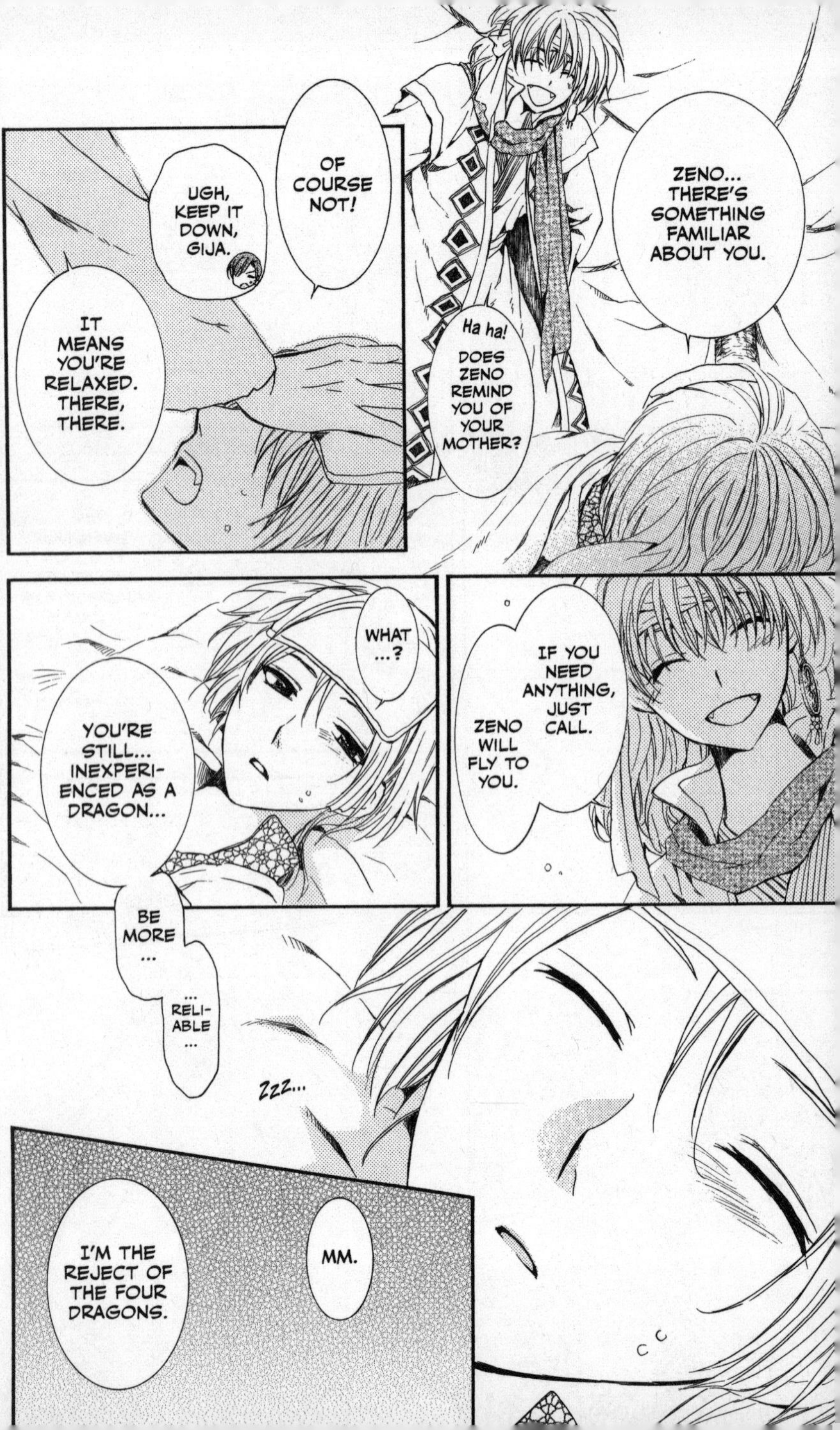
ZENO... THERE'S SOMETHING FAMILIAR ABOUT YOU.
Ha ha! DOES ZENO REMIND YOU OF YOUR MOTHER?
OF COURSE NOT!
UGH, KEEP IT DOWN, GIJA.
IT MEANS YOU'RE RELAXED. THERE, THERE.
IF YOU NEED ANYTHING, JUST CALL.
ZENO WILL FLY TO YOU.
WHAT ...?
YOU'RE STILL... INEXPERIENCED AS A DRAGON...
BE MORE ...
... RELIABLE ...
Zzz...
MM.
I'M THE REJECT OF THE FOUR DRAGONS.

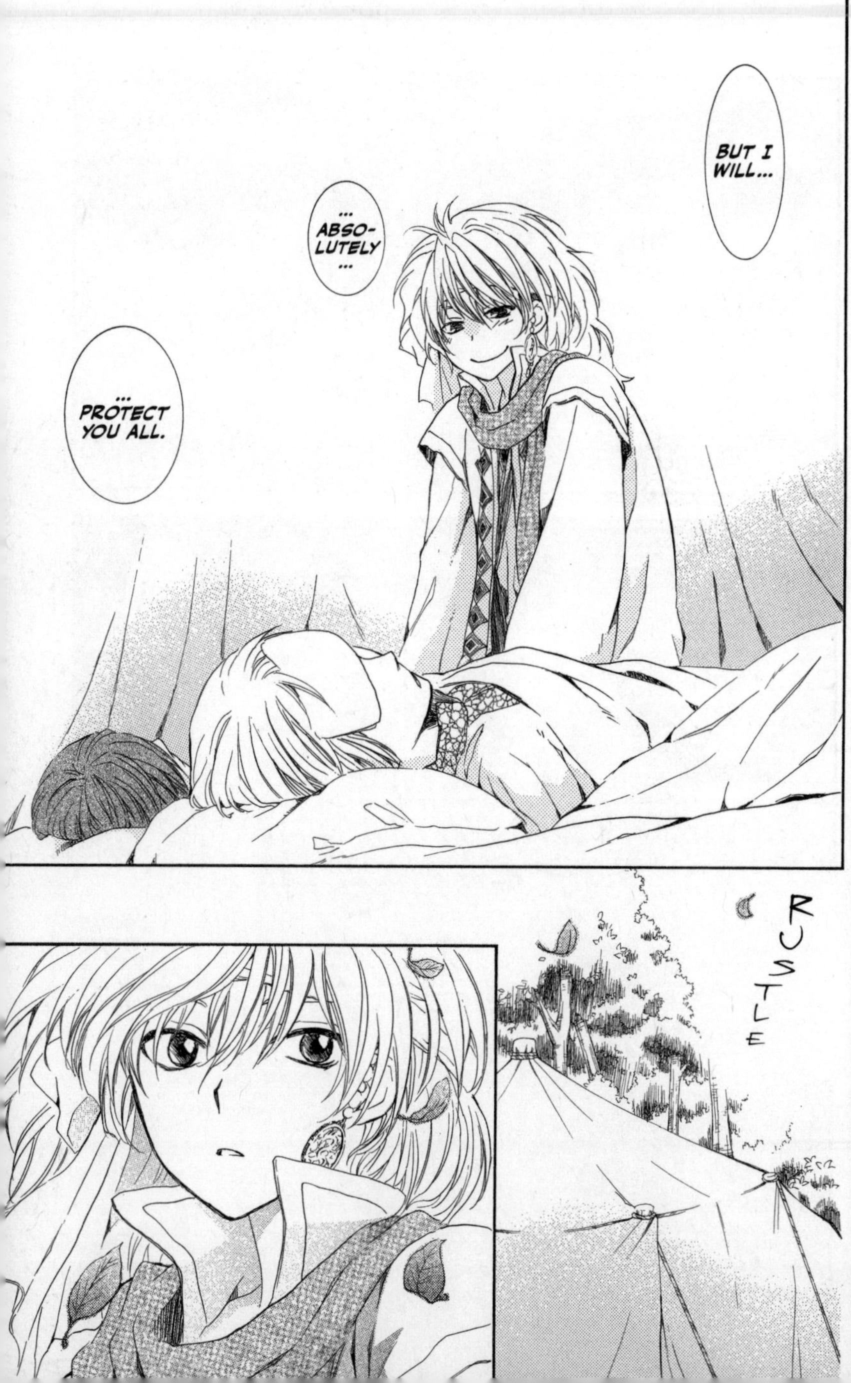
BUT I WILL...
...ABSO-LUTELY...
...PROTECT YOU ALL.
RUSTLE

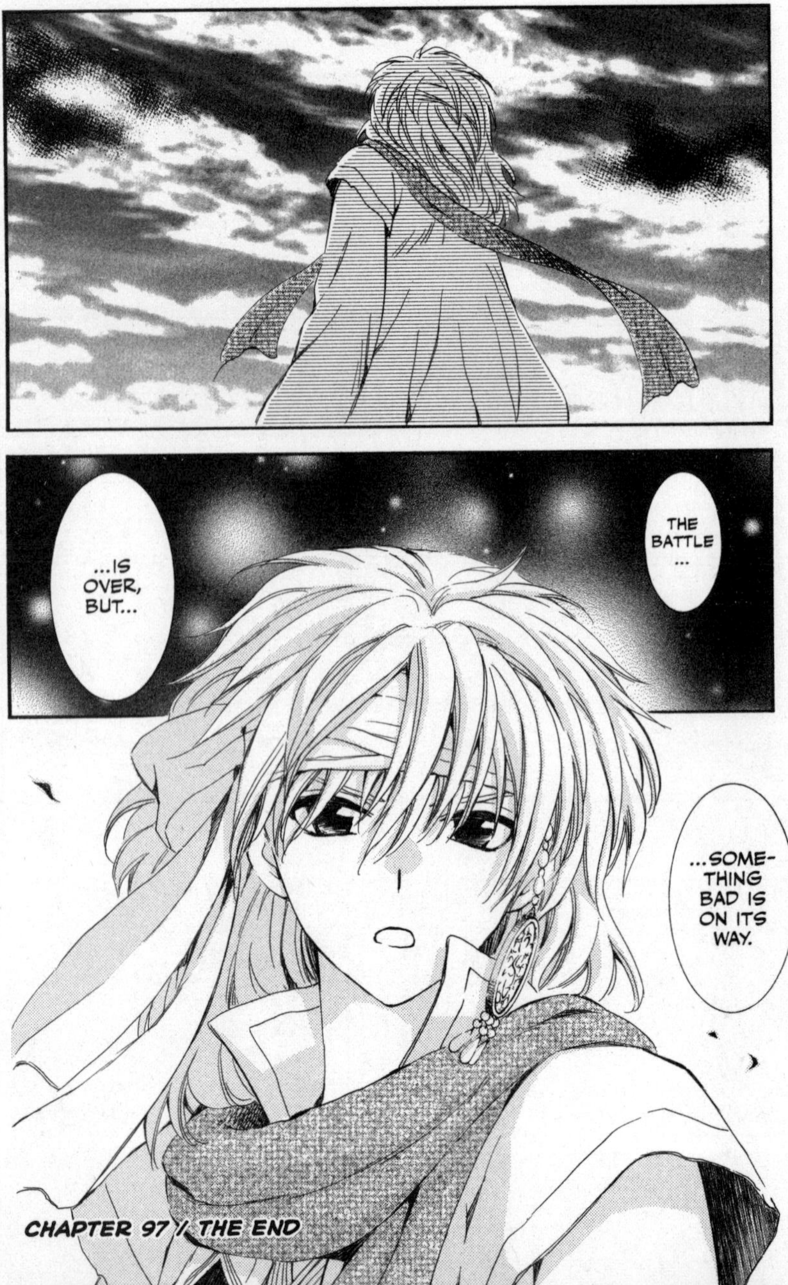
THE BATTLE ...
...IS OVER, BUT...
...SOME-THING BAD IS ON ITS WAY.
CHAPTER 97 / THE END

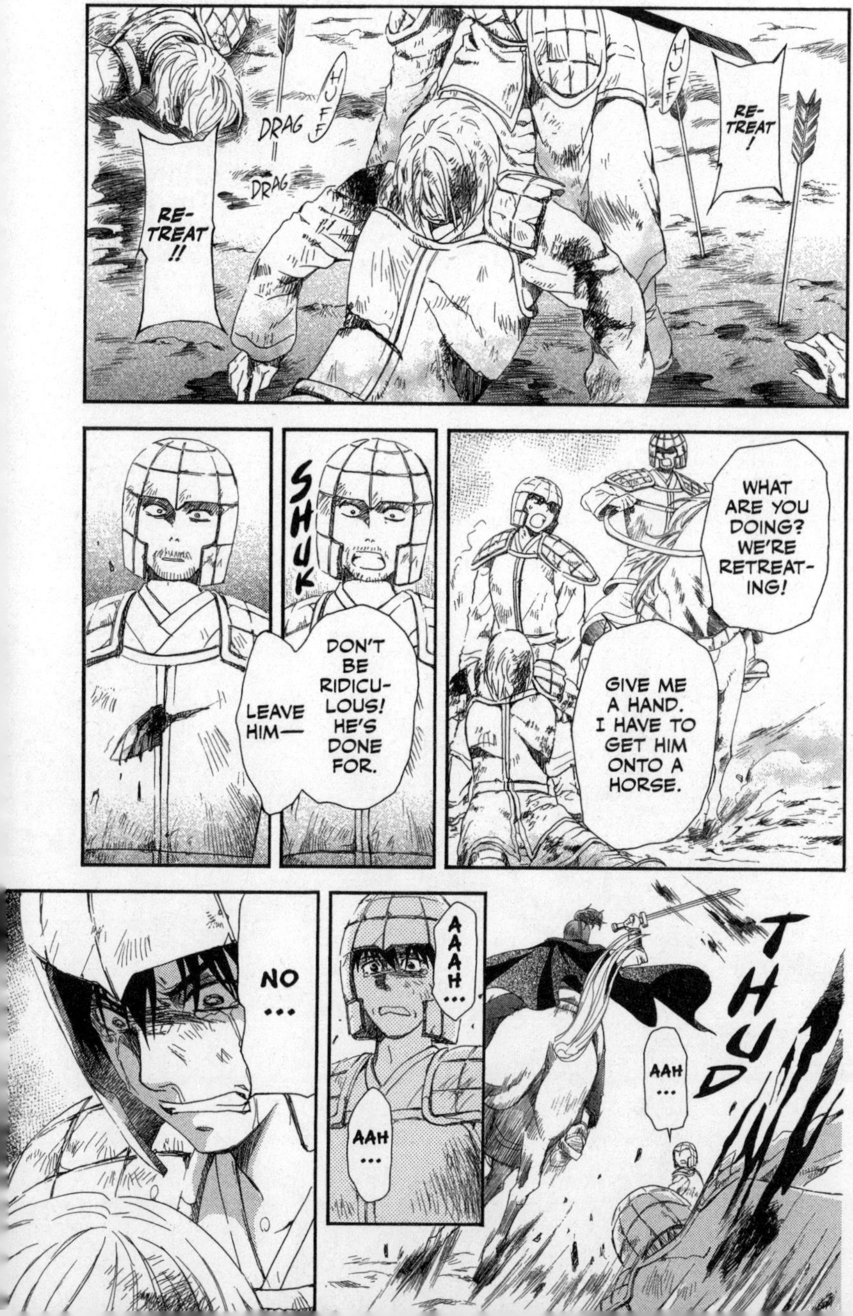
RE-TREAT!
HUFF
HUFF
DRAG DRAG
RE-TREAT!!
WHAT ARE YOU DOING? WE'RE RETREATING!
GIVE ME A HAND. I HAVE TO GET HIM ONTO A HORSE.
SHUK
DON'T BE RIDICULOUS! HE'S DONE FOR.
LEAVE HIM—
THUD
AAH...
AAAH...
AAH...
NO...

# CHAPTER 98: RUN AWAY

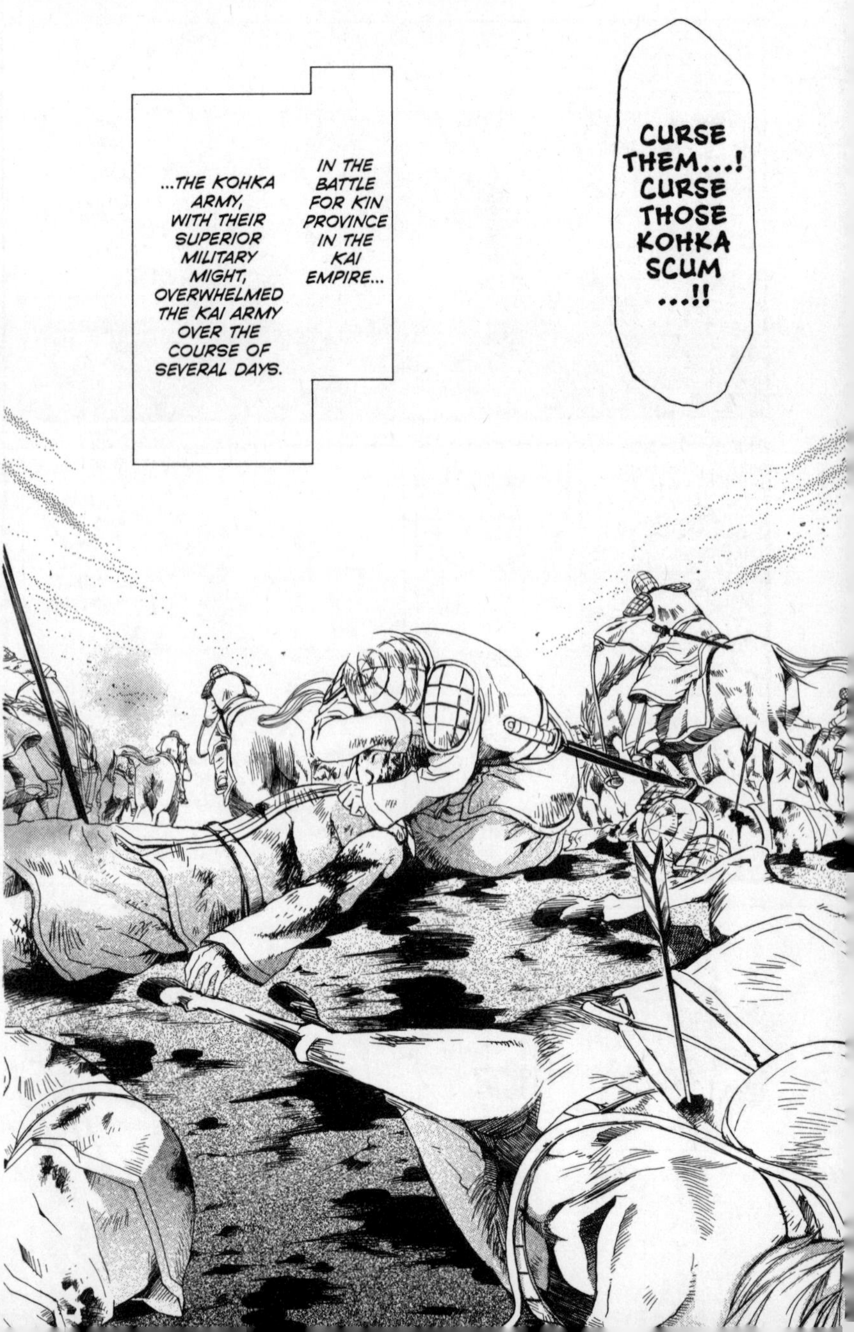
CURSE THEM...! CURSE THOSE KOHKA SCUM ...!!
IN THE BATTLE FOR KIN PROVINCE IN THE KAI EMPIRE...
...THE KOHKA ARMY, WITH THEIR SUPERIOR MILITARY MIGHT, OVERWHELMED THE KAI ARMY OVER THE COURSE OF SEVERAL DAYS.

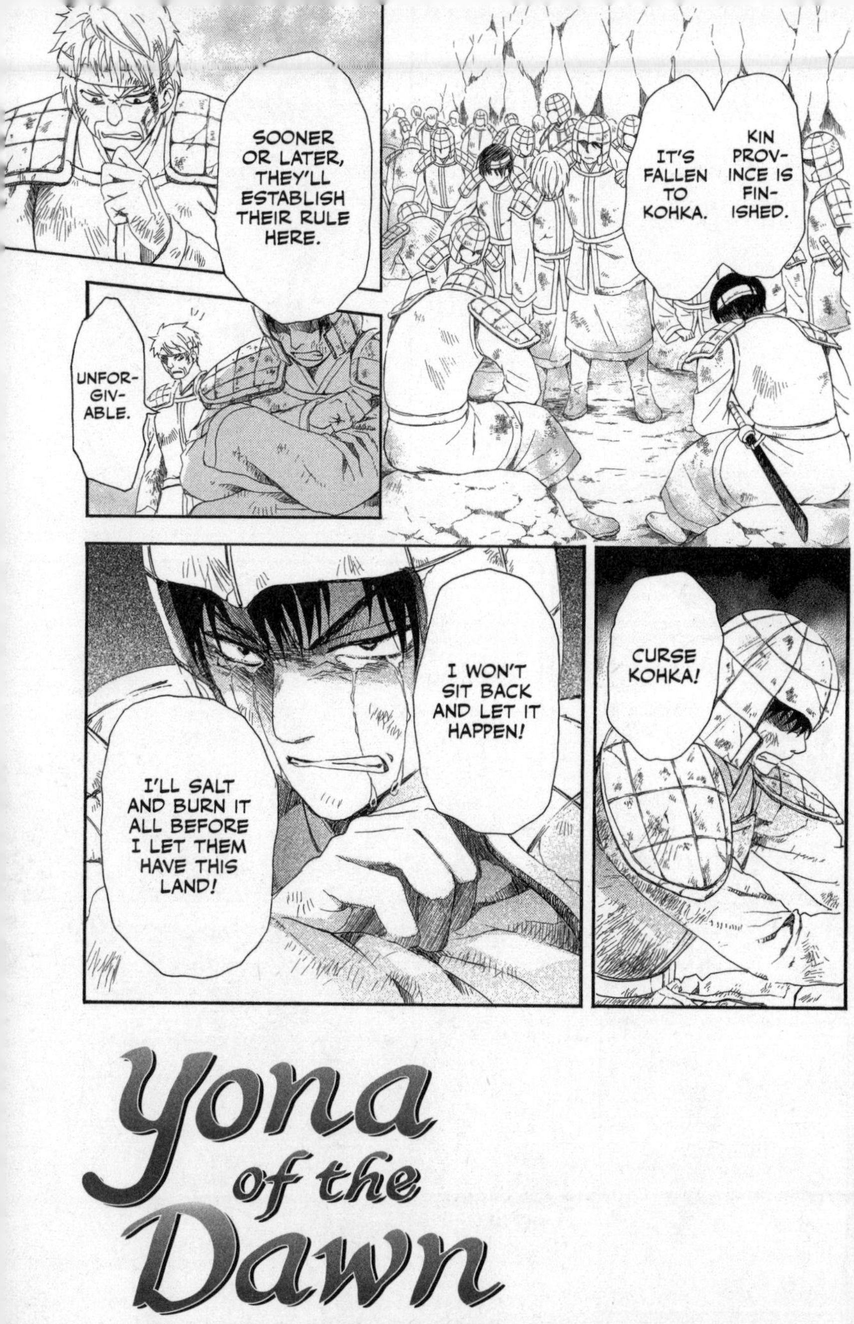
KIN PROVINCE IS FINISHED.
IT'S FALLEN TO KOHKA.
SOONER OR LATER, THEY'LL ESTABLISH THEIR RULE HERE.
UNFORGIVABLE.
CURSE KOHKA!
I WON'T SIT BACK AND LET IT HAPPEN!
I'LL SALT AND BURN IT ALL BEFORE I LET THEM HAVE THIS LAND!

# Yona of the Dawn

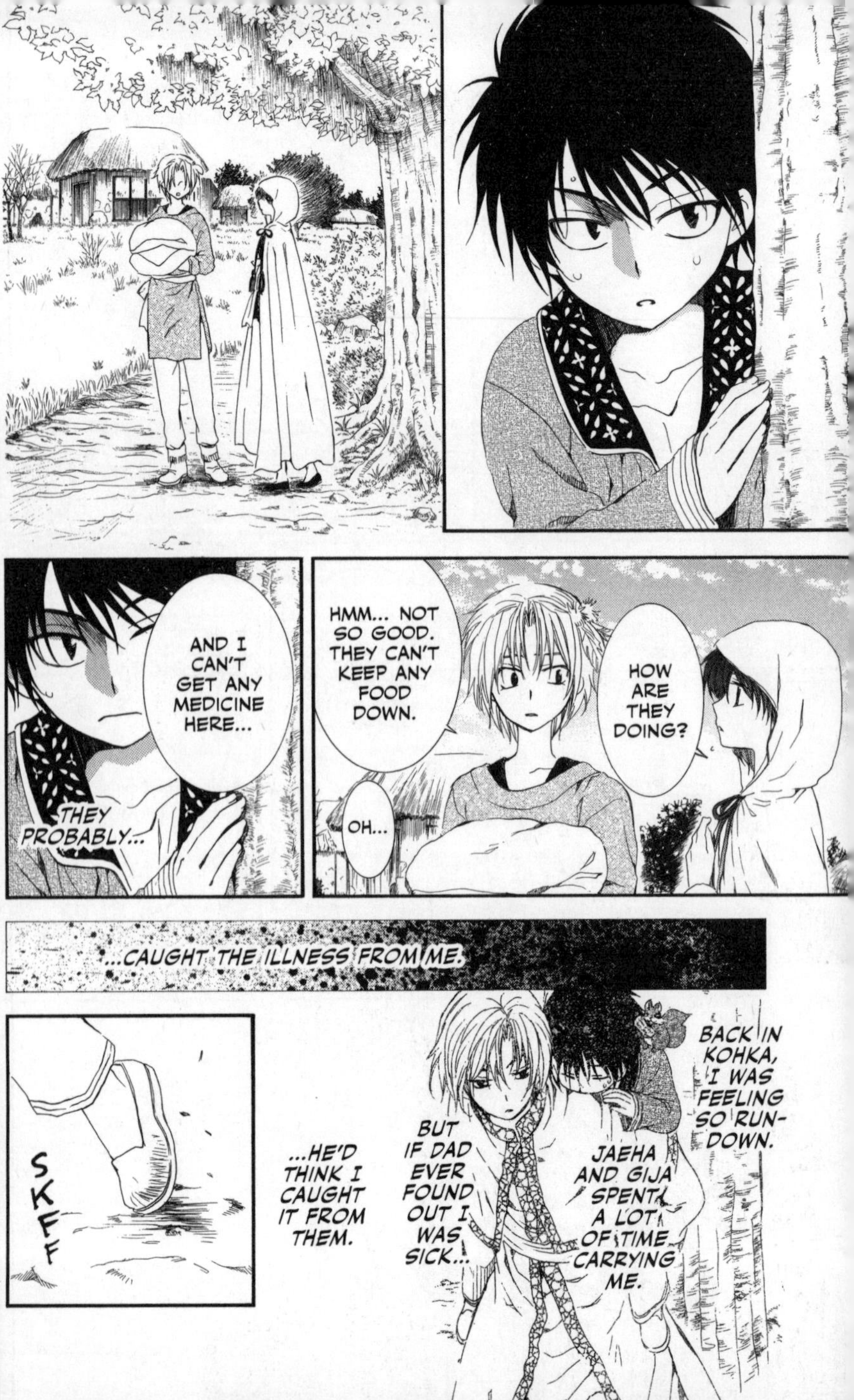
HOW ARE THEY DOING?
HMM... NOT SO GOOD. THEY CAN'T KEEP ANY FOOD DOWN.
OH...
AND I CAN'T GET ANY MEDICINE HERE...
THEY PROBABLY...
...CAUGHT THE ILLNESS FROM ME.
BACK IN KOHKA, I WAS FEELING SO RUN-DOWN.
JAEHA AND GIJA SPENT A LOT OF TIME CARRYING ME.
BUT IF DAD EVER FOUND OUT I WAS SICK...
...HE'D THINK I CAUGHT IT FROM THEM.
SKFF

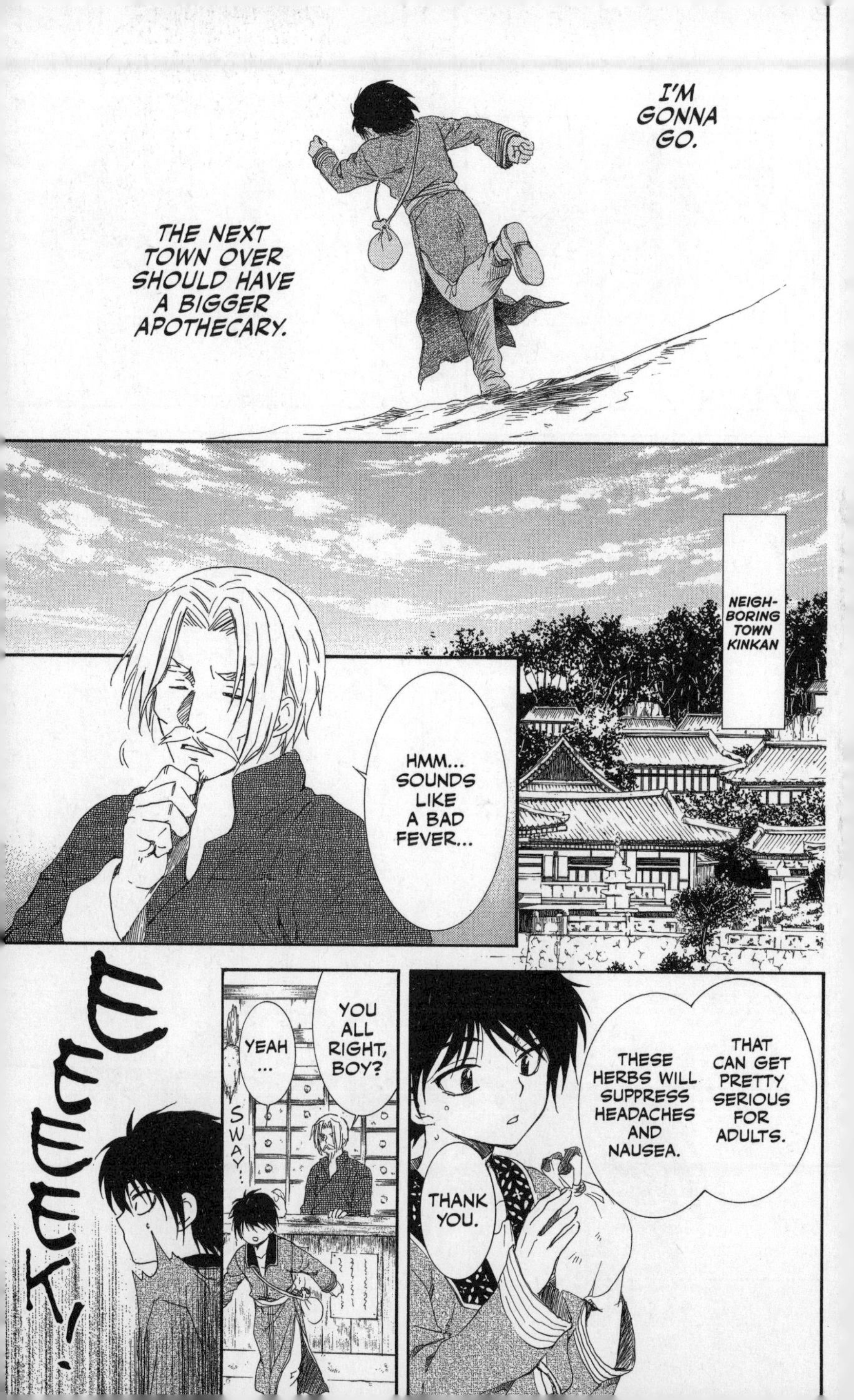
I'M GONNA GO.
THE NEXT TOWN OVER SHOULD HAVE A BIGGER APOTHECARY.
NEIGHBORING TOWN KINKAN
HMM... SOUNDS LIKE A BAD FEVER...
THAT CAN GET PRETTY SERIOUS FOR ADULTS.
THESE HERBS WILL SUPPRESS HEADACHES AND NAUSEA.
THANK YOU.
YOU ALL RIGHT, BOY?
YEAH...
SWAY...
EEEEEK!

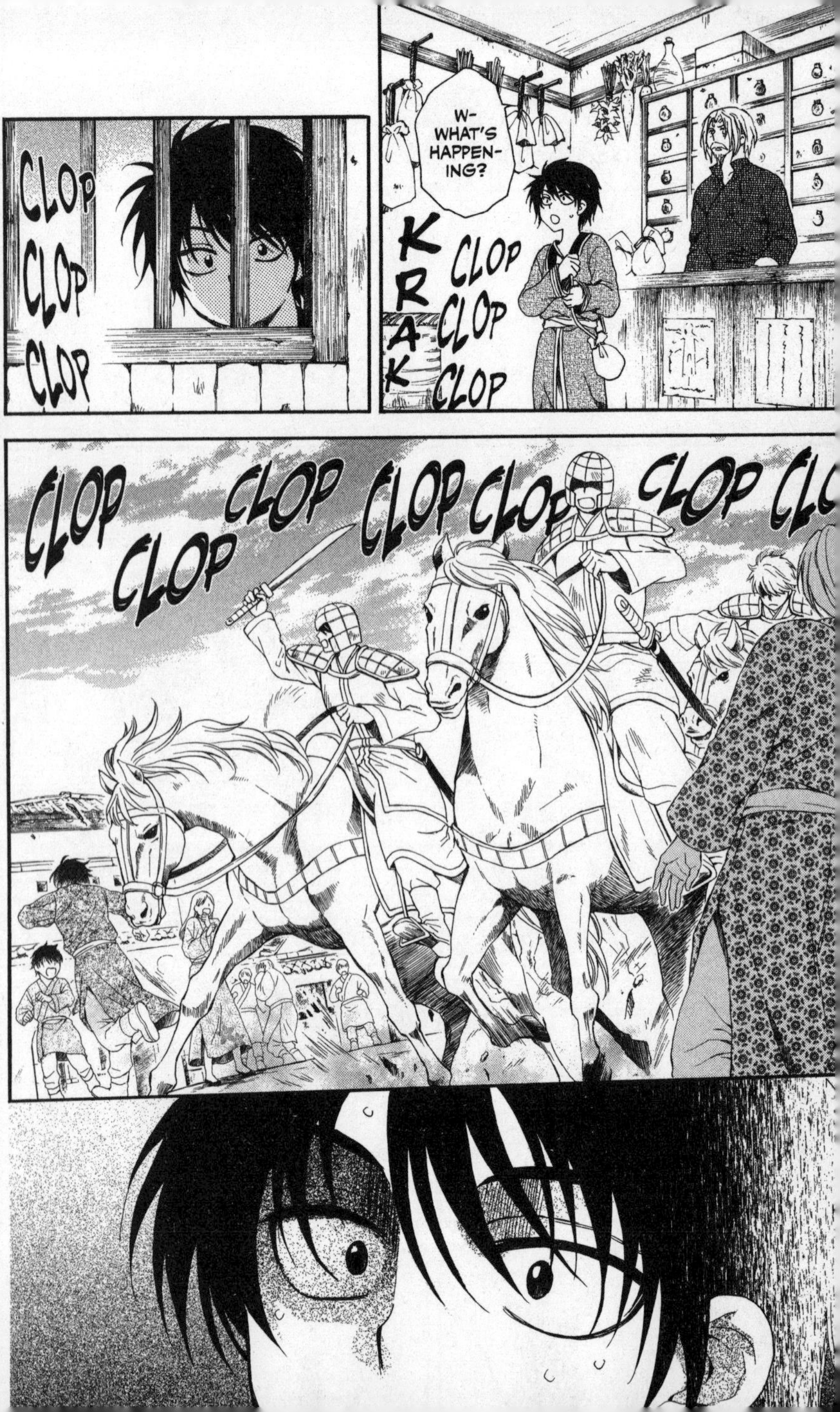
W-WHAT'S HAPPENING?
KRAK
CLOP CLOP CLOP
CLOP CLOP CLOP
CLOP
CLOP
CLOP
CLOP
CLOP
CLOP

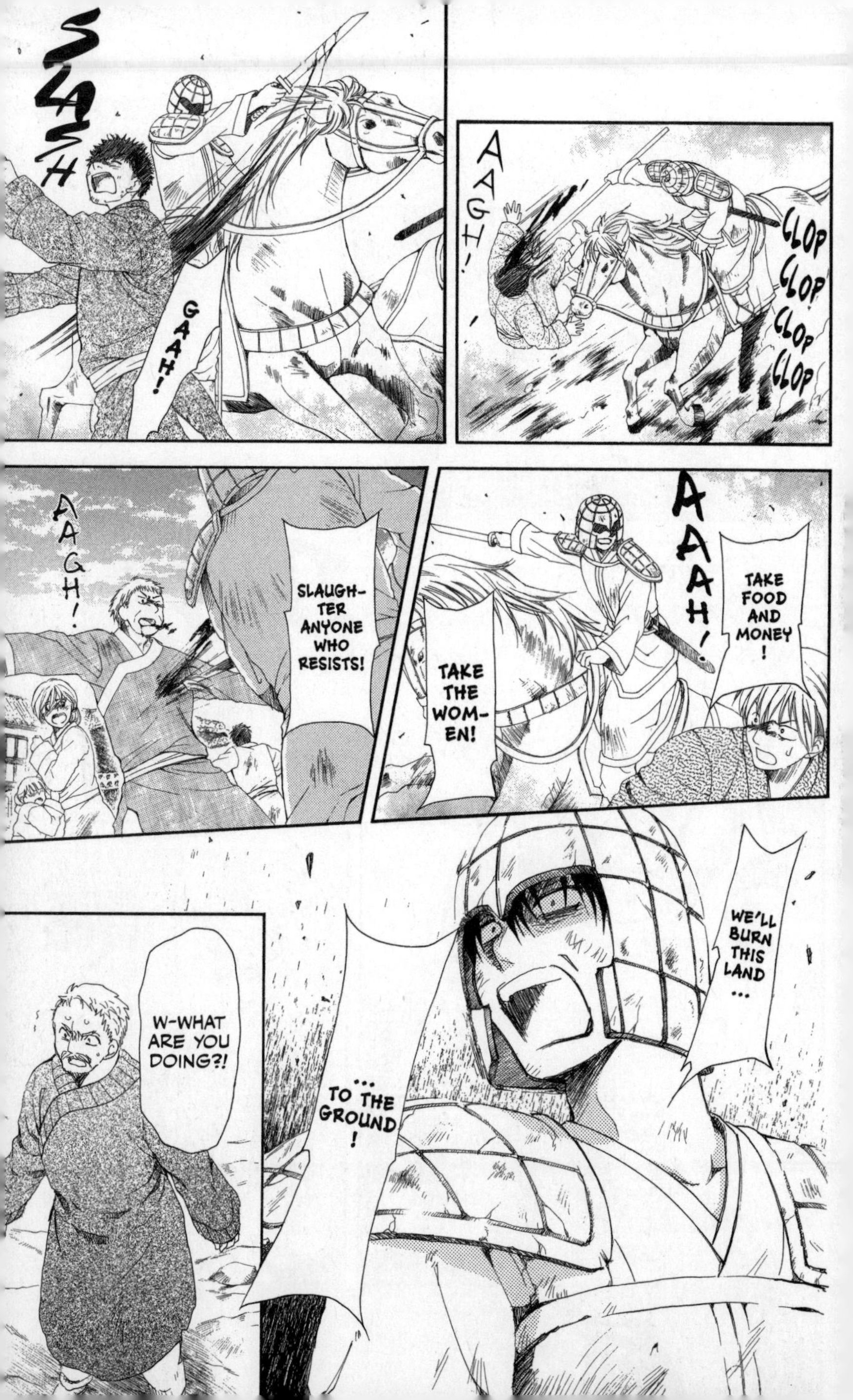
AAGH!
CLOP CLOP CLOP CLOP
SLASH
GAAH!
AAAH!
TAKE FOOD AND MONEY!
TAKE THE WOMEN!
AAGH!
SLAUGHTER ANYONE WHO RESISTS!
WE'LL BURN THIS LAND...
...TO THE GROUND!
W-WHAT ARE YOU DOING?!

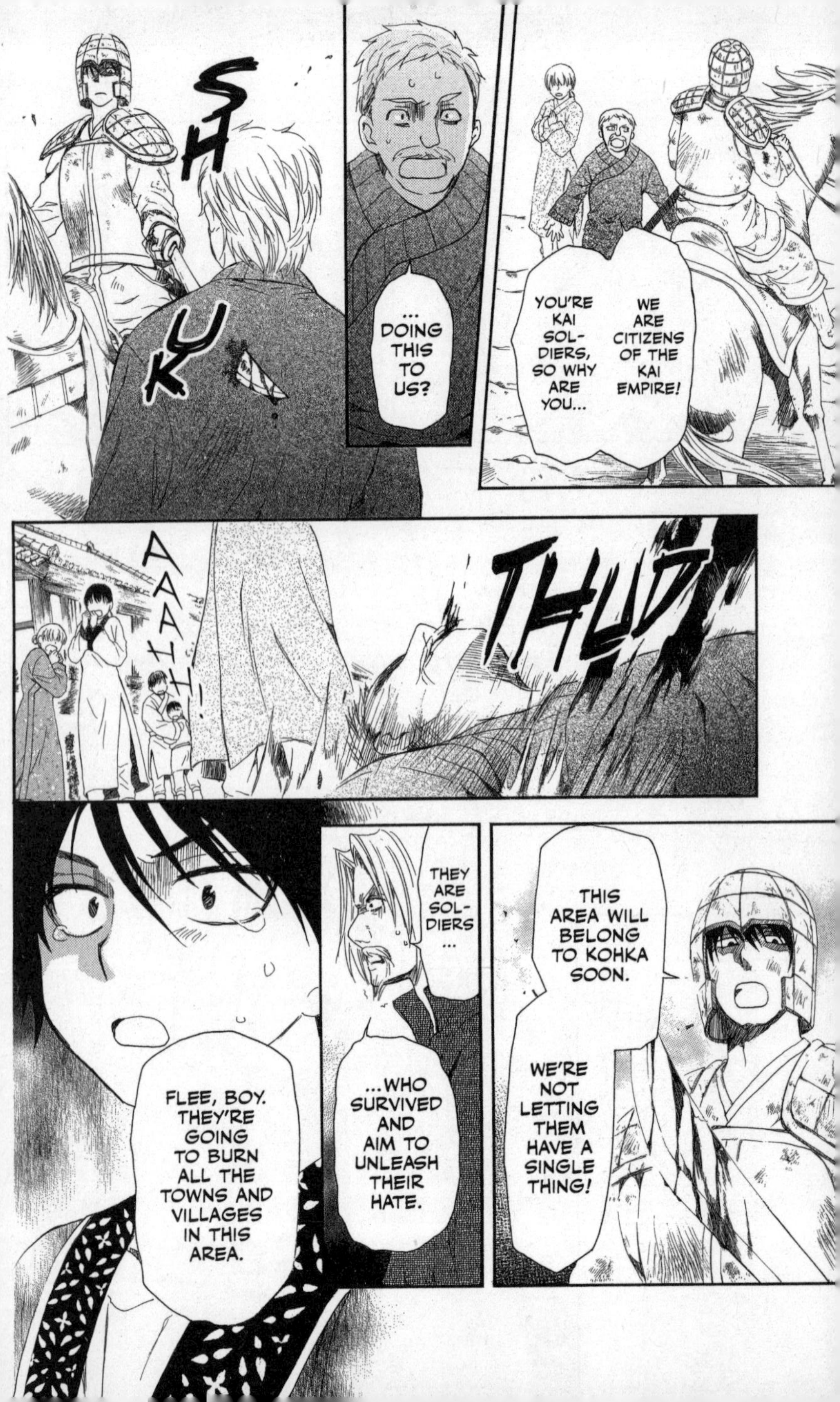
WE ARE CITIZENS OF THE KAI EMPIRE!
YOU'RE KAI SOLDIERS, SO WHY ARE YOU...
...DOING THIS TO US?
SHUK
THUD
AAAAHH!
THIS AREA WILL BELONG TO KOHKA SOON.
WE'RE NOT LETTING THEM HAVE A SINGLE THING!
THEY ARE SOLDIERS...
...WHO SURVIVED AND AIM TO UNLEASH THEIR HATE.
FLEE, BOY. THEY'RE GOING TO BURN ALL THE TOWNS AND VILLAGES IN THIS AREA.

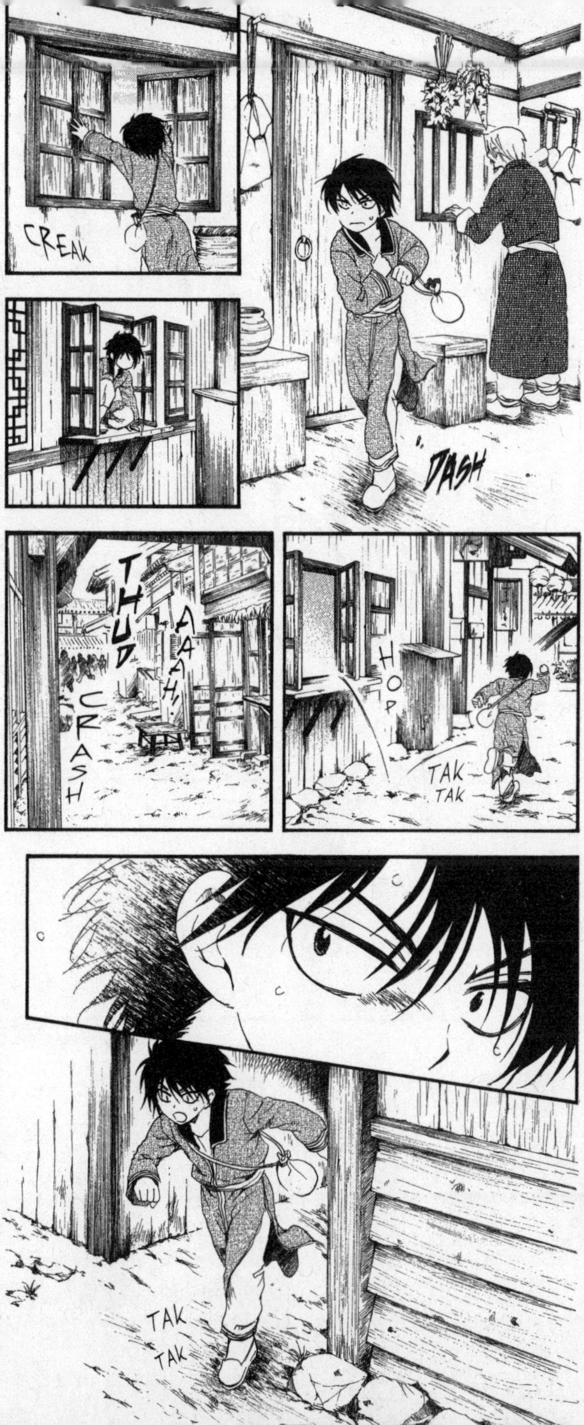
DASH
CREAK
HOP
TAK TAK
THUD
AAAAH!
CRASH
TAK TAK

Continuation

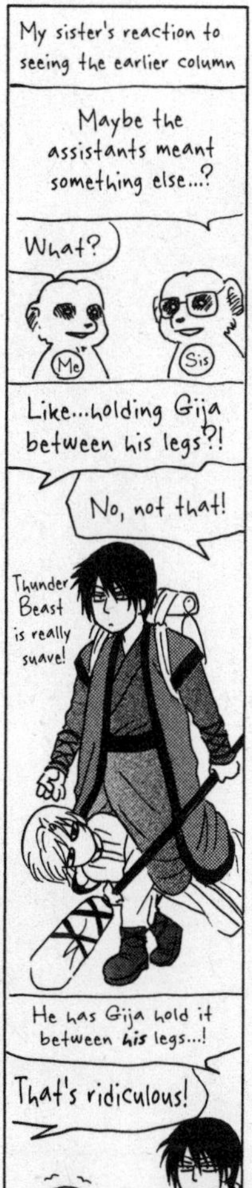
My sister's reaction to seeing the earlier column
Maybe the assistants meant something else...?
What?
Me
Sis
Like...holding Gija between his legs?!
No, not that!
Thunder Beast is really suave!
He has Gija hold it between *his* legs...!
That's ridiculous!

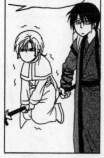

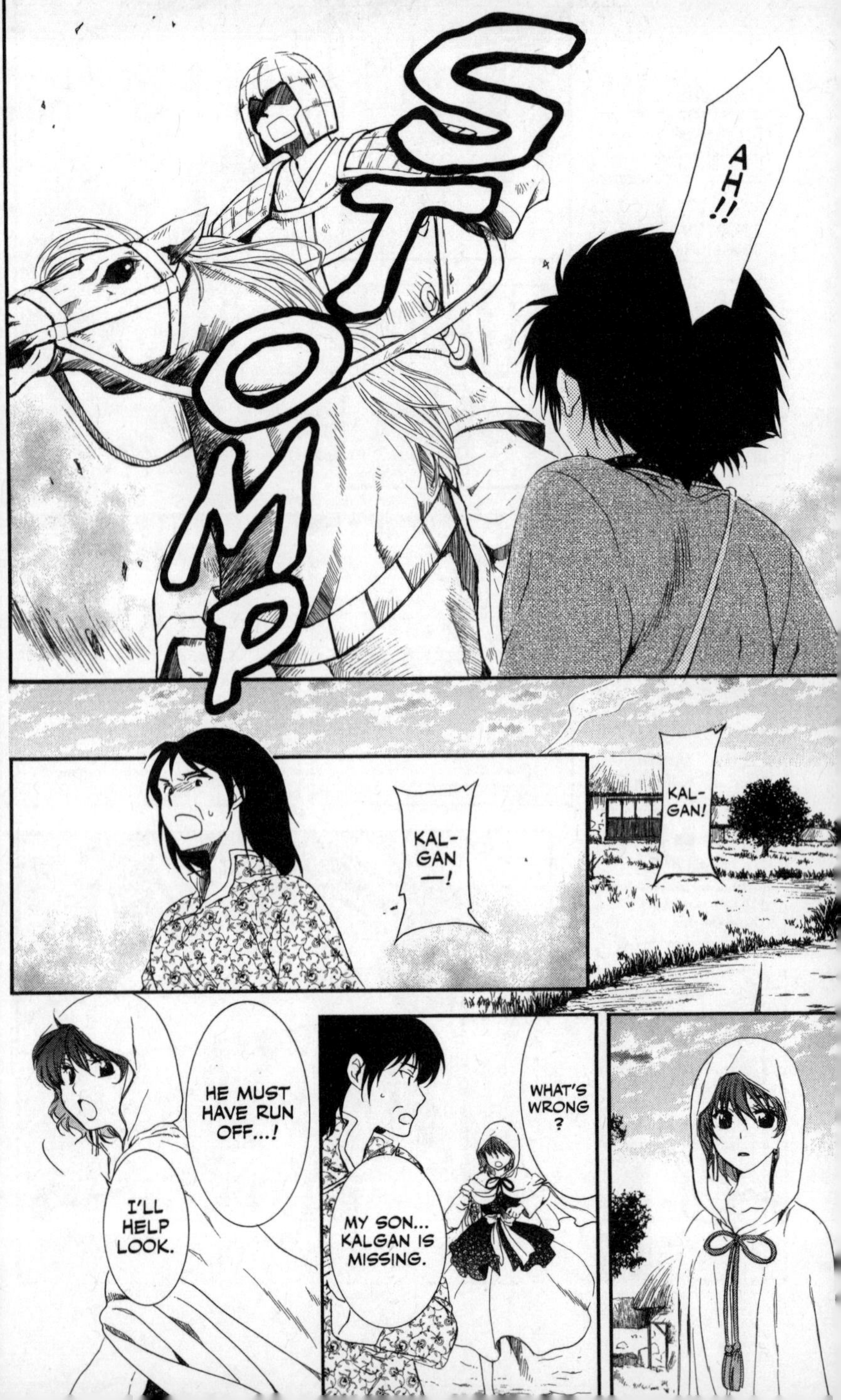
AH!!
STOMP
KALGAN!
KALGAN—!
WHAT'S WRONG?
MY SON... KALGAN IS MISSING.
HE MUST HAVE RUN OFF...!
I'LL HELP LOOK.

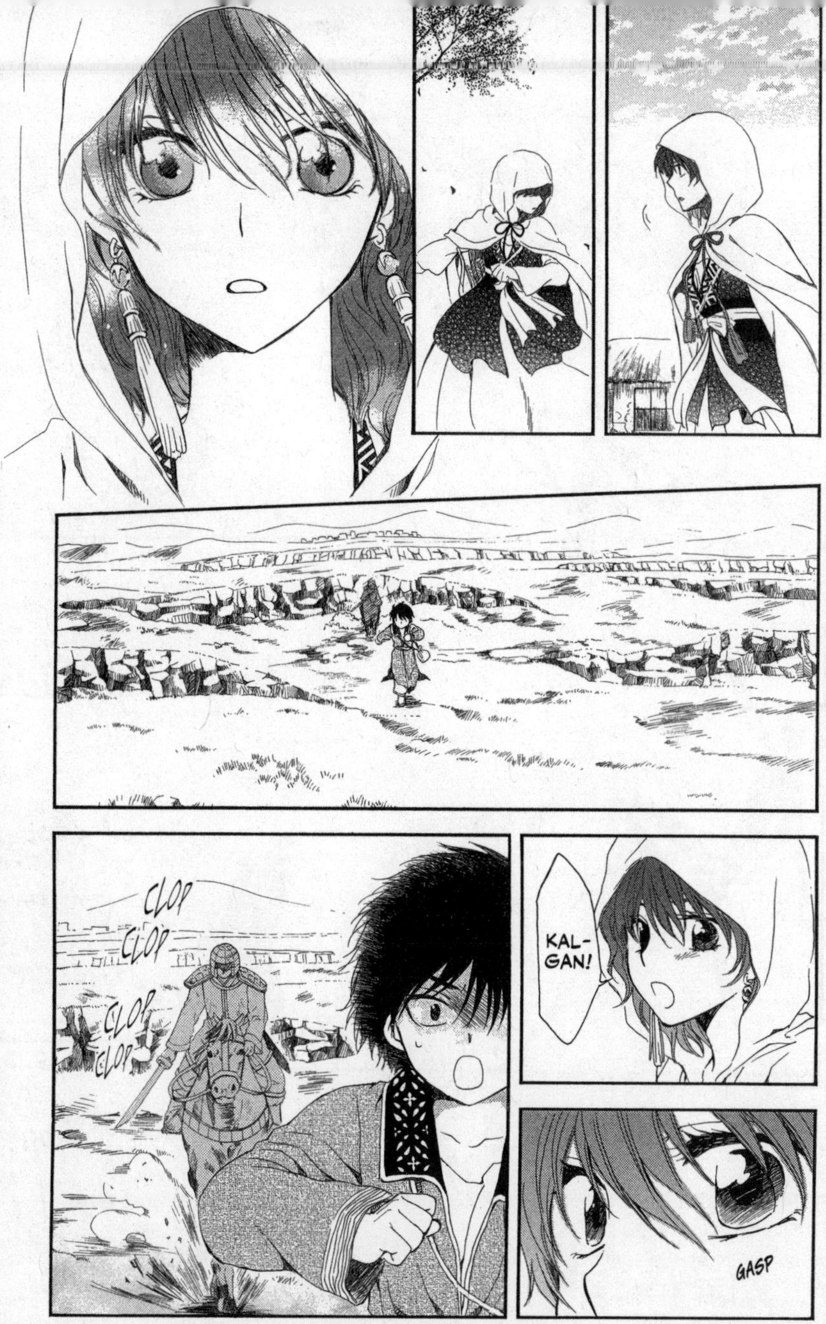
KAL-GAN!
CLOP
CLOP
CLOP
CLOP
GASP

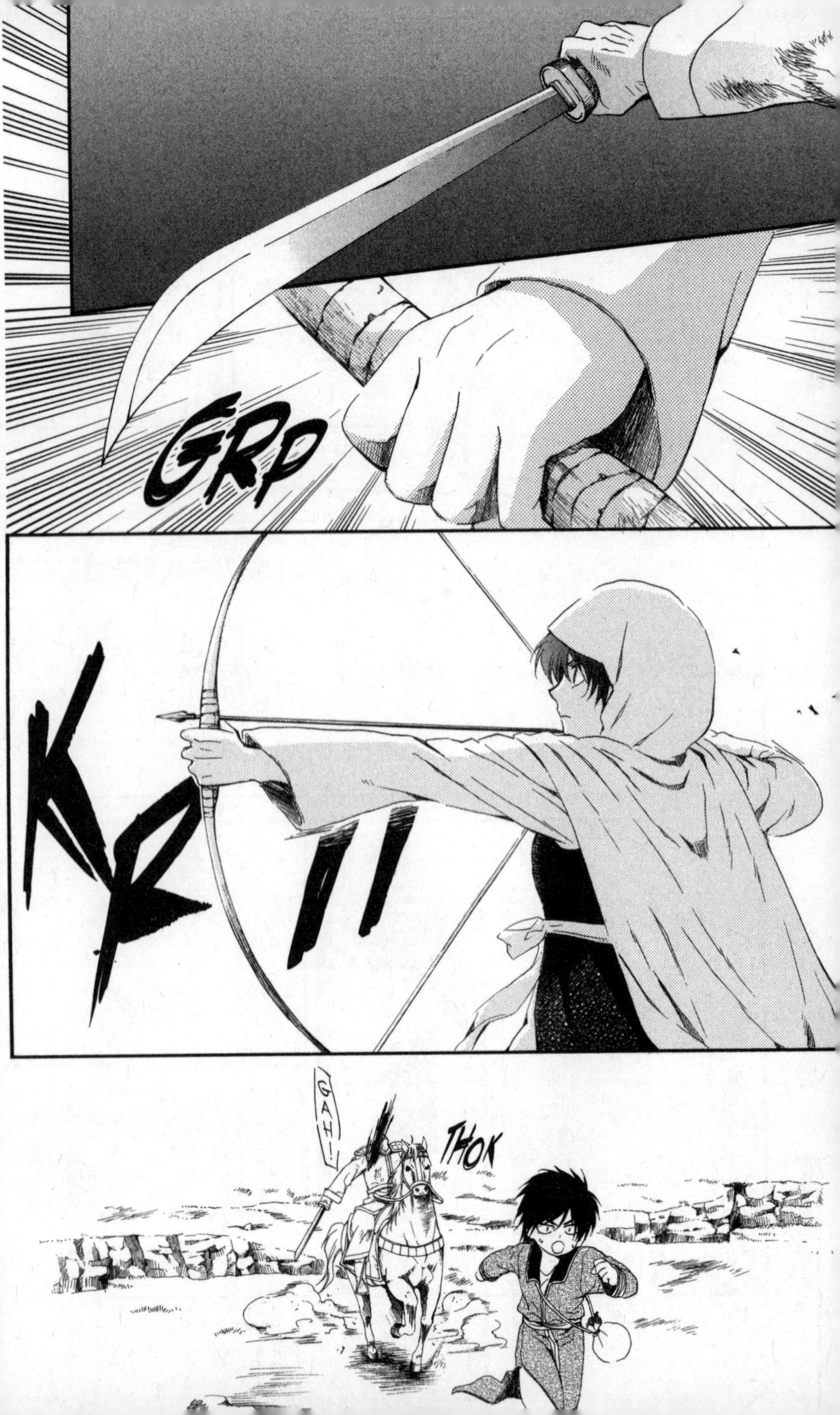
GRP
GAH!
THOK

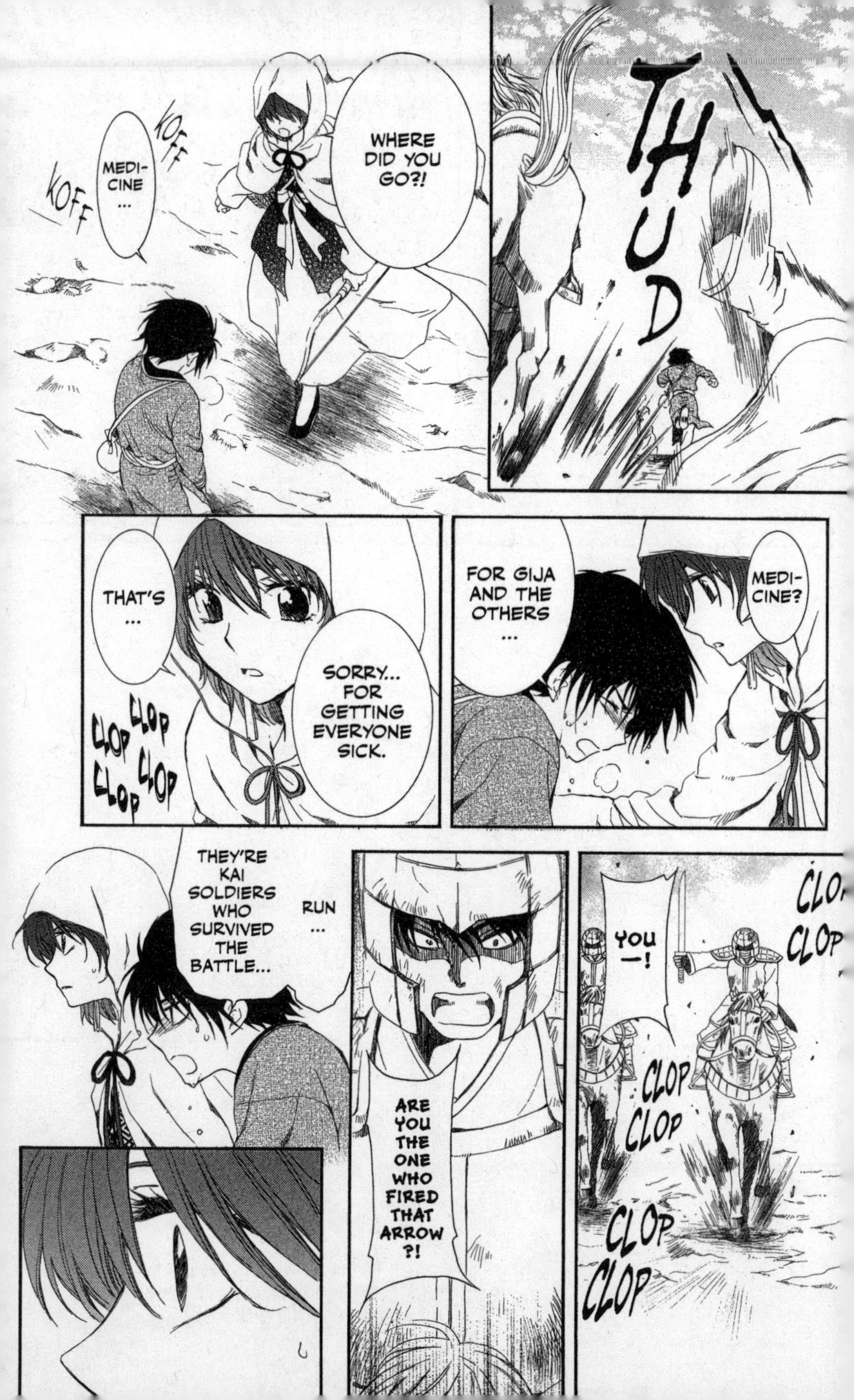
THUD
WHERE DID YOU GO?!
KOFF
KOFF
MEDI-CINE...
MEDI-CINE?
FOR GIJA AND THE OTHERS...
THAT'S...
SORRY... FOR GETTING EVERYONE SICK.
CLOP CLOP CLOP CLOP
CLOP CLOP
YOU—!
CLOP CLOP
CLOP CLOP
ARE YOU THE ONE WHO FIRED THAT ARROW?!
RUN...
THEY'RE KAI SOLDIERS WHO SURVIVED THE BATTLE...

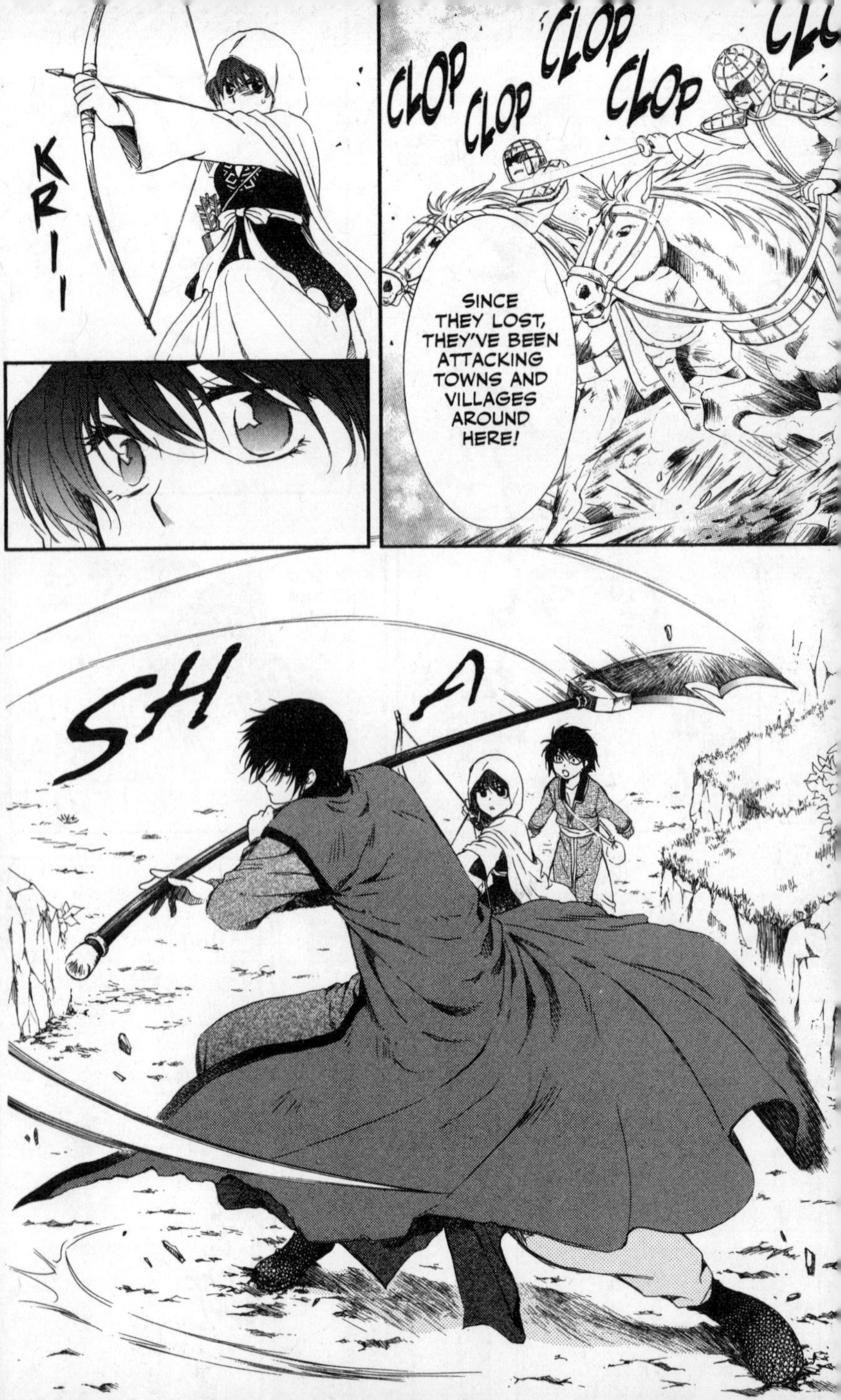
CLOP CLOP CLOP CLOP
SINCE THEY LOST, THEY'VE BEEN ATTACKING TOWNS AND VILLAGES AROUND HERE!
KRII
SHA

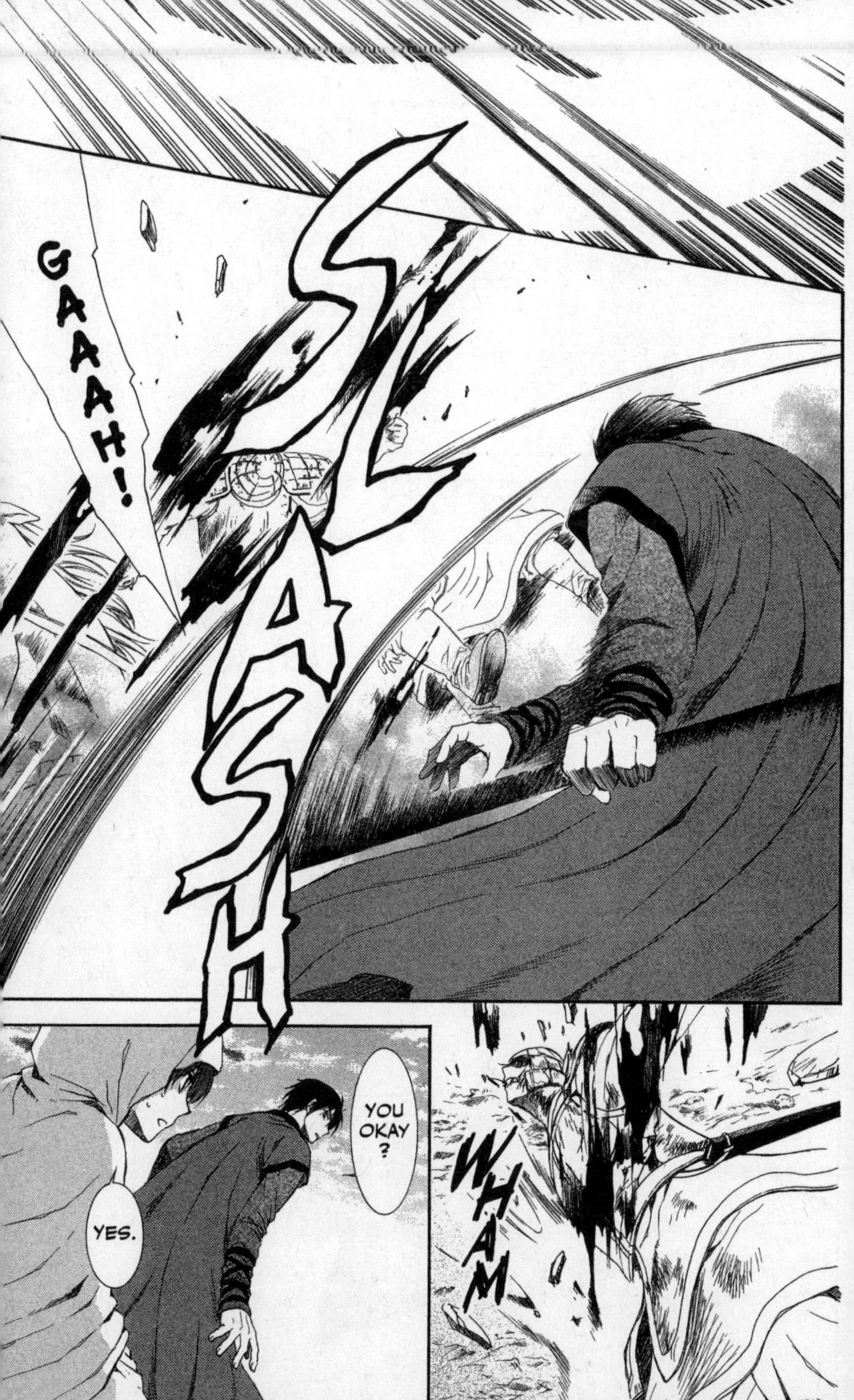
SLASH
GAAAH!
WHAM
YOU OKAY?
YES.

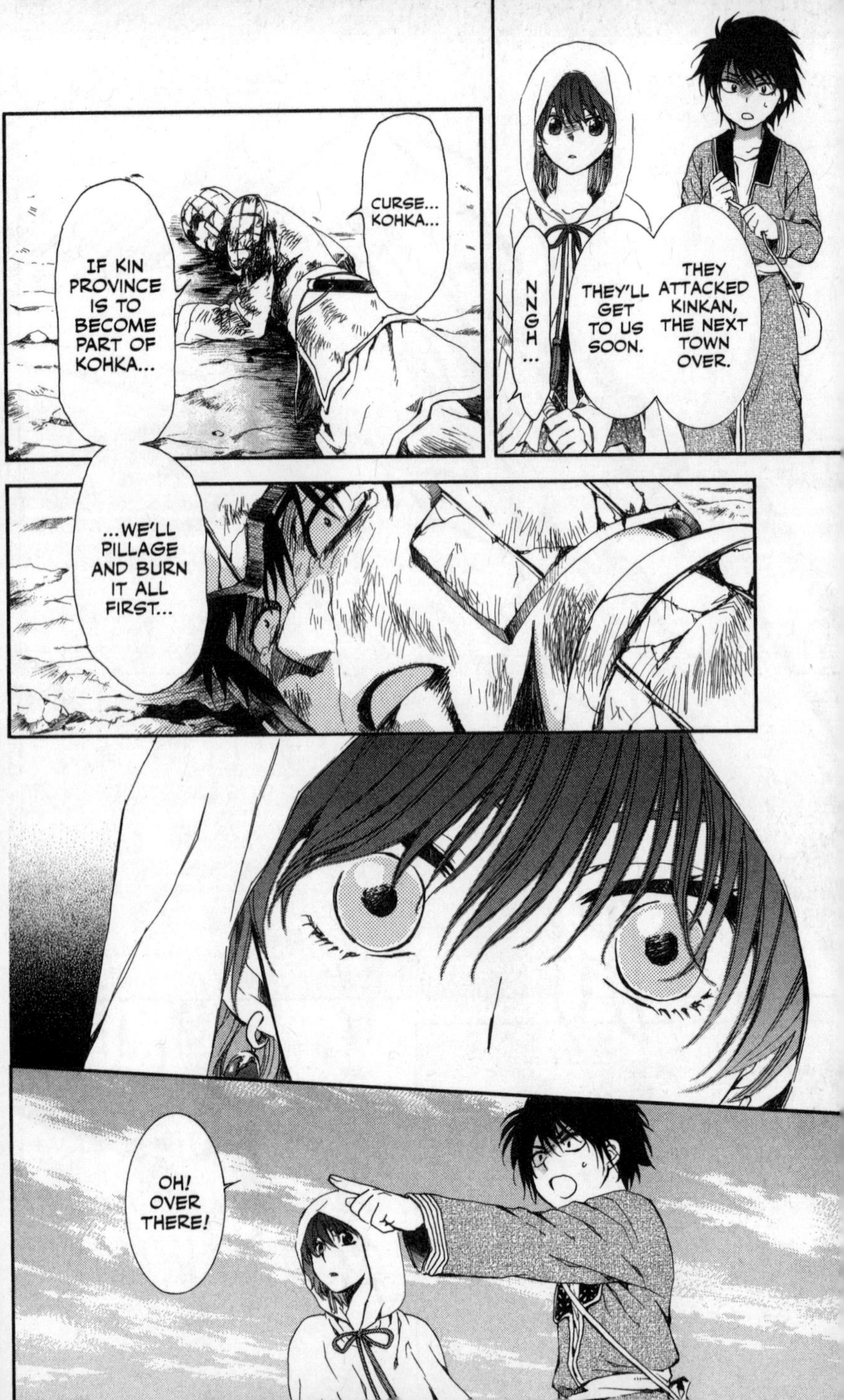
THEY ATTACKED KINKAN, THE NEXT TOWN OVER.
THEY'LL GET TO US SOON.
NNGH...
CURSE... KOHKA...
IF KIN PROVINCE IS TO BECOME PART OF KOHKA...
...WE'LL PILLAGE AND BURN IT ALL FIRST...
OH! OVER THERE!

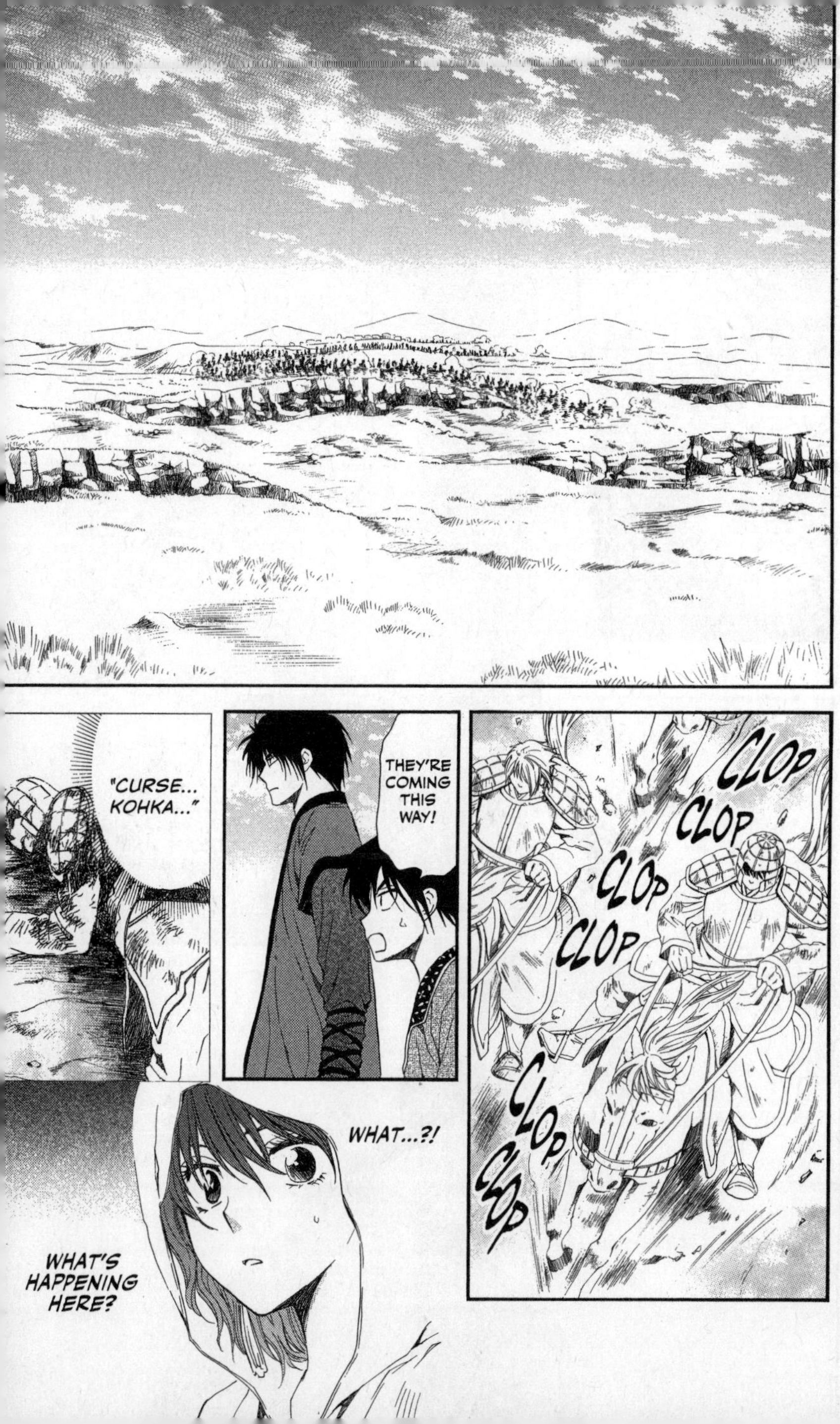
CLOP
CLOP
CLOP
CLOP
CLOP
CLOP
THEY'RE COMING THIS WAY!
"CURSE... KOHKA..."
WHAT...?!
WHAT'S HAPPENING HERE?

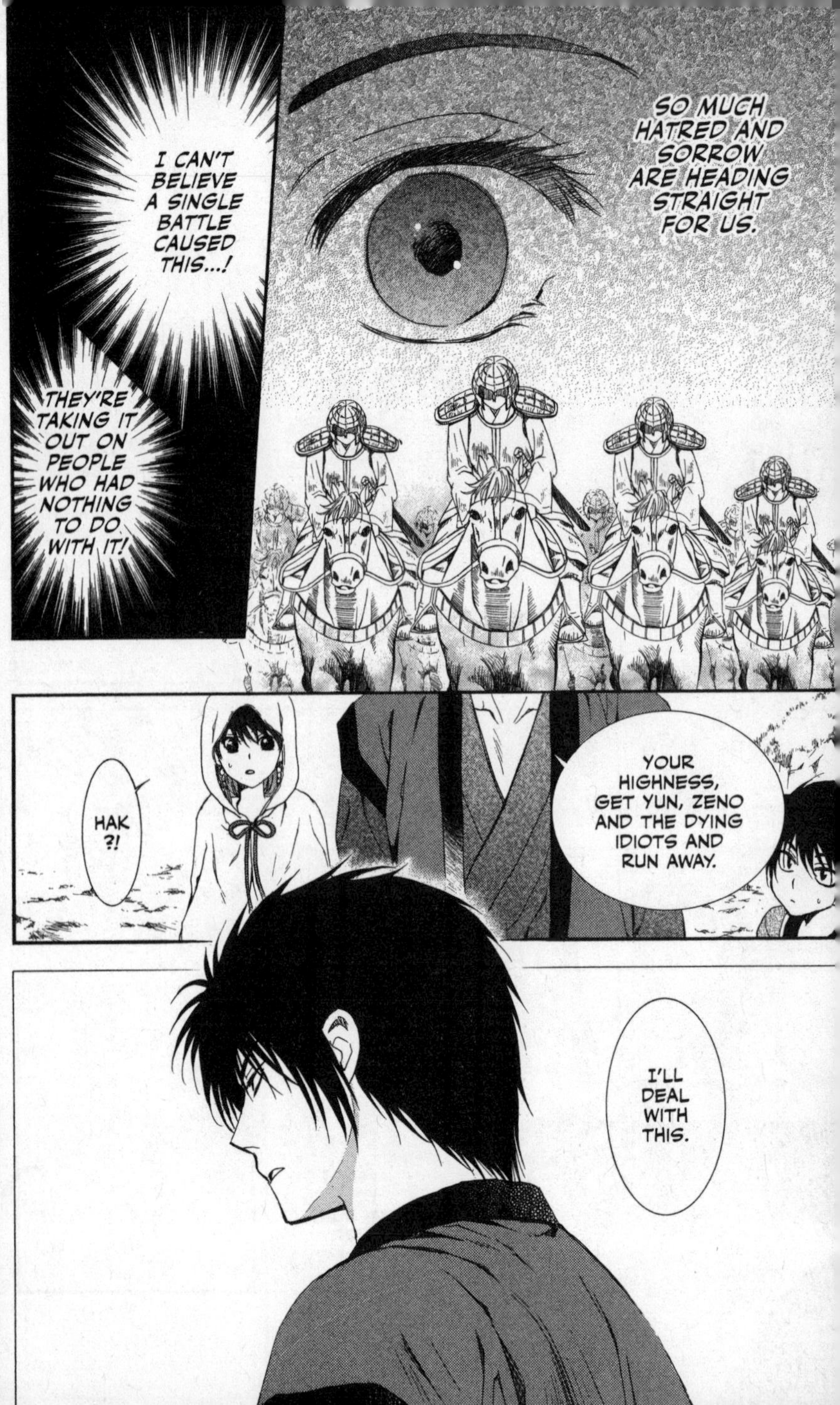
SO MUCH HATRED AND SORROW ARE HEADING STRAIGHT FOR US.
I CAN'T BELIEVE A SINGLE BATTLE CAUSED THIS...!
THEY'RE TAKING IT OUT ON PEOPLE WHO HAD NOTHING TO DO WITH IT!
YOUR HIGHNESS, GET YUN, ZENO AND THE DYING IDIOTS AND RUN AWAY.
HAK ?!
I'LL DEAL WITH THIS.

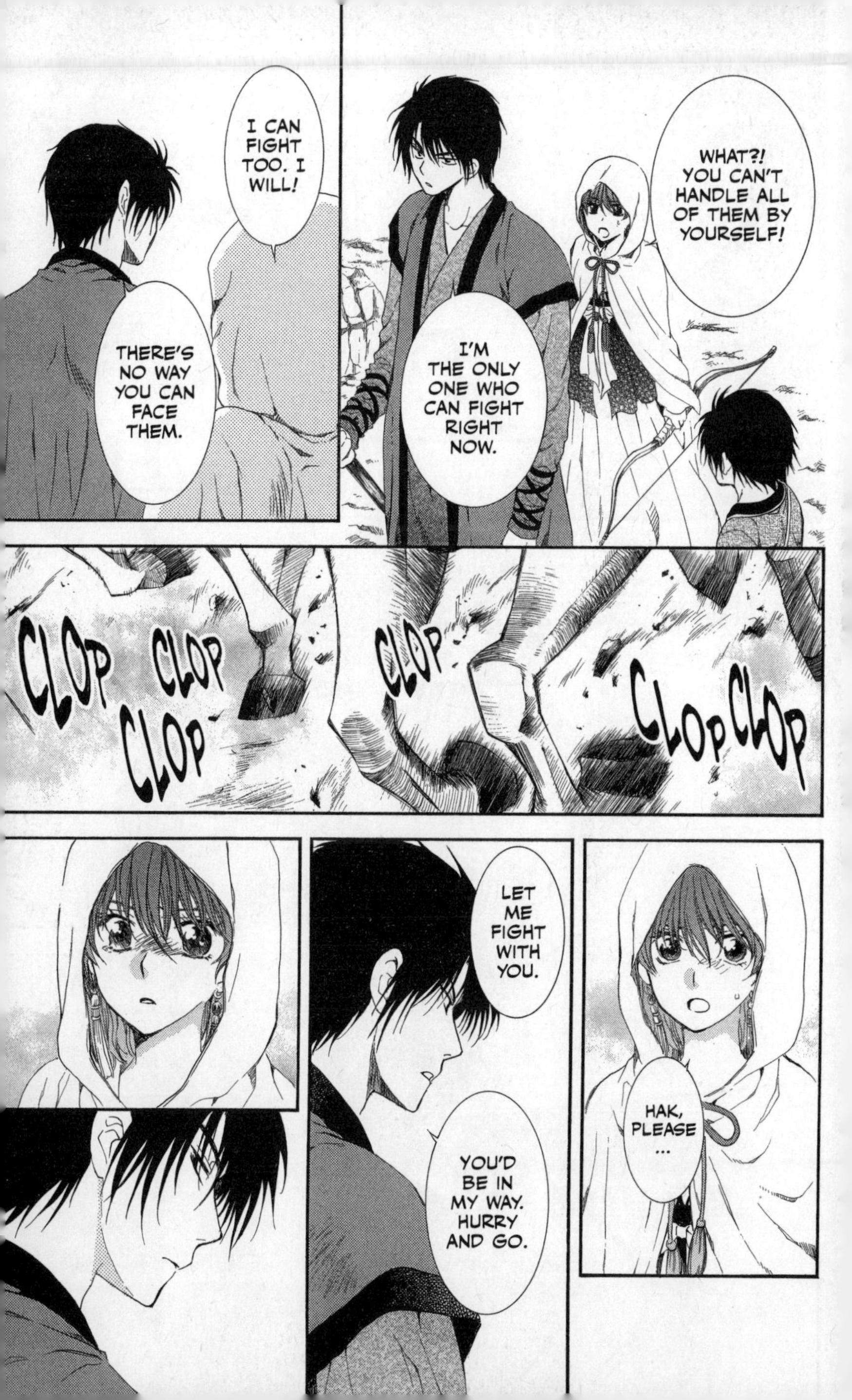
WHAT?! YOU CAN'T HANDLE ALL OF THEM BY YOURSELF!
I'M THE ONLY ONE WHO CAN FIGHT RIGHT NOW.
I CAN FIGHT TOO. I WILL!
THERE'S NO WAY YOU CAN FACE THEM.
CLOP CLOP
CLOP
CLOP
CLOP
CLOP
HAK, PLEASE ...
LET ME FIGHT WITH YOU.
YOU'D BE IN MY WAY. HURRY AND GO.

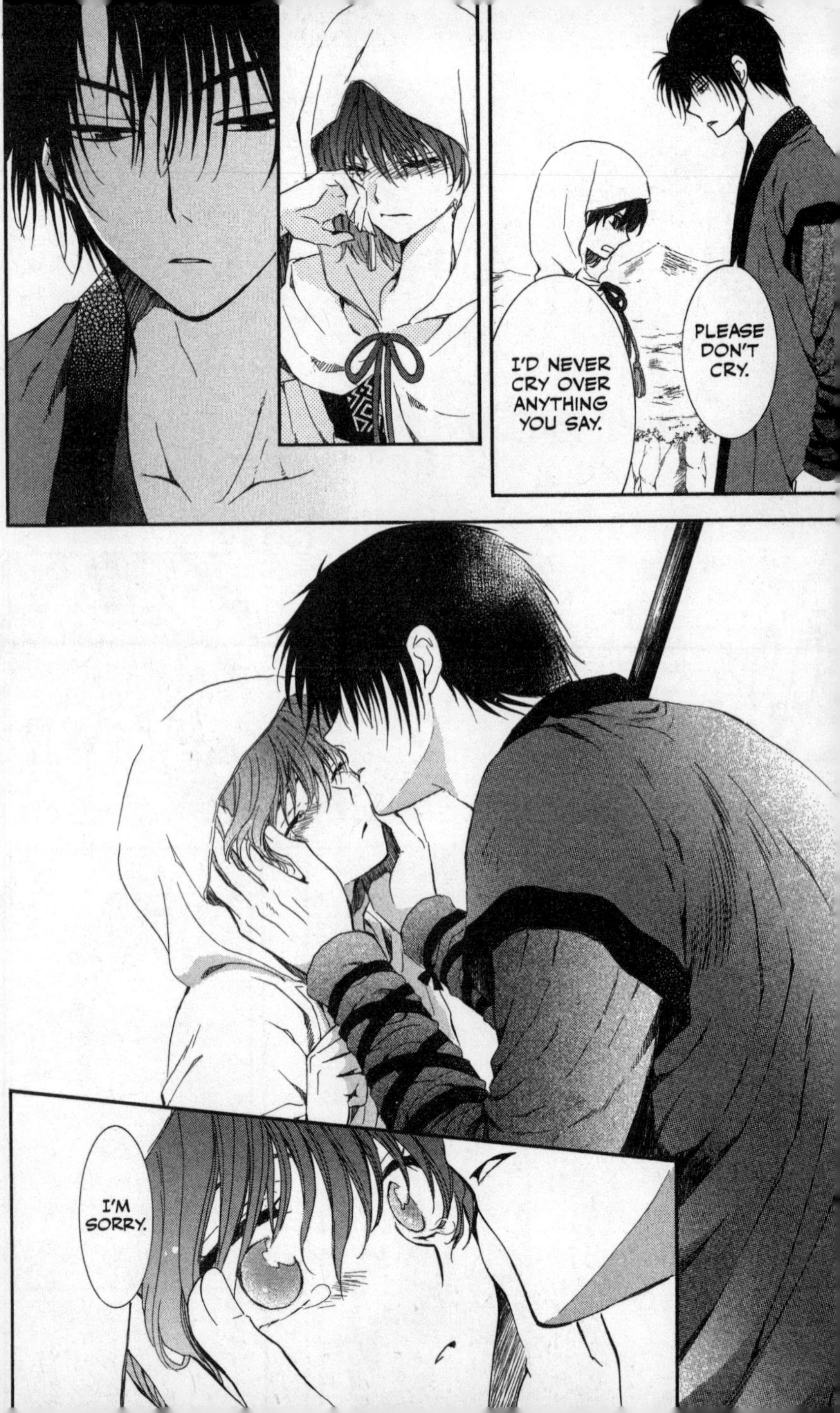
PLEASE DON'T CRY.
I'D NEVER CRY OVER ANYTHING YOU SAY.
I'M SORRY.

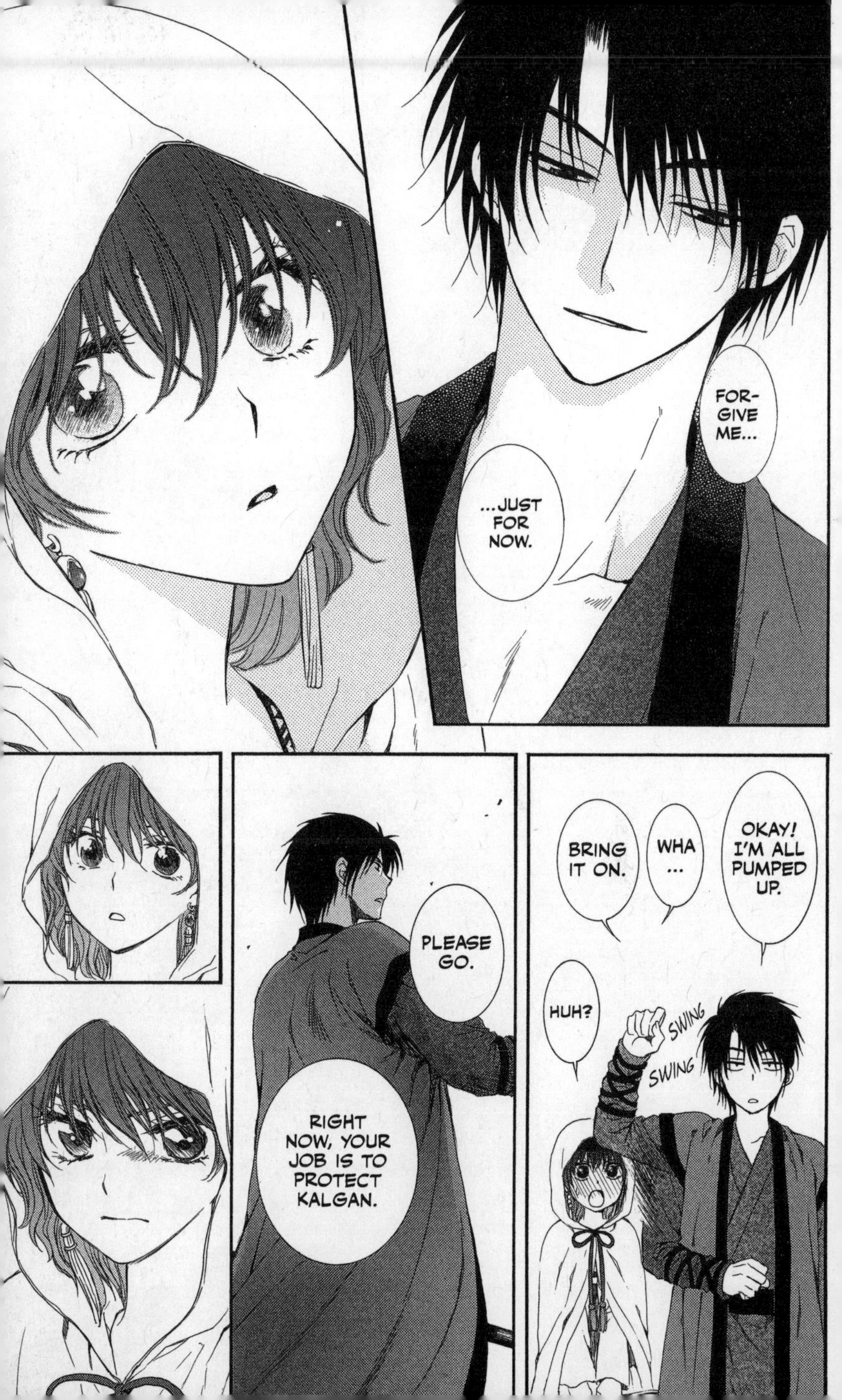
FOR-
GIVE
ME...
...JUST
FOR
NOW.
OKAY!
I'M ALL
PUMPED
UP.
WHA
...
BRING
IT ON.
HUH?
SWING
SWING
PLEASE
GO.
RIGHT
NOW, YOUR
JOB IS TO
PROTECT
KALGAN.

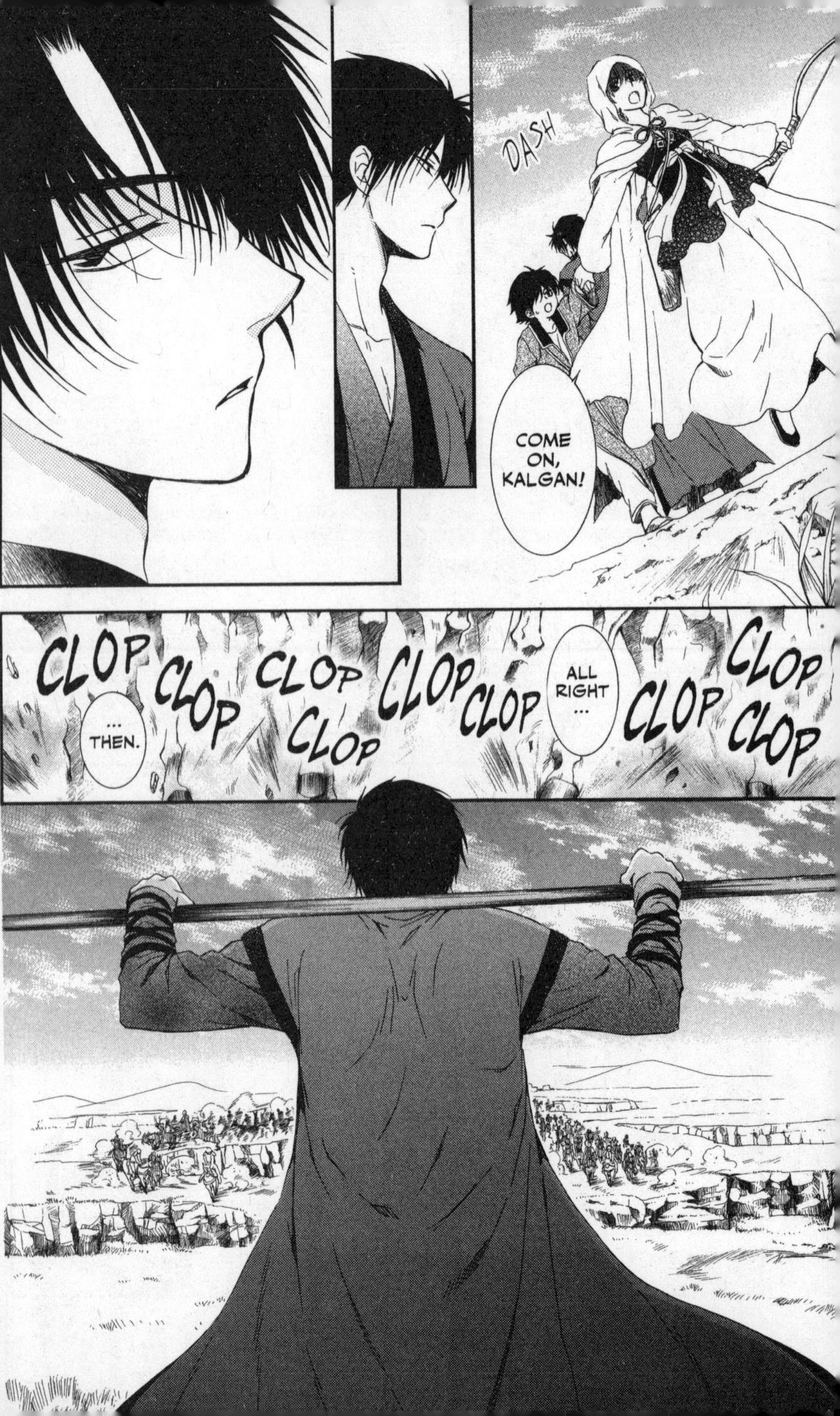
DASH
COME ON, KALGAN!
CLOP
CLOP
CLOP
ALL RIGHT...
CLOP
CLOP
CLOP
CLOP
CLOP
... THEN.
CLOP
CLOP

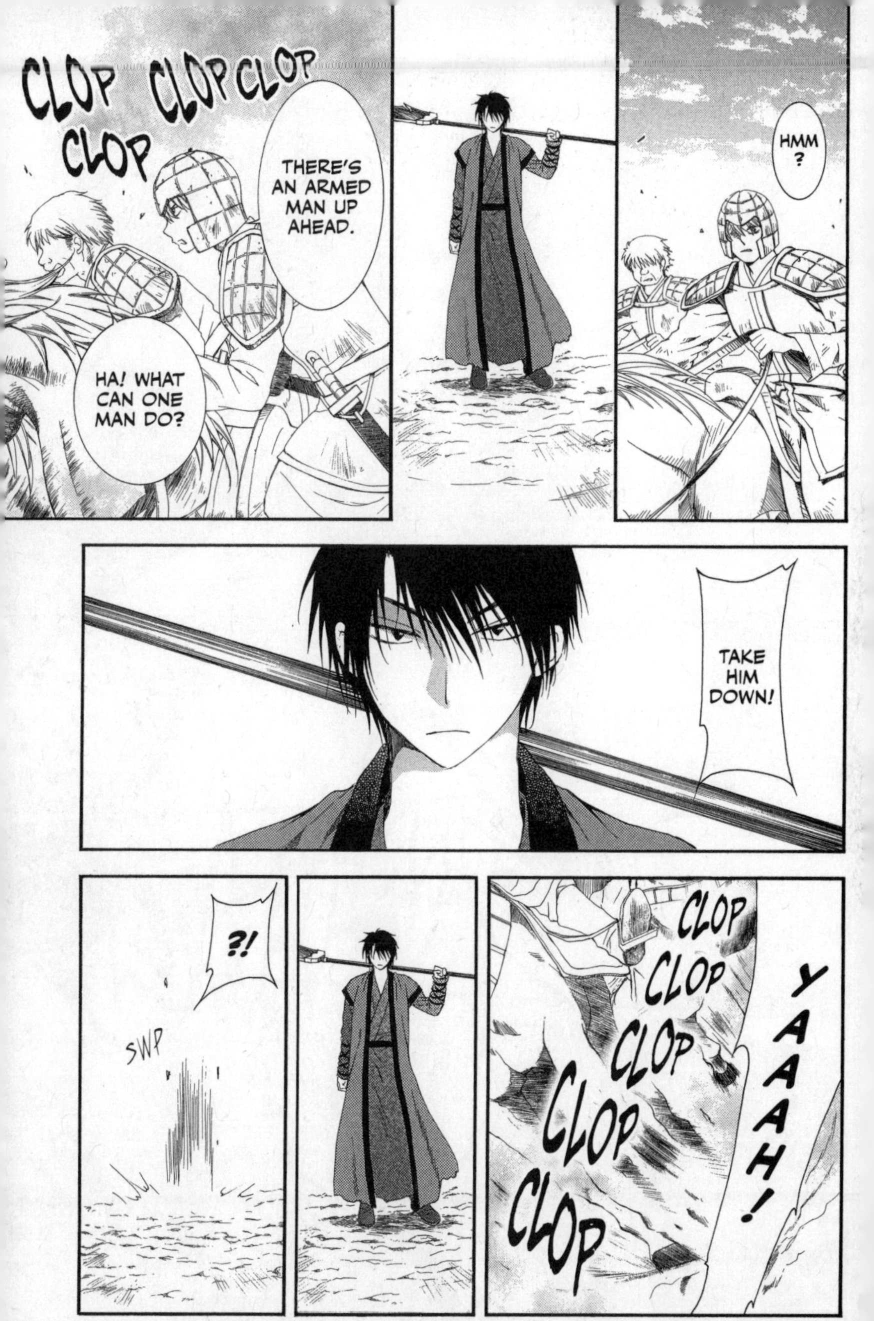
HMM?
THERE'S AN ARMED MAN UP AHEAD.
CLOP CLOP CLOP CLOP
HA! WHAT CAN ONE MAN DO?
TAKE HIM DOWN!
CLOP CLOP CLOP CLOP CLOP
YAAAAH!
?!
SWP

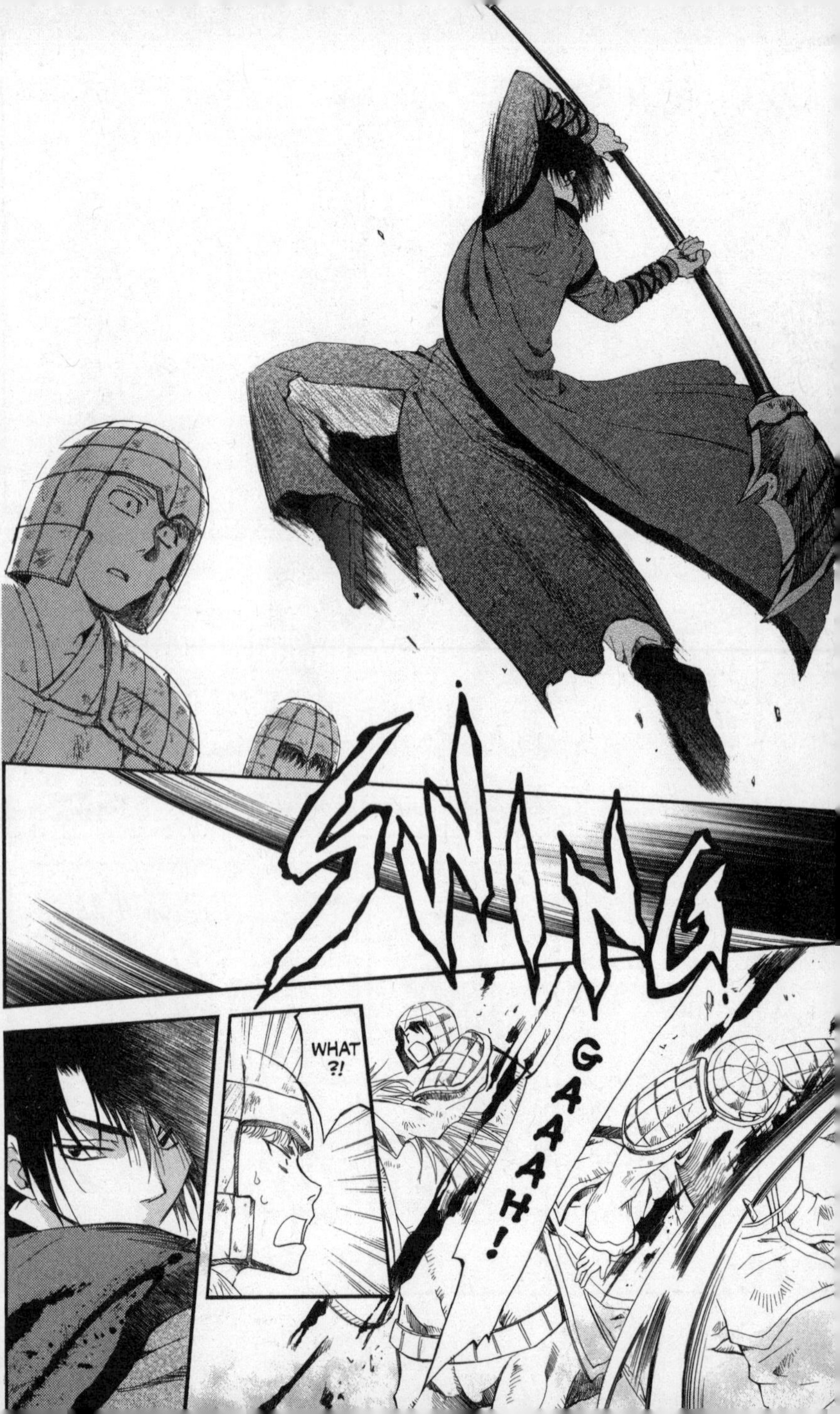
SWING
WHAT ?!
GAAAH!

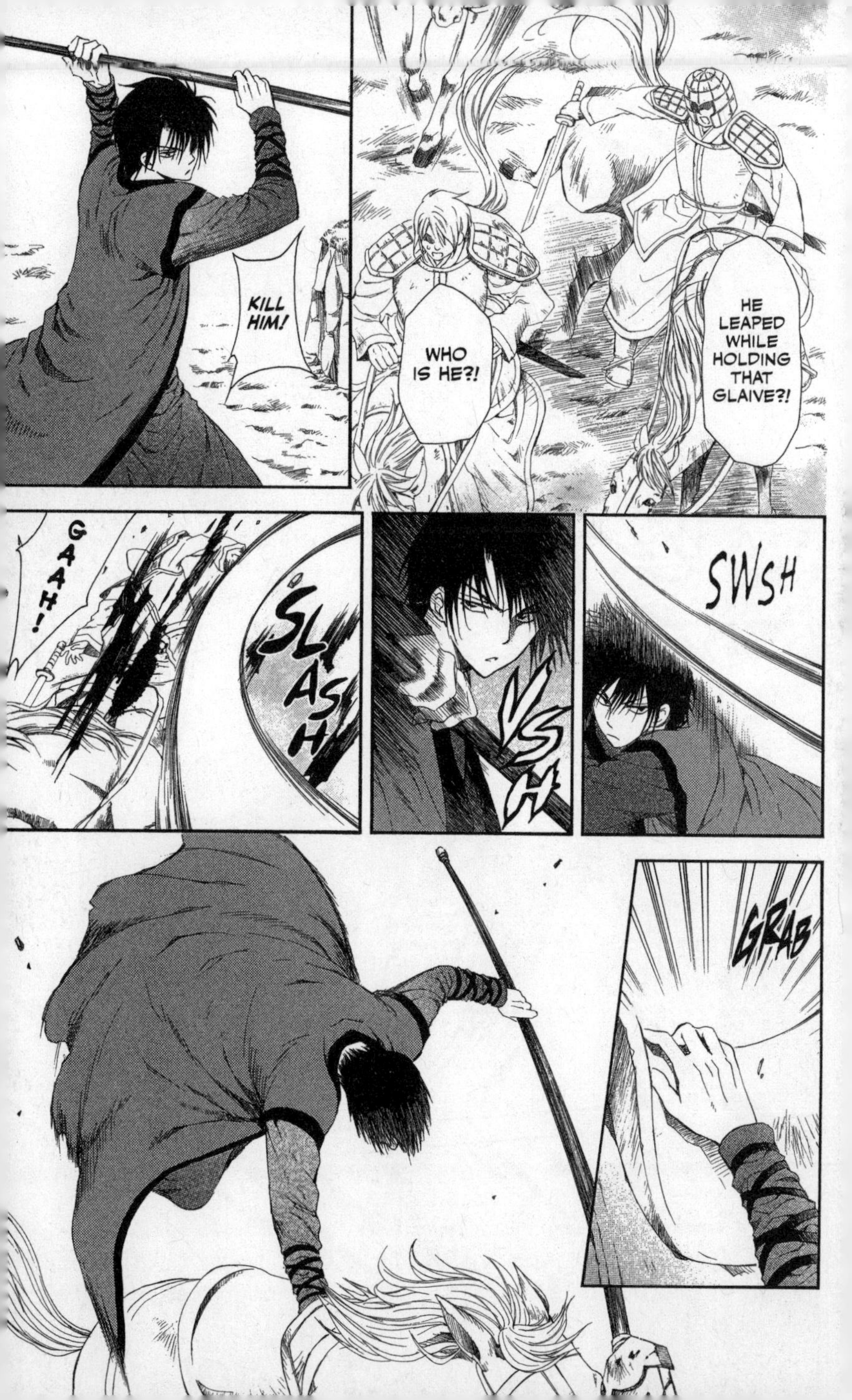
HE LEAPED WHILE HOLDING THAT GLAIVE?!
WHO IS HE?!
KILL HIM!
SWSH
VSH
SLASH
GAAH!
GRAB

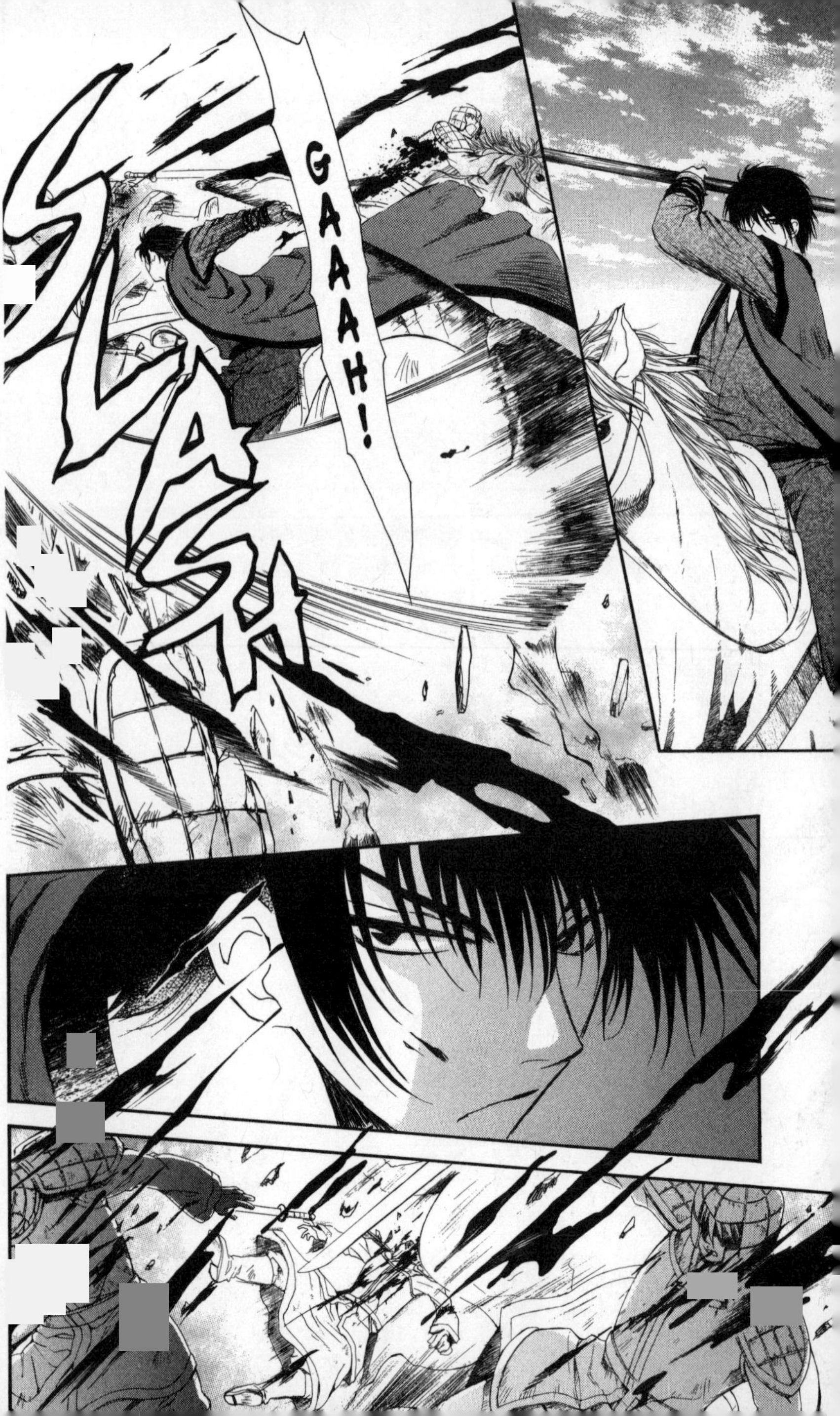
GAAAAH!
SLASH

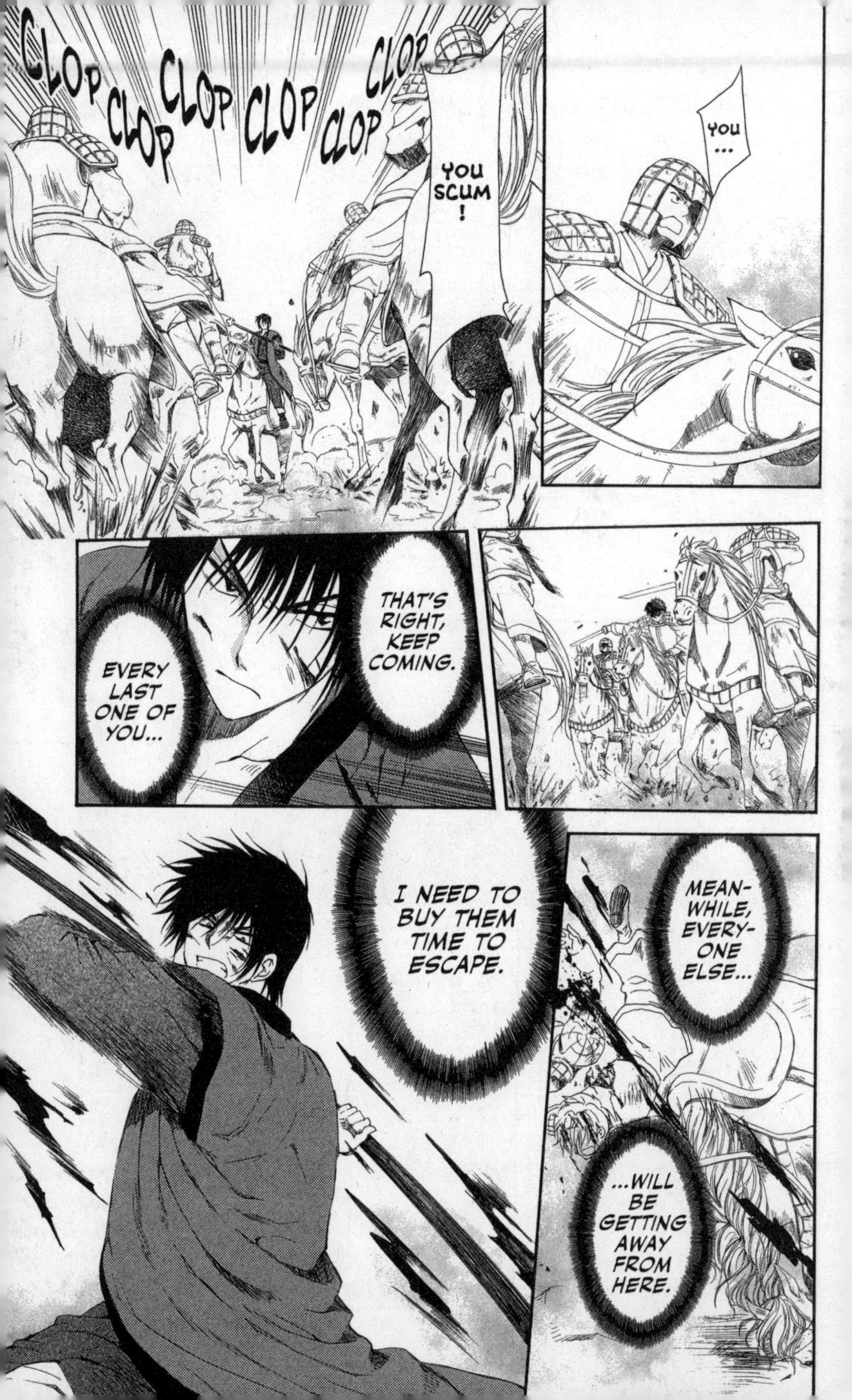
YOU ...
CLOP CLOP CLOP CLOP CLOP CLOP
YOU SCUM !
THAT'S RIGHT, KEEP COMING.
EVERY LAST ONE OF YOU...
MEAN-WHILE, EVERY-ONE ELSE...
...WILL BE GETTING AWAY FROM HERE.
I NEED TO BUY THEM TIME TO ESCAPE.

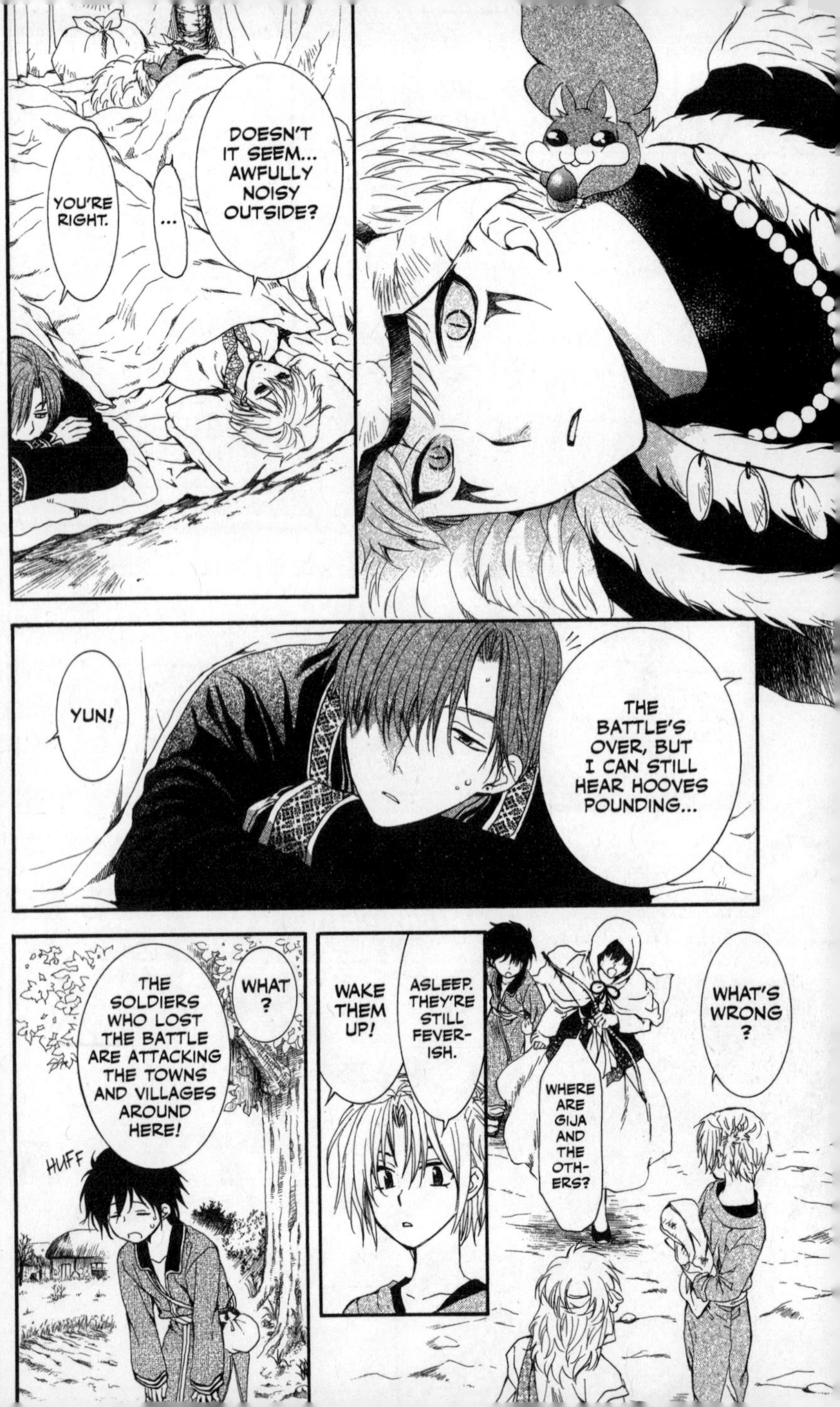
DOESN'T IT SEEM... AWFULLY NOISY OUTSIDE?
...
YOU'RE RIGHT.
THE BATTLE'S OVER, BUT I CAN STILL HEAR HOOVES POUNDING...
YUN!
WHAT'S WRONG?
WHERE ARE GIJA AND THE OTHERS?
ASLEEP. THEY'RE STILL FEVERISH.
WAKE THEM UP!
WHAT?
THE SOLDIERS WHO LOST THE BATTLE ARE ATTACKING THE TOWNS AND VILLAGES AROUND HERE!
HUFF

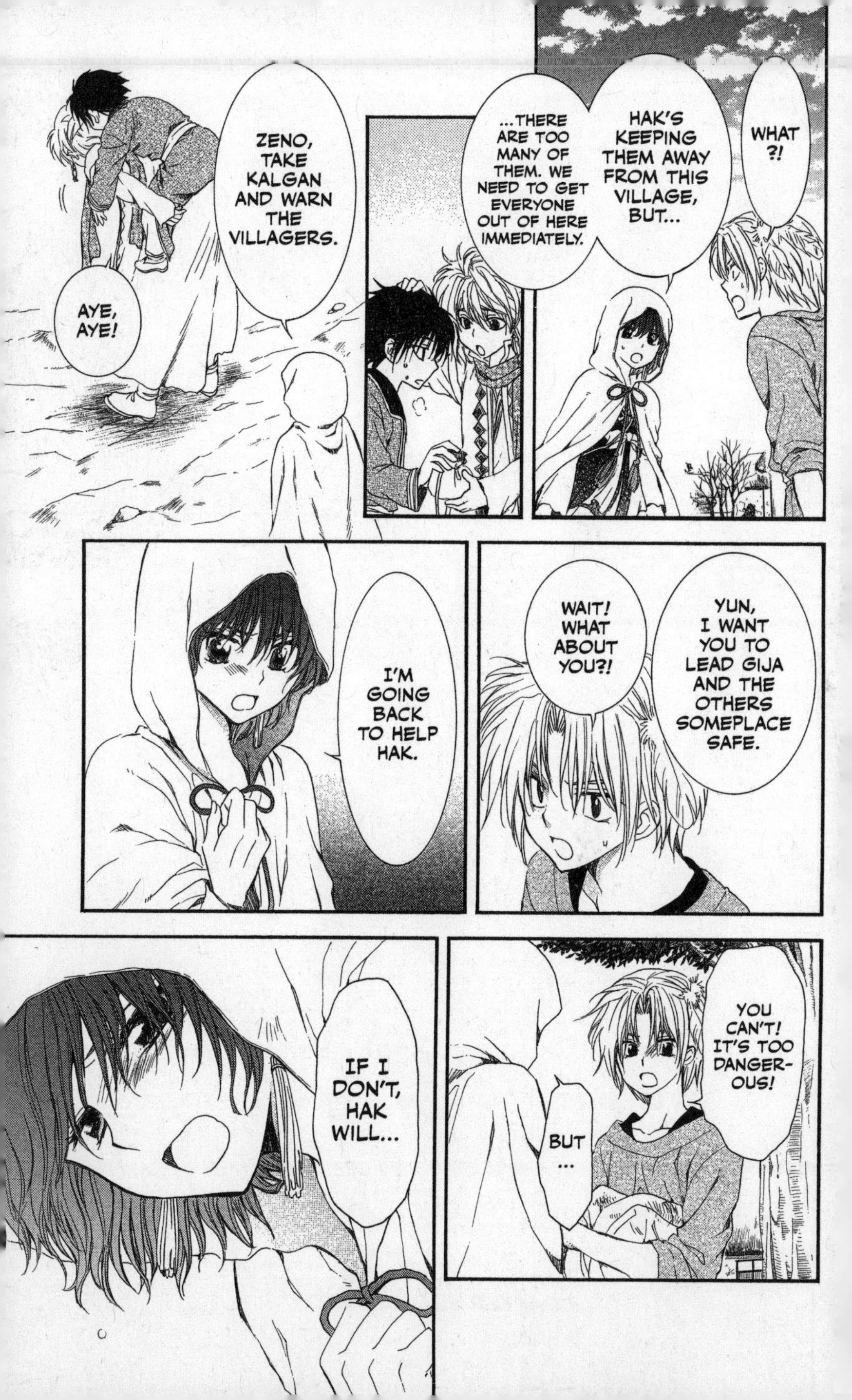
WHAT?!
HAK'S KEEPING THEM AWAY FROM THIS VILLAGE, BUT...
...THERE ARE TOO MANY OF THEM. WE NEED TO GET EVERYONE OUT OF HERE IMMEDIATELY.
ZENO, TAKE KALGAN AND WARN THE VILLAGERS.
AYE, AYE!
YUN, I WANT YOU TO LEAD GIJA AND THE OTHERS SOMEPLACE SAFE.
WAIT! WHAT ABOUT YOU?!
I'M GOING BACK TO HELP HAK.
YOU CAN'T! IT'S TOO DANGER-OUS!
BUT ...
IF I DON'T, HAK WILL...

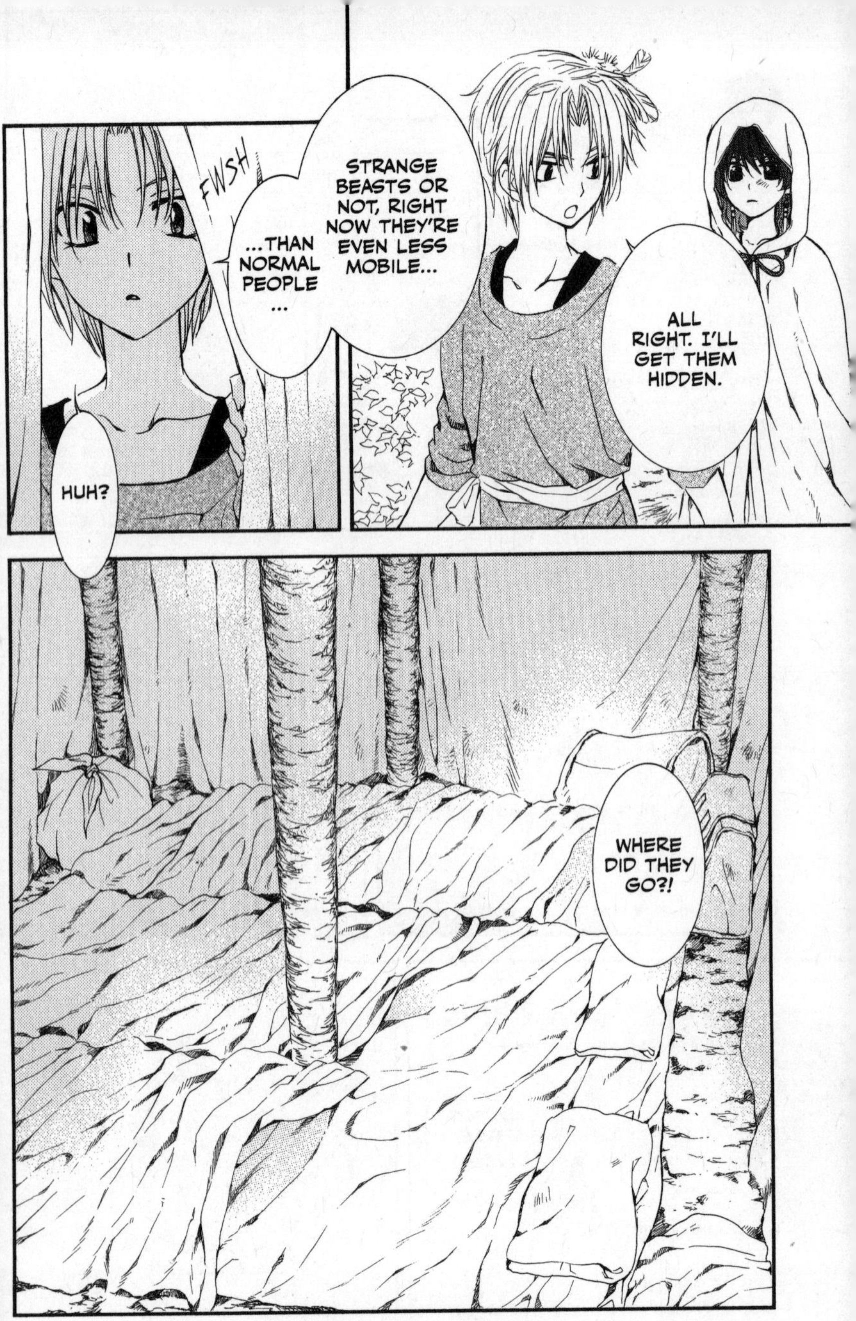
STRANGE BEASTS OR NOT, RIGHT NOW THEY'RE EVEN LESS MOBILE...
...THAN NORMAL PEOPLE ...
ALL RIGHT. I'LL GET THEM HIDDEN.
FWSH
HUH?
WHERE DID THEY GO?!

***CHAPTER 98 / THE END***

People often ask me about the Yona characters' birthdays. I wasn't sure how to create a calendar for this world, so I decided to do something readers would enjoy. I'm only doing the main characters for now. (Hak's birthday was already decided for a *Hana to Yume* campaign, but forget about that.) As you can see, I've picked these dates entirely for fun. I'm totally into it!

Yona→4/7 (Because she's Yo [4]-na [7]*)
Hak→8/9 (Because he's Ha [8]-ku [9])
Su-won → 2/3 (Insomnia (Fu [2]-min [3]) Day)
Yun → 9/25 (Housewife Day of Rest)
Gija → 4/6 (Day of White (Shi [4]-ro [6]))
Sinha →1/3 (Eye (Hito [1] - mi [3]) Day)
Jaeha → 5/4 (Greenery Day)
Zeno→8/30 (Happy Sunshine Day, a day on which you smile as bright as the sun and feel happy.)

Su-won seems like he's an insomniac (according to my sister), so I made it 2/3. 2/3 is also Setsubun and my birthday, so I was a bit hesitant, but I suppose it shouldn't influence my decision. Another option I had for Yun was Genius (Ten [10]-sa [3]-i [1]) Day, but I ended up choosing Housewife Day of Rest.

On the next page are the results of a character popularity poll in *Hana to Yume*!

*The numbers in brackets correspond with the phonetic syllables listed next to them.

Bonus

**Happy birthday**

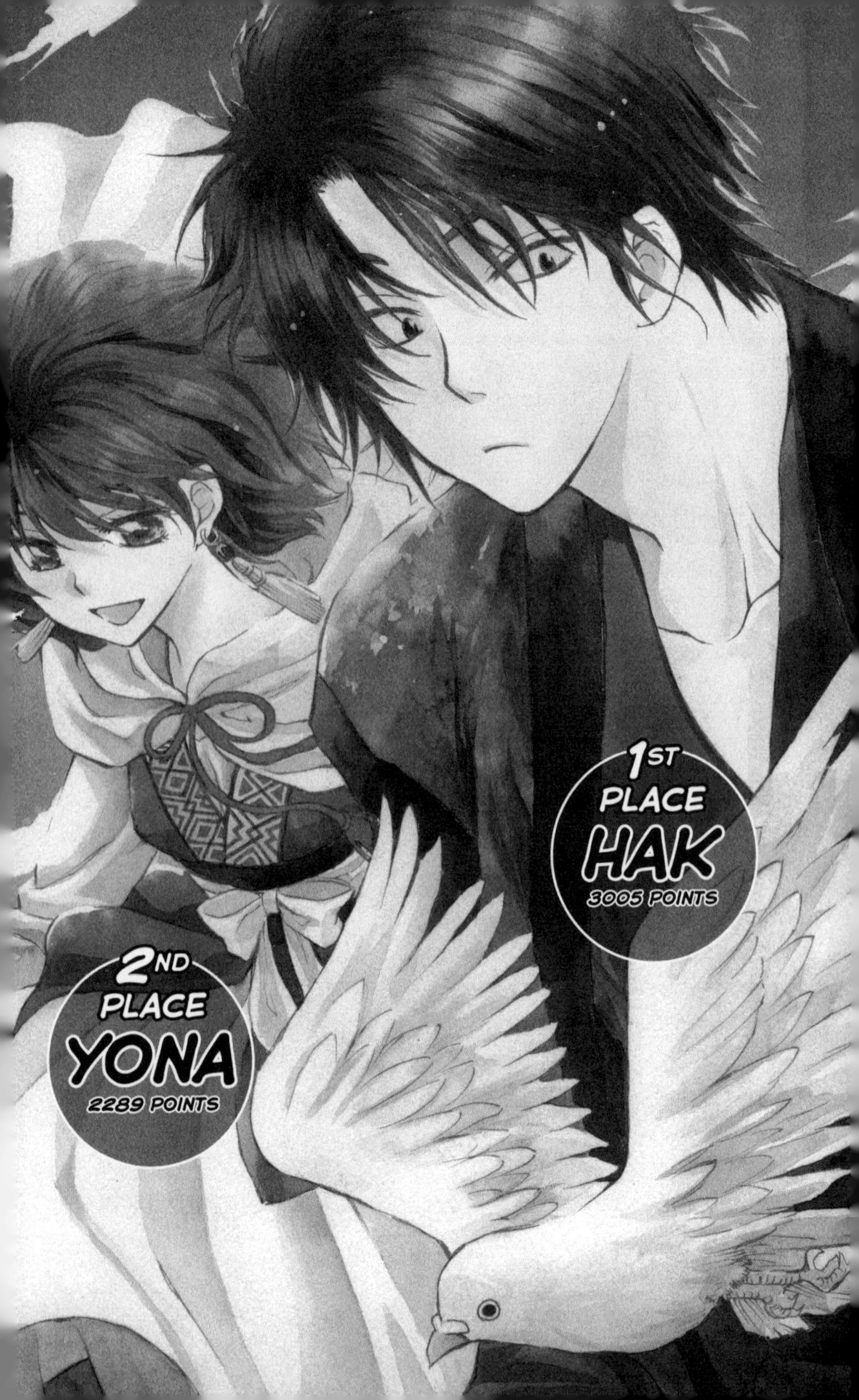
1ST PLACE
HAK
3005 POINTS
2ND PLACE
YONA
2289 POINTS

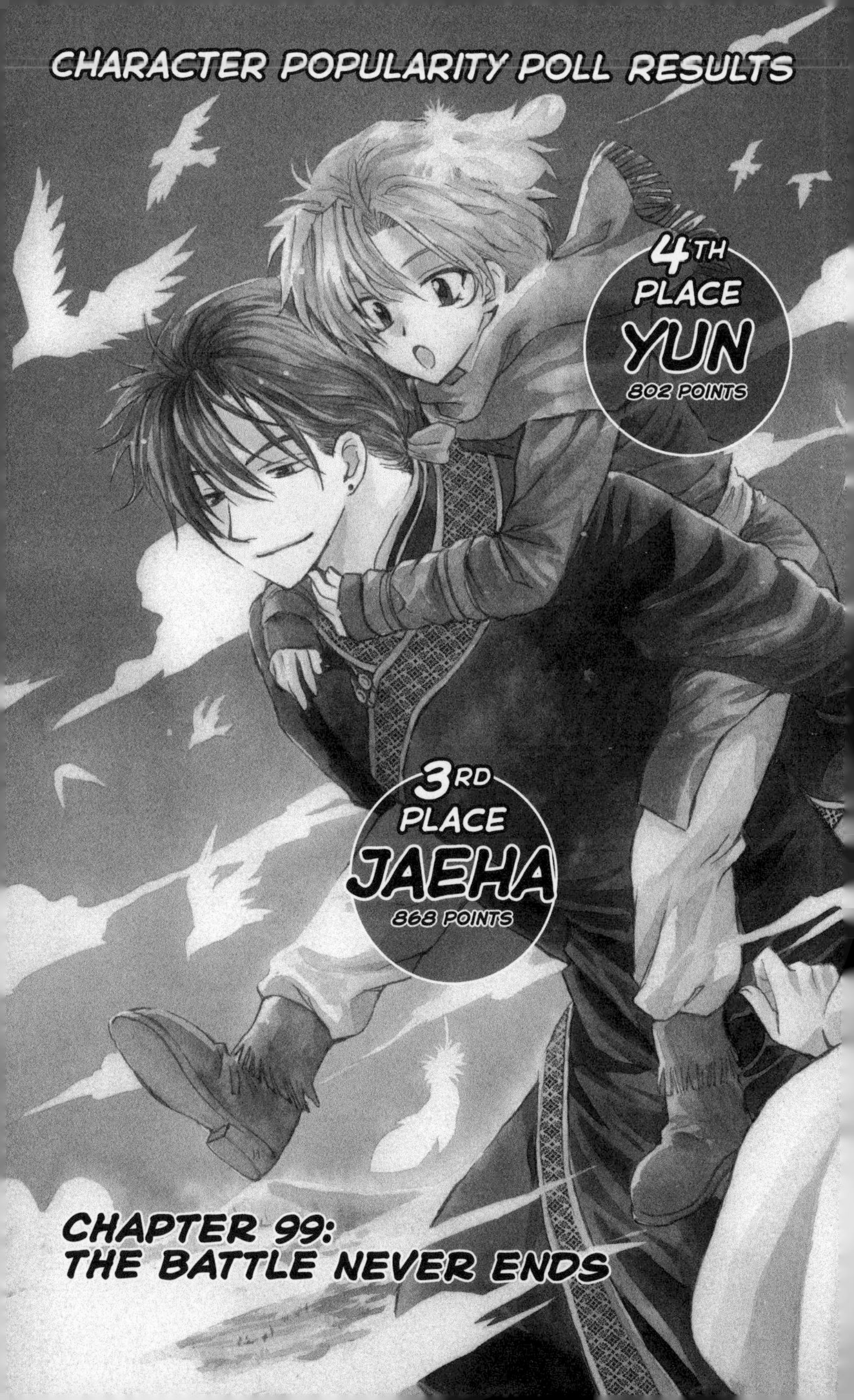
CHARACTER POPULARITY POLL RESULTS
4TH PLACE
YUN
802 POINTS
3RD PLACE
JAEHA
868 POINTS
CHAPTER 99:
THE BATTLE NEVER ENDS

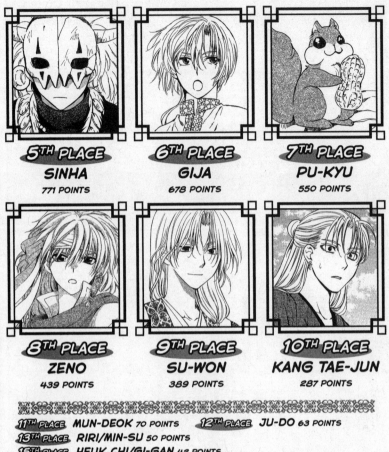

**5TH PLACE**
**SINHA**
771 POINTS

**6TH PLACE**
**GIJA**
678 POINTS

**7TH PLACE**
**PU-KYU**
550 POINTS

**8TH PLACE**
**ZENO**
439 POINTS

**9TH PLACE**
**SU-WON**
389 POINTS

**10TH PLACE**
**KANG TAE-JUN**
287 POINTS

11TH PLACE **MUN-DEOK** 70 POINTS
12TH PLACE **JU-DO** 63 POINTS
13TH PLACE **RIRI/MIN-SU** 50 POINTS
15TH PLACE **HEUK CHI/GI-GAN** 42 POINTS
17TH PLACE **YI GEUN-TAE** 28 POINTS
18TH PLACE **YUNO** 24 POINTS
19TH PLACE **TAE-U** 22 POINTS
20TH PLACE **HYEONG-DAE** 13 POINTS
21ST PLACE **AHN JUNG-GI** 12 POINTS
22ND PLACE **TAE-YEON** 11 POINTS
23RD PLACE **AYURA/ KIL-SON** 8 POINTS
25TH PLACE **TETRA** 7 POINTS
26TH PLACE **KEISHUK/IL** 6 POINTS
28TH PLACE **PREVIOUS BLUE DRAGON** 5 POINTS
29TH PLACE **KANG KYO-GA/YU-HON/IK-SU** 4 POINTS
32ND PLACE **MIZUHO KUSANAGI** 3 POINTS
33RD PLACE **KALGAN/GRANNY/MEERCAT** 2 POINTS
36TH PLACE **OGI/CHUL-RANG/GAROU/GIJA'S DAD** 1 POINT

*3 POINTS WERE GIVEN TO THE FIRST FAVORITE, 2 POINTS FOR THE SECOND FAVORITE AND 1 POINT FOR THE THIRD FAVORITE

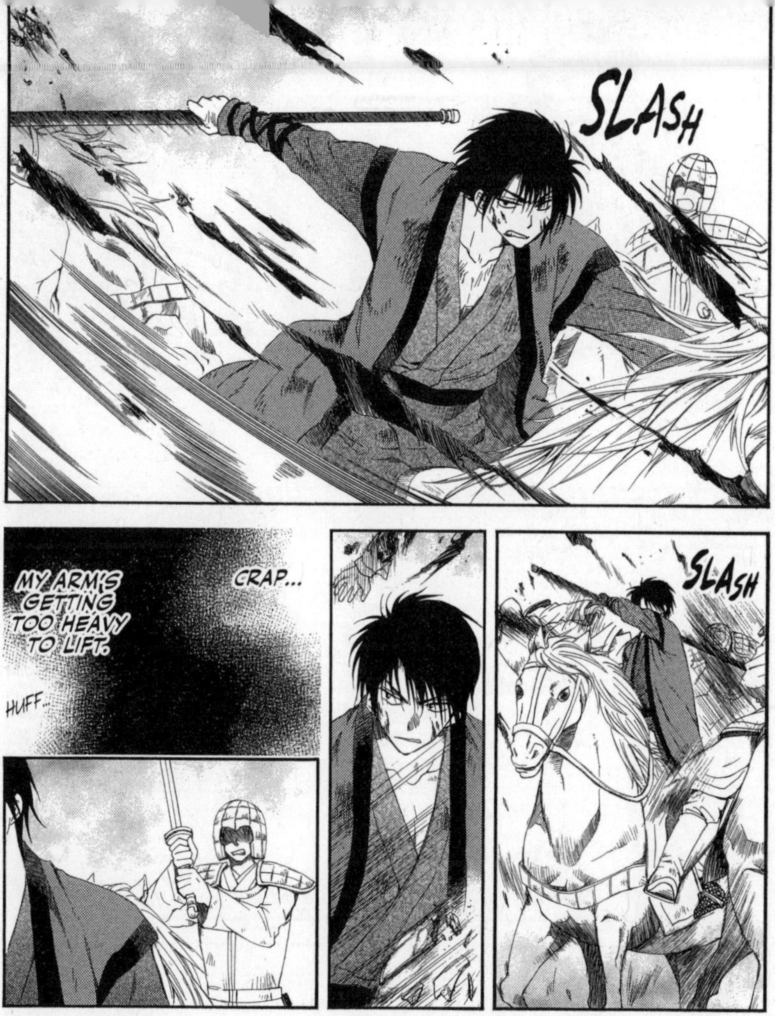
SLASH
SLASH
CRAP...
MY ARM'S GETTING TOO HEAVY TO LIFT.
HUFF...

Special thanks to all the people who've helped me.
My assistants → Mikorun, C.F., Oka, Awafuji, Ryo Sakura, Ryo, Eika and my little sister...
My editors Ishihara and Takizawa, my previous editors and the *Hana to Yume* editorial office...
Everyone who's involved in creating and selling *Yona*-related merchandise...
Family and friends who've always supported me...
And of course you, for reading this! Thank you so much.
I'll keep doing my very best, so I hope to see you around!
I make announcements on my blog and on Twitter, where I'm @KusanagiMizuho.

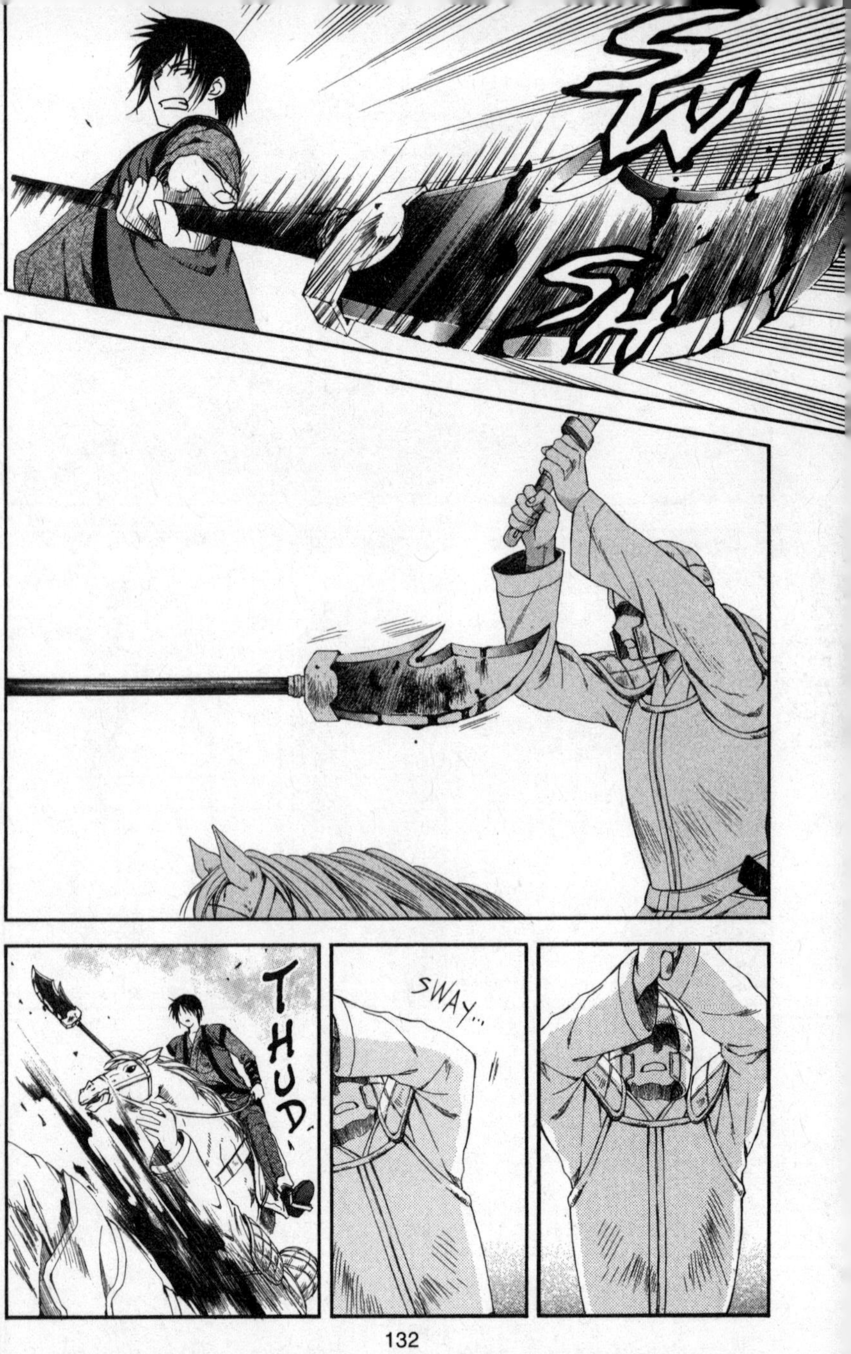
SWSH
SWAY...
THUD

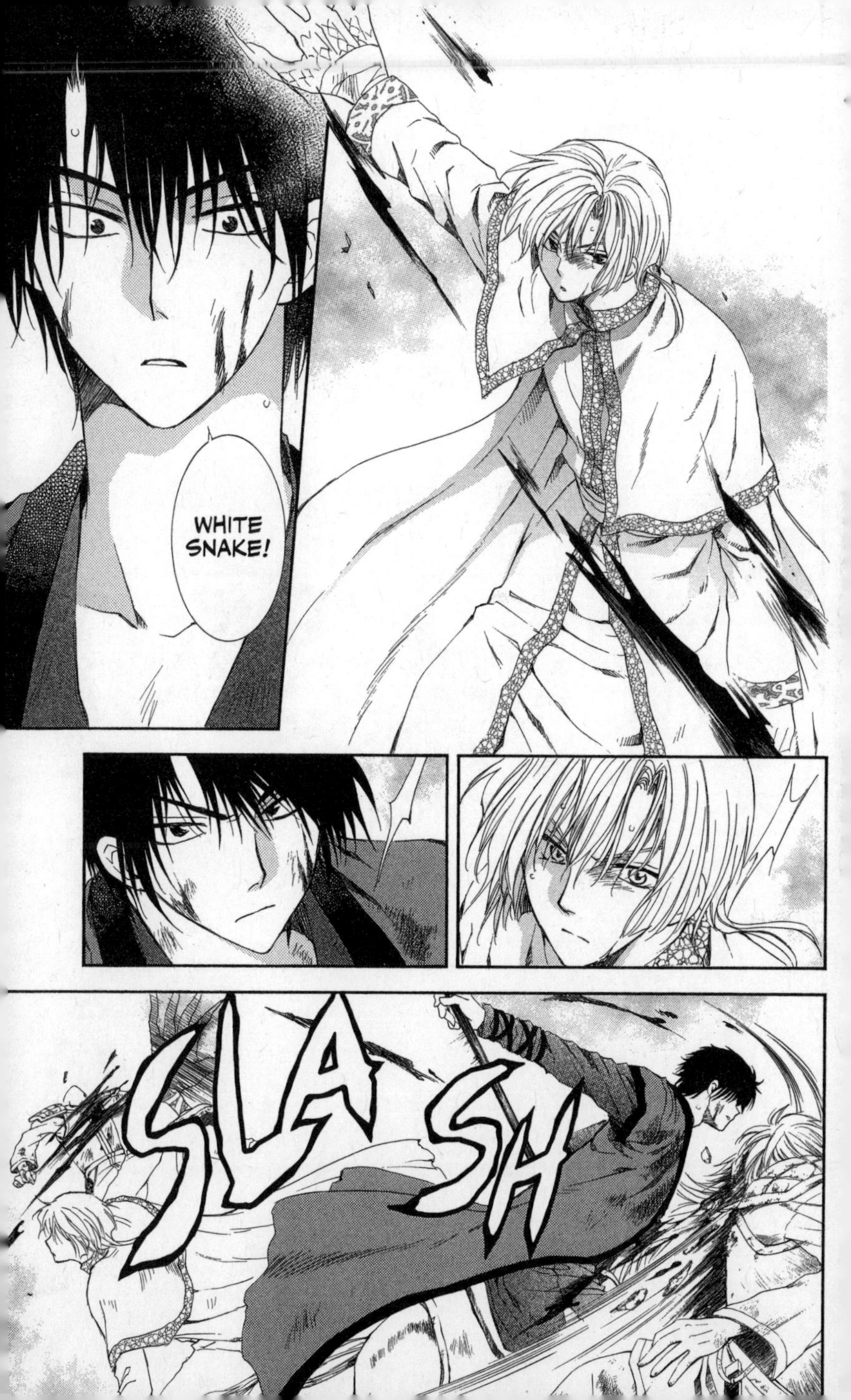
WHITE SNAKE!
SLASH

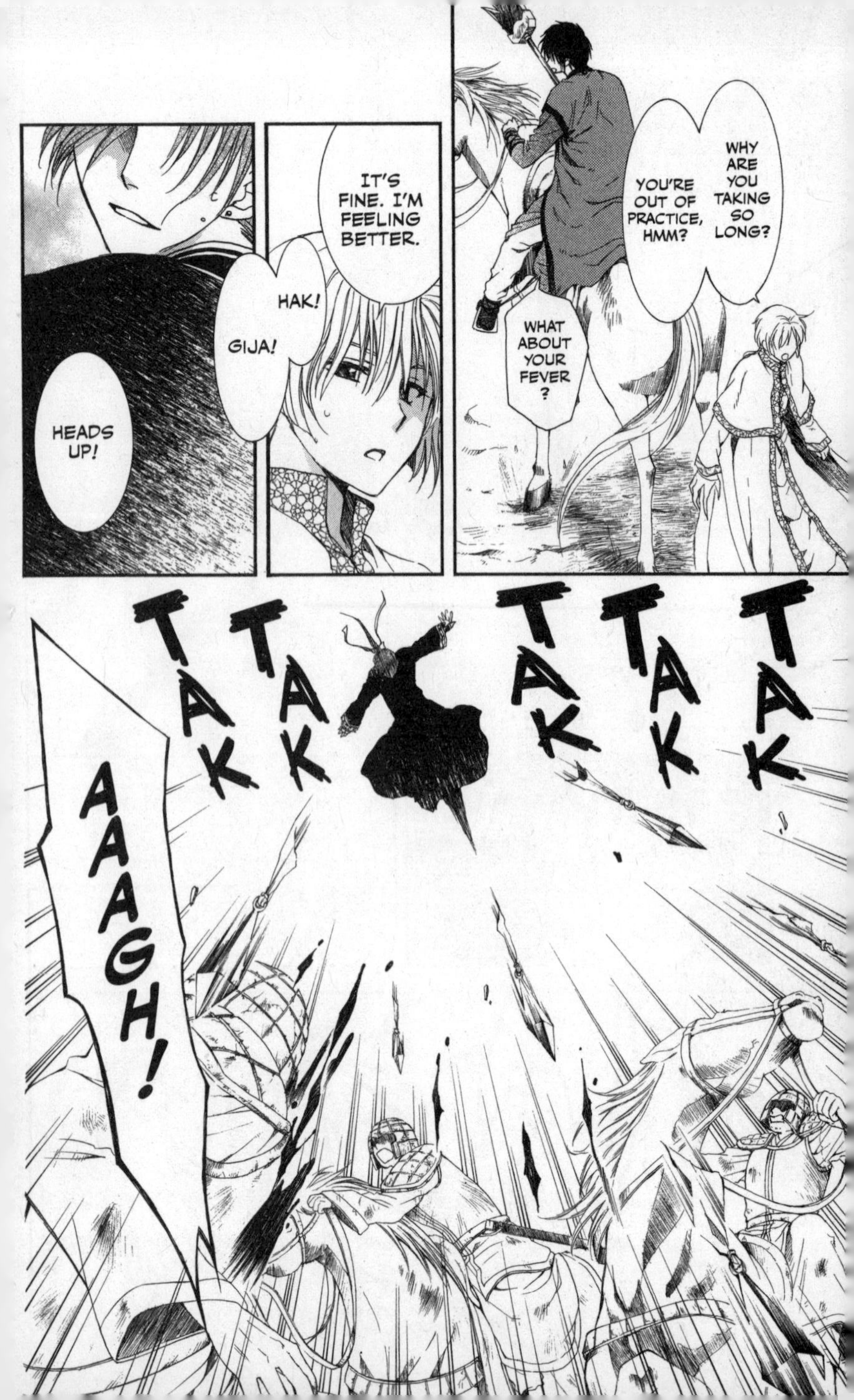
WHY ARE YOU TAKING SO LONG?
YOU'RE OUT OF PRACTICE, HMM?
WHAT ABOUT YOUR FEVER?
IT'S FINE. I'M FEELING BETTER.
HAK!
GIJA!
HEADS UP!
TAK
TAK
TAK
TAK
TAK
AAAGH!

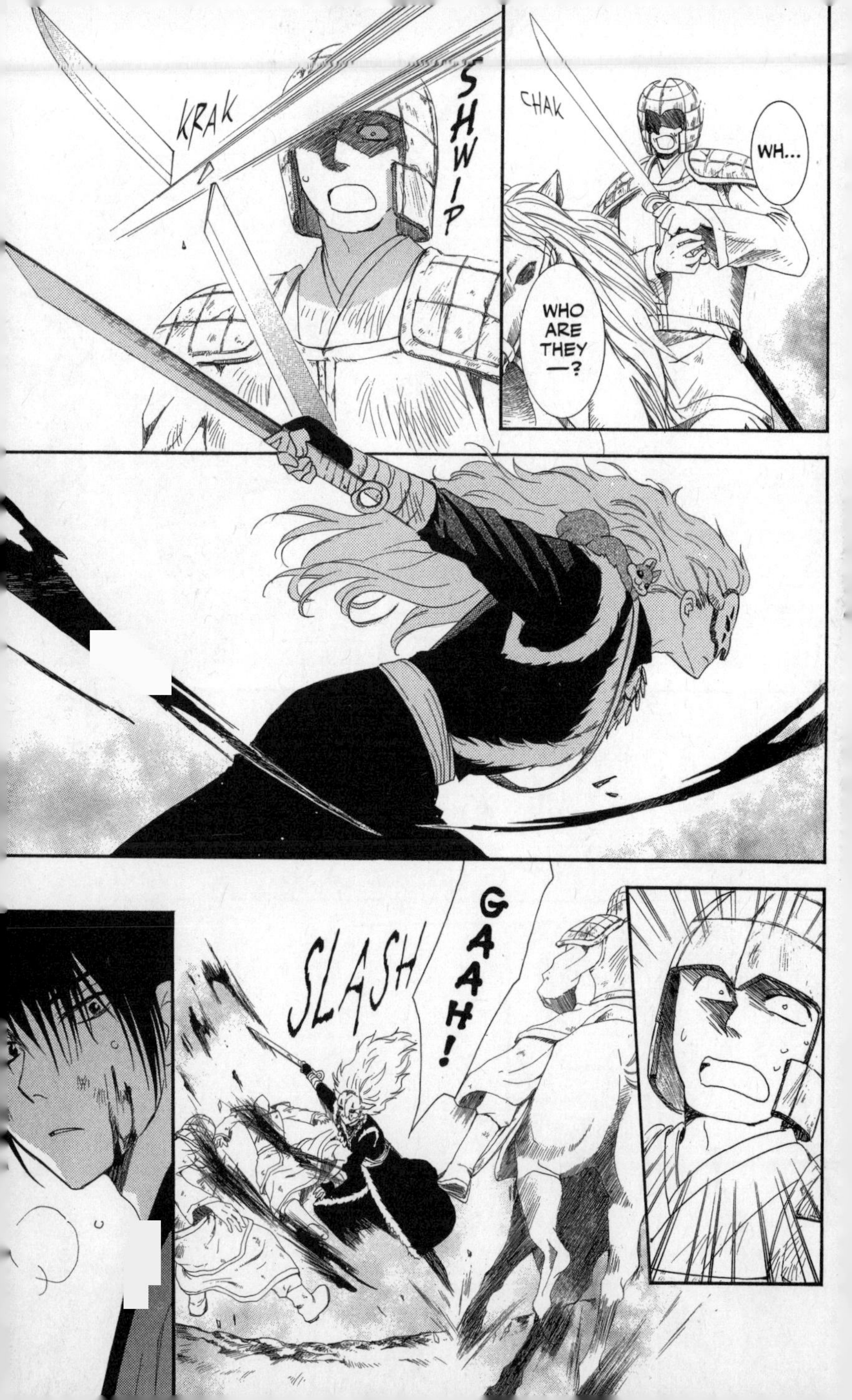
CHAK
WH...
WHO ARE THEY —?
KRAK
SHWIP
GAAH!
SLASH

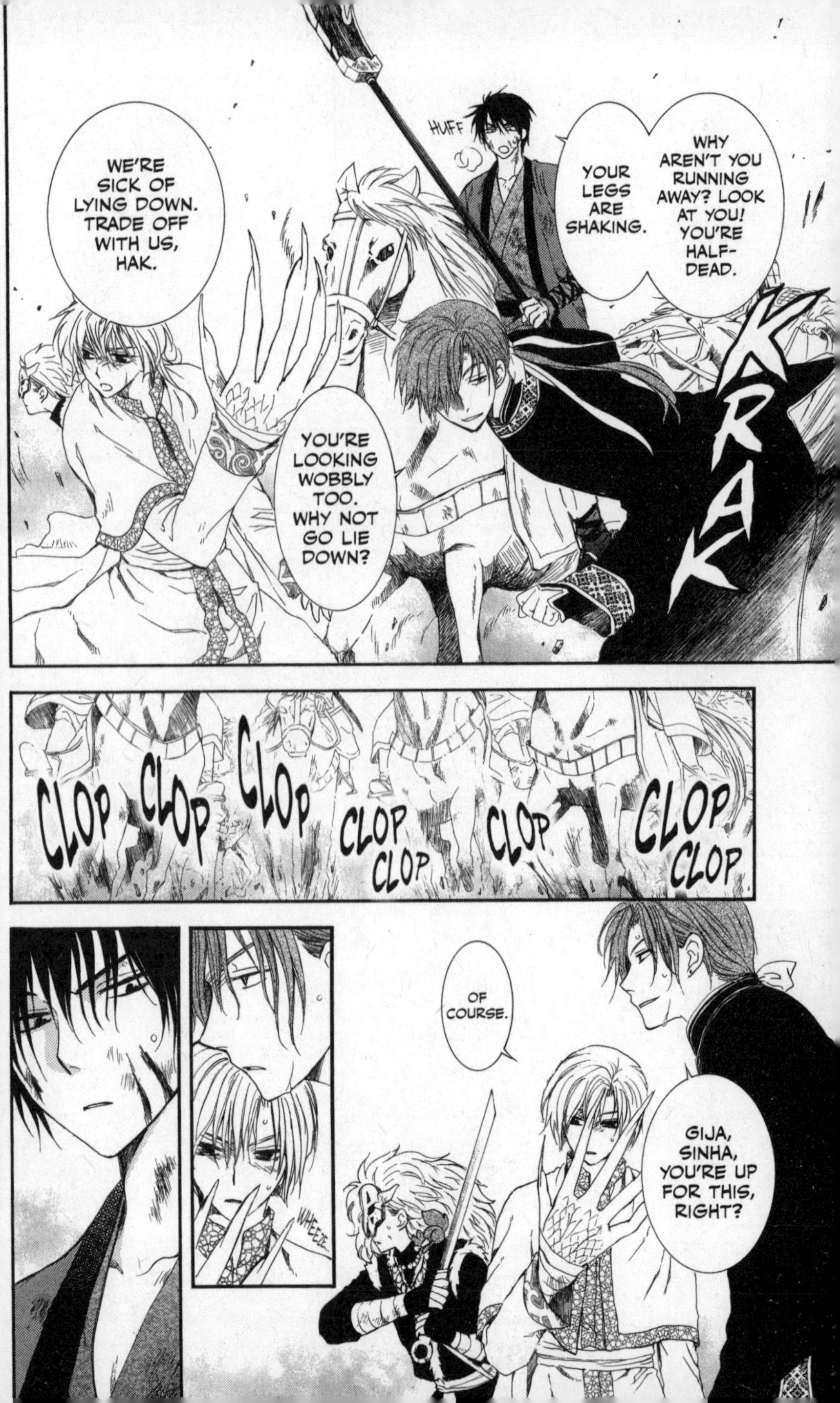
WHY AREN'T YOU RUNNING AWAY? LOOK AT YOU! YOU'RE HALF-DEAD.
YOUR LEGS ARE SHAKING.
HUFF
WE'RE SICK OF LYING DOWN. TRADE OFF WITH US, HAK.
KRAK
YOU'RE LOOKING WOBBLY TOO. WHY NOT GO LIE DOWN?
CLOP CLOP CLOP CLOP CLOP CLOP CLOP CLOP CLOP
GIJA, SINHA, YOU'RE UP FOR THIS, RIGHT?
OF COURSE.
WHEEZE...

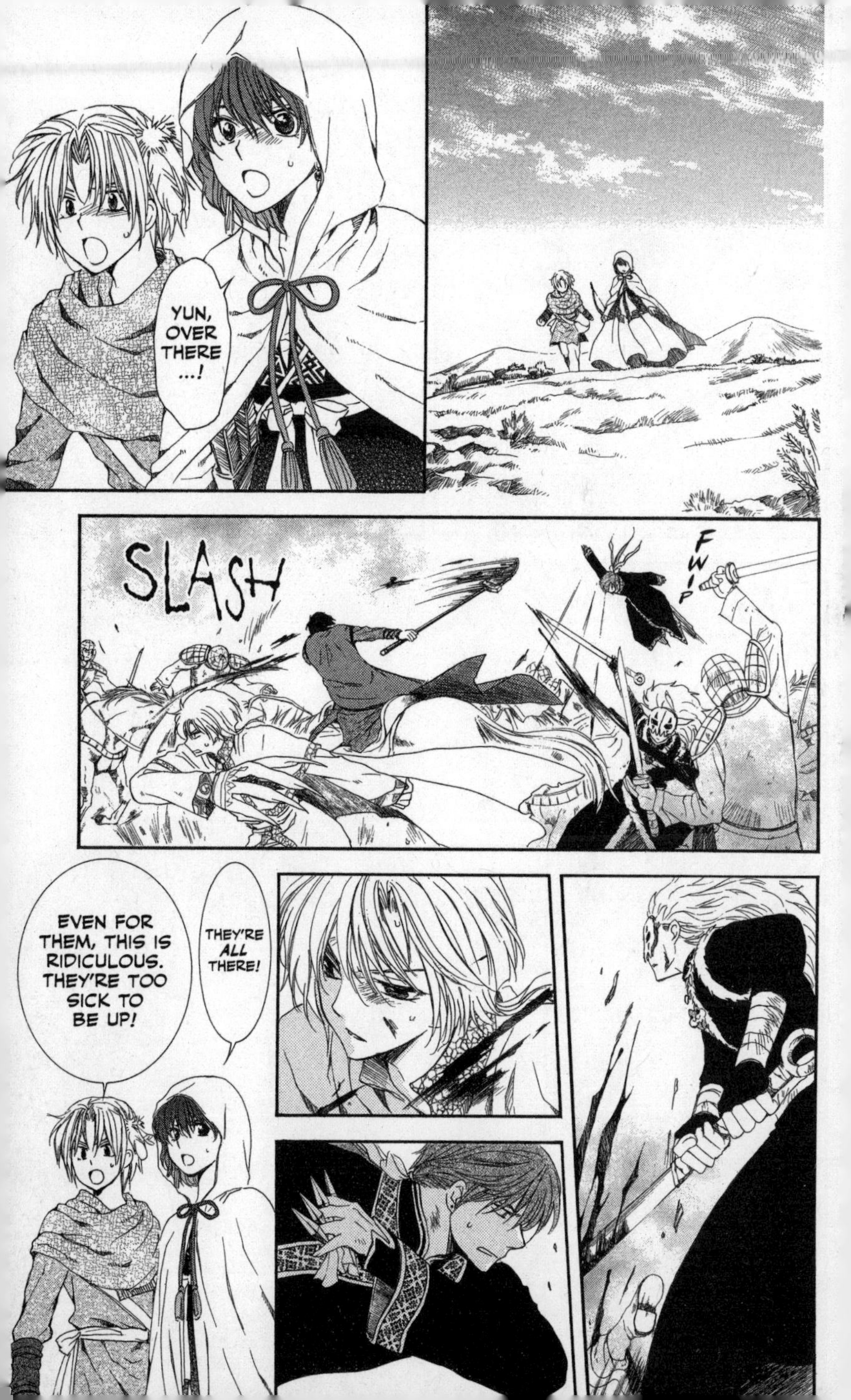
YUN, OVER THERE ...!
FWIP
SLASH
THEY'RE *ALL* THERE!
EVEN FOR THEM, THIS IS RIDICULOUS. THEY'RE TOO SICK TO BE UP!

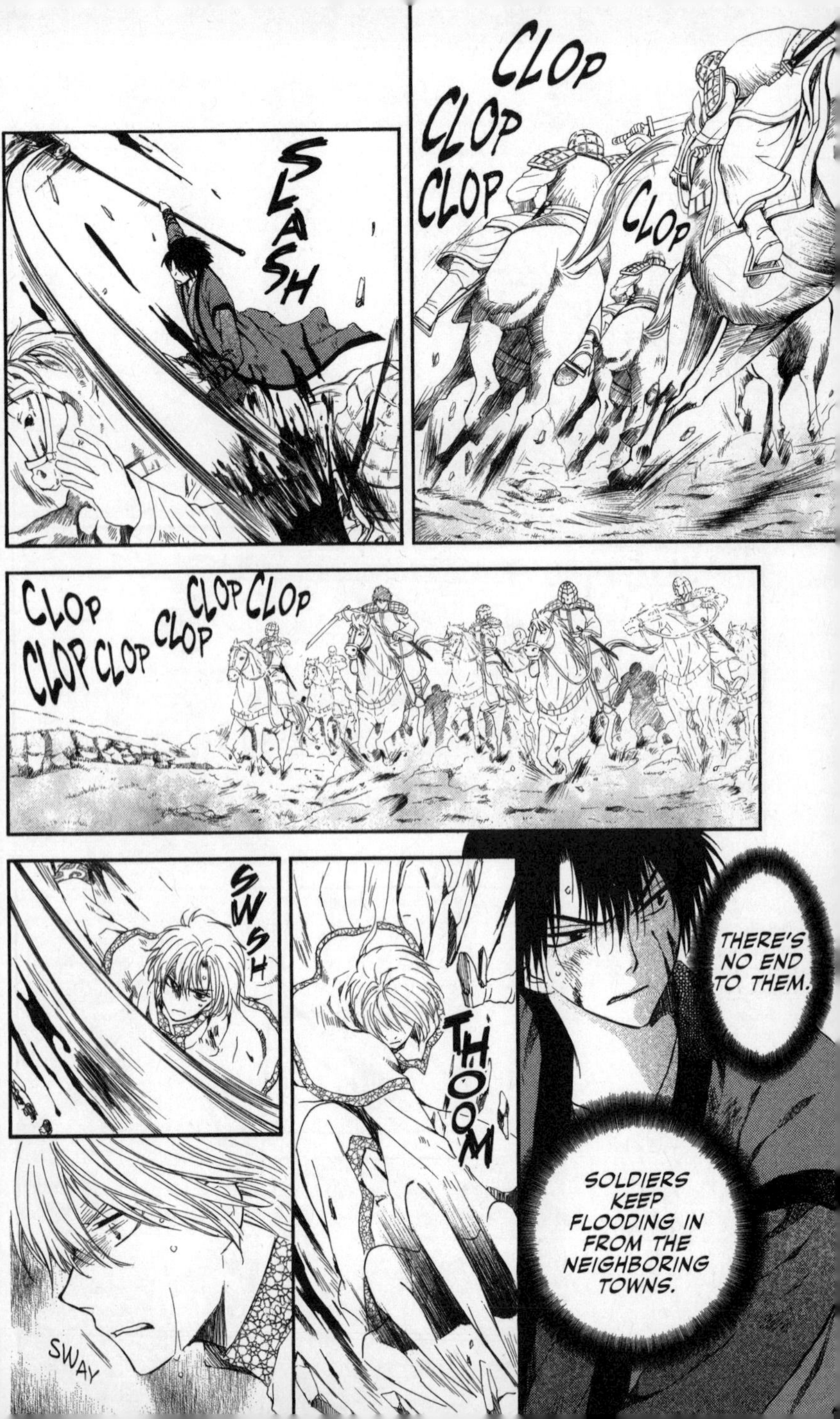
CLOP
CLOP
CLOP
CLOP
SLASH
CLOP CLOP
CLOP
CLOP
CLOP CLOP
THERE'S NO END TO THEM.
SOLDIERS KEEP FLOODING IN FROM THE NEIGHBORING TOWNS.
THOOM
SWSH
SWAY

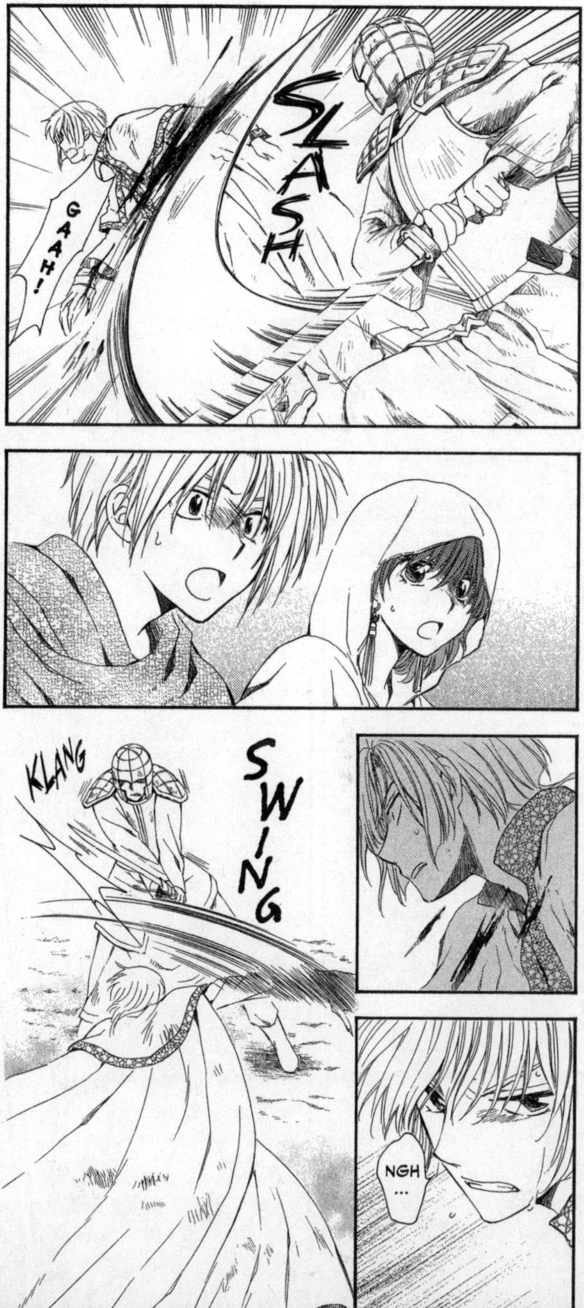
SLASH
GAAH!
NGH...
SWING
KLANG

Thanks to the anime, the people in Gi-gan's pirate crew from the Awa arc have names! I always wanted them to, so I'm delighted. It's a bit late in the game, but let me introduce you to Jaeha's old friends.

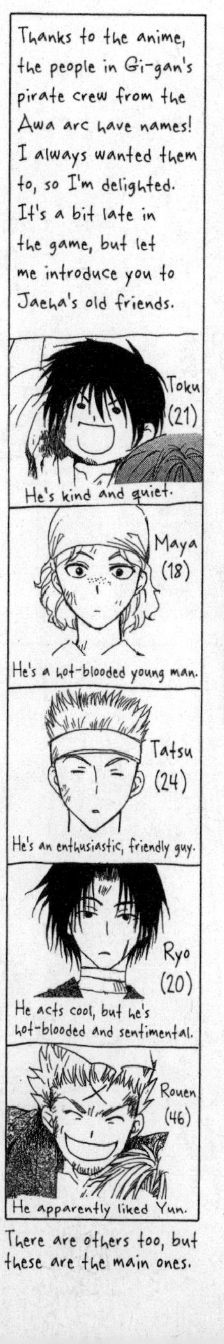
Toku (21)
He's kind and quiet.
Maya (18)
He's a hot-blooded young man.
Tatsu (24)
He's an enthusiastic, friendly guy.
Ryo (20)
He acts cool, but he's hot-blooded and sentimental.
Rouen (46)
He apparently liked Yun.

There are others too, but these are the main ones.

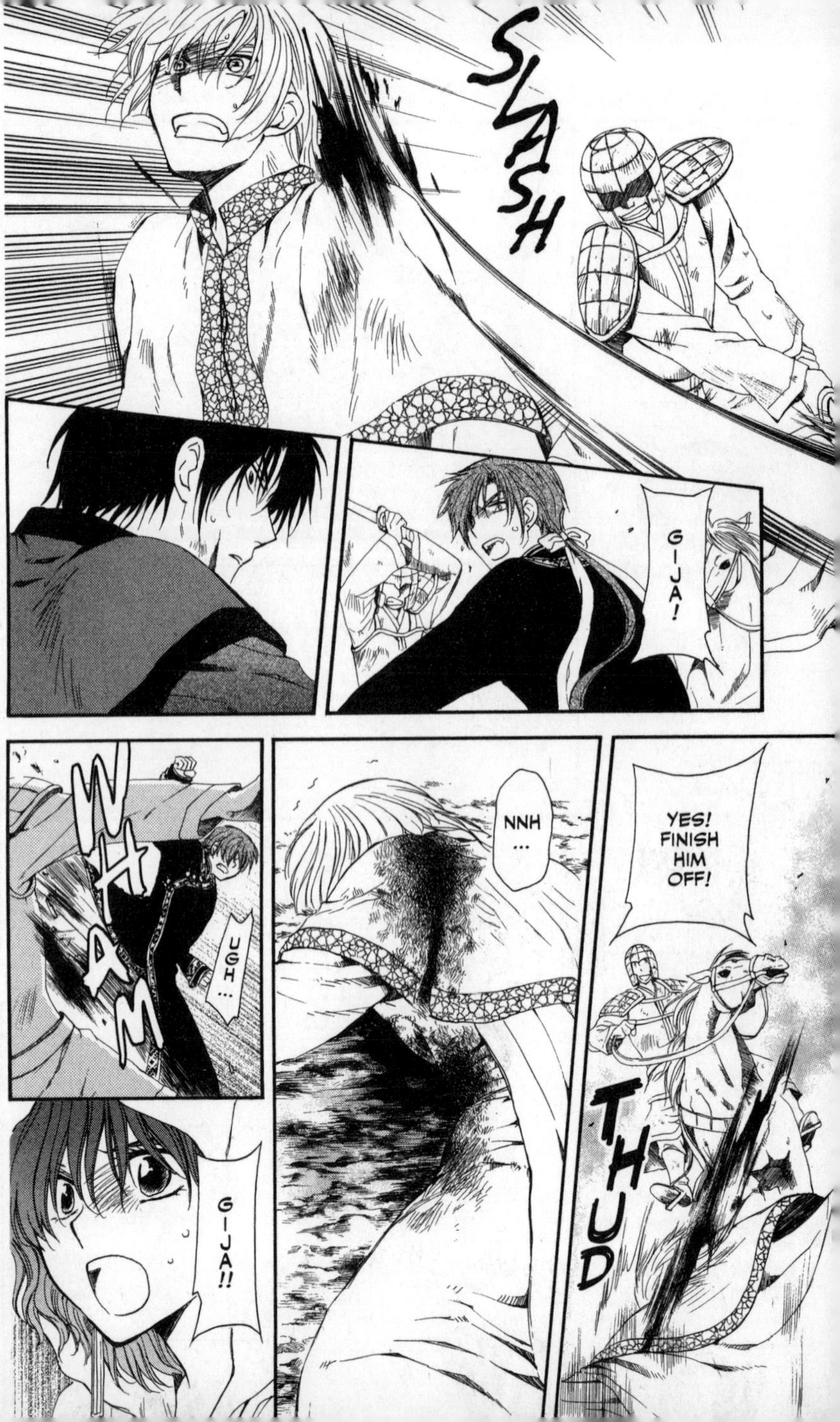
SLASH
GIJA!
YES! FINISH HIM OFF!
NNH ...
WHAM
UGH ...
THUD
GIJA!!

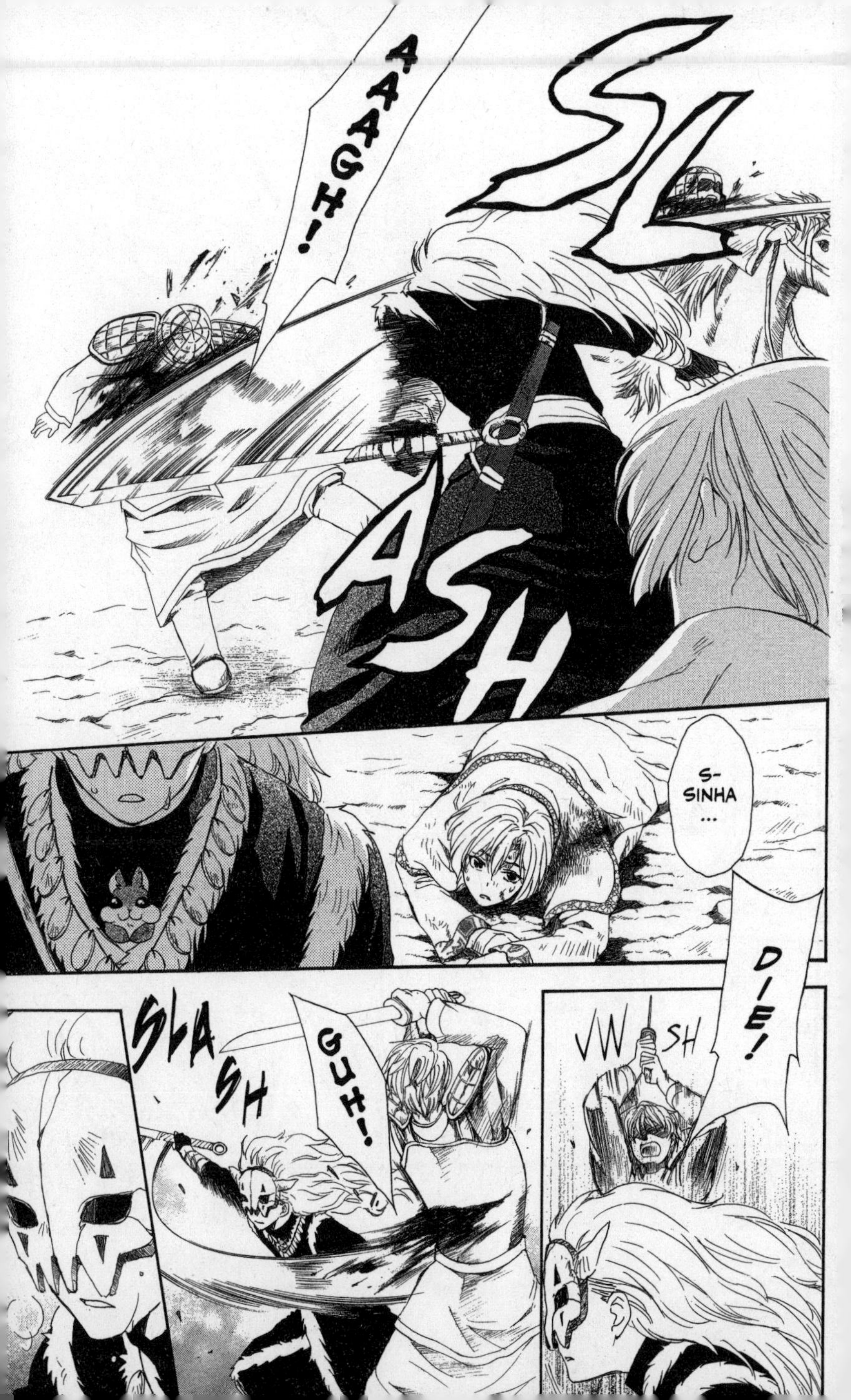
SL
AAAGH!
ASH
S-SINHA...
DIE!
VW SH
GUH!
SLASH

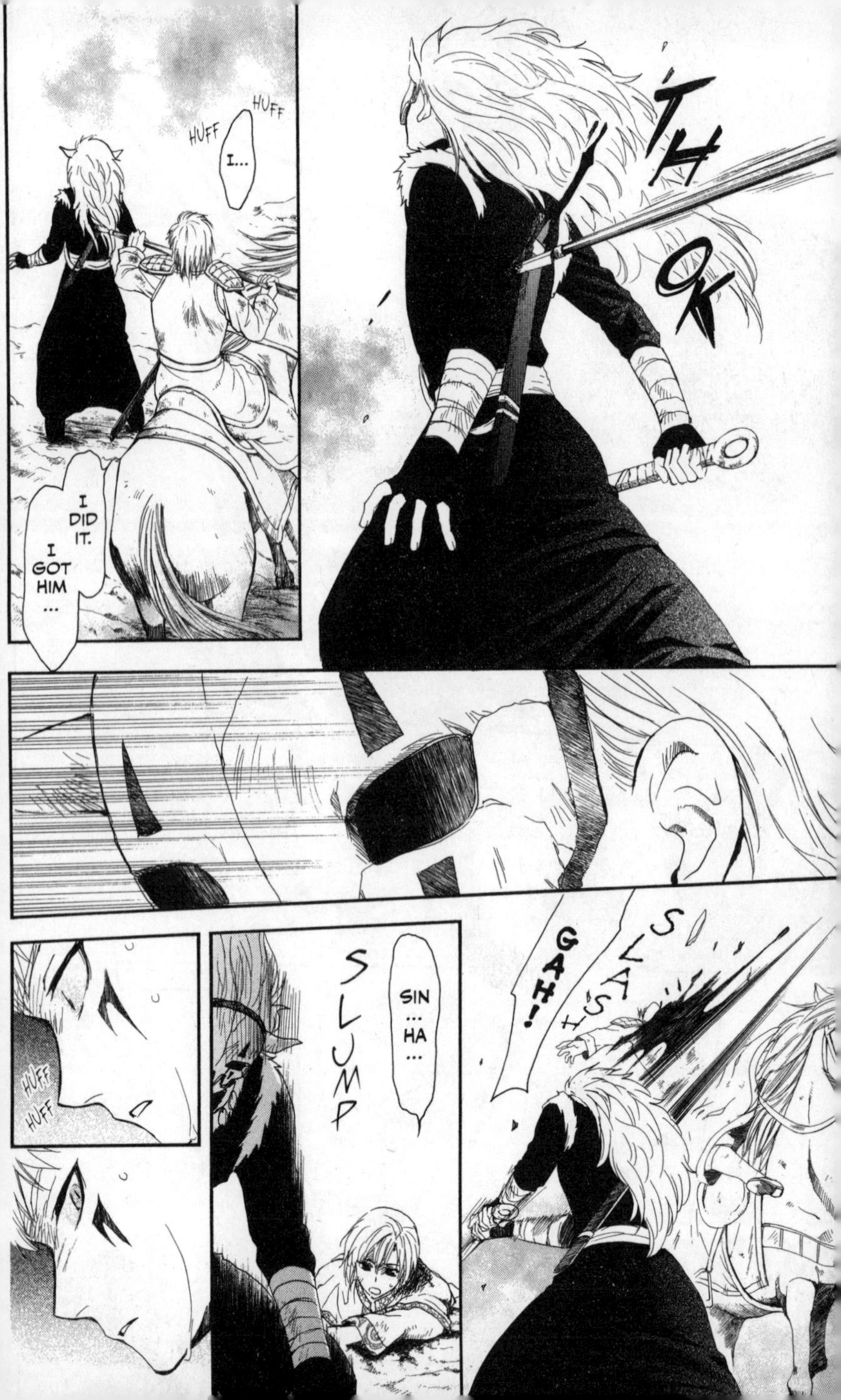
THOK
HUFF
HUFF
I...
I DID IT. I GOT HIM...
SLASH
GAH!
SIN... HA...
SLUMP
HUFF
HUFF

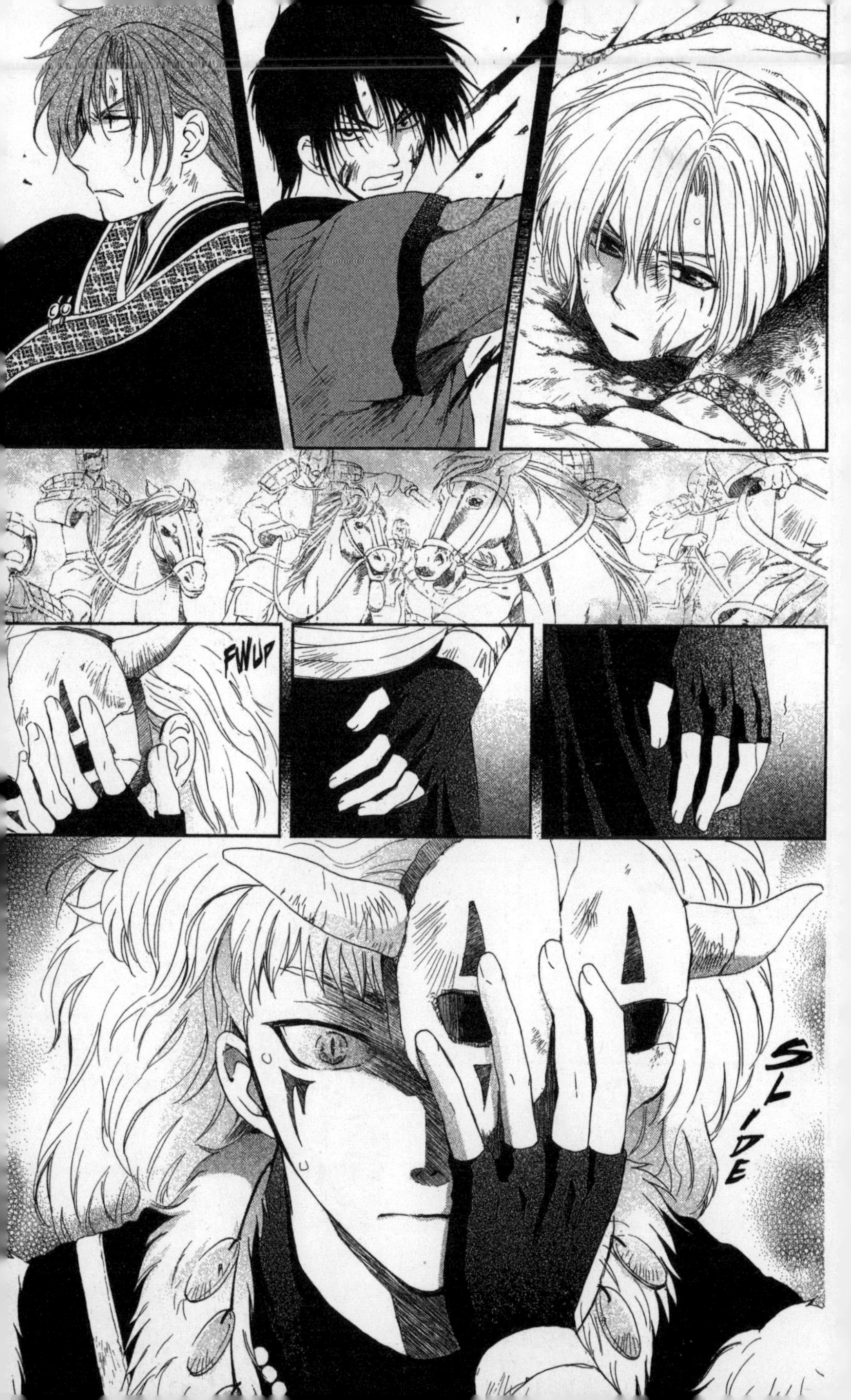
FWUP
SLIDE

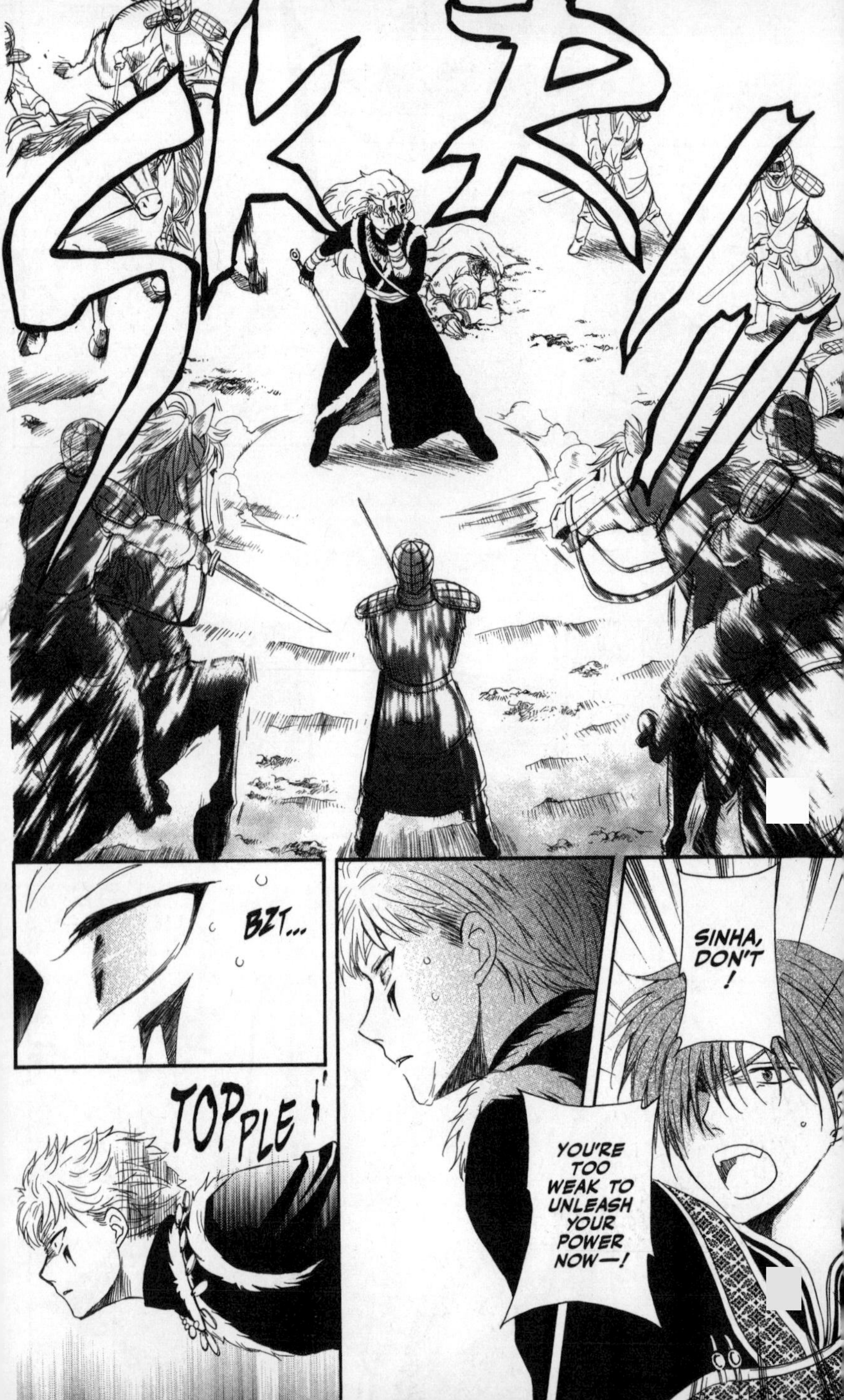
SINHA, DON'T!
YOU'RE TOO WEAK TO UNLEASH YOUR POWER NOW—!
BZT...
TOPPLE

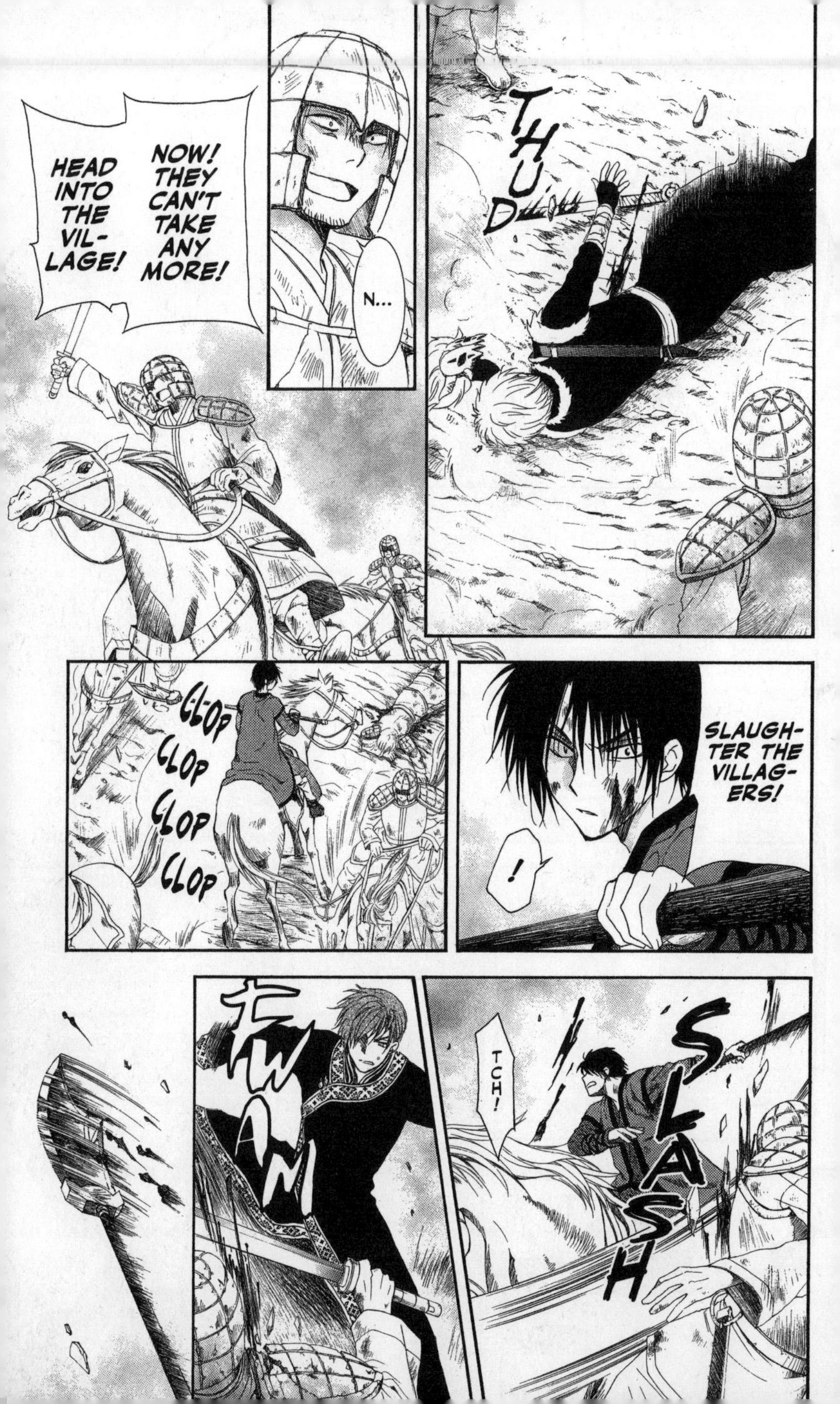
THUD
N...
NOW! THEY CAN'T TAKE ANY MORE!
HEAD INTO THE VIL-LAGE!
SLAUGH-TER THE VILLAG-ERS!
!
CLOP CLOP CLOP CLOP
TCH!
SLASH
TWAM

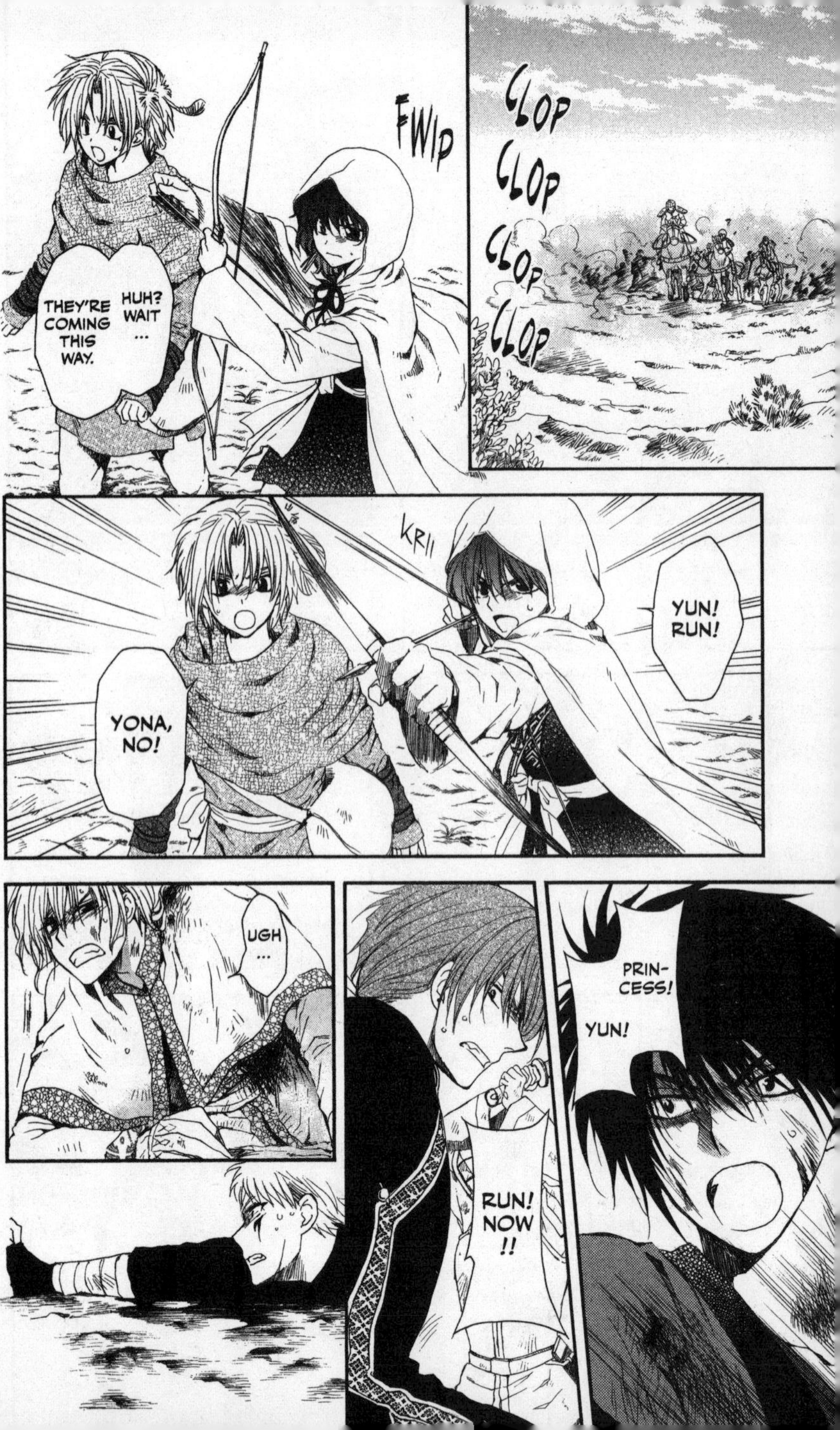
CLOP
CLOP
CLOP
CLOP
FWIP
HUH? WAIT ...
THEY'RE COMING THIS WAY.
KRII
YUN! RUN!
YONA, NO!
PRIN-CESS!
YUN!
RUN! NOW !!
UGH ...

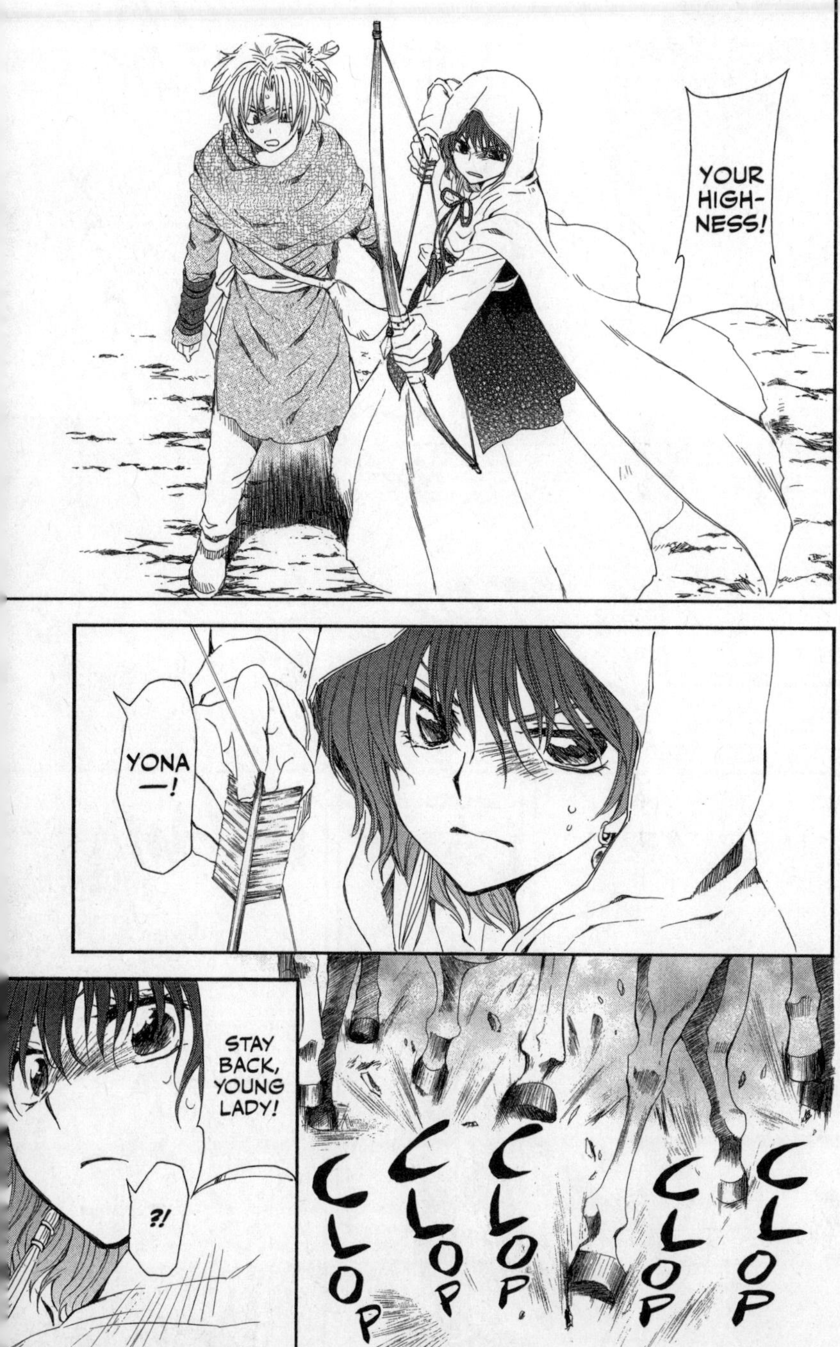
YOUR HIGH-NESS!
YONA—!
CLOP
CLOP
CLOP.
CLOP
CLOP
STAY BACK, YOUNG LADY!
?!

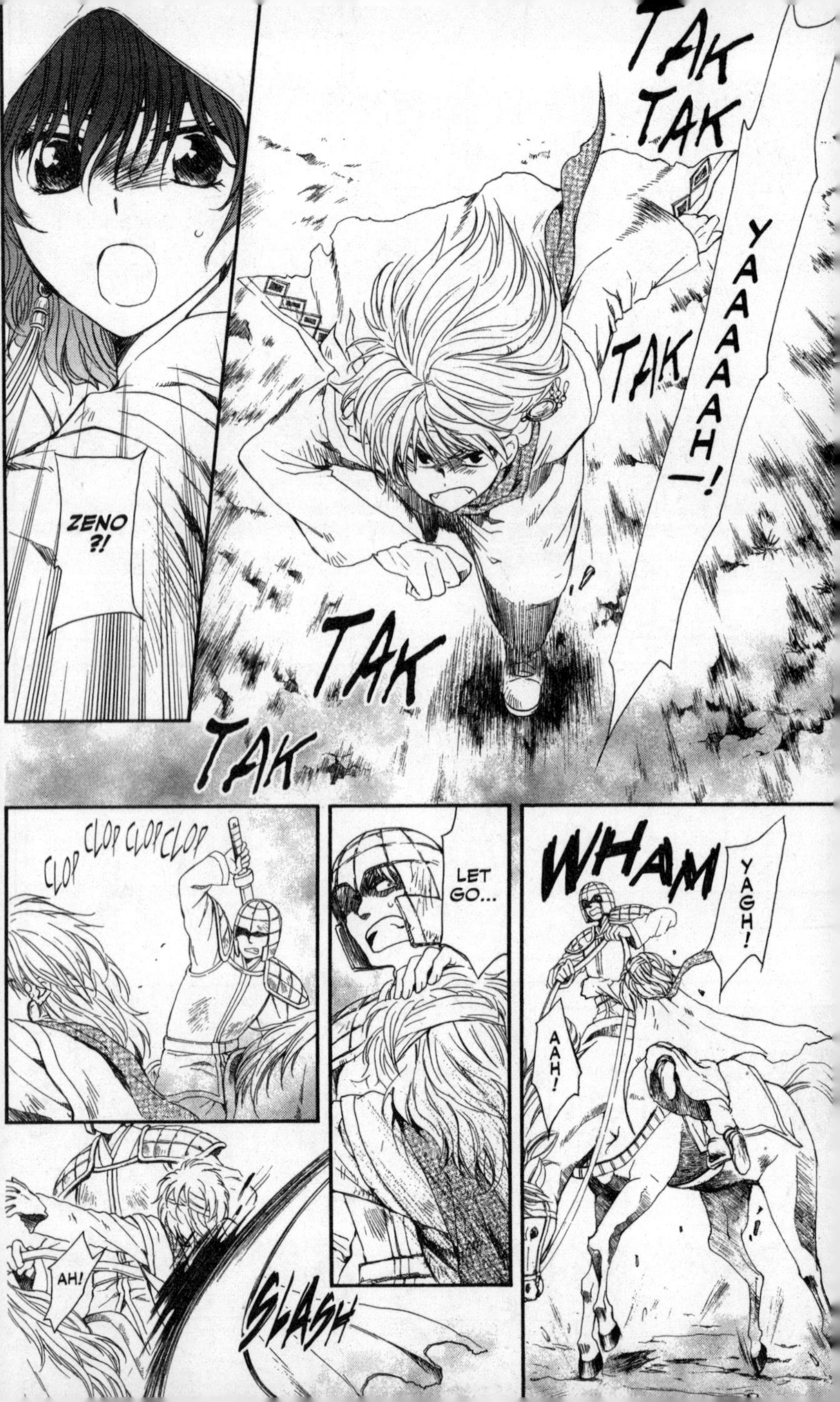
TAK
TAK
YAAAAAAH—!
TAK
TAK
TAK
ZENO?!
WHAM
YAGH!
AAH!
LET GO...
CLOP CLOP CLOP CLOP
AH!
SLASH

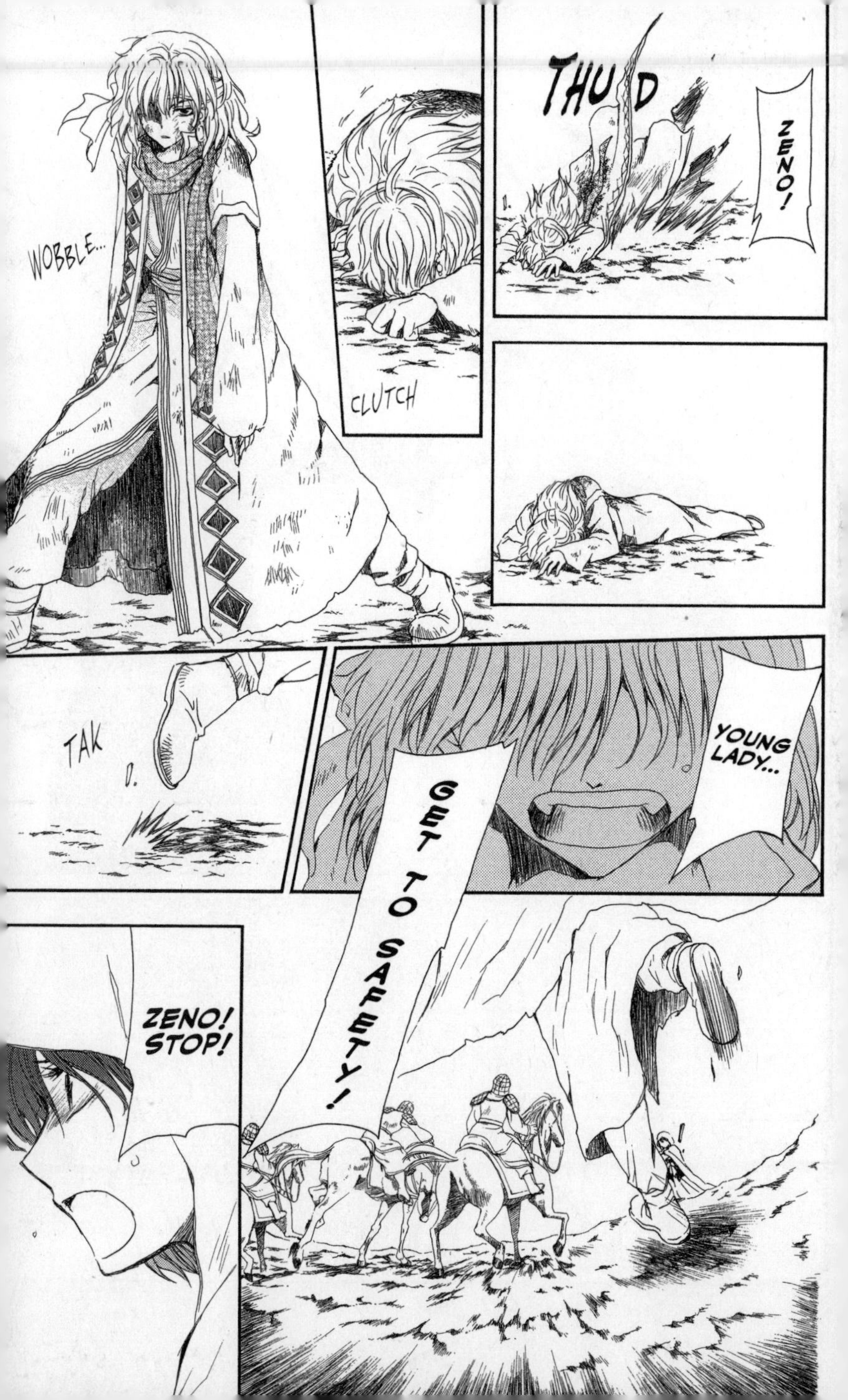
THUD
ZENO!
CLUTCH
WOBBLE...
YOUNG LADY...
TAK
GET TO SAFETY!
ZENO! STOP!

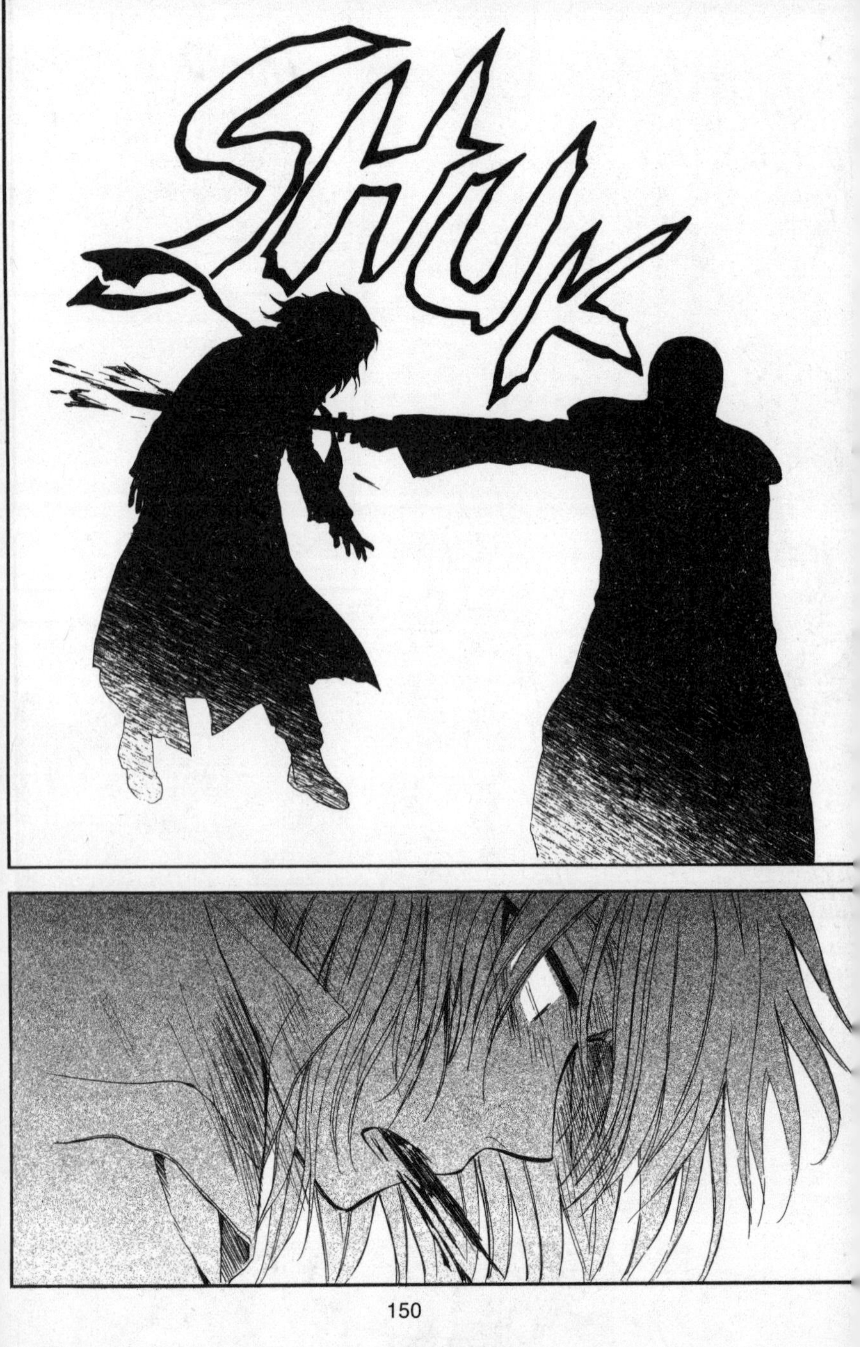
SHTUK

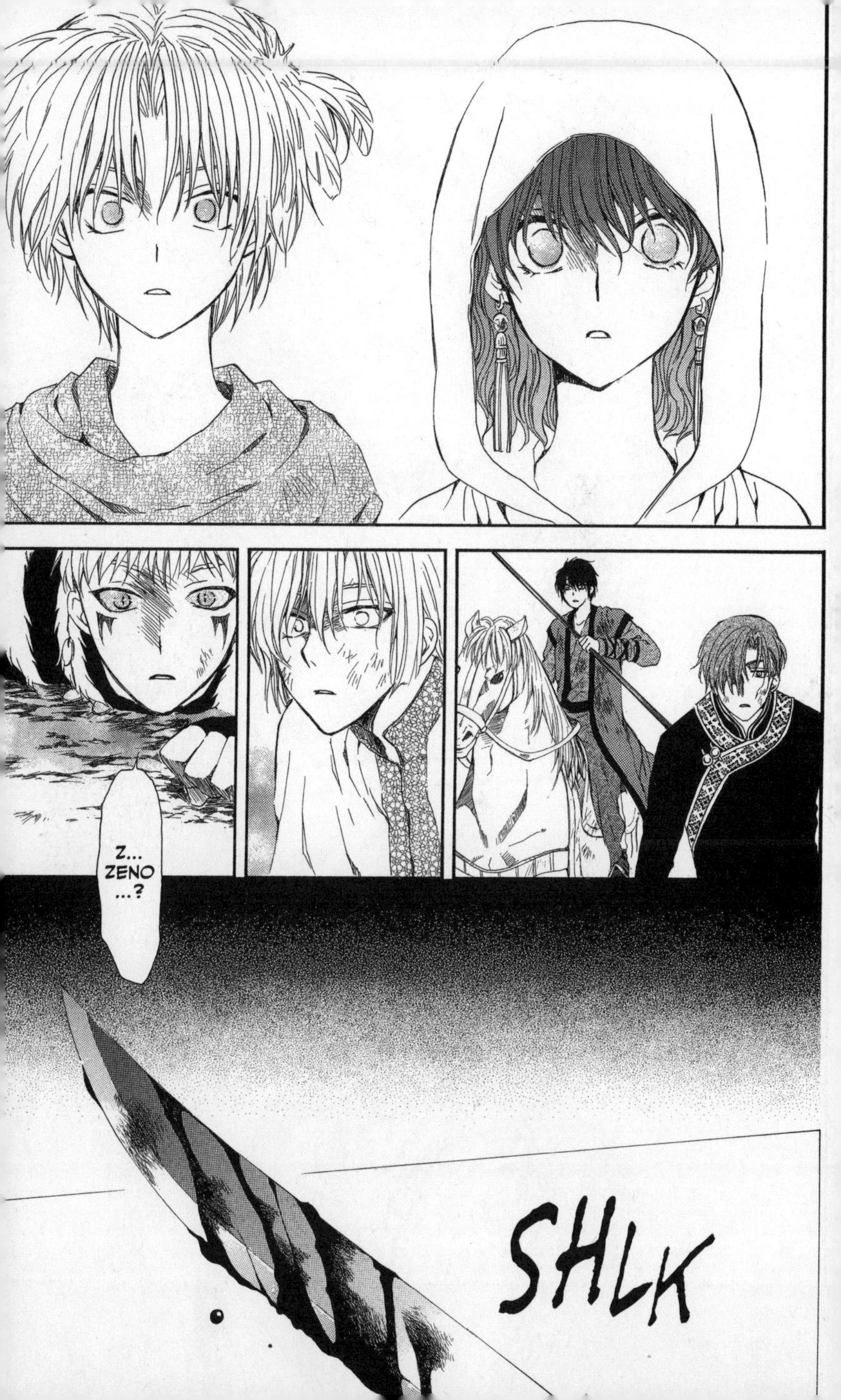
Z... ZENO ...?
SHLK

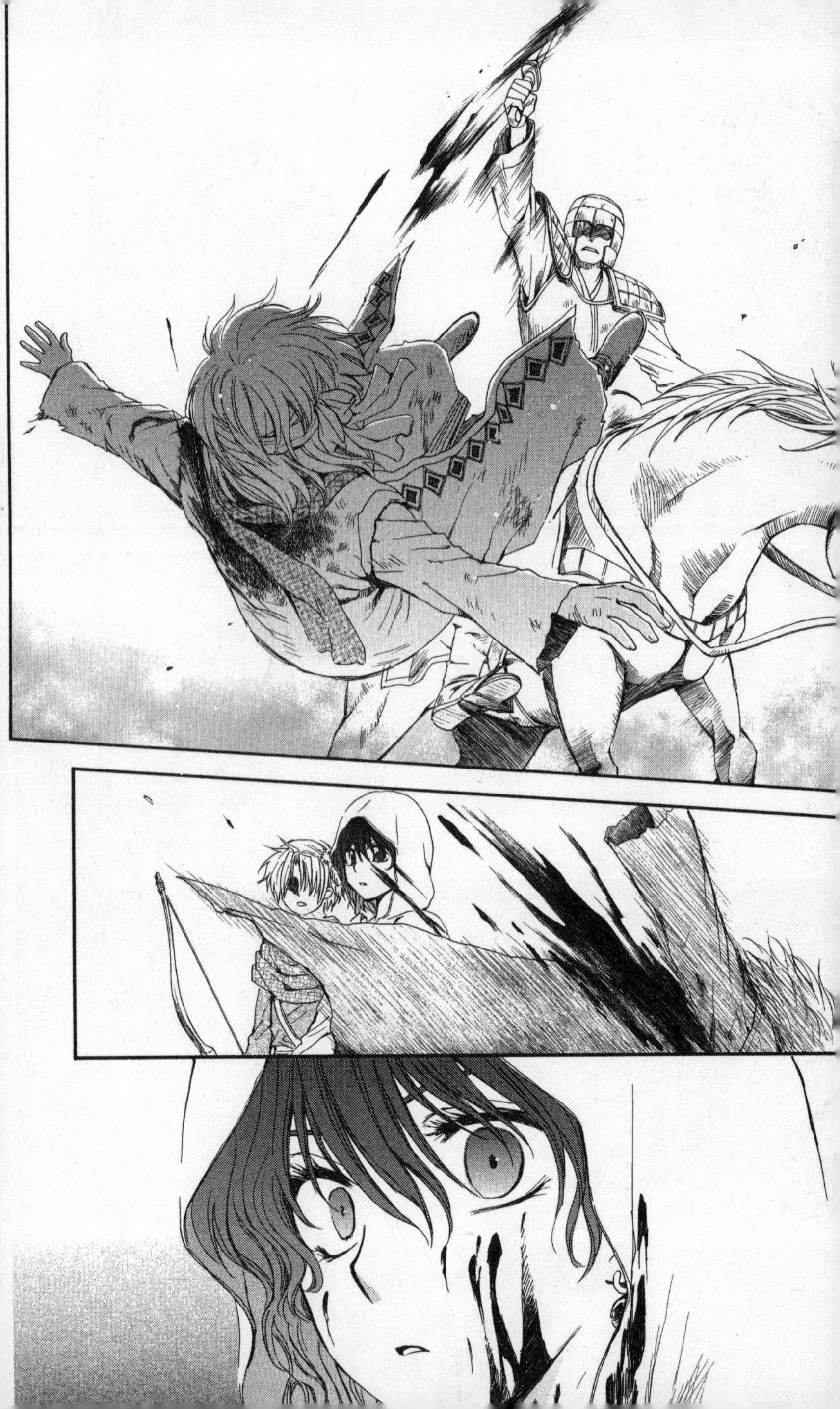

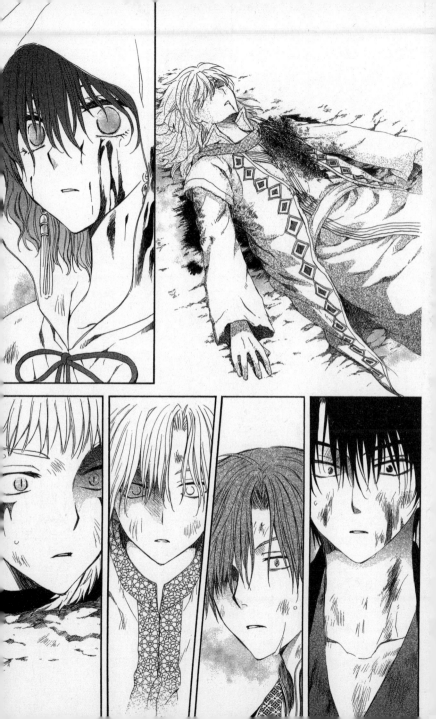

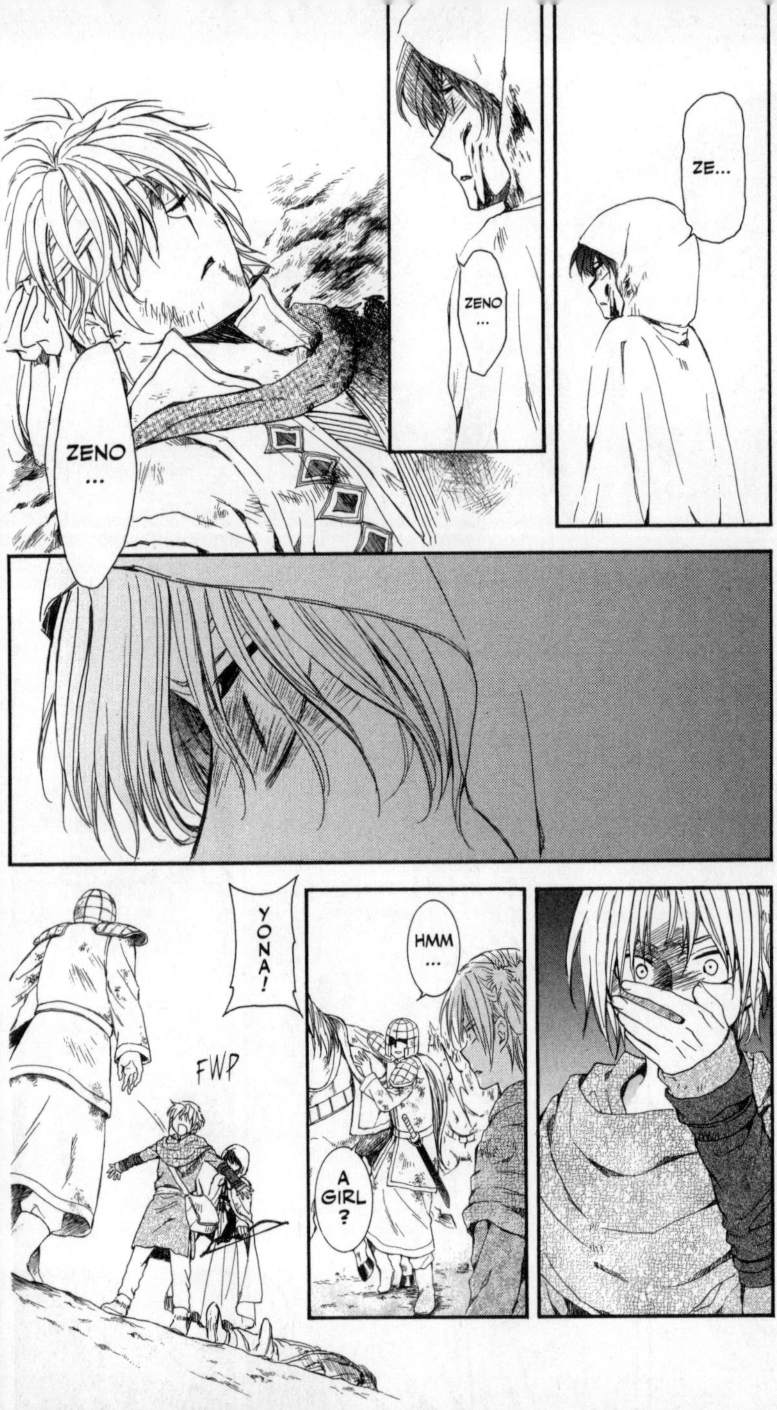
ZE...
ZENO ...
ZENO ...
HMM ...
A GIRL ?
YONA!
FWP

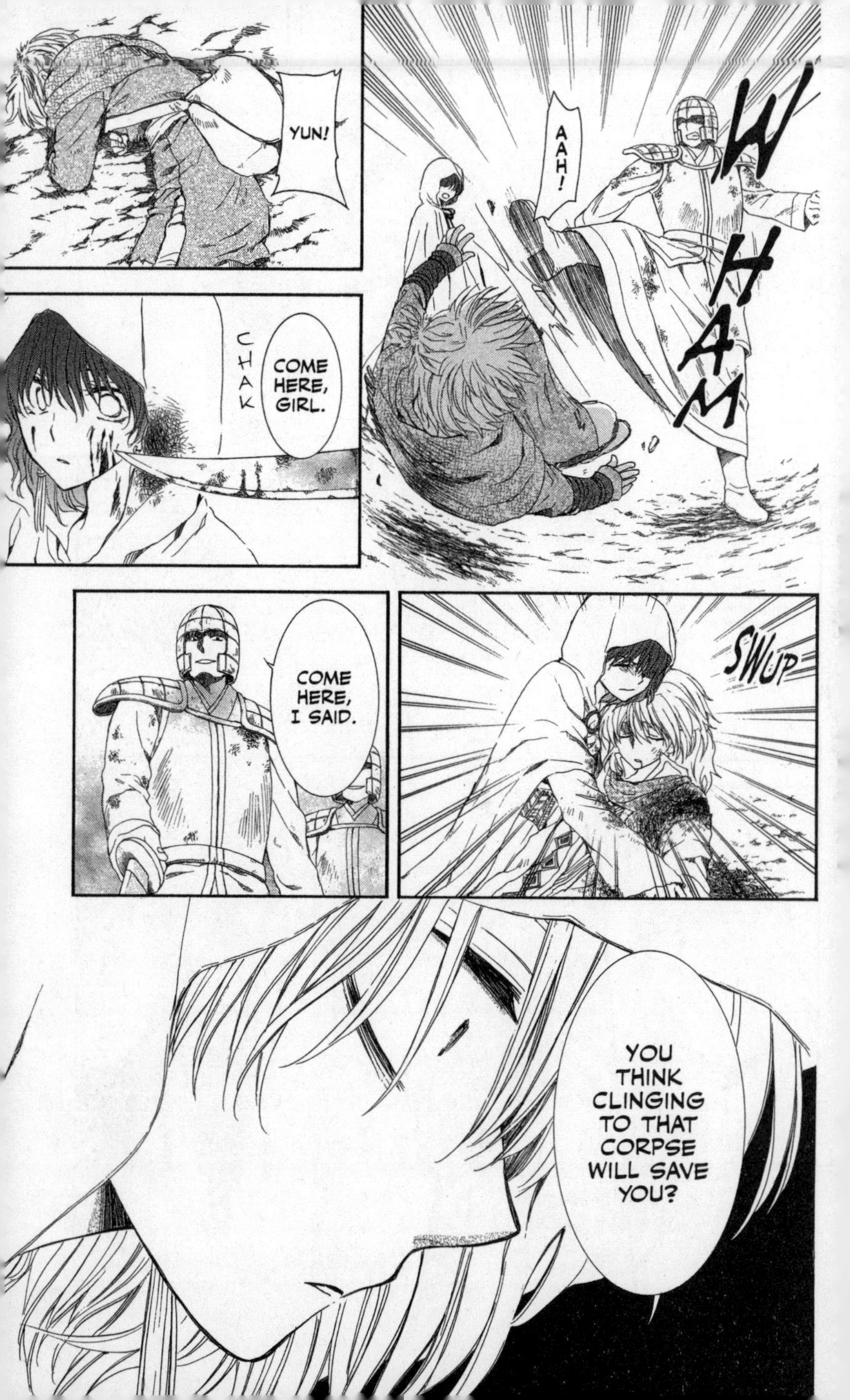
AAH!
WHAM
YUN!
CHAK
COME HERE, GIRL.
SWUP
COME HERE, I SAID.
YOU THINK CLINGING TO THAT CORPSE WILL SAVE YOU?

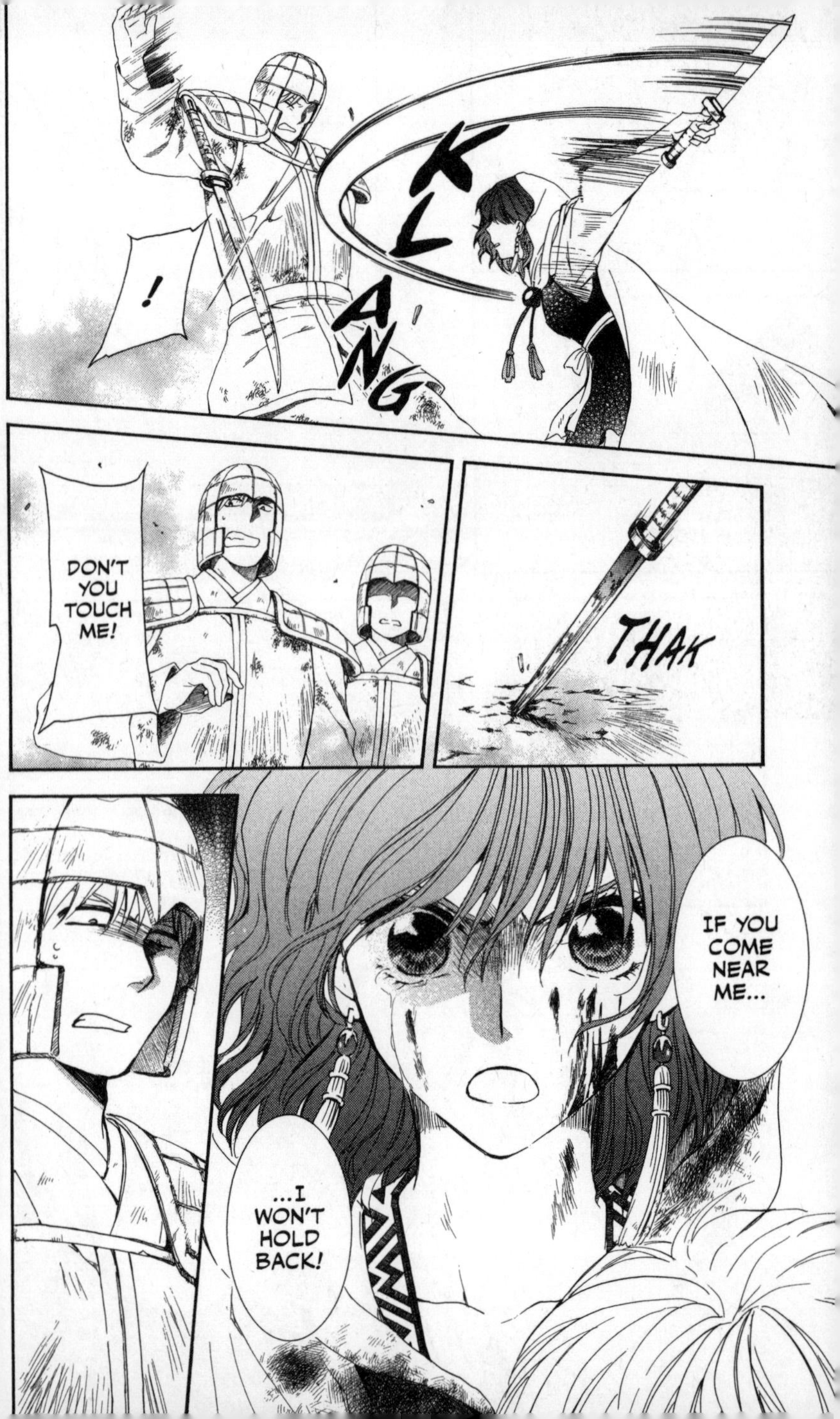
KLANG
!
THAK
DON'T YOU TOUCH ME!
IF YOU COME NEAR ME...
...I WON'T HOLD BACK!

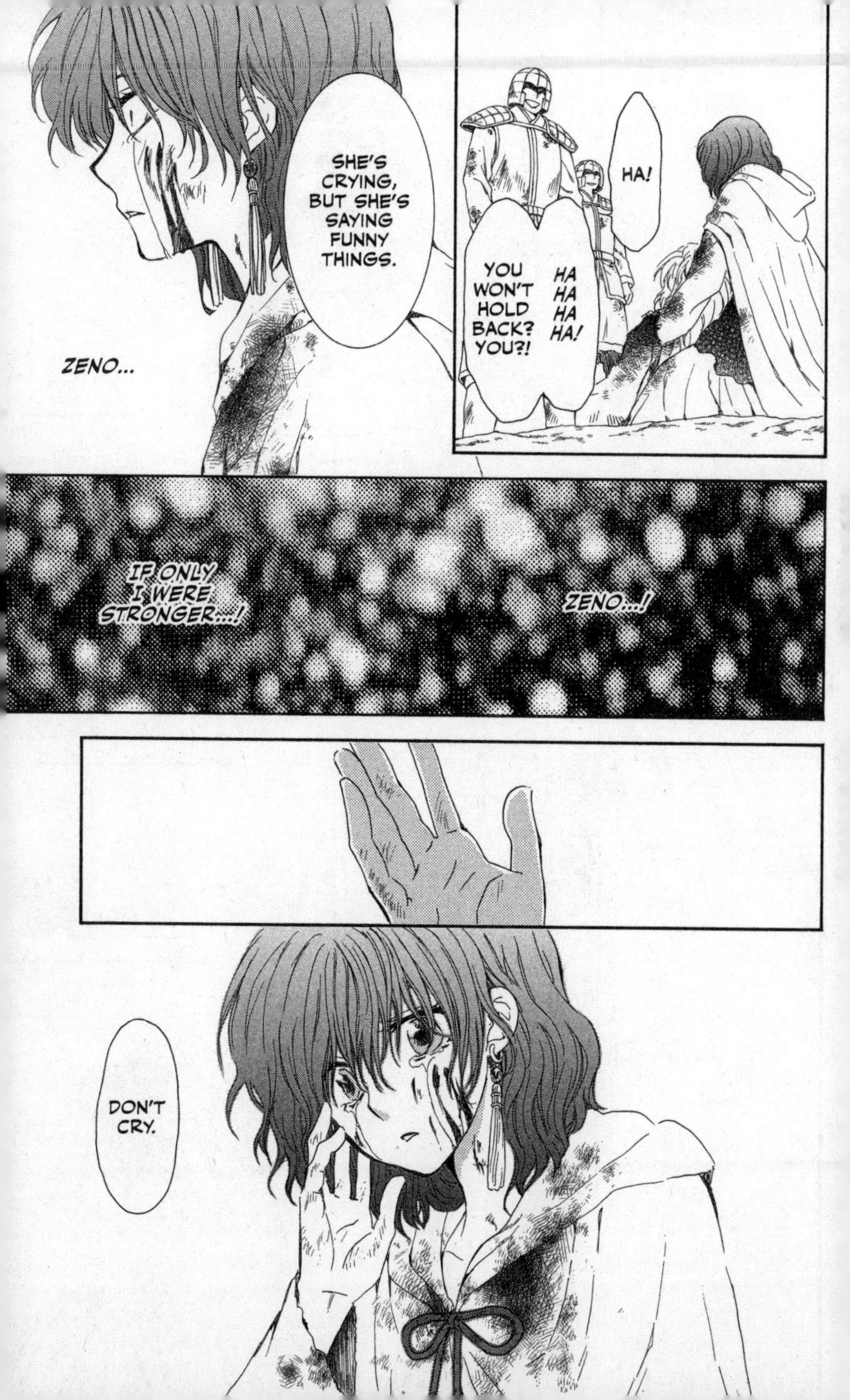
HA!
YOU WON'T HOLD BACK? YOU?!
HA HA HA HA!
SHE'S CRYING, BUT SHE'S SAYING FUNNY THINGS.
ZENO...
ZENO...!
IF ONLY I WERE STRONGER...!
DON'T CRY.

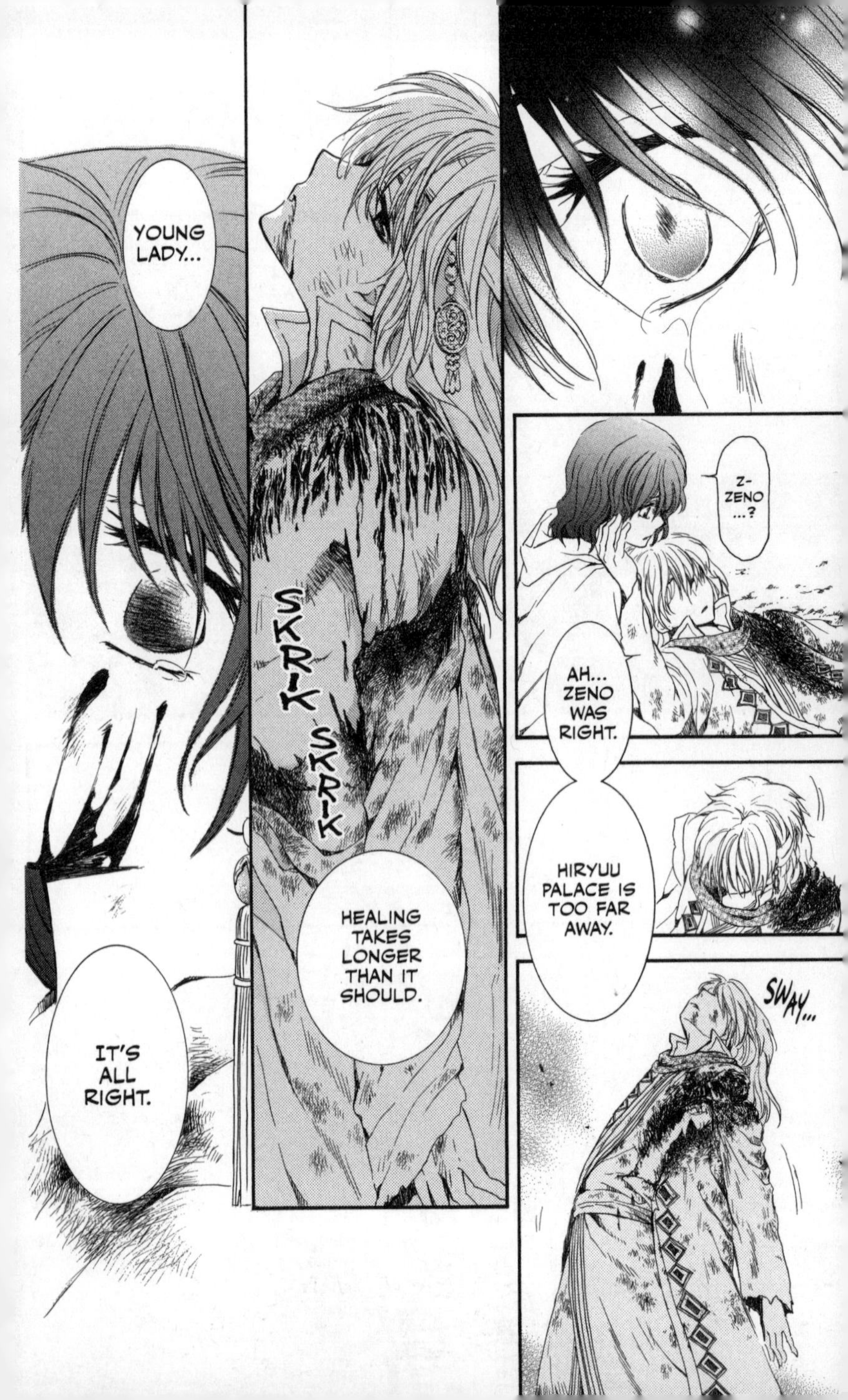
Z-ZENO ...?
AH... ZENO WAS RIGHT.
HIRYUU PALACE IS TOO FAR AWAY.
SWAY...
SKRIK SKRIK
HEALING TAKES LONGER THAN IT SHOULD.
YOUNG LADY...
IT'S ALL RIGHT.

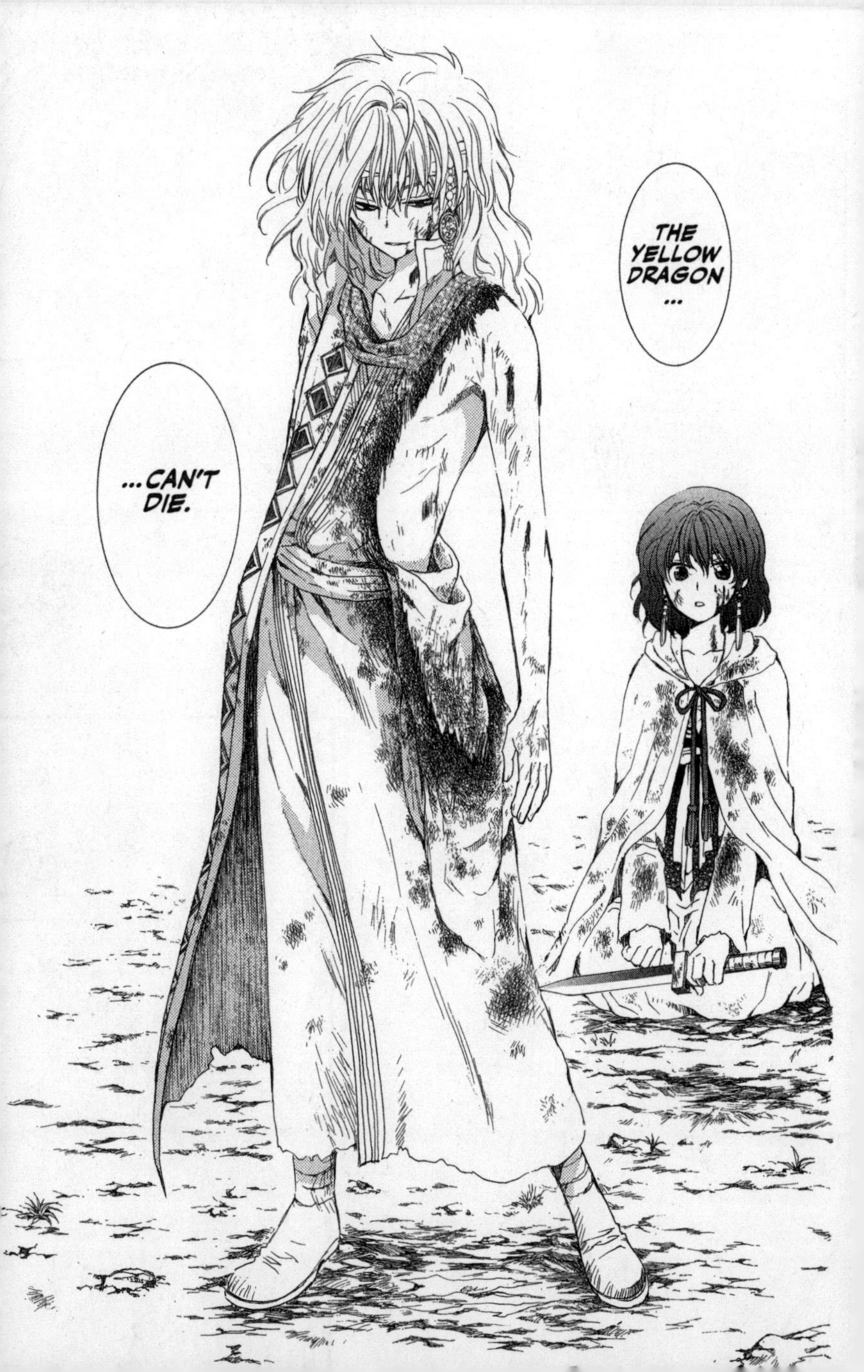
THE YELLOW DRAGON ...
...CAN'T DIE.

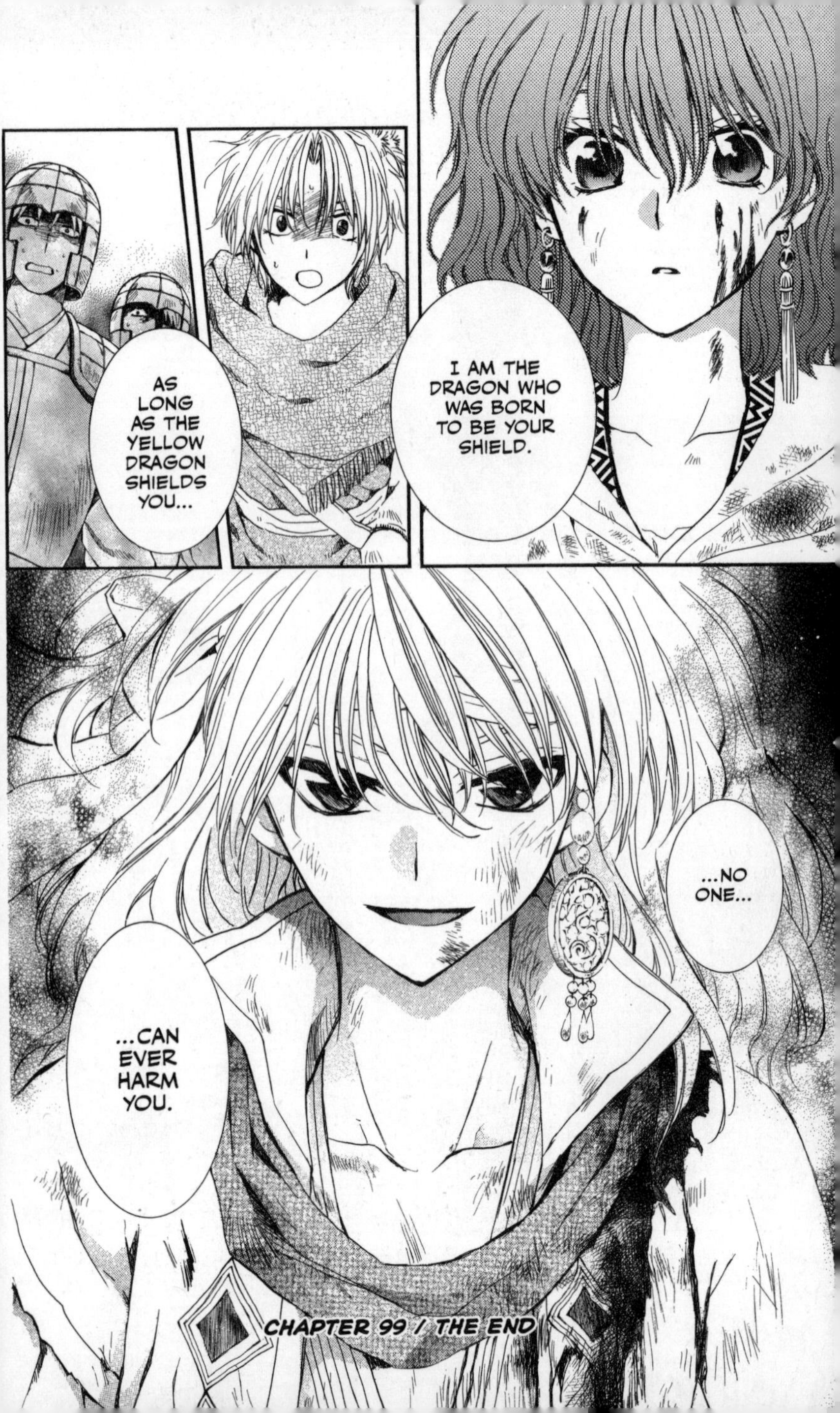
I AM THE DRAGON WHO WAS BORN TO BE YOUR SHIELD.
AS LONG AS THE YELLOW DRAGON SHIELDS YOU...
...NO ONE...
...CAN EVER HARM YOU.
CHAPTER 99 / THE END

# BONUS CHAPTER: FLY AWAY

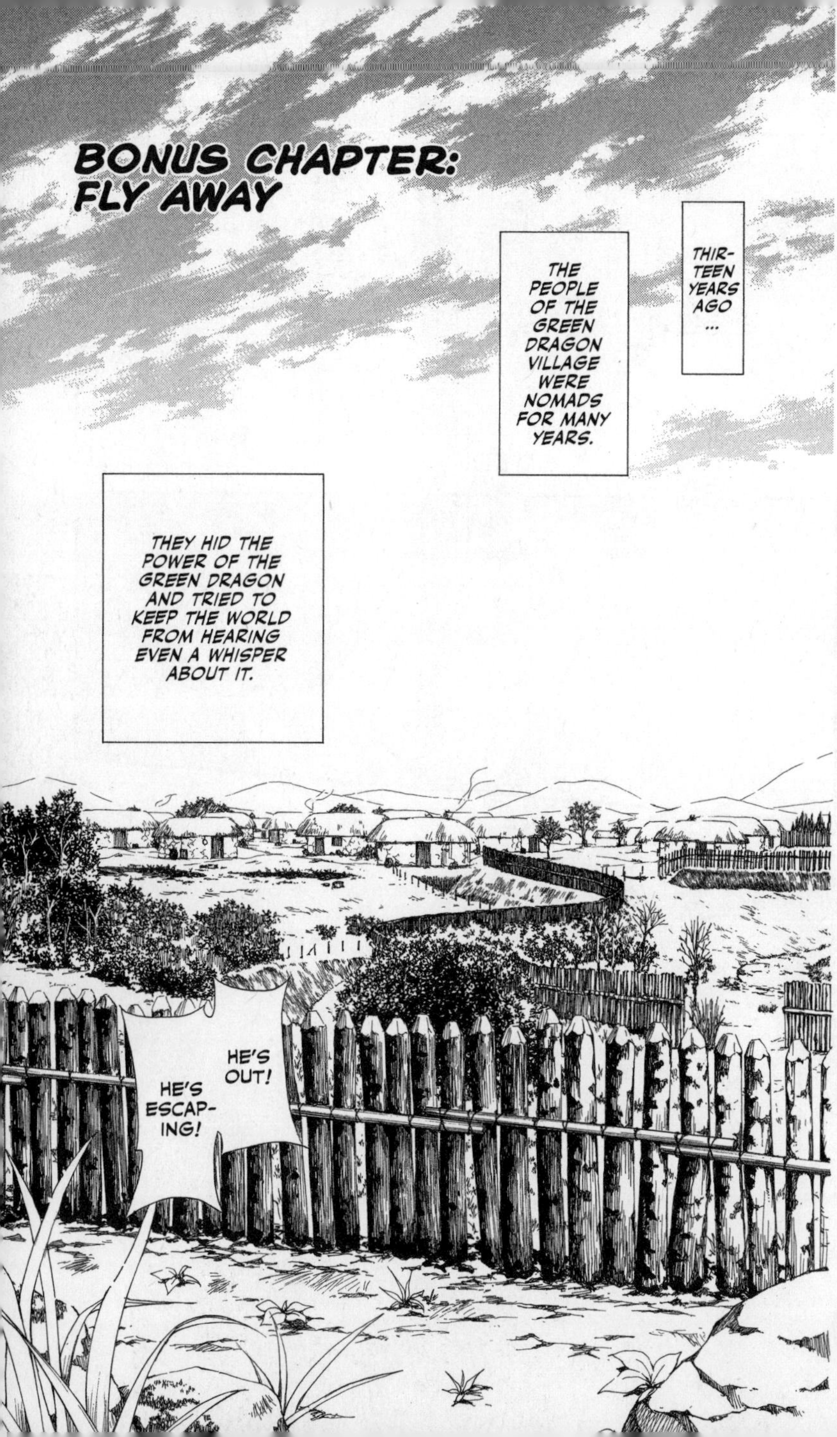
THIRTEEN YEARS AGO...
THE PEOPLE OF THE GREEN DRAGON VILLAGE WERE NOMADS FOR MANY YEARS.
THEY HID THE POWER OF THE GREEN DRAGON AND TRIED TO KEEP THE WORLD FROM HEARING EVEN A WHISPER ABOUT IT.
HE'S OUT!
HE'S ESCAPING!

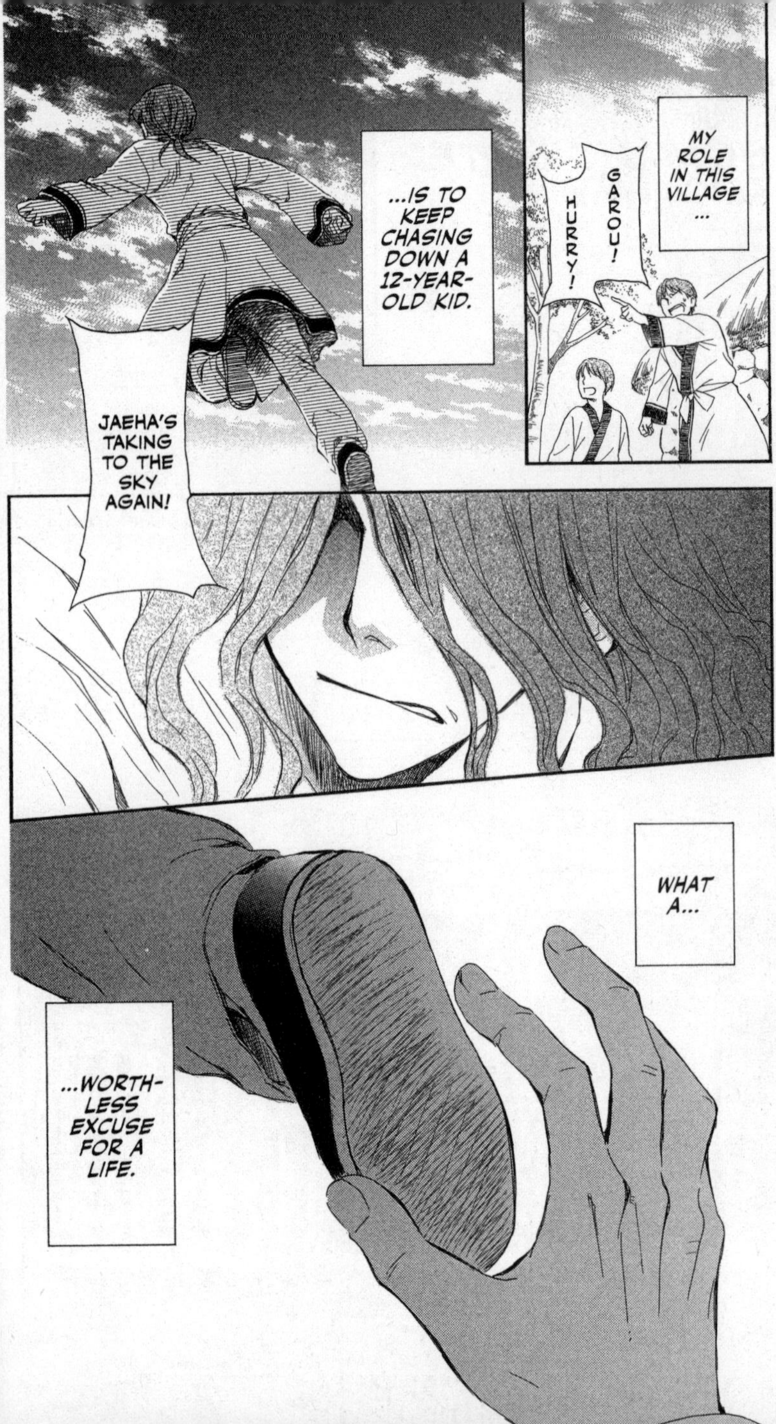
MY ROLE IN THIS VILLAGE ...
GAROU!
HURRY!
...IS TO KEEP CHASING DOWN A 12-YEAR-OLD KID.
JAEHA'S TAKING TO THE SKY AGAIN!
WHAT A...
...WORTH-LESS EXCUSE FOR A LIFE.

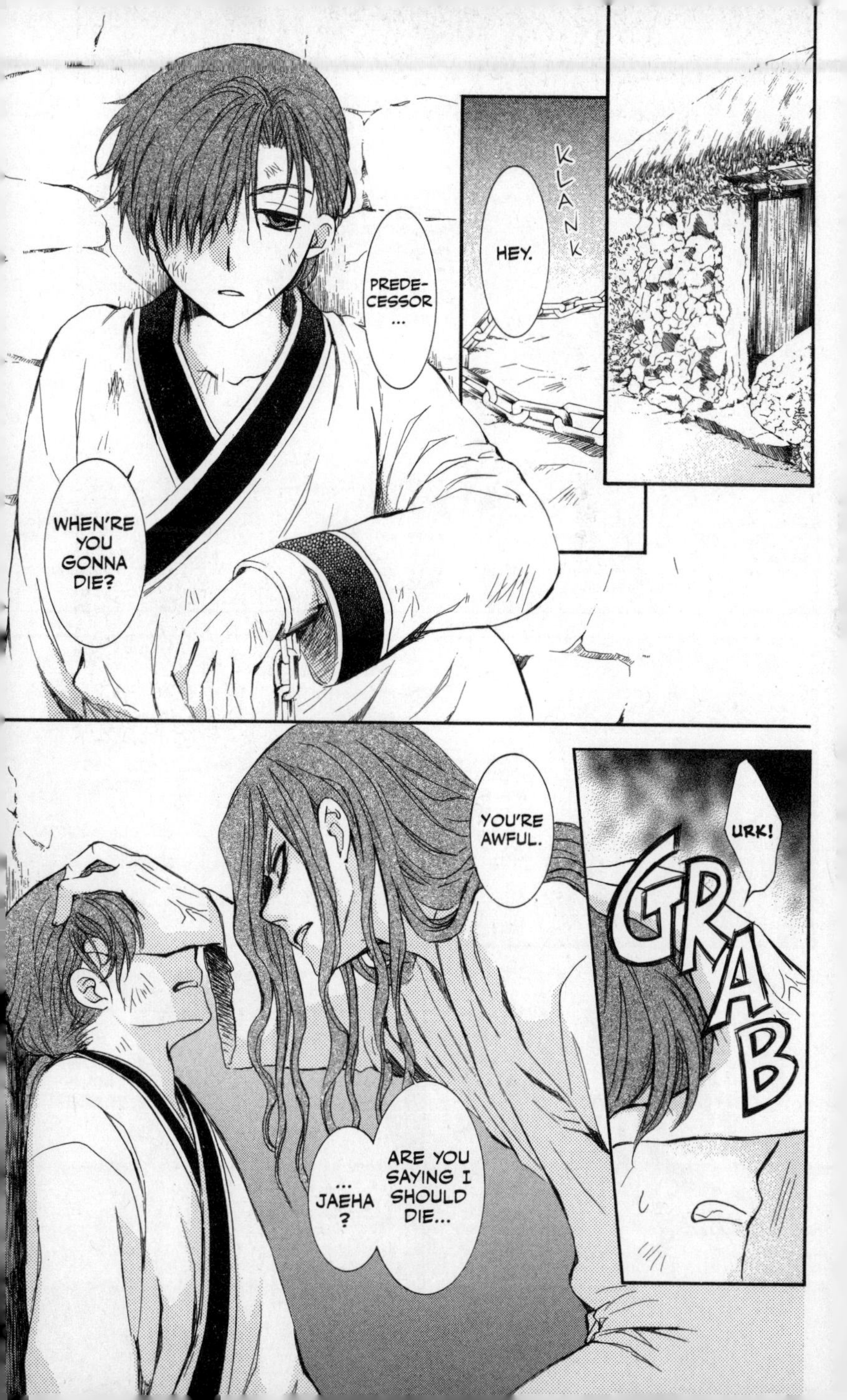
KLANK
HEY.
PREDE-CESSOR...
WHEN'RE YOU GONNA DIE?
URK!
GRAB
YOU'RE AWFUL.
ARE YOU SAYING I SHOULD DIE...
...JAEHA?

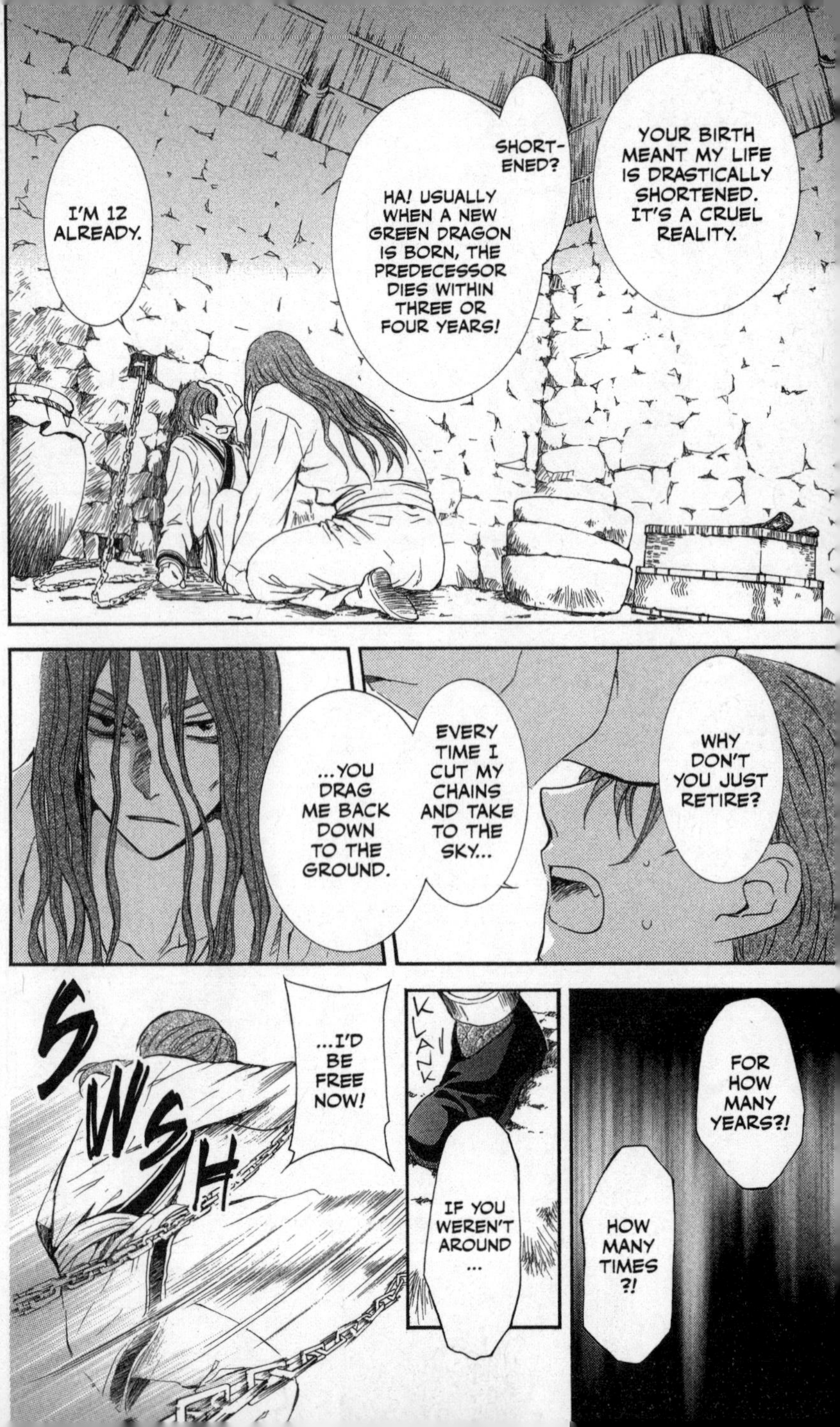
YOUR BIRTH MEANT MY LIFE IS DRASTICALLY SHORTENED. IT'S A CRUEL REALITY.
SHORTENED?
HA! USUALLY WHEN A NEW GREEN DRAGON IS BORN, THE PREDECESSOR DIES WITHIN THREE OR FOUR YEARS!
I'M 12 ALREADY.
WHY DON'T YOU JUST RETIRE?
EVERY TIME I CUT MY CHAINS AND TAKE TO THE SKY...
...YOU DRAG ME BACK DOWN TO THE GROUND.
FOR HOW MANY YEARS?!
HOW MANY TIMES?!
KLANK
IF YOU WEREN'T AROUND...
...I'D BE FREE NOW!
SWSH

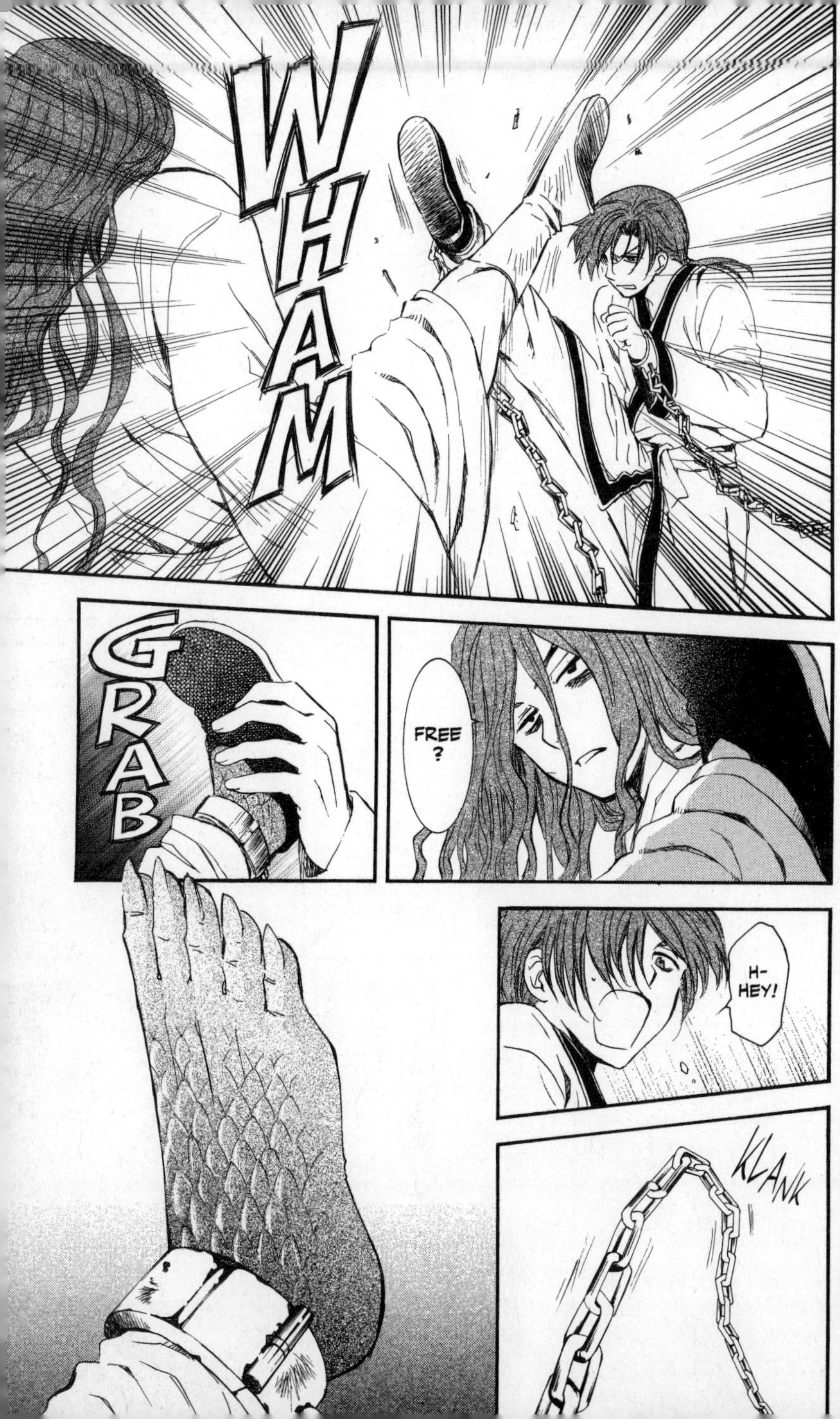
WHAM
FREE ?
GRAB
H- HEY!
KLANK

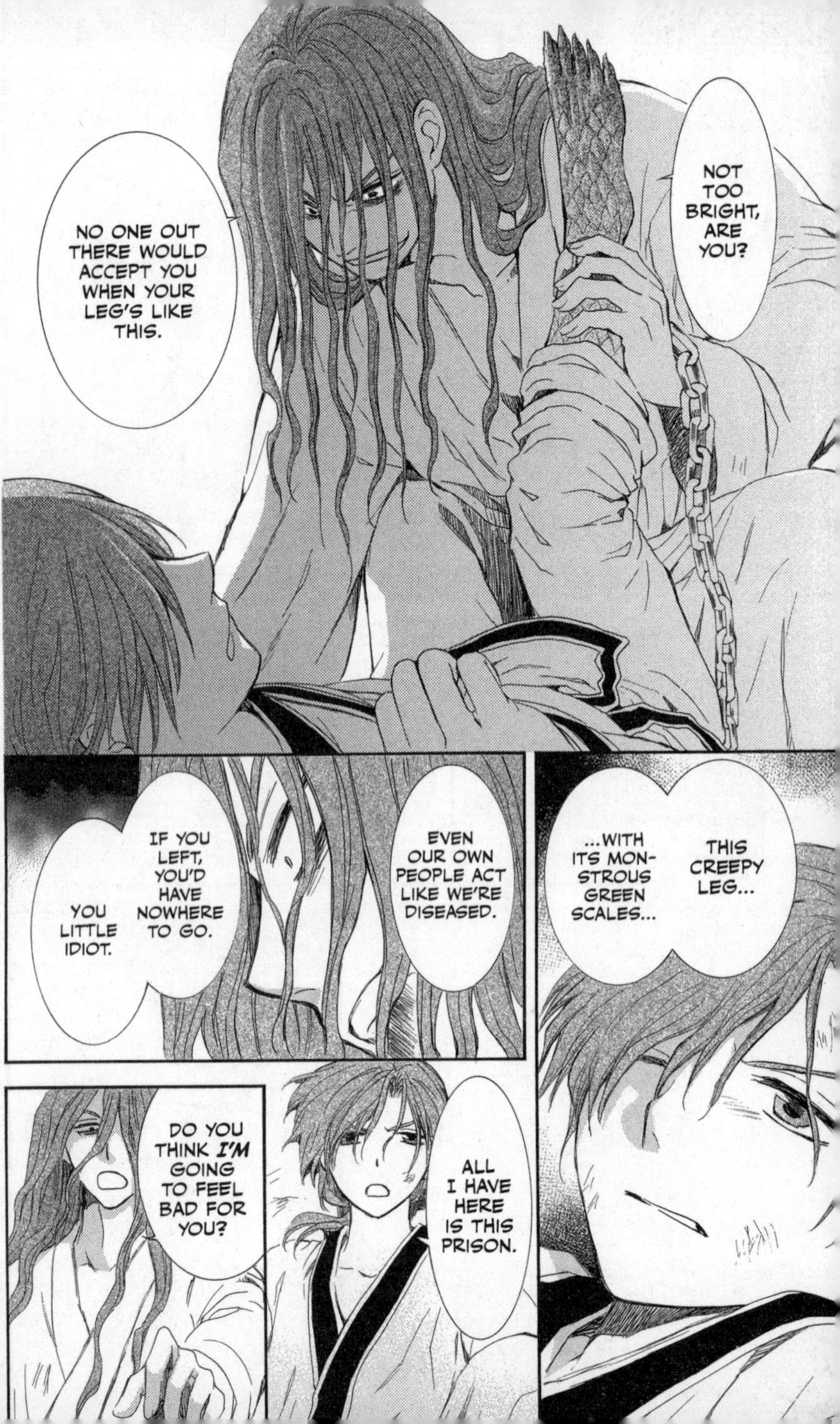
NOT TOO BRIGHT, ARE YOU?
NO ONE OUT THERE WOULD ACCEPT YOU WHEN YOUR LEG'S LIKE THIS.
THIS CREEPY LEG...
...WITH ITS MON-STROUS GREEN SCALES...
EVEN OUR OWN PEOPLE ACT LIKE WE'RE DISEASED.
IF YOU LEFT, YOU'D HAVE NOWHERE TO GO.
YOU LITTLE IDIOT.
ALL I HAVE HERE IS THIS PRISON.
DO YOU THINK *I'M* GOING TO FEEL BAD FOR YOU?

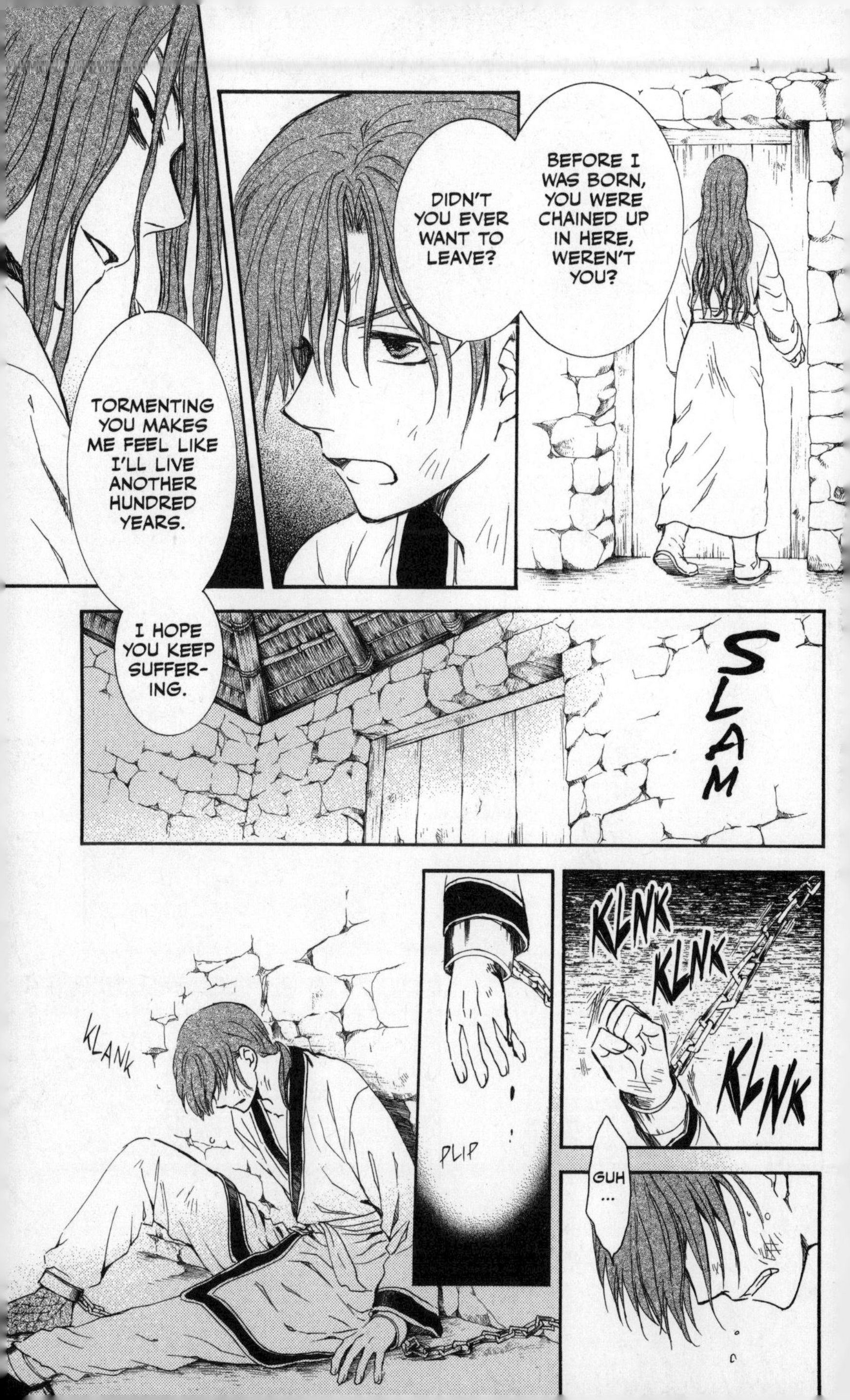
BEFORE I WAS BORN, YOU WERE CHAINED UP IN HERE, WEREN'T YOU?
DIDN'T YOU EVER WANT TO LEAVE?
TORMENTING YOU MAKES ME FEEL LIKE I'LL LIVE ANOTHER HUNDRED YEARS.
I HOPE YOU KEEP SUFFER-ING.
SLAM
KLNK
KLNK
KLNK
GUH...
PLIP
KLANK

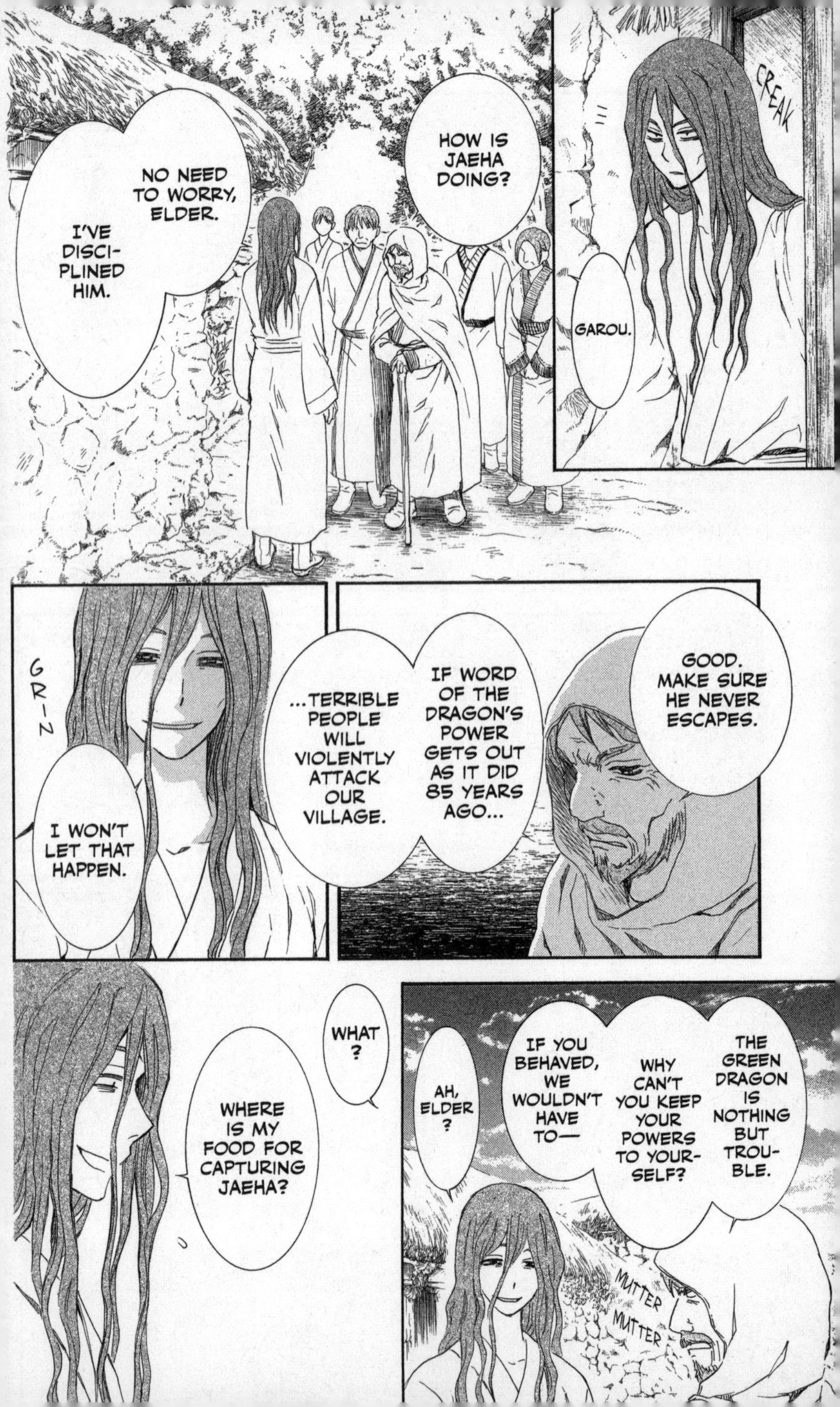
CREAK
GAROU.
HOW IS JAEHA DOING?
NO NEED TO WORRY, ELDER.
I'VE DISCIPLINED HIM.
GOOD. MAKE SURE HE NEVER ESCAPES.
IF WORD OF THE DRAGON'S POWER GETS OUT AS IT DID 85 YEARS AGO...
...TERRIBLE PEOPLE WILL VIOLENTLY ATTACK OUR VILLAGE.
GRIN
I WON'T LET THAT HAPPEN.
THE GREEN DRAGON IS NOTHING BUT TROUBLE.
WHY CAN'T YOU KEEP YOUR POWERS TO YOURSELF?
IF YOU BEHAVED, WE WOULDN'T HAVE TO—
MUTTER MUTTER
AH, ELDER?
WHAT?
WHERE IS MY FOOD FOR CAPTURING JAEHA?

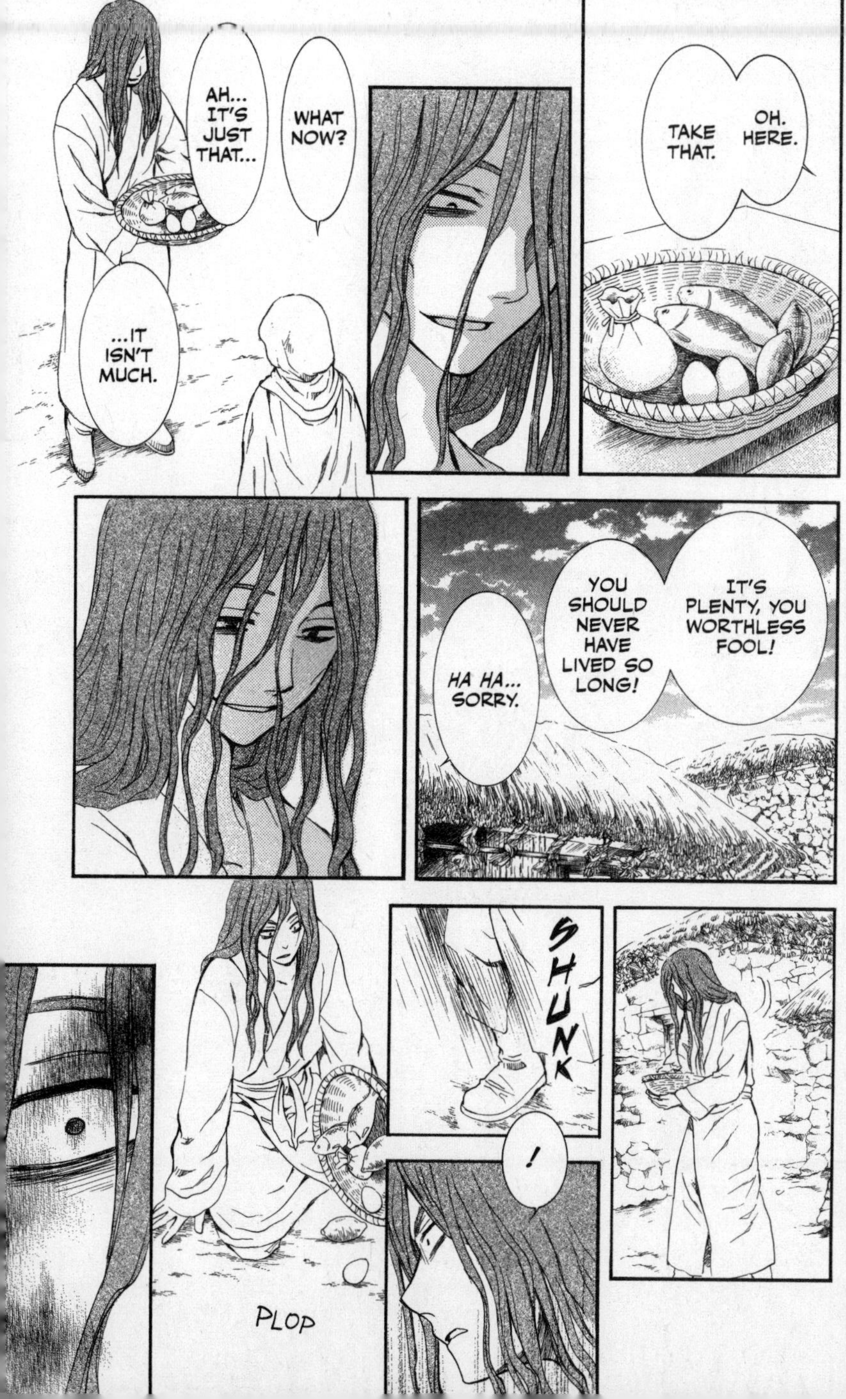

OH. HERE.
TAKE THAT.
WHAT NOW?
AH... IT'S JUST THAT...
...IT ISN'T MUCH.
IT'S PLENTY, YOU WORTHLESS FOOL!
YOU SHOULD NEVER HAVE LIVED SO LONG!
HA HA... SORRY.
SHUNK
!
PLOP

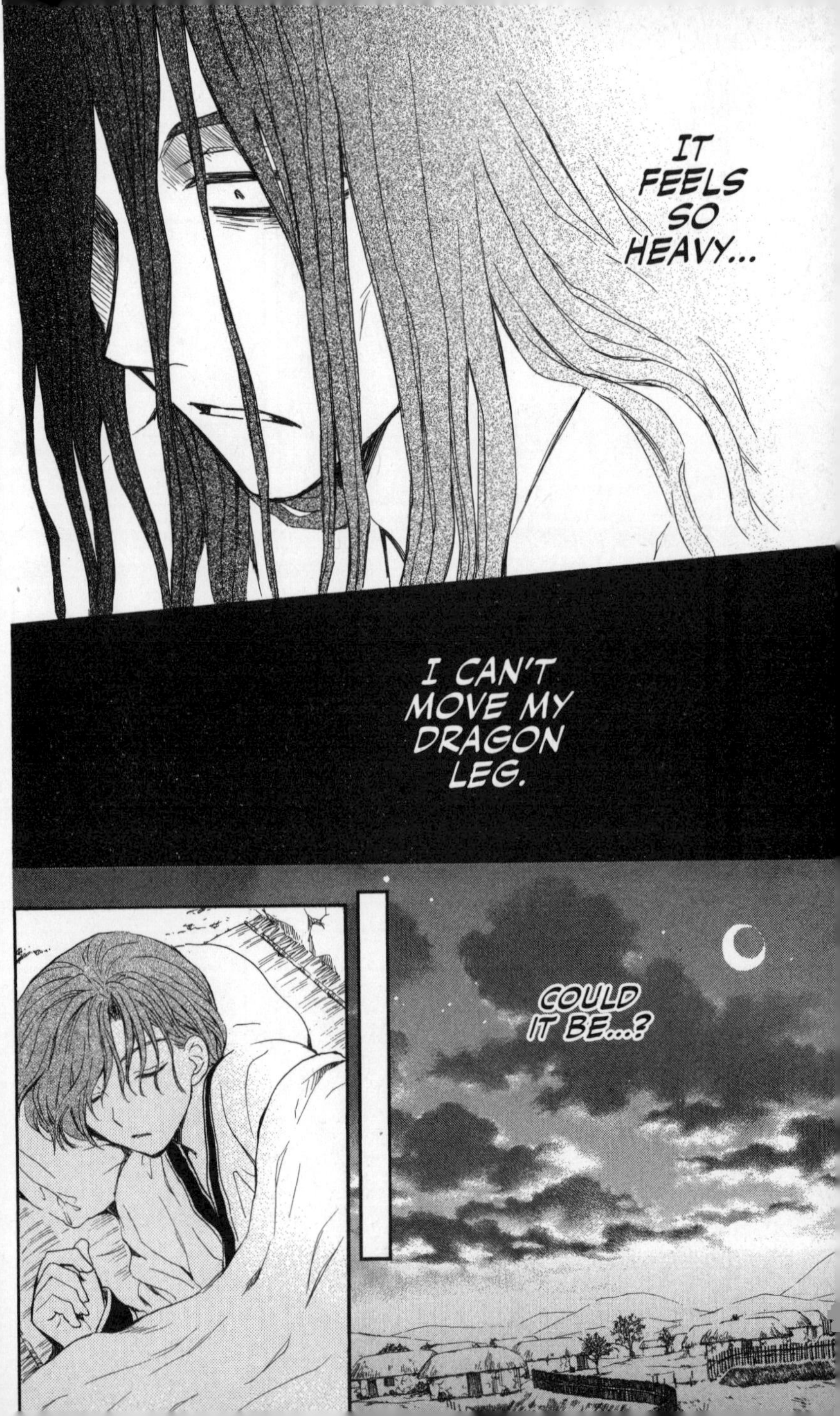
IT FEELS SO HEAVY...
I CAN'T MOVE MY DRAGON LEG.
COULD IT BE...?

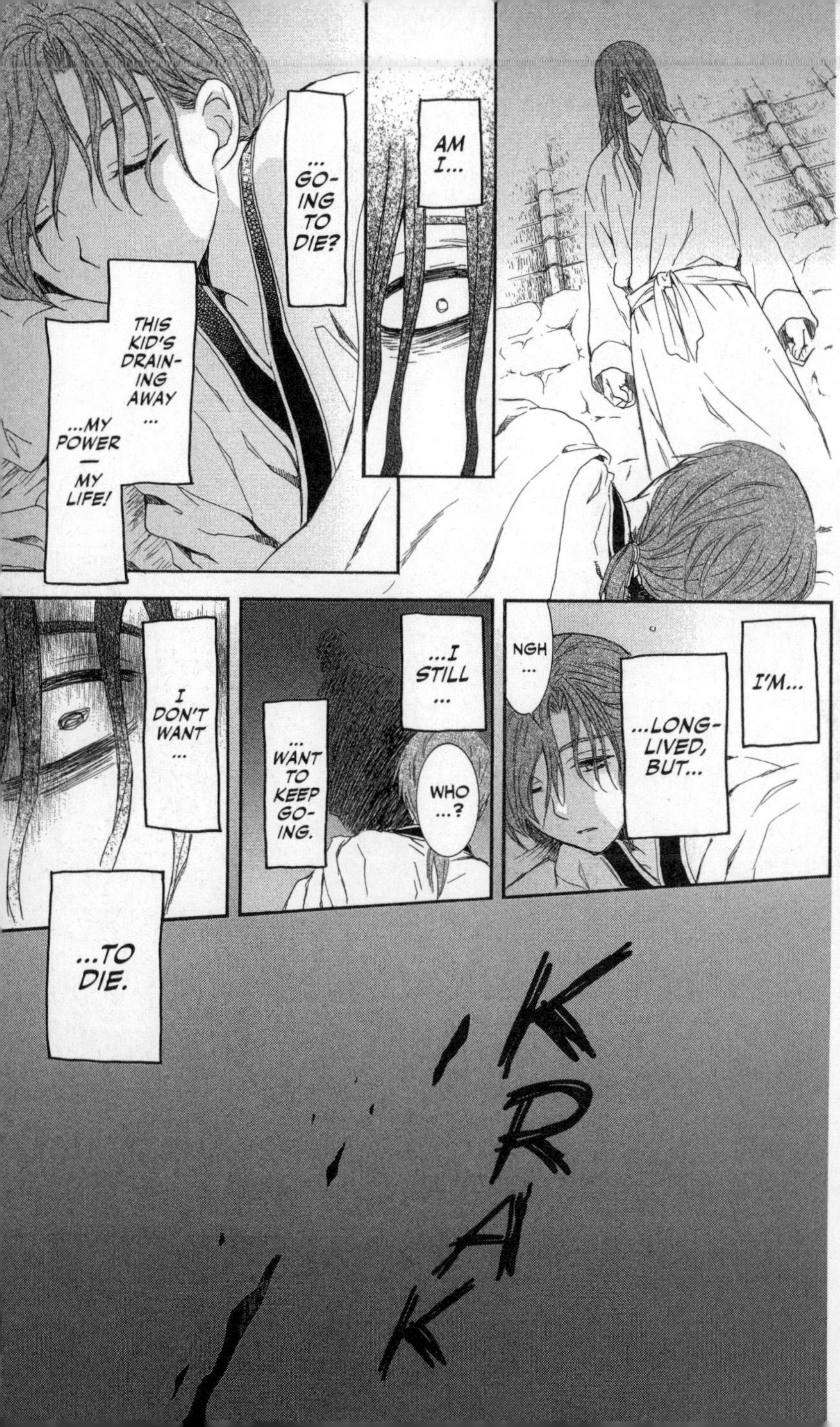
AM I...
...GO-ING TO DIE?
THIS KID'S DRAIN-ING AWAY...
...MY POWER—MY LIFE!
I'M...
...LONG-LIVED, BUT...
NGH...
...I STILL...
...WANT TO KEEP GO-ING.
WHO...?
I DON'T WANT...
...TO DIE.
KRAK

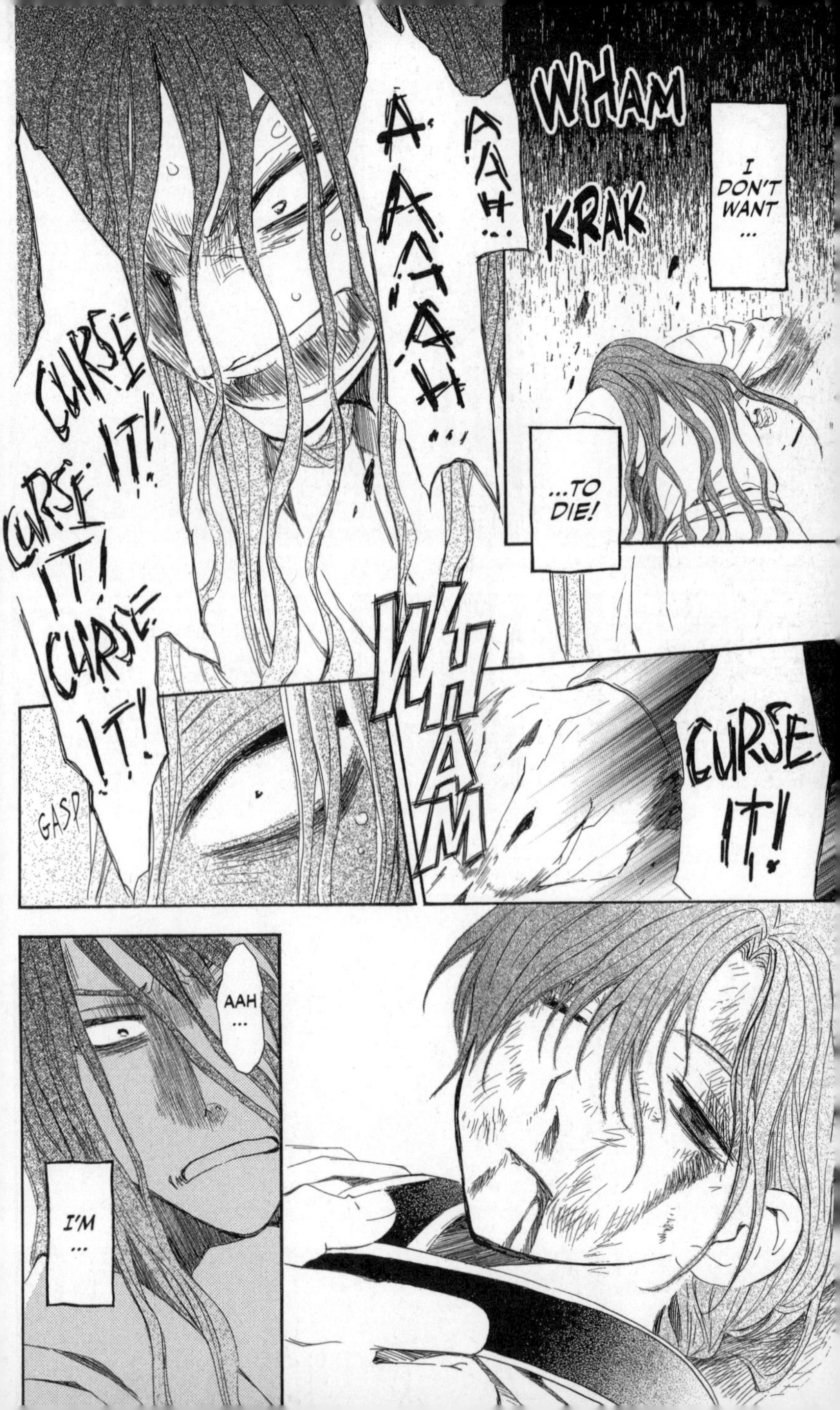
WHAM
KRAK
I DON'T WANT...
...TO DIE!
AAH...!
AAAAAH...
CURSE IT!
CURSE IT!
CURSE IT!
WHAM
CURSE IT!
GASP
AAH...
I'M...

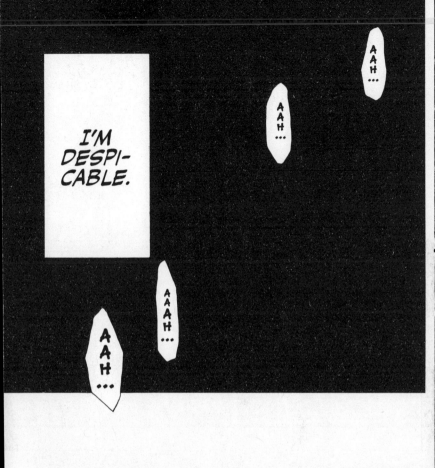

I'M DESPI-CABLE.

AAH...

AAH...

AAAH...

AAH...

I...

...HATE YOU, BUT...

H-HOW CAN THAT BE ENOUGH?

I WANT TO KILL YOU.

ARE YOU DONE?

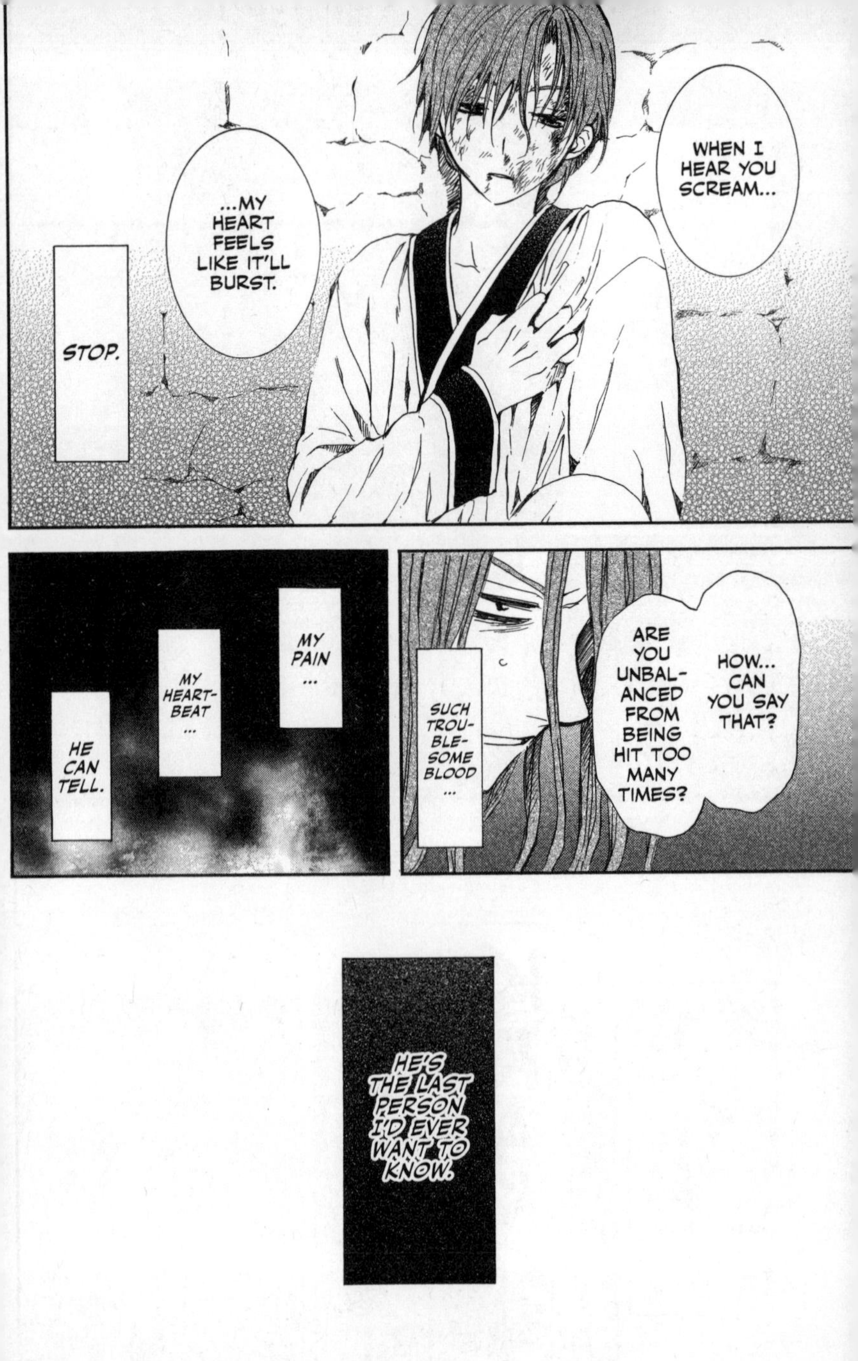
WHEN I HEAR YOU SCREAM...
...MY HEART FEELS LIKE IT'LL BURST.
STOP.
HOW... CAN YOU SAY THAT?
ARE YOU UNBAL-ANCED FROM BEING HIT TOO MANY TIMES?
SUCH TROU-BLE-SOME BLOOD...
MY PAIN...
MY HEART-BEAT...
HE CAN TELL.
HE'S THE LAST PERSON I'D EVER WANT TO KNOW.

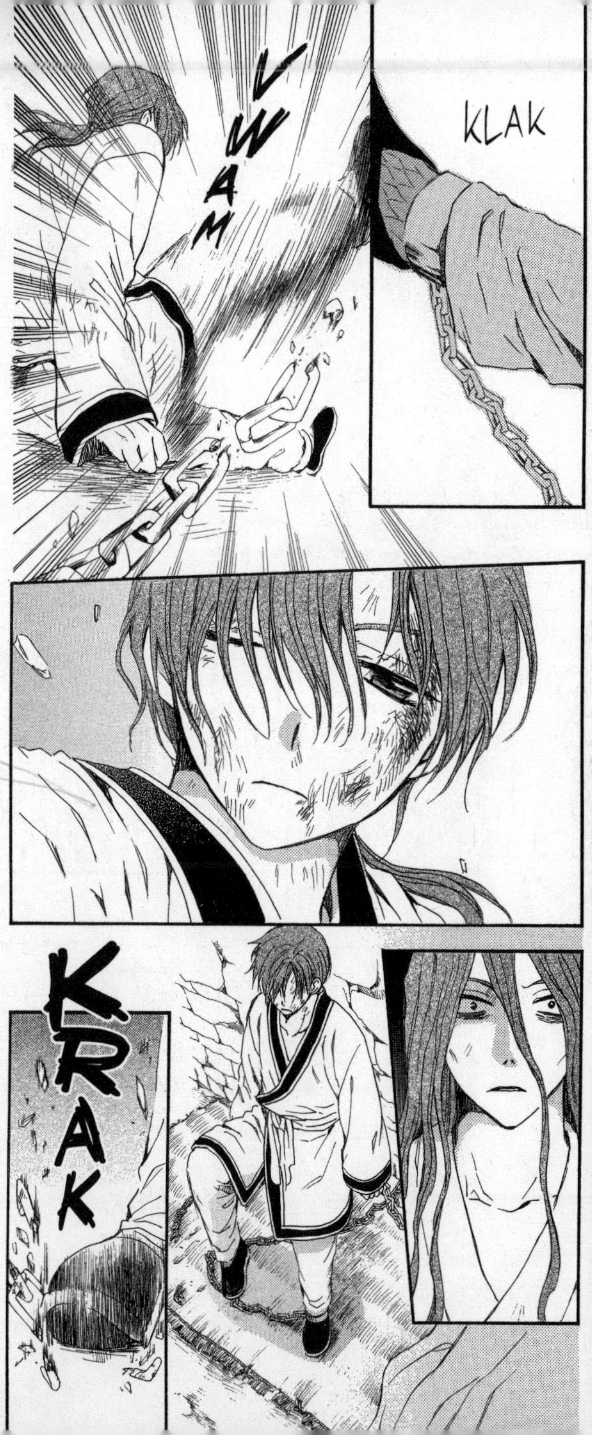
KLAK
VWAM
KRAK

Bonus Chapter

This is a story about Jaeha's childhood, although in practice, his predecessor, Garou, seems to be the protagonist. I wanted to spend a little more time drawing it.

Jaeha likes beautiful things. He likes his clothes and his powers, but he doesn't really like the way his dragon leg looks. He rarely removes his shoes, and he keeps his leg wrapped up, the same way Gija wraps his arm.

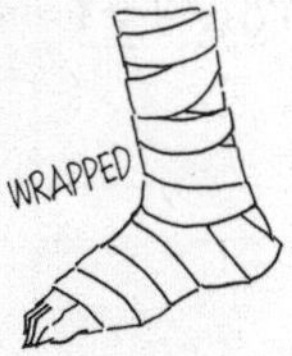
WRAPPED

Gija, on the other hand, doesn't dislike his dragon arm, but he wraps it up because the people in his village (especially his granny) taught him not to let anyone find out about it.

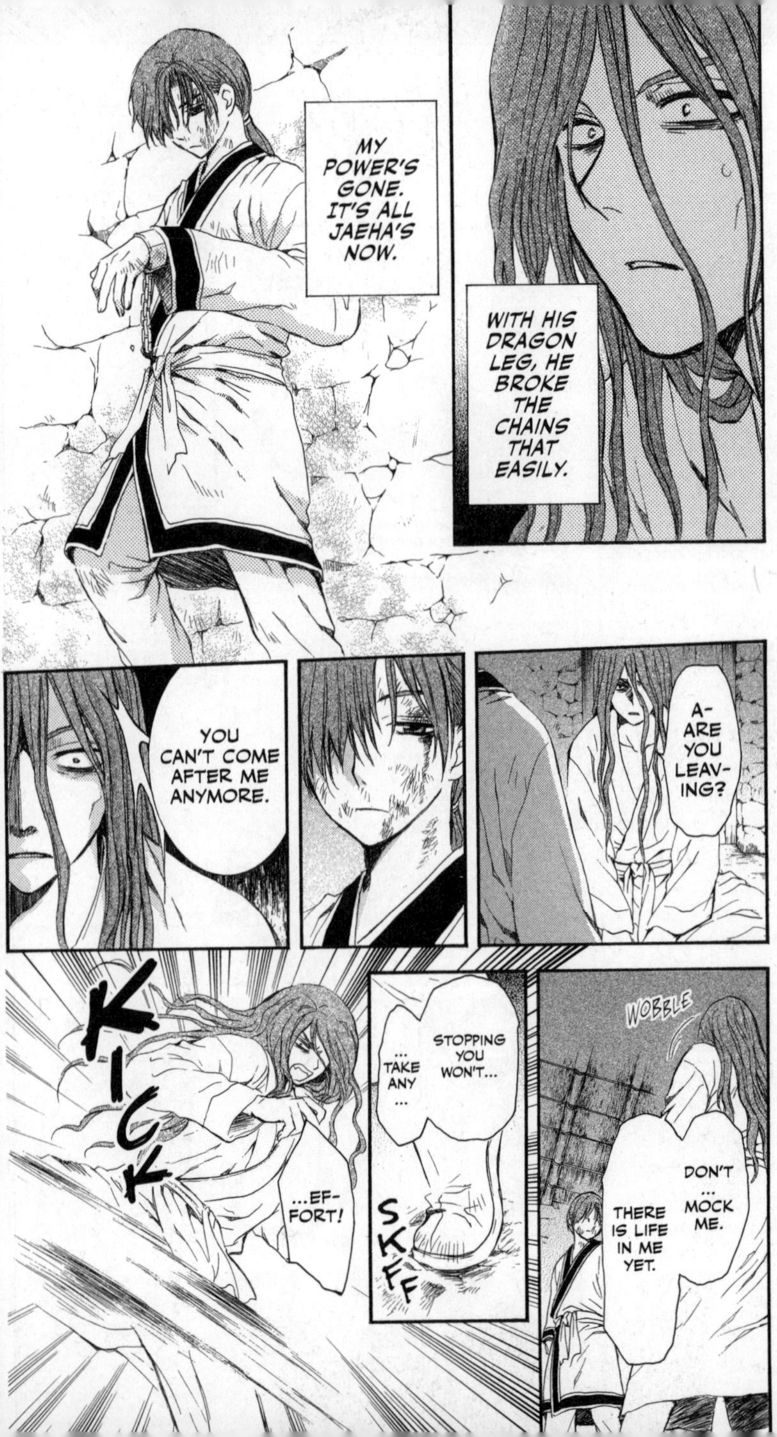
WITH HIS DRAGON LEG, HE BROKE THE CHAINS THAT EASILY.
MY POWER'S GONE. IT'S ALL JAEHA'S NOW.
A- ARE YOU LEAV- ING?
YOU CAN'T COME AFTER ME ANYMORE.
WOBBLE
DON'T ... MOCK ME.
THERE IS LIFE IN ME YET.
STOPPING YOU WON'T...
... TAKE ANY ...
SKFF
KICK
...EF- FORT!

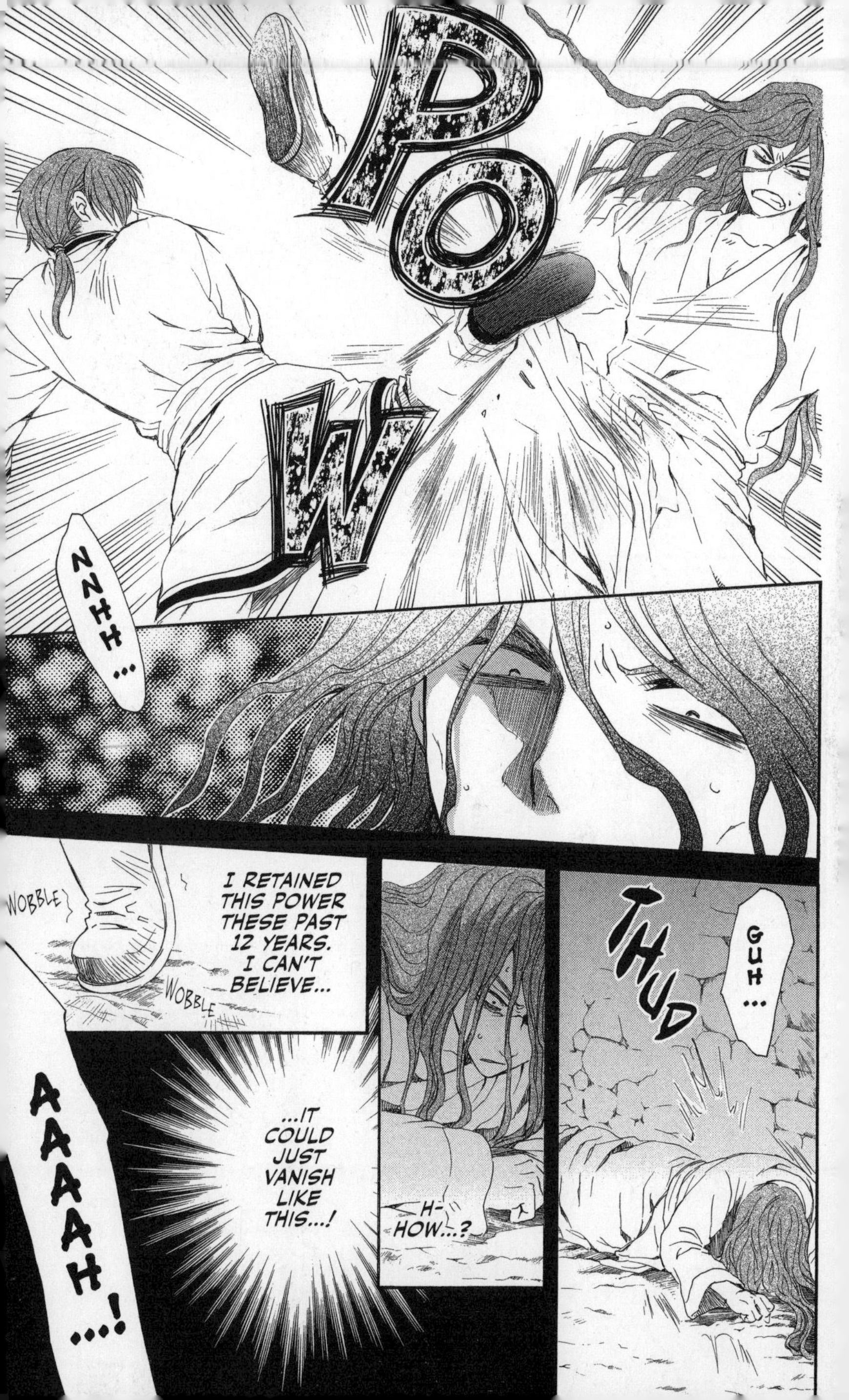
POW
NNHH...
THUD
GUH...
H-HOW...?
WOBBLE
I RETAINED THIS POWER THESE PAST 12 YEARS. I CAN'T BELIEVE...
WOBBLE
...IT COULD JUST VANISH LIKE THIS...!
AAAAH...!

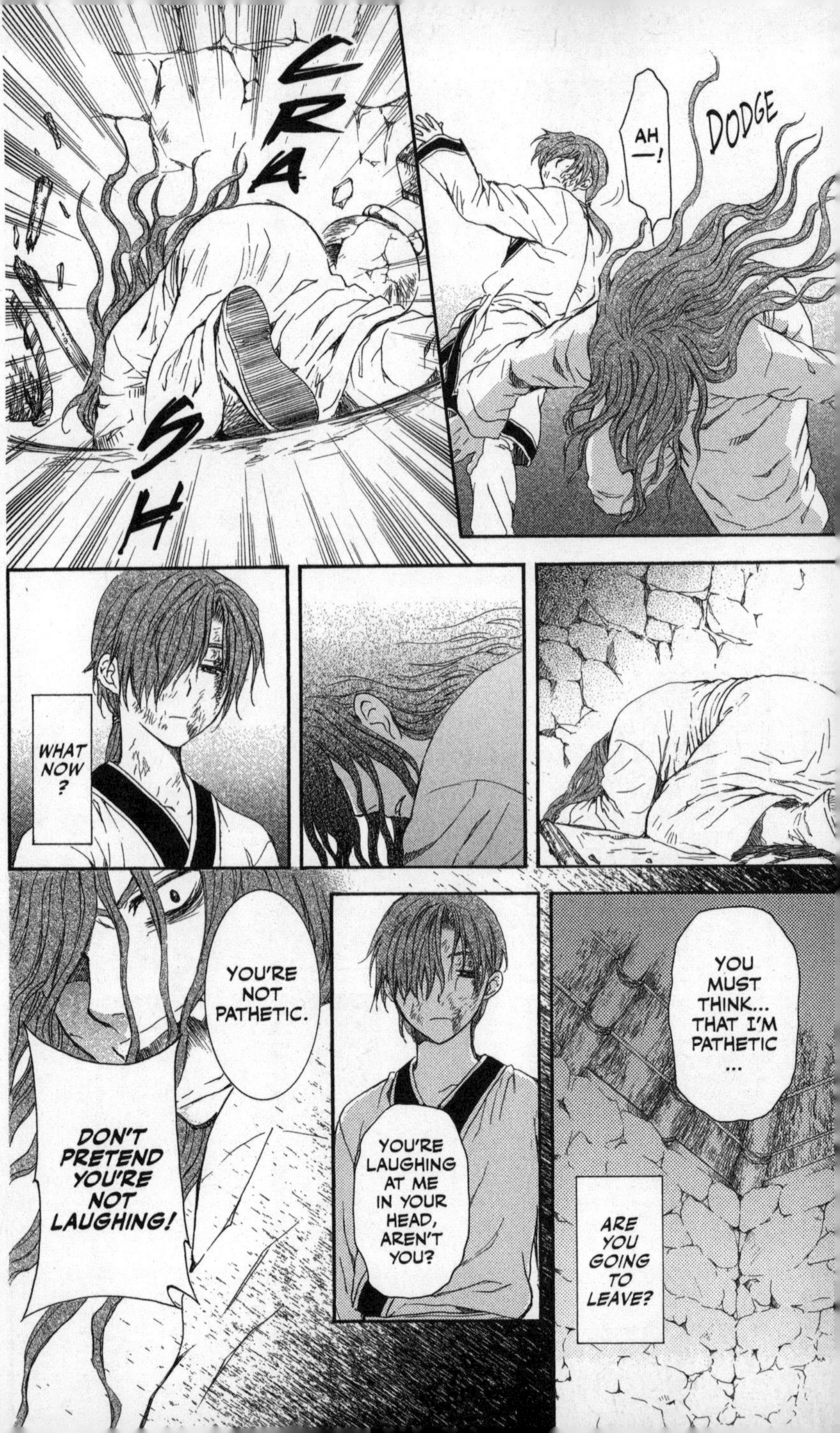
DODGE
AH—!
CRASH
WHAT NOW?
YOU MUST THINK... THAT I'M PATHETIC...
ARE YOU GOING TO LEAVE?
YOU'RE LAUGHING AT ME IN YOUR HEAD, AREN'T YOU?
YOU'RE NOT PATHETIC.
DON'T PRETEND YOU'RE NOT LAUGHING!

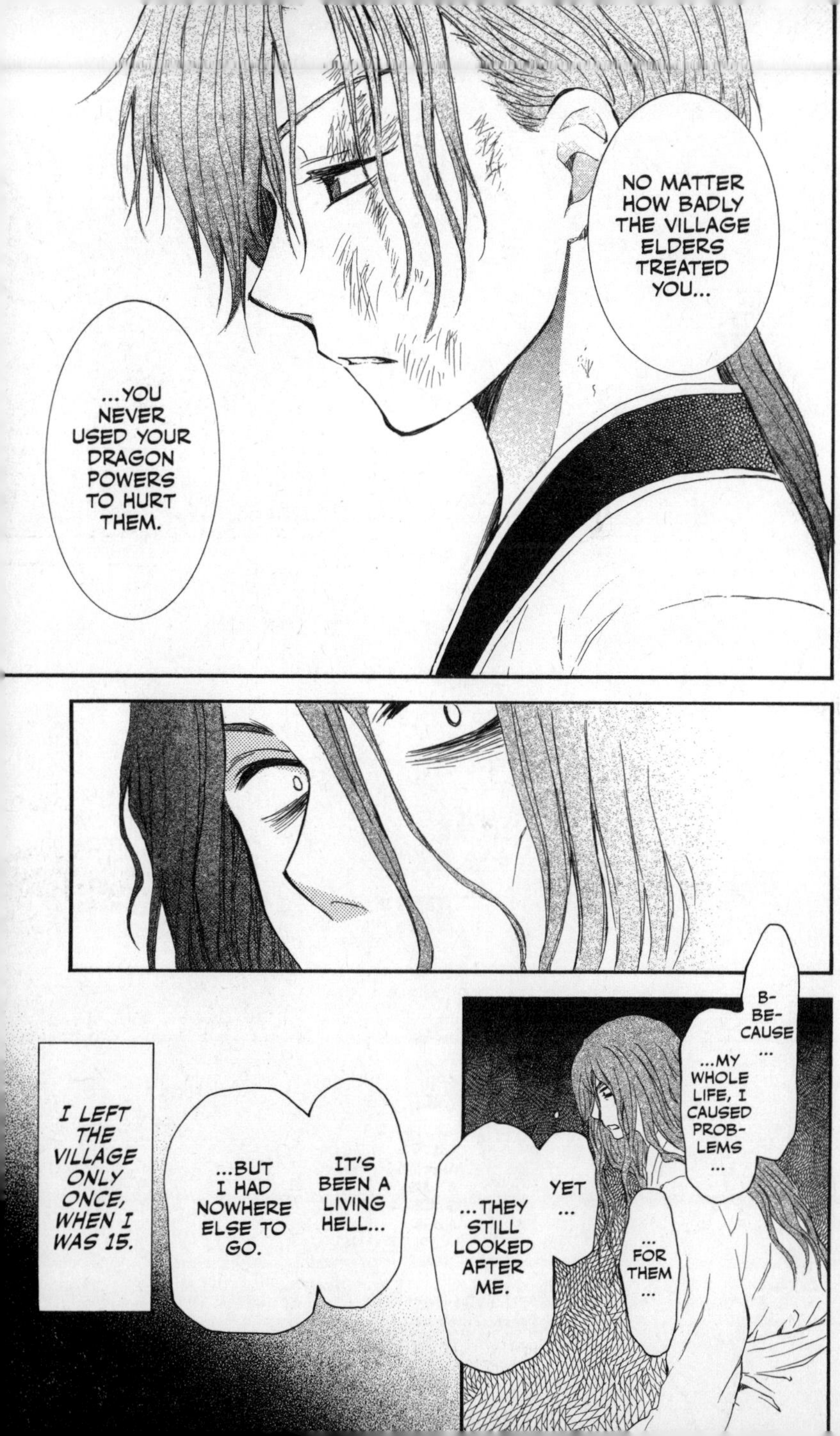
NO MATTER HOW BADLY THE VILLAGE ELDERS TREATED YOU...
...YOU NEVER USED YOUR DRAGON POWERS TO HURT THEM.
B-BE-CAUSE ...
...MY WHOLE LIFE, I CAUSED PROB-LEMS ...
... FOR THEM ...
YET ...
...THEY STILL LOOKED AFTER ME.
IT'S BEEN A LIVING HELL...
...BUT I HAD NOWHERE ELSE TO GO.
I LEFT THE VILLAGE ONLY ONCE, WHEN I WAS 15.

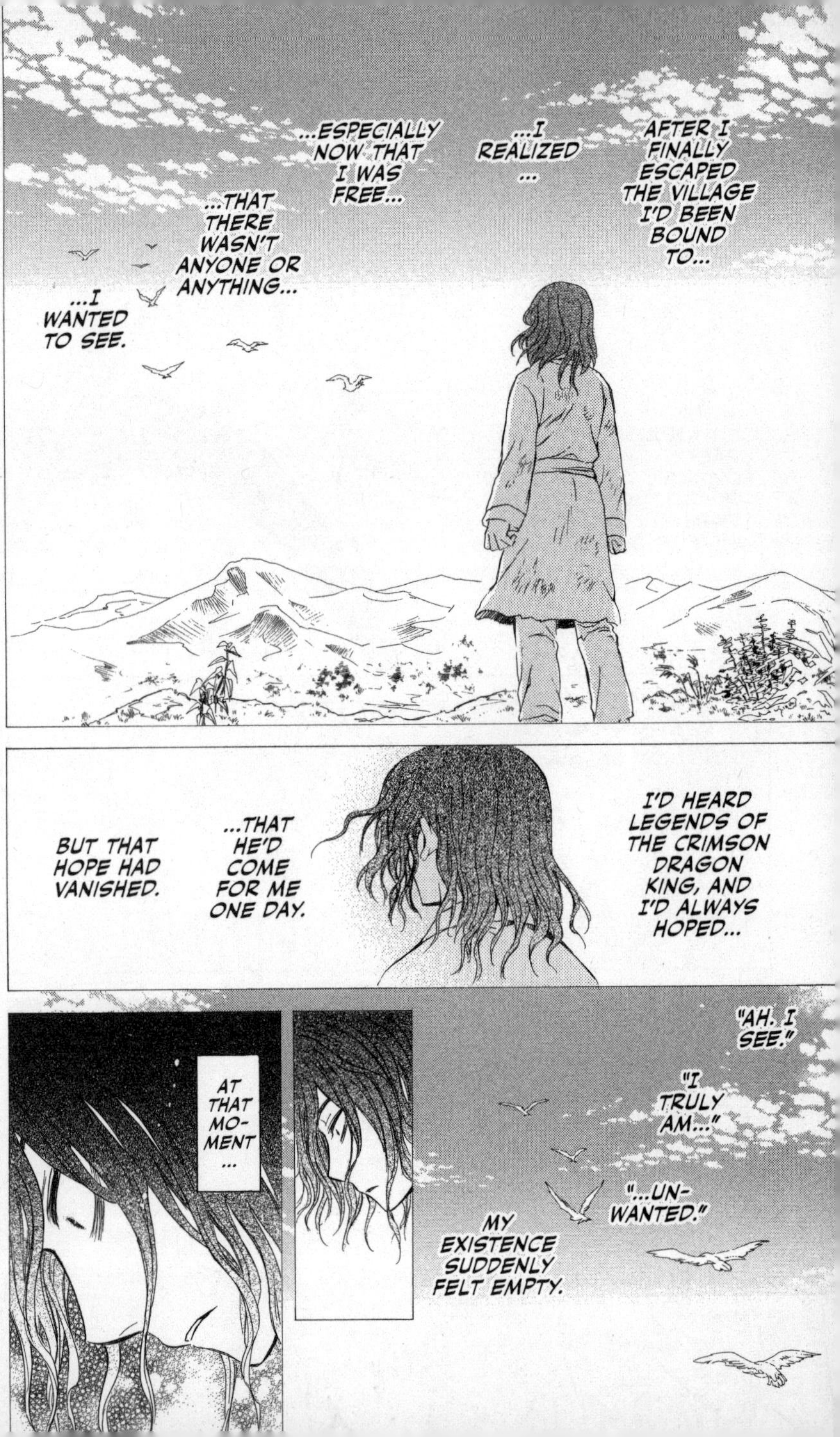
AFTER I FINALLY ESCAPED THE VILLAGE I'D BEEN BOUND TO...
...I REALIZED...
...ESPECIALLY NOW THAT I WAS FREE...
...THAT THERE WASN'T ANYONE OR ANYTHING...
...I WANTED TO SEE.
I'D HEARD LEGENDS OF THE CRIMSON DRAGON KING, AND I'D ALWAYS HOPED...
...THAT HE'D COME FOR ME ONE DAY.
BUT THAT HOPE HAD VANISHED.
"AH. I SEE."
"I TRULY AM..."
"...UN-WANTED."
MY EXISTENCE SUDDENLY FELT EMPTY.
AT THAT MO-MENT...

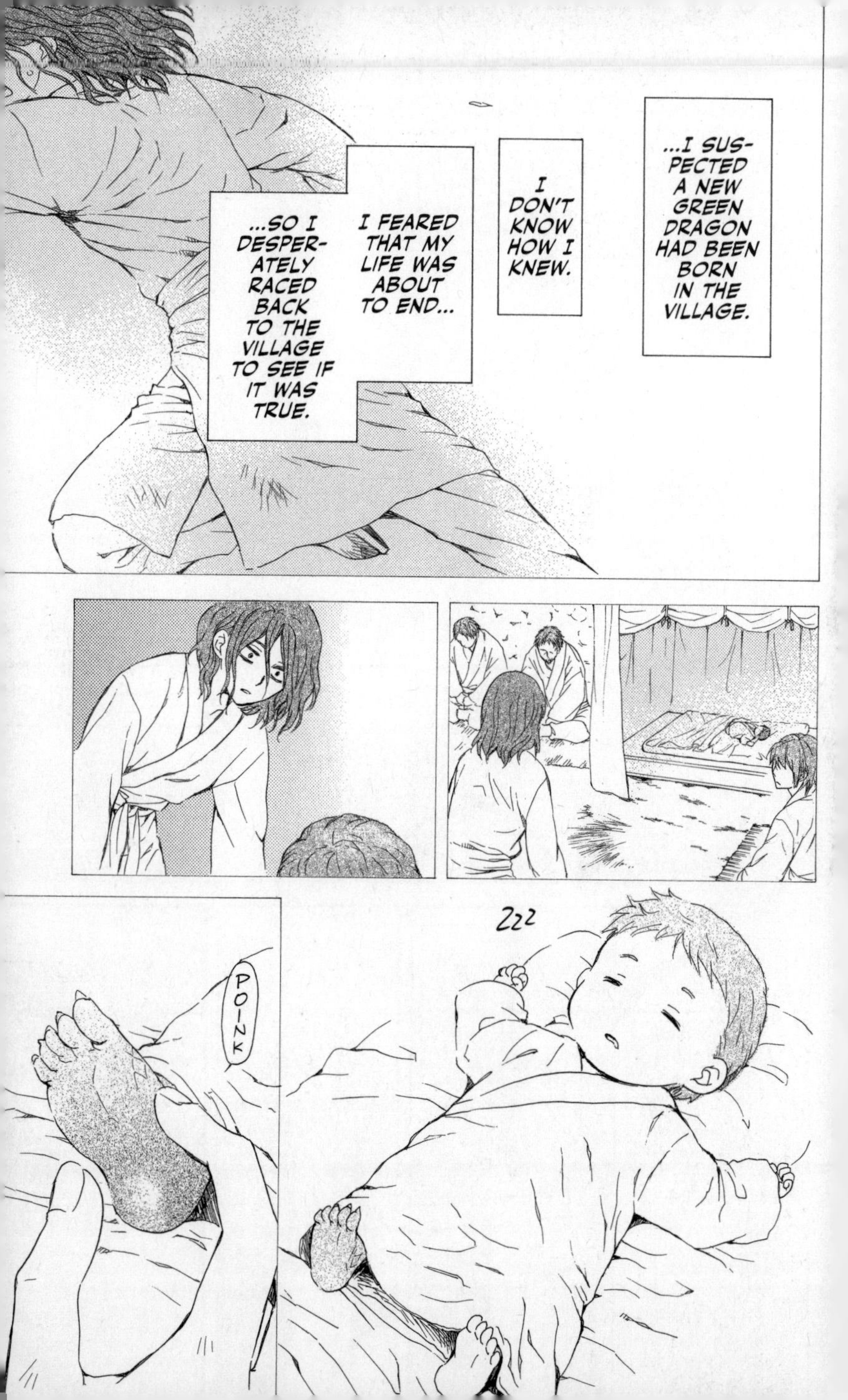
...I SUS-PECTED A NEW GREEN DRAGON HAD BEEN BORN IN THE VILLAGE.
I DON'T KNOW HOW I KNEW.
I FEARED THAT MY LIFE WAS ABOUT TO END...
...SO I DESPER-ATELY RACED BACK TO THE VILLAGE TO SEE IF IT WAS TRUE.
ZZZ
POINK

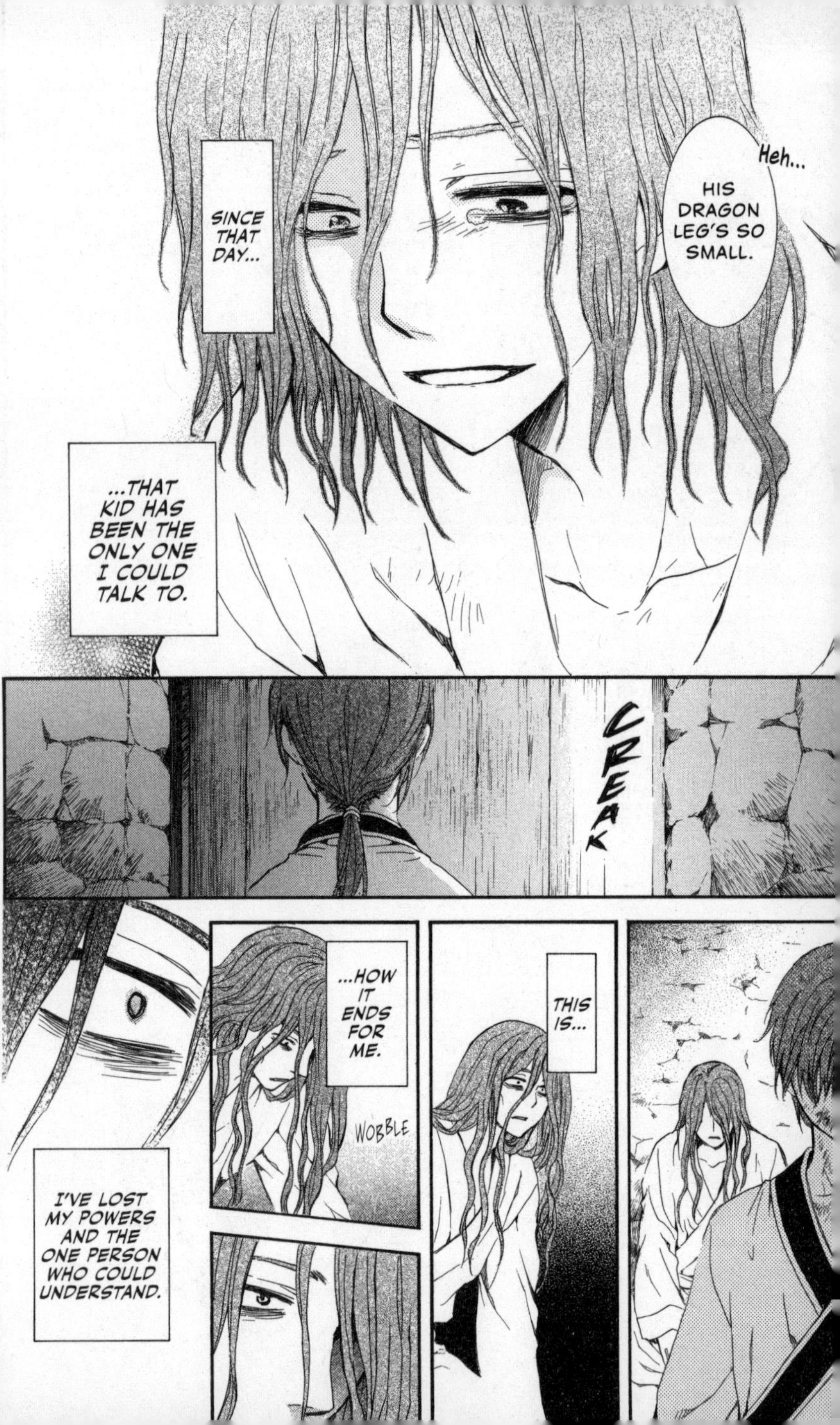
Heh...
HIS DRAGON LEG'S SO SMALL.
SINCE THAT DAY...
...THAT KID HAS BEEN THE ONLY ONE I COULD TALK TO.
CREAK
THIS IS...
...HOW IT ENDS FOR ME.
WOBBLE
I'VE LOST MY POWERS AND THE ONE PERSON WHO COULD UNDERSTAND.

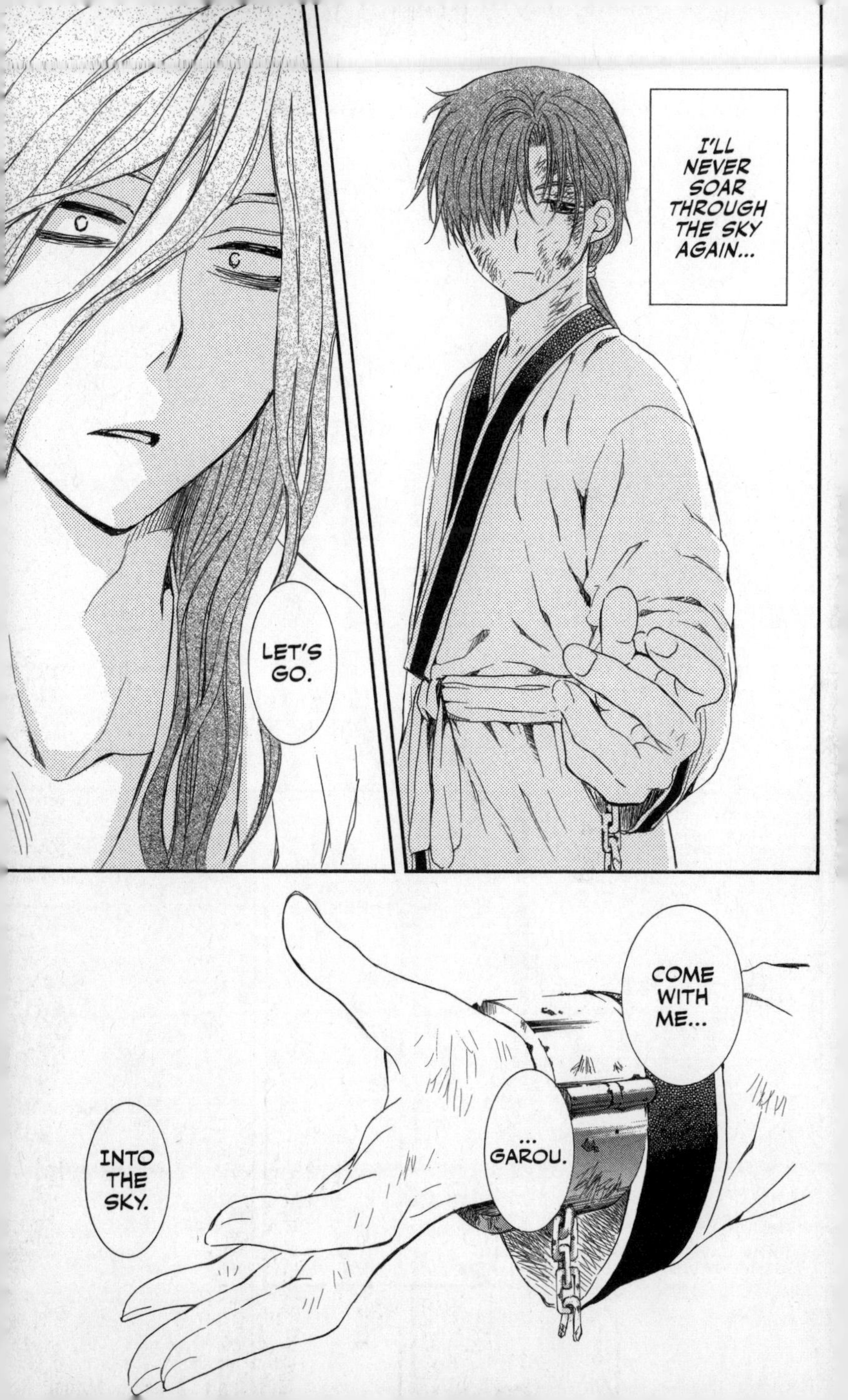
I'LL NEVER SOAR THROUGH THE SKY AGAIN...
LET'S GO.
COME WITH ME...
...GAROU.
INTO THE SKY.

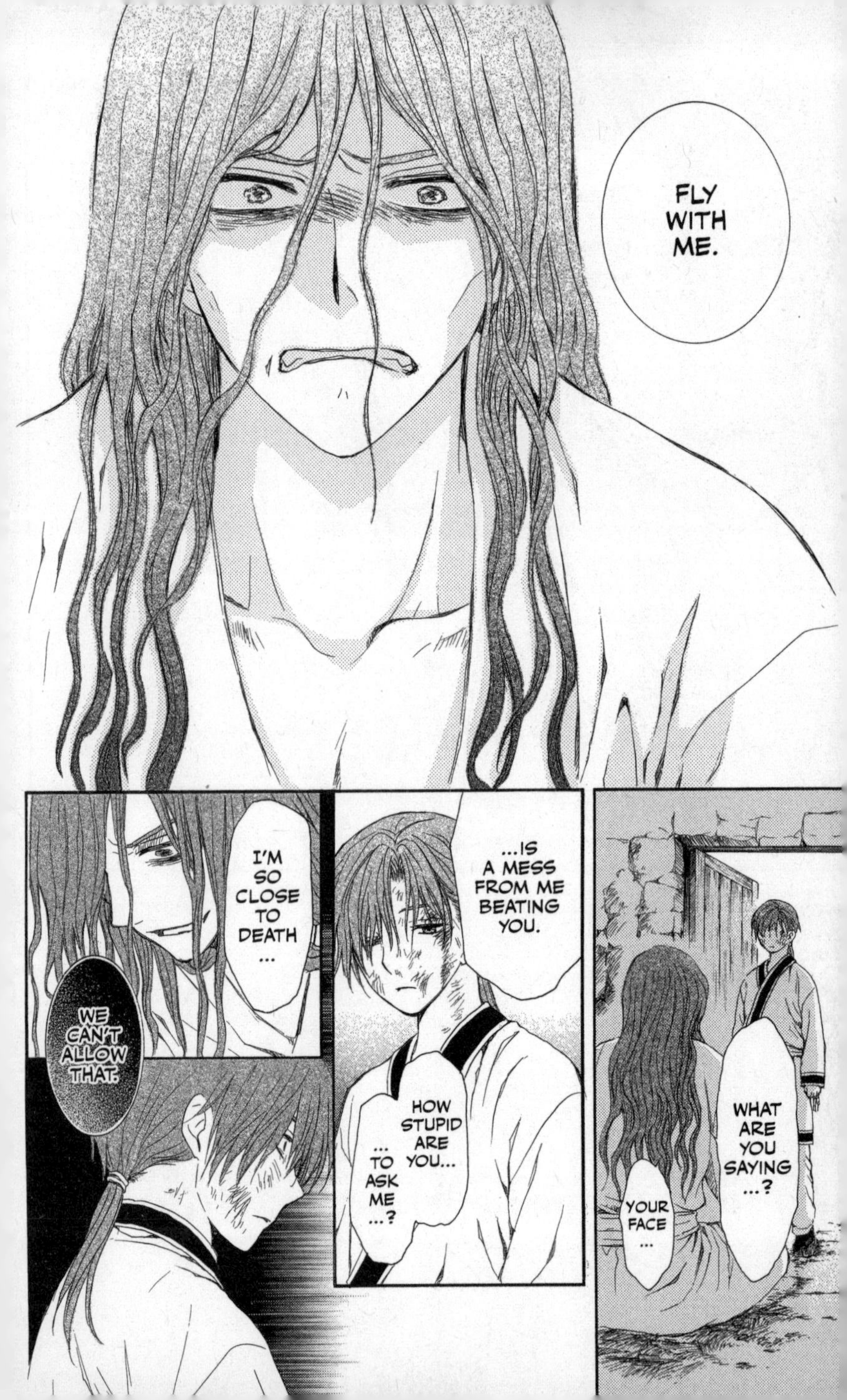
FLY WITH ME.
WHAT ARE YOU SAYING ...?
YOUR FACE ...
...IS A MESS FROM ME BEATING YOU.
HOW STUPID ARE YOU...
... TO ASK ME ...?
I'M SO CLOSE TO DEATH ...
WE CAN'T ALLOW THAT.

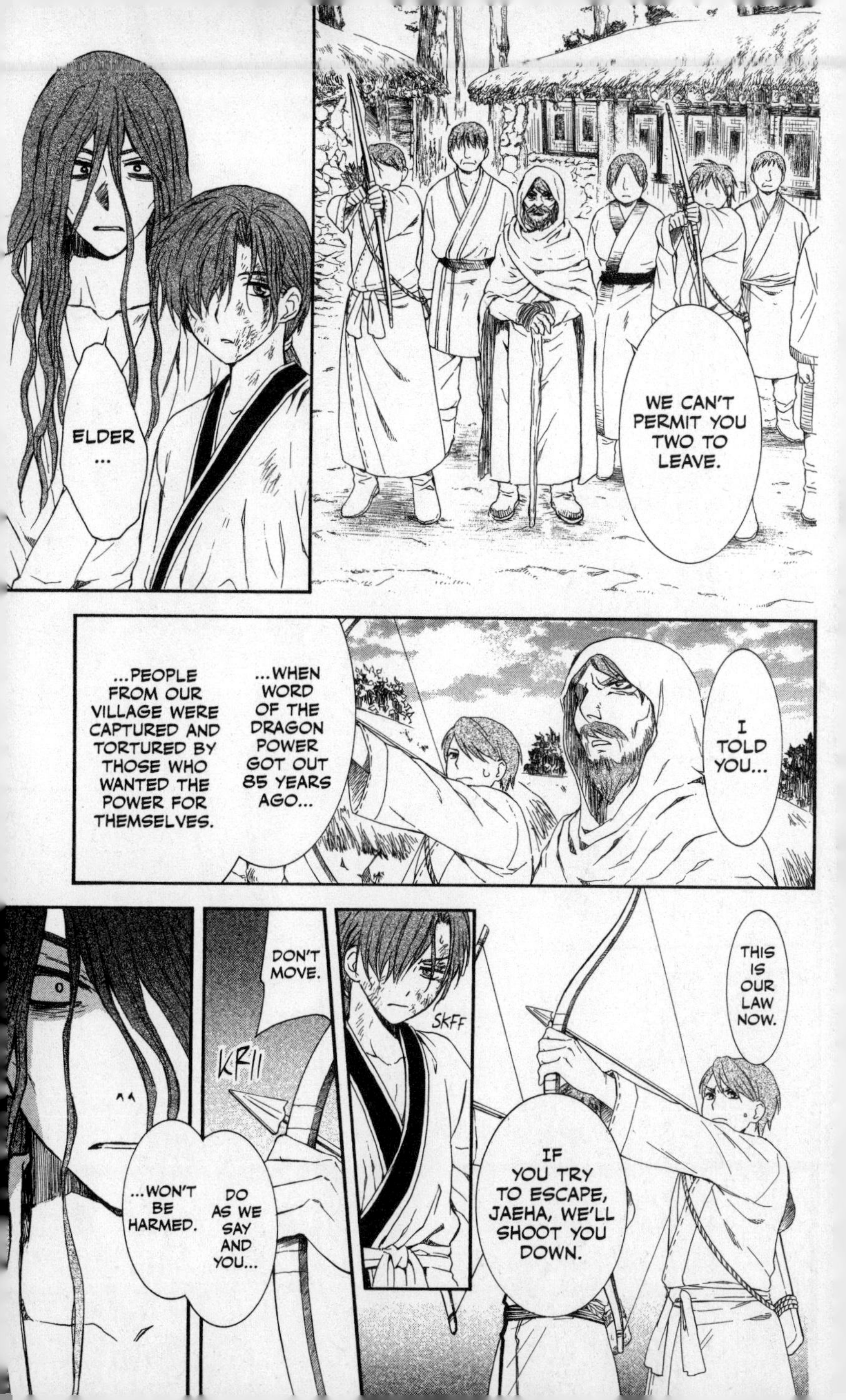
WE CAN'T PERMIT YOU TWO TO LEAVE.
ELDER ...
I TOLD YOU...
...WHEN WORD OF THE DRAGON POWER GOT OUT 85 YEARS AGO...
...PEOPLE FROM OUR VILLAGE WERE CAPTURED AND TORTURED BY THOSE WHO WANTED THE POWER FOR THEMSELVES.
THIS IS OUR LAW NOW.
IF YOU TRY TO ESCAPE, JAEHA, WE'LL SHOOT YOU DOWN.
SKFF
DON'T MOVE.
KRII
DO AS WE SAY AND YOU...
...WON'T BE HARMED.

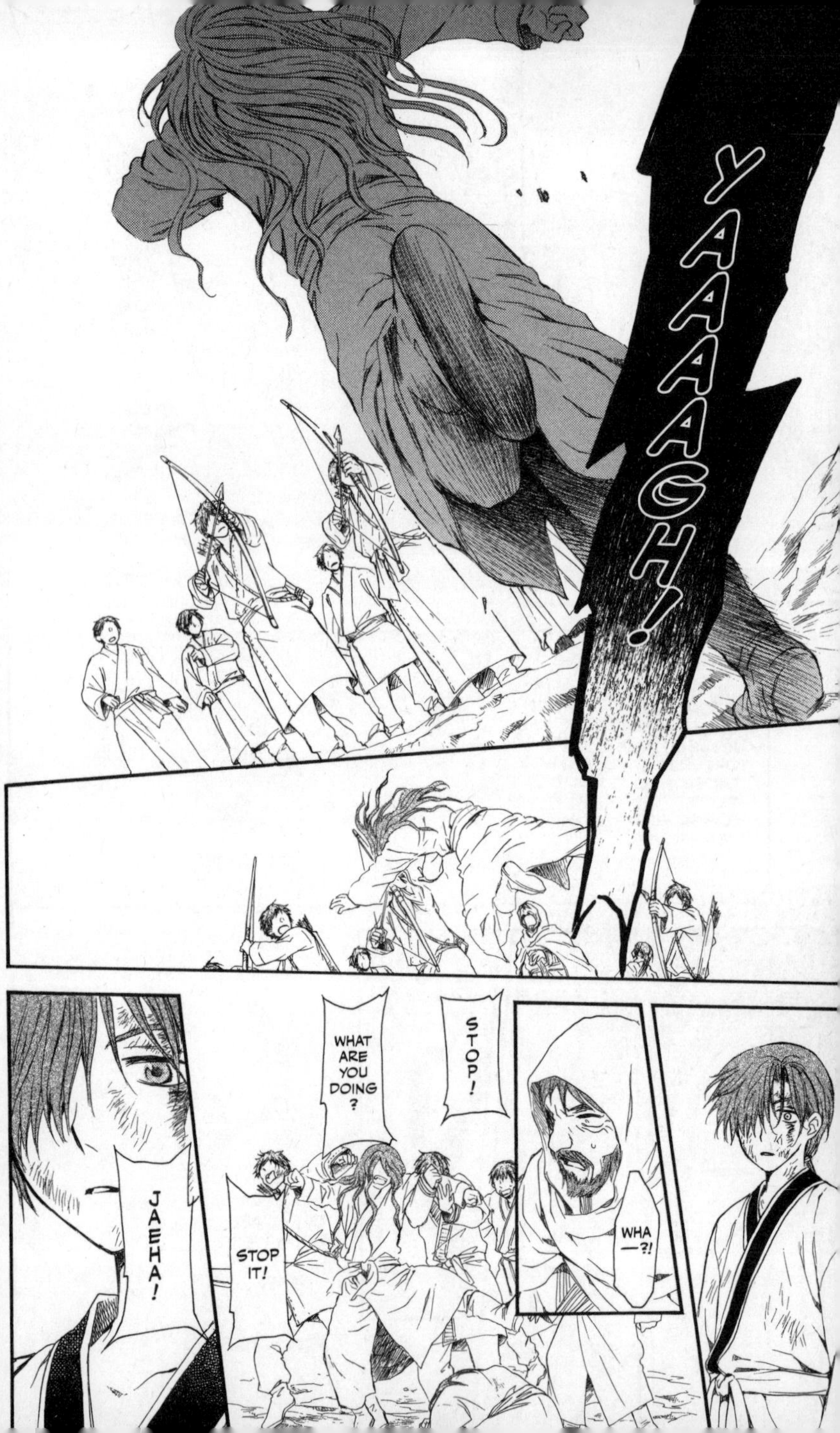
YAAAAAGH!
WHA—?!
STOP!
WHAT ARE YOU DOING?
STOP IT!
JAEHA!

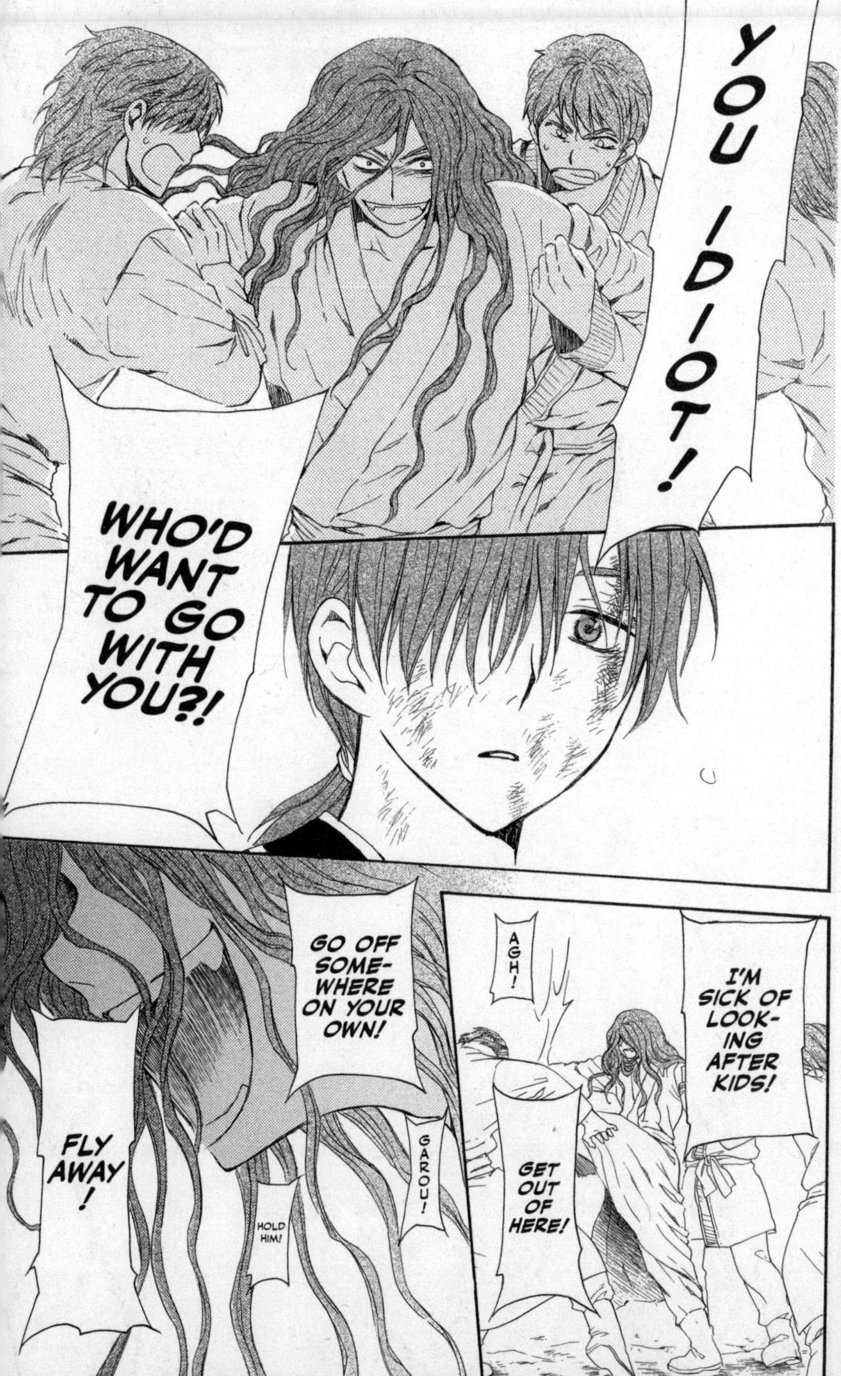
YOU IDIOT!
WHO'D WANT TO GO WITH YOU?!
I'M SICK OF LOOK-ING AFTER KIDS!
AGH!
GET OUT OF HERE!
GO OFF SOME-WHERE ON YOUR OWN!
GAROU!
HOLD HIM!
FLY AWAY!

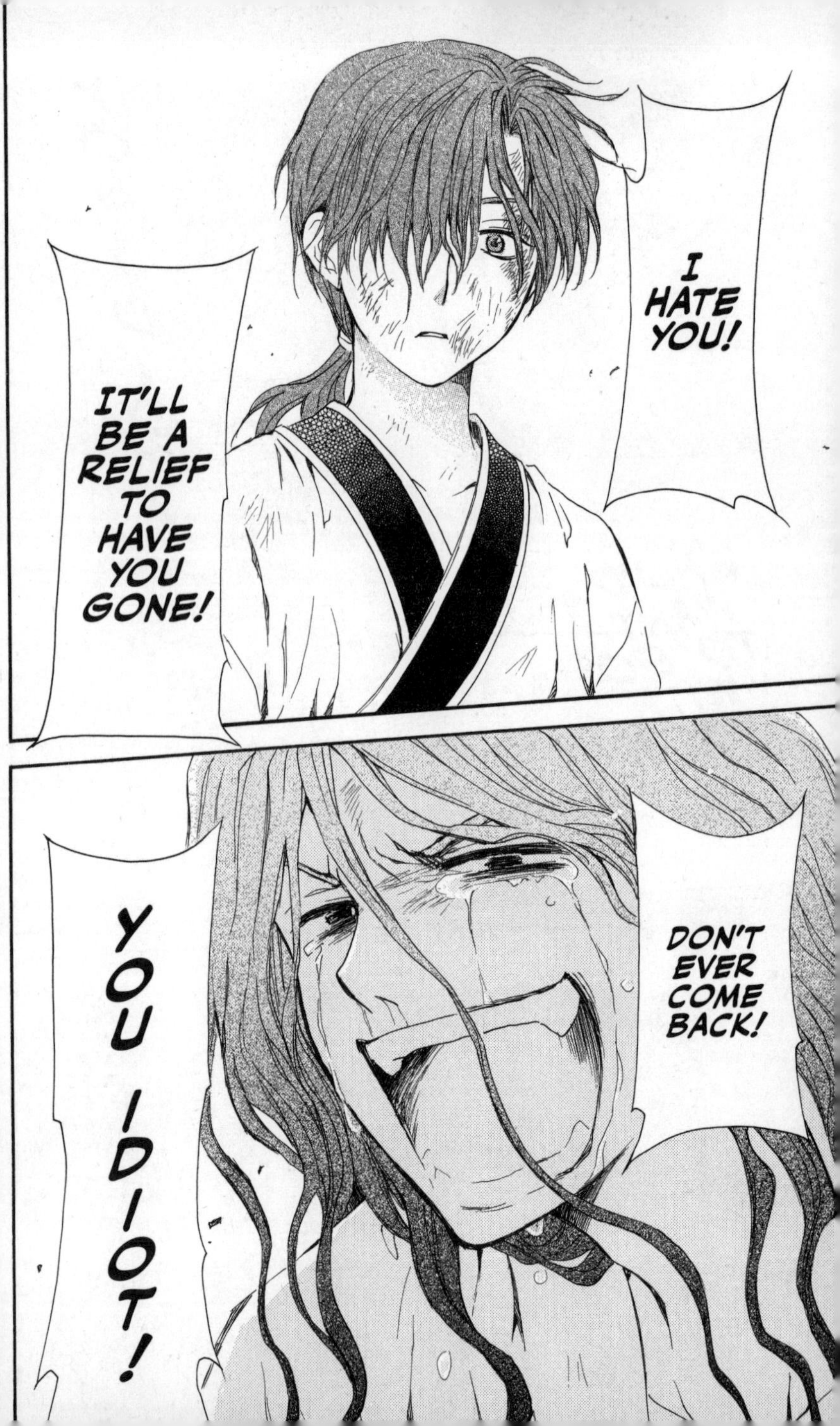
I HATE YOU!
IT'LL BE A RELIEF TO HAVE YOU GONE!
DON'T EVER COME BACK!
YOU IDIOT!

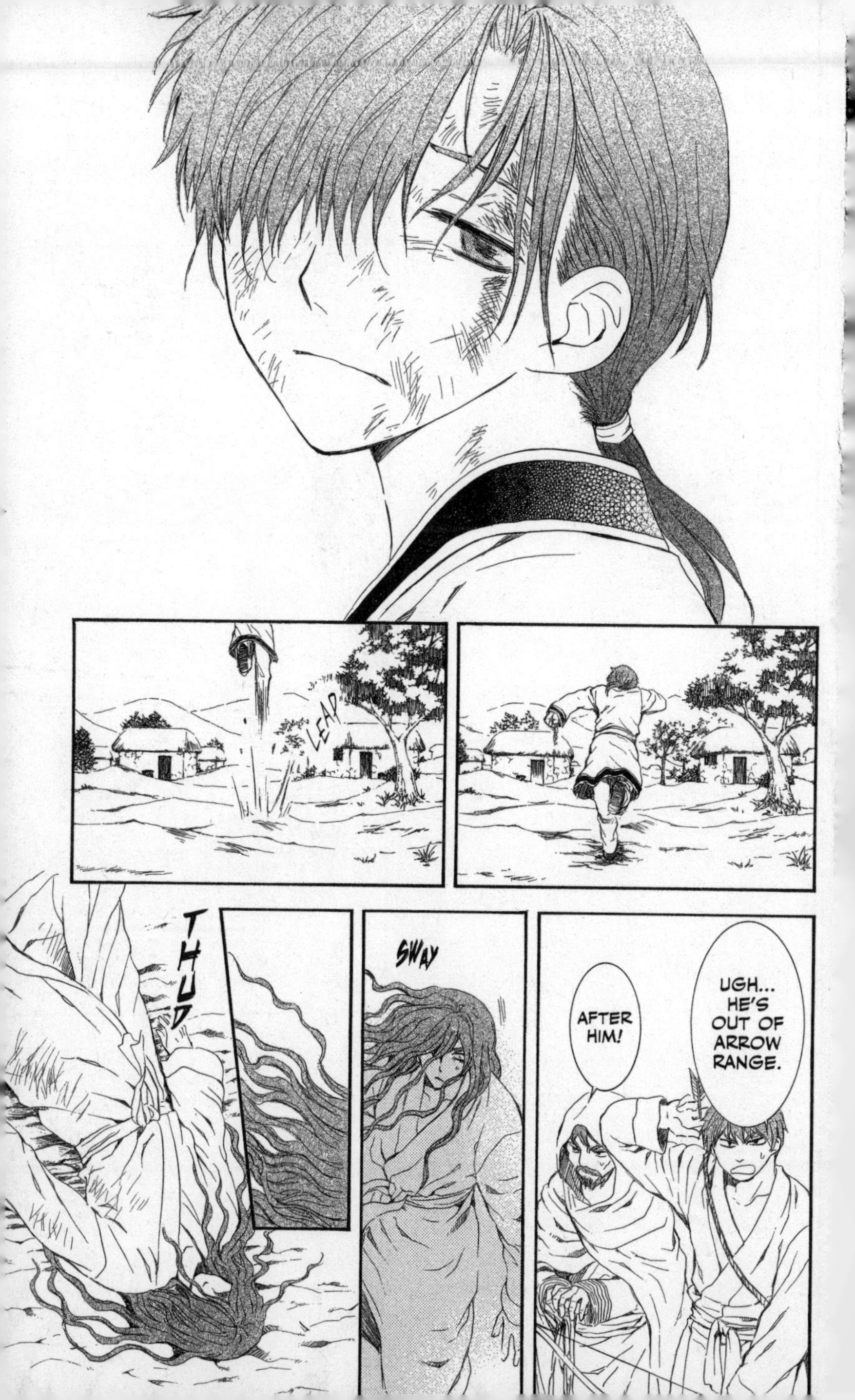
LEAP
UGH... HE'S OUT OF ARROW RANGE.
AFTER HIM!
SWAY
THUD

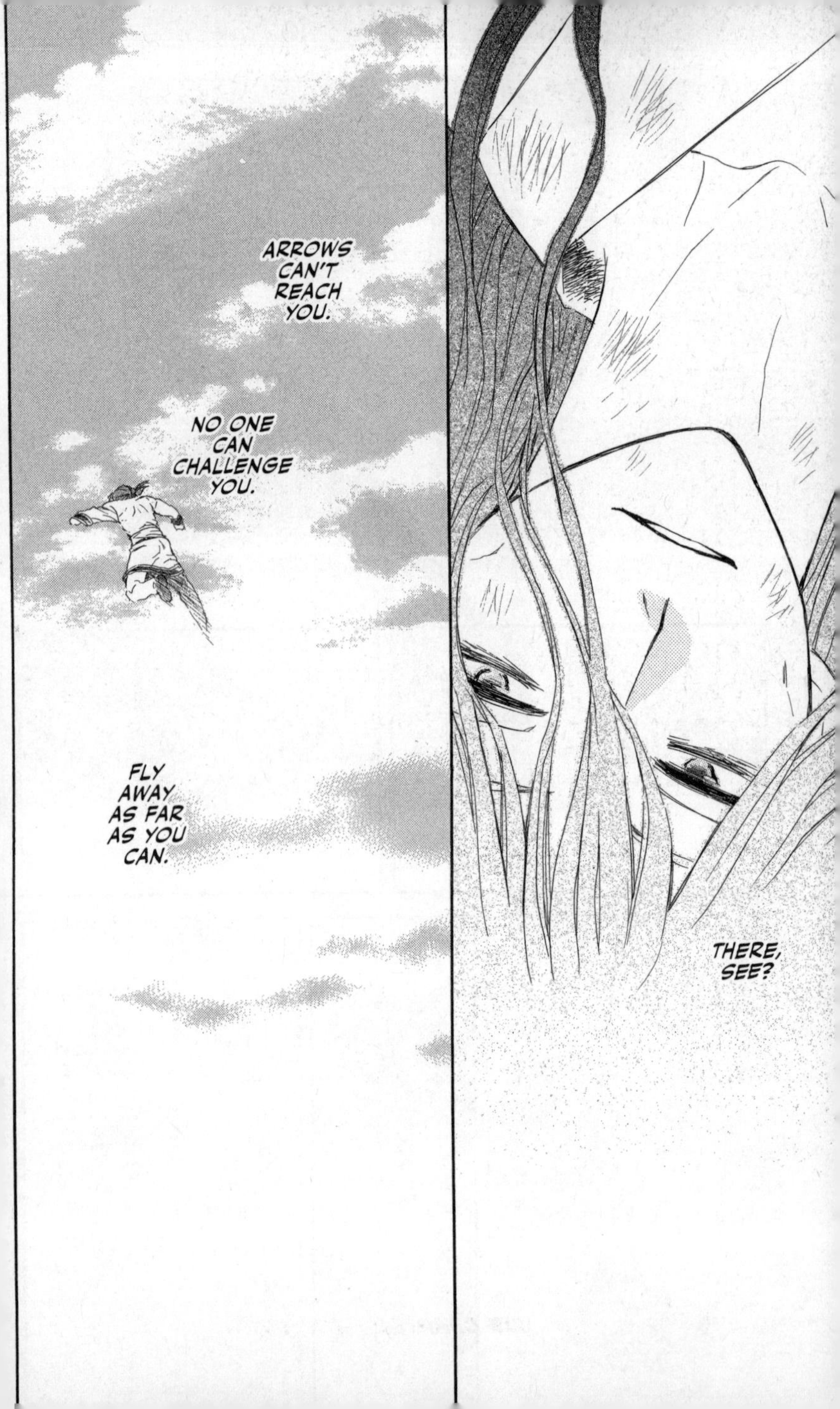
THERE, SEE?
ARROWS CAN'T REACH YOU.
NO ONE CAN CHALLENGE YOU.
FLY AWAY AS FAR AS YOU CAN.

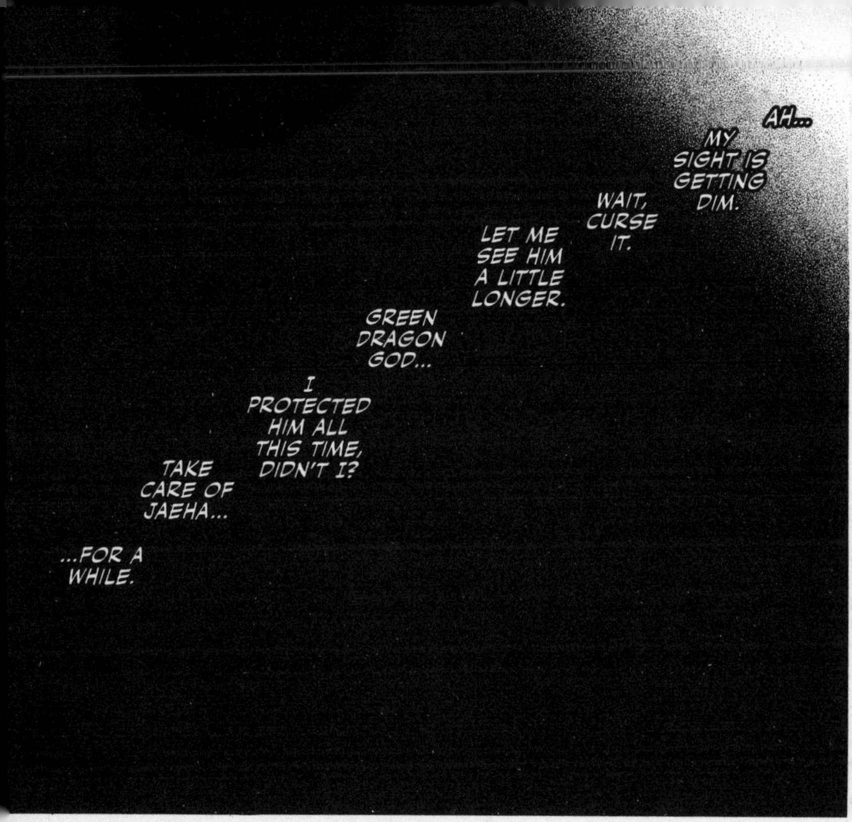
AH...
MY SIGHT IS GETTING DIM.
WAIT, CURSE IT.
LET ME SEE HIM A LITTLE LONGER.
GREEN DRAGON GOD...
I PROTECTED HIM ALL THIS TIME, DIDN'T I?
TAKE CARE OF JAEHA...
...FOR A WHILE.

PLEASE...

...PROTECT...

...HIM.

**BONUS CHAPTER / THE END**

The cover art for this volume features three dragons. They are feeling dizzy because of their high fevers.

—Mizuho Kusanagi

Born on February 3 in Kumamoto Prefecture in Japan, Mizuho Kusanagi began her professional manga career with *Yoiko no Kokoroe* (The Rules of a Good Child) in 2003. Her other works include *NG Life*, which was serialized in *Hana to Yume* and *The Hana to Yume* magazines and published by Hakusensha in Japan. *Yona of the Dawn* was adapted into an anime in 2014.

# YONA OF THE DAWN
## VOL. 17
### Shojo Beat Edition

STORY AND ART BY
MIZUHO KUSANAGI

English Adaptation/Ysabet Reinhardt MacFarlane
Translation/JN Productions
Touch-Up Art & Lettering/Lys Blakeslee
Design/Yukiko Whitley
Editor/Amy Yu

Akatsuki no Yona by Mizuho Kusanagi
© Mizuho Kusanagi 2015
All rights reserved.
First published in Japan in 2015 by HAKUSENSHA, Inc., Tokyo.
English language translation rights arranged with
HAKUSENSHA, Inc., Tokyo.

The stories, characters and incidents mentioned in this publication
are entirely fictional.

No portion of this book may be reproduced or transmitted in
any form or by any means without written permission from the
copyright holders.

Printed in the U.S.A.

Published by VIZ Media, LLC
P.O. Box 77010
San Francisco, CA 94107

10 9 8 7 6 5 4 3 2 1
First printing, April 2019

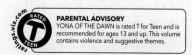

**PARENTAL ADVISORY**
YONA OF THE DAWN is rated T for Teen and is
recommended for ages 13 and up. This volume
contains violence and suggestive themes.

viz.com
shojobeat.com

# Takane &* Hana

**STORY AND ART BY**
**Yuki Shiwasu**

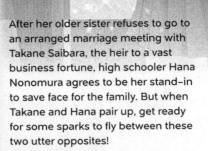

After her older sister refuses to go to an arranged marriage meeting with Takane Saibara, the heir to a vast business fortune, high schooler Hana Nonomura agrees to be her stand-in to save face for the family. But when Takane and Hana pair up, get ready for some sparks to fly between these two utter opposites!

Takane to Hana © Yuki Shiwasu 2015/HAKUSENSHA, Inc.

RATED **T** TEEN

**Beat**
shojobeat.com

**VIZ**
viz.com

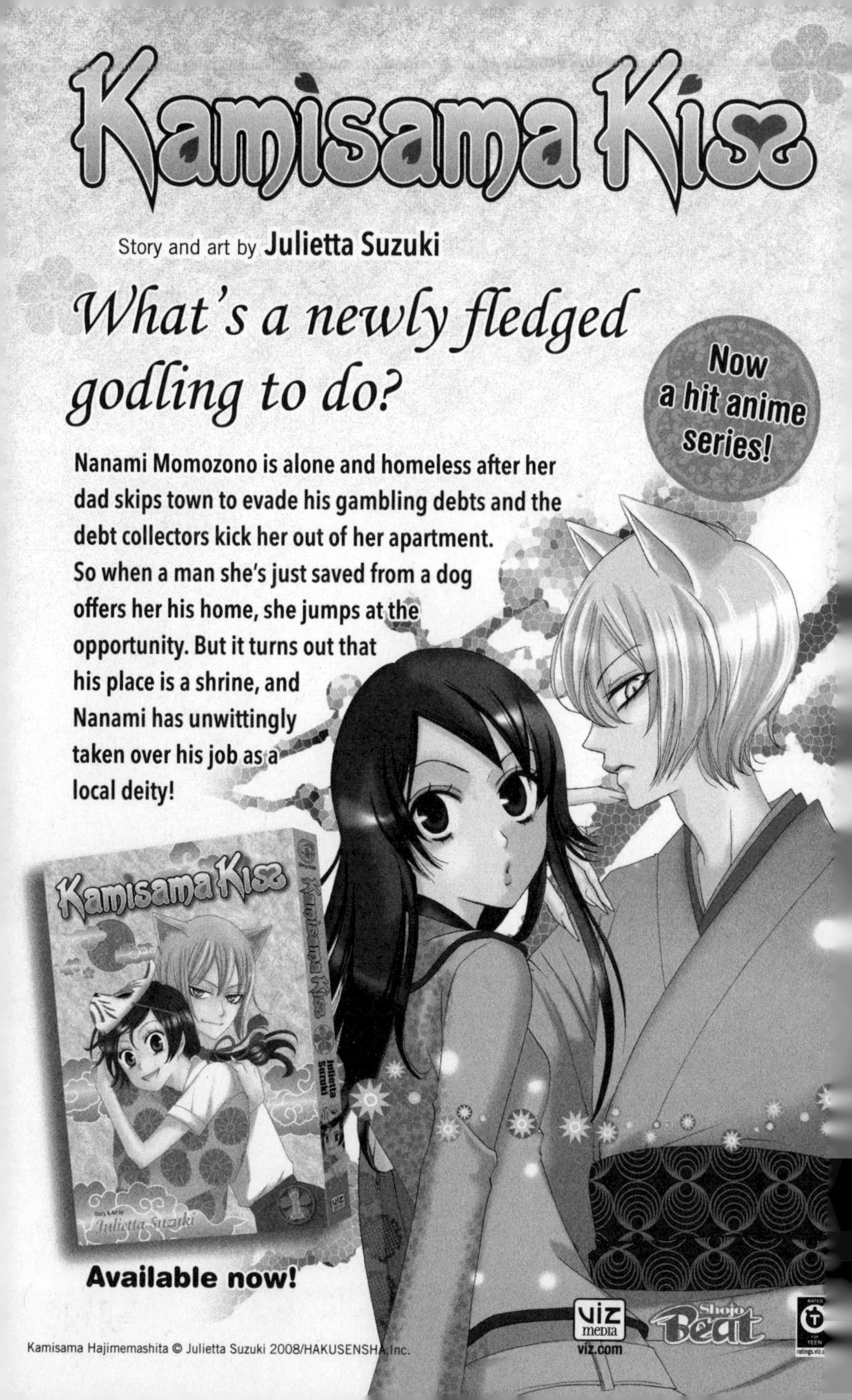
Kamisama Kiss
Story and art by Julietta Suzuki
What's a newly fledged godling to do?
Now a hit anime series!
Nanami Momozono is alone and homeless after her dad skips town to evade his gambling debts and the debt collectors kick her out of her apartment. So when a man she's just saved from a dog offers her his home, she jumps at the opportunity. But it turns out that his place is a shrine, and Nanami has unwittingly taken over his job as a local deity!
Kamisama Kiss
Story & Art by Julietta Suzuki
Available now!
VIZ media
viz.com
Shojo Beat
RATED T FOR TEEN
Kamisama Hajimemashita © Julietta Suzuki 2008/HAKUSENSHA, Inc.

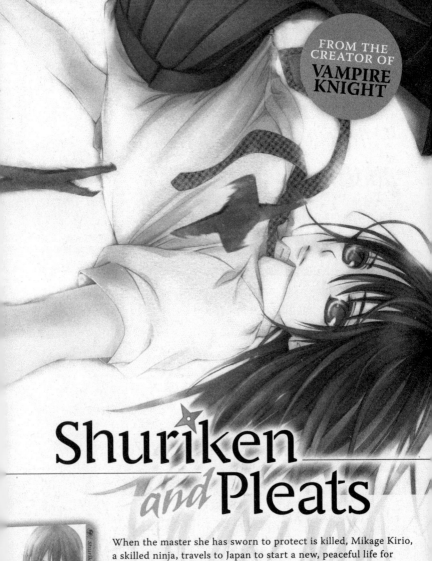

FROM THE
CREATOR OF
**VAMPIRE
KNIGHT**

# Shuriken *and* Pleats

When the master she has sworn to protect is killed, Mikage Kirio, a skilled ninja, travels to Japan to start a new, peaceful life for herself. But as soon as she arrives, she finds herself fighting to protect the life of Mahito Wakashimatsu, a man who is under attack by a band of ninja. From that time on, Mikage is drawn deeper into the machinations of his powerful family.

www.viz.com

ratings.viz.com

Shuriken to Pleats © Matsuri Hino 2015/HAKUSENSHA, Inc.

Kyoko Mogami followed her true love Sho to Tokyo to support him while he made it big as an idol. But he's casting her out now that he's famous enough! Kyoko won't suffer in silence— she's going to get her sweet revenge by beating Sho in show biz!

Vol. 1 ISBN: 978-1-4215-4226-3

Vol. 2 ISBN: 978-1-4215-4227-0

Vol. 3 ISBN: 978-1-4215-4228-7

Show biz is sweet...but revenge is sweeter!

In Stores Now!

# Skip·Beat!

Story and Art by YOSHIKI NAKAMURA

Skip•Beat! © Yoshiki Nakamura 2002/HAKUSENSHA, Inc.

Nino Arisugawa, a girl who loves to sing, experiences her first heart-wrenching goodbye when her beloved childhood friend, Momo, moves away. And after Nino befriends Yuzu, a music composer, she experiences another sad parting! With music as their common ground and only outlet, how will everyone's unrequited loves play out?

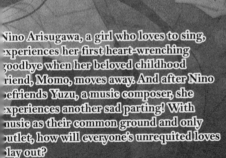

# ANONYMOUS NOISE

**viz** media
viz.com

Shojo Beat

Story & Art by
Ryoko Fukuyama

Fukumenkei Noise © Ryoko Fukuyama 2013/HAKUSENSHA, Inc.

# THE YOUNG MASTER'S REVENGE

When Leo was a young boy, he had his pride torn to shreds by Tenma, a girl from a wealthy background who was always getting him into trouble. Now, years after his father's successful clothing business has made him the heir to a fortune, he searches out Tenma to enact a dastardly plan—he'll get his revenge by making her fall in love with him!

STORY & ART BY Meca Tanaka

THE YOUNG MASTER'S REVENGE

1

Kimi no Kotonado Zettaini © Meca Tanaka 2015/HAKUSENSHA, Inc.

RATED TEEN

VIZ
viz.com

# This is the last page.

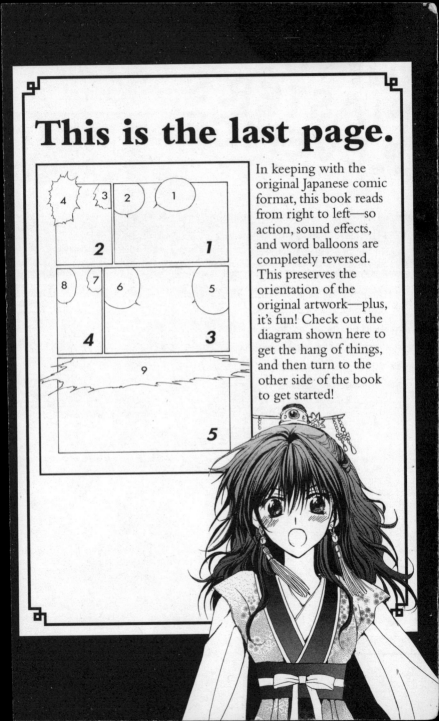

In keeping with the original Japanese comic format, this book reads from right to left—so action, sound effects, and word balloons are completely reversed. This preserves the orientation of the original artwork—plus, it's fun! Check out the diagram shown here to get the hang of things, and then turn to the other side of the book to get started!